Global Islamophobia and the Rise of Populism

Global Islamophobia and the Rise of Populism

Edited by

SAHAR F. AZIZ AND JOHN L. ESPOSITO

OXFORD
UNIVERSITY PRESS

Oxford University Press is a department of the University of Oxford. It furthers
the University's objective of excellence in research, scholarship, and education
by publishing worldwide. Oxford is a registered trade mark of Oxford University
Press in the UK and certain other countries.

Published in the United States of America by Oxford University Press
198 Madison Avenue, New York, NY 10016, United States of America.

© Oxford University Press 2024

All rights reserved. No part of this publication may be reproduced, stored in
a retrieval system, or transmitted, in any form or by any means, without the
prior permission in writing of Oxford University Press, or as expressly permitted
by law, by license, or under terms agreed with the appropriate reproduction
rights organization. Inquiries concerning reproduction outside the scope of the
above should be sent to the Rights Department, Oxford University Press, at the
address above.

You must not circulate this work in any other form
and you must impose this same condition on any acquirer.

CIP data is on file at the Library of Congress

ISBN 978-0-19-764900-8 (pbk.)
ISBN 978-0-19-764899-5 (hbk.)

DOI: 10.1093/oso/9780197648995.001.0001

Paperback printed by Marquis Book Printing, Canada
Hardback printed by Bridgeport National Bindery, Inc., United States of America

Contents

Foreword   vii
    Barbara A. Lee

1. Introduction   1
    Sahar F. Aziz and John L. Esposito

PART I ISLAMOPHOBIA IN NORTH AMERICA: RACE, RELIGION, AND CITIZENSHIP

2. The Price of Recognition: The One Islam and the Many   23
    Joseph Massad

3. The Politics of Vulnerability: Today's Threat to American Muslims' Religious Freedom   36
    Asma T. Uddin

4. Anti-Muslim Racism and the Rise of Ethnonationalist Populism in the United States   56
    Saher Selod

PART II ISLAMOPHOBIA IN EUROPE: XENOPHOBIA, ANTI-SEMITISM, AND NATIONALISM

5. Postcolonialism, Post–National Socialism, German Reunification, and the Rise of the Far Right: Making Sense of Islamophobia in Germany   75
    Farid Hafez

6. Islamophobia: How the Far Right Went Mainstream in Britain   94
    Mobashra Tazamal

7. France's Islamophobic Bloc and the "Mainstreamization" of the Far Right   112
    Marwan Mohammed

8. Islamophobia without Muslims? Not Only in Eastern Europe   132
    Ivan Kalmar

vi CONTENTS

9. Islamophobia in Russia: Ethnicity, Migration, and
   National Security   151
   Sarah Calderone and Sahar F. Aziz

10. Muslim Life in Belgium: In Search of a *Vivre ensemble*   169
    John Farmer and Ava Majlesi

PART III ISLAMOPHOBIA IN ASIA: GENOCIDE, POGROMS, AND DETENTION

11. Displacing and Disciplining Muslims in India's Burgeoning
    Hindu *Rashtra*   183
    Audrey Truschke

12. Contesting the Spatialization of Islamophobia in Urban India 201
    Stuti Govil and D. Asher Ghertner

13. (Un)Made in China: Uyghur Muslims at the Intersection of
    Islamophobia and Ethnic Cleansing   218
    Khaled A. Beydoun

14. Islamophobia and Genocide: Myanmar's Rohingya Genocide   233
    Ronan Lee

PART IV CONCLUSION: LESSONS FROM SOUTH AFRICA

15. Confronting Islamophobia: Defeating Colonial Bigotries,
    Learning from South Africa   257
    Ebrahim Rasool

Index   275

Foreword

Since the late winter of 2020, much has been written and discussed about the "twin pandemics" of COVID-19 and racism—in the United States and around the world. While in the United States much of the attention has, understandably, been given to racism involving nonwhites (particularly Blacks and Asians), less attention has been given to the long-standing problem of Islamophobia, not only in the United States but globally. Schools and colleges throughout the United States are discussing how to incorporate antiracism into their curricula and into their missions. This book is an important reminder that anti-Islamophobia is also a significant issue that needs to be confronted squarely and treated with the seriousness and passion that support antiracism efforts.

Although Western democracies have somewhat different histories with respect to the growth of Islamophobia (in the United States, the horrific attacks of September 11, 2001; in England, Germany, and France, multiple attacks by terrorists against concertgoers, shoppers, commuters, and pedestrians; and the diaspora resulting from the Syrian civil war that drove refugees to Europe), the victimization of and discrimination against Muslims show similar patterns. Adherents of white supremacy, xenophobia encouraged by politicians in both the United States and Europe, and individuals' fear of "replacement" by individuals and groups of different cultures, religions, and priorities have fueled an increase in Islamophobia that requires examination and explanation.

This book, a collection of essays written by fourteen scholars who have been studying Islamophobia, in some cases for decades, is designed to inform and analyze the causes of Islamophobia—political, social, religious, economic, and historical—in both the United States and globally. It is particularly important that the next generation of political leaders, voters, and citizens understands and appreciates these trends and the many forces that have exacerbated this global problem. These future leaders and citizens are now in high school and college, and giving them the critical thinking skills to address not only the problem of Islamophobia but the problem of racism and hatred more generally is critical to building a more civil society.

A common theme throughout these essays is that fear is a powerful motivator of Islamophobia—fear of having one's culture, political power, values, and priorities superseded by the "Other" whose culture, values, and priorities are viewed as different and inferior. According to Uddin, Islamophobia in the United States is driven by fear of a diminution of Christian identity and Christian

viii FOREWORD

values—the bedrock upon which the United States, founded by white Christian Europeans—was established. Selod traces the rise of ethnonationalist populism in the United States that was exacerbated by the rhetoric and policies of former President Donald Trump and explains the appeal of Trump's "Make America Great Again" in the context of the fear of foreigners and their culture. And Massad discusses the many forms of Islam and the pressures exerted by the United States and Western European nations to secularize Islam in order to facilitate the assimilation process toward Western values as a mechanism for reducing fear of the "other."

Similarly, Hafez, Mohammed, and Farmer and Majlesi dissect the fears of white Europeans in Germany, France, and Belgium, respectively, saying that although the fear is similar, it is expressed as concern for the weakening of secular democratic rule rather than religious diversity. Tazamal discusses the overt Islamophobia of Conservative British government leaders, as not only an element in the Brexit vote by British citizens but a more general fear that they have been "invaded" by groups whose culture will obliterate British identity and culture. Kalmar discusses the rise of Islamophobia in east-central Europe (Poland, the Czech Republic, Slovakia, and Hungary) despite, or because of, the relatively small number of Muslims living in those countries. His discussion of "peripherality"—the feeling of an individual or ethnic group that they are on the outside of the core of privilege, which thus convinces them of the need to differentiate themselves from and to distrust "the Other"—can be applied to the problem of Islamophobia more generally. And in Russia, the history and current climate of prejudice and discrimination against Muslims on the basis of religion and ethnicity and through national security and migration law are traced by Aziz and Calderone.

Beydoun and Lee describe the brutal actions of the leaders of China and Myanmar, respectively, to effect a form of "ethnic cleansing" against Muslim religious and ethnic groups, many of whose members are citizens, to ensure that each country's citizenry retains the dominance of the Han ethnic group, in the case of China, and in Myanmar, the Buddhist religious and ethnic social and political elite. With respect to the treatment of Muslims in India, Truschke traces historical and recent actions by a Hindu majority government to marginalize and vilify Muslims and to deny or complicate efforts to become citizens as well as the support the government has provided for violence against Muslims in that country. Govil and Ghertner add to the discussion of the challenges faced by Muslims in India by addressing how "substantive citizenship entitlements pertaining to material needs—including clean water and sanitation, residential tenure security, freedom of movement, and access to public space and resources—are inflected by municipal belonging as much as by national belonging"—all in addition to the political, social, and humanitarian needs experienced by Muslims living in India.

Rasool's concluding chapter traces the development of the participation of Muslims as full members of society in South Africa, from their initial status as slaves to full citizenship and their alliance with Nelson Mandela's work to abolish apartheid. He describes how political alliances, compromise with other disenfranchised groups, and the willingness of Muslim leaders to work for the common good rather than the good of their constituents has led to positive change in a country not so long ago rocked with discrimination, violence, and religious intolerance.

These essays raise many interesting questions, too numerous to enumerate in this foreword. Why, for example, do citizens of the nation to which refugees and migrants travel expect these individuals to assimilate completely, obliterating their culture, their religion, and their history? How can global organizations such as the United Nations prohibit or punish those countries that practice ethnic cleansing, apparently without restraint? How can a democracy persuade its voters to consider the collective good rather than the personal benefits provided or promised to them by those in public office? Will what appears to be a shift to far-right political power in Britain, some European Union countries, and east-central Europe spread more widely, and what are the implications in those countries for minority ethnic groups with different religions and cultures?

And while, of course, fear is neither a justification nor an excuse for criminal, political, or legal attacks on followers of Islam, the discussions in these essays offer readers—especially those young adults who are learning to think critically and to evaluate what they may have been taught by family members, politicians, or religious leaders about "terrorism" and its relationship to a particular religion—an explanation (but not an excuse) for the virulence of Islamophobia.

It seems obvious that our students, and our citizens, need to be educated about the topics addressed in this collection of essays. Colleges and universities can play an important role in helping us understand the causes, effects, and antidotes to Islamophobia. Policymakers, as well, need to understand the sources and effects of Islamophobia so that they can exercise true leadership rather than simply deferring to their constituents' fears and biases. Citizens need to inform themselves in order to differentiate between propaganda and facts. The history of discrimination and serious mistreatment of Muslims is a disgrace, particularly for those nations that preach devotion to human rights and "justice for all." This book cannot reverse this history or even stop the rhetoric of the uninformed. But it can help people who value truth and fairness to evaluate the rhetoric and work to combat it.

The fact that this conference with its ensuing essays was sponsored by Rutgers University, one of the most diverse public universities in the United States, is no accident. I commend the organizers of the conference, Professors Sahar Aziz and John Esposito, for bringing together a truly learned and knowledgeable group of scholars and journalists who have enlightened us and whose observations and commentary provide important insights for our students and ourselves.

Barbara A. Lee
University Professor
Former Senior Vice President for Academic Affairs
Rutgers University

1

Introduction

Sahar F. Aziz and John L. Esposito

An inherent risk in compiling an edited volume of this nature is the waning relevance of the topic. Nothing could be further from the truth here. Far from abating over time, global Islamophobia and right-wing populism have grown and intensified. Far-right groups and ethnonationalist leaders are expanding their influence in the United States, Europe, and Asia where sizable Muslim minorities live.[1] In Europe, Muslims are the quintessential racial trope of the dangerous "other" that threatens the imagined White Christian civilized nation. In the United States, Muslims are the latest minority in a long history of xenophobia that blames new immigrants for domestic social, political, and economic grievances. And in India, China, and Myanmar (formerly Burma), Muslim minorities native to the land are suspected of usurping social and political dominance from the Hindu, Han, and Buddhist majorities, in the latest iteration of domestic racism.

On the global stage, Islamophobia is propagated by Western nations' national security practices in a US-led "Global War on Terror" (GWOT).[2] The GWOT arguably has been the single most effective political weapon in legitimizing anti-Muslim racism by state and private actors across continents. Claiming the mantle of self-defense after the worst terrorist attack in US history, on September 11, 2001, the American government mobilized countries worldwide to surveil, investigate, prosecute, and kill any Muslim individual or group suspected of supporting terrorism against a Western nation.

---

[1] See, for example, Cassie Miller, "SPLC Poll Finds Substantial Support for 'Great Replacement' Theory and Other Hard-Right Ideas," Southern Poverty Law Center, June 1, 2022, https://www.splcenter.org/news/2022/06/01/poll-finds-support-great-replacement-hard-right-ideas; Michel Martin, "What the Recent Wins for Far-Right Parties in Europe Could Mean for the Region," NPR, October 1, 2022, https://www.npr.org/2022/10/01/1126419403/what-the-recent-wins-for-far-right-parties-in-europe-could-mean-for-the-region; Hartosh Singh Bal, "The Unstoppable Rise of Hindu Nationalism," *Foreign Affairs*, April 13, 2022, https://www.foreignaffairs.com/articles/india/2022-04-13/unstoppable-rise-hindu-nationalism; Camila Vergara, "How Christian Nationalism Is Taking Root across the World," *Politico*, October 27, 2022, https://www.politico.com/news/magazine/2022/10/27/global-far-right-christian-nationalists-00063400.

[2] Saher Selod, "Islamophobia and the Rise of Ethnonationalist Populism in the United States," ch. 4 in this volume.

Sahar F. Aziz and John L. Esposito, *Introduction* In: *Global Islamophobia and the Rise of Populism*. Edited by: Sahar F. Aziz and John L. Esposito, Oxford University Press. © Oxford University Press 2024. DOI: 10.1093/oso/9780197648995.003.0001

For authoritarian regimes in the Middle East and North Africa, the post–9/11 era was an opportune political moment to systematically (and openly) repress domestic opposition to their regimes, without being held politically accountable by their Western allies.[3] Nonviolent political movements animated by Islamic principles were conflated with violent, extremist militias fighting in civil wars. In Europe, the GWOT unleashed deeply held Islamophobic societal prejudice.[4] Nations with colonialist histories, orientalist beliefs, and White-supremacist practices had long otherized their Muslim minorities as inferior and uncivilized, notwithstanding those same nations' contemporary pledges to pluralism.[5] Whatever stigma was associated with anti-Muslim discrimination in these purportedly liberal states was replaced with racist notions of patriotism that equated national security with criminalizing Muslim identity.[6]

The muted criticism of liberals within the US and European governments against other countries' human rights violations offered little reassurance to Muslims. Indefinite detention of hundreds of Muslim men without due process in Guantanamo Bay, pervasive torture in the CIA's rendition program and US military prisons in Abu Ghraib, and mass surveillance of Muslim communities sent a clear message to the world: Muslims' lives and dignity do not matter.

Counterterrorism gave carte blanche to Western governments to disregard liberal principles of civil liberties, anti-discrimination principles, rule of law, and religious pluralism. While the first people to pay the costs of such retraction of liberalism were Muslims, the rights infringements soon spread to other minority groups and, in some cases, the society at large.[7]

Concurrent with the spread of Islamophobia within the GWOT were substantial shifts in demographics and migration patterns from the global east and global south to the global north.[8] Decades of neoliberal capitalist globalization have caused seismic socioeconomic changes across the world. Multinational corporations have moved high-paying jobs out of the United States and Europe to

---

[3] Sahar F. Aziz, "The Authoritarianization of US Counterterrorism," *Washington and Lee Law Review* 75, no. 3 (2018): p. 1573.

[4] Beth Elise Whitaker, "Exporting the Patriot Act? Democracy and the 'War on Terror' in the Third World," *Third World Quarterly* 28, no. 5 (2007): pp. 1017–32; Khaled A. Beydoun, "Exporting Islamophobia in the Global 'War on Terror,'" *New York University Law Review* 95 (2020): pp. 81–100.

[5] Joseph A. Massad, *Islam in Liberalism* (Chicago, IL: University of Chicago Press, 2015).

[6] Sahar Aziz, *The Racial Muslim: When Racism Quashes Religious Freedom* (Berkeley: University of California Press, 2021).

[7] Miller, "SPLC Poll"; "Eastern and Western Europeans Differ on Importance of Religion, Views of Minorities, and Key Social Issues," Pew Research Center, October 29, 2018, https://www.pewr esearch.org/religion/2018/10/29/eastern-and-western-europeans-differ-on-importance-of-relig ion-views-of-minorities-and-key-social-issues/; Neli Esipova, Julie Ray, and Anita Pugliese, "World Grows Less Accepting of Migrants," Gallup, September 23, 2020, https://news.gallup.com/poll/320 678/world-grows-less-accepting-migrants.aspx.

[8] Anusha Natarajan, Mohamad Moslimani, and Mark Hugo Lopez, "Key Facts about Recent Trends in Global Migration," Pew Research Center, December 16, 2022, https://www.pewresearch. org/fact-tank/2022/12/16/key-facts-about-recent-trends-in-global-migration/.

developing nations where workers are paid much less for more work.[9] Corporate profits are not reinvested in the host countries, nor do they pay sufficient local taxes, leaving governments struggling to meet the basic needs of their people.[10] The increasing domestic poverty in turn presses people to seek work in wealthier countries in the global north where they often find a society in need of low-wage workers but hostile to foreigners.[11]

This steady flow of economic migrants into Europe and the United States has changed the racial and ethnic demographics of societies that have always been majority White and Christian.[12] The now defunct practices of affordable housing, quality public education, and gainful employment that were once provided by western European governments to their citizens have left them collectively worse off—and resentful.[13] Within this toxic mix of xenophobia, White Christian nationalism, and decreasing social mobility, the phoenix of right-wing populism arises. Nationalist political parties, marginalized since World War II, are exploiting Islamophobia to gain followers. Right-wing populists' blaming of Muslims (and other ethnic minorities) for White citizens' economic grievances and perceived loss of status has been a political boon.[14]

Islamophobia and Right-Wing Populism

The definition of Islamophobia in this volume is the exaggerated fear, hatred, and hostility toward Islam and Muslims by state and private actors arising from imputed inferior biological or cultural traits that are based on religious identity. More specifically, Islamophobia portrays Muslims as "(1) monolithic and

---

[9] "Offshoring US Labor Increasing," PRB, September 30, 2008, https://www.prb.org/resources/offshoring-u-s-labor-increasing/.

[10] "Inequality and Poverty: The Hidden Costs of Tax Dodging," Oxfam International, accessed January 4, 2023, https://www.oxfam.org/en/inequality-and-poverty-hidden-costs-of-tax-dodging.

[11] Natarajan, Moslimani, and Lopez, "Key Facts."

[12] PRRI Staff, "The 2020 Census of American Religion," PRRI, July 8, 2020, https://www.prri.org/research/2020-census-of-american-religion/; "Less Than Half of England and Wales Population Christian, Census 2021 Shows," BBC News, November 29, 2022, https://www.bbc.com/news/uk-63792408; Jade Le Deley, "Immigrant Population Rises in France, but So Does Discrimination," *Christian Science Monitor*, July 18, 2022, https://www.csmonitor.com/World/Europe/2022/0718/Immigrant-population-rises-in-France-but-so-does-discrimination.

[13] Peter Taylor Gooby, Benjamin Leruth, and Heejung Chung, eds., "The Context: How European Welfare States Have Responded to Post-Industrialism, Ageing Populations, and Populist Nationalism," in *After Austerity: Welfare State Transformation in Europe After the Great Recession*, ed. Peter Taylor Gooby, Benjamin Leruth, and Heejung Chung (Oxford: Oxford University Press, 2017), 1–26. See, for example, Susi Meret and Andreas Beyer Gregersen, "Islam as a 'Floating Signifier': Right-Wing Populism and Perceptions of Muslims in Denmark," Brookings Institution, July 24, 2019, https://www.brookings.edu/research/islam-as-a-floating-signifier-right-wing-populism-and-perceptions-of-muslims-in-denmark/.

[14] Bart Bonikowski, "Three Lessons of Contemporary Populism in Europe and the United States," *Brown Journal of World Affairs* 23, no. 1 (Fall–Winter 2016): pp. 9–24.

4 SAHAR F. AZIZ AND JOHN L. ESPOSITO

static; (2) separate and 'other', not sharing the values of other cultures; (3) irrational, primitive and inferior to the West; (4) aggressive, violent and implicated in a clash of civilizations; (5) [possessing] an ideology used to promote political and military interests; (6) intolerant towards Western critiques; (7) deserving of the discriminatory practices towards and exclusion of Muslims; and (8) making anti-Muslim hostility natural and normal."[15] As a result, Islamophobia produces systemic bias, discrimination, marginalization, and exclusion of Muslims from social, political, and civic life.[16]

Each chapter in this volume demonstrates how the ubiquity of these negative and fallacious stereotypes across continents has harmed Muslims economically, politically, and socially. In the most egregious cases, Islamophobia has cost Muslims their lives and liberty. In India, for example, Muslims are bearing the brunt of the alarming rise of Hindutva—a right-wing Hindu-supremacist political movement endorsed by Prime Minister Narendra Modi.[17] Thousands of Muslim Indians have been killed by sectarianism fueled by Hindutva.[18] Millions of Chinese Uyghur Muslims have been rounded up into labor and so-called reeducation camps intended to coercively convert them out of Islam and to assimilate them into Han culture.[19] In Europe, right-wing populists leveraged anti-Muslim racism after 9/11 to further polarize Western societies for their political gain. Right-wing politicians' core principles that are opposed to the European Union (EU) and immigrants are deliberately framed in Islamophobic terms.[20] In all the nations examined in this volume, populism is a powerful mechanism through which Islamophobia spreads.

Populism comes in many varieties that are not specific to right- or left-wing politics. It "is an ideology or political movement that 'considers society to be ultimately separated into two homogeneous and antagonistic groups, the pure people versus the corrupt elite, and which argues that politics should be an expression of the volonté générale (general will) of the people.'"[21] As a result, populists separate society into two homogeneous and antagonistic groups,

[15] Raymond Taras, "Islamophobia Never Stands Still," *Ethnic and Racial Studies* 36, no. 3 (2013): pp. 417–18.

[16] Aziz, *Racial Muslim*, p. 21.

[17] Audrey Truschke, "Displacing and Disciplining Muslims in India's Burgeoning Hindu *Rashtra*," ch. 11 in this volume.

[18] Truschke, "Displacing," ch. 11 in this volume; Raheel Dhattiwala and Michael Biggs, "The Political Logic of Ethnic Violence: The Anti-Muslim Pogrom in Gujarat, 2002," *Politics and Society* 40, no. 4 (2012): pp. 483–516.

[19] Khaled A. Beydoun, "(Un)Made in China: Uyghur Muslims at the Intersection of Islamophobia and Ethnic Cleansing," ch. 13 in this volume.

[20] Farid Hafez, "Postcolonialism, Post–National Socialism, German Reunification, and the Rise of the Far Right: Making Sense of Islamophobia in Germany," ch. 5 in this volume.

[21] Bojan Bugaric, "The Two Faces of Populism: Between Authoritarian and Democratic Populism," *German Law Journal* 20 (2019): pp. 390–400 (quoting Cas Mudde, "The Populist Zeitgeist," *Government and Opposition* 20 (2004): p. 543.

the people versus *the elites*. The elites are purportedly depriving (or attempting to deprive) the sovereign people of their rights, values, and voice.[22] Populism distinguishes itself politically as prioritizing popular sovereignty and direct democracy; hence, populists claim to speak in the name of the common people while denouncing the elites. Beyond these features, populism emerges in a variety of forms such as agrarian, socioeconomic, reactionary, authoritarian, and progressive populism.[23]

Xenophobic, ethnonationalist populism is the most prevalent strain fueling global Islamophobia. It adopts a historical narrative that centers the values and experiences of a particular native-born ethnic group as the definitive founding dogma of that nation. Ethnonationalist populists, thus, define the *people* as excluding the nonnative, the foreigner, and even the co-citizen who does not fit into an imagined homogeneous majority. Intrinsically anti-pluralist, populists intentionally create an us-versus-them distinction as a means of pitting their preferred ethnic group against immigrants, refugees, or ethnic minorities who are scapegoated as threatening the native culture and security of the people.[24] Populist politics consequently prioritize the interests and will of the favored ethnonationalist *people* over the *others*.[25] Anyone from the majority group who opposes populists' xenophobic political agenda is a traitor siding with the invading immigrants.

Populist discourse accuses the elites of being lazy parasites at the top of a social and economic order that exploits hard-working ordinary citizens. Ethnonationalist populists blame the elites for allowing Muslim (and other) immigrants to enter the country to take jobs that rightfully belong to the majority ethnic and religious group. The lower wages of immigrants allegedly enrich the elite while impoverishing the native born. Moreover, right-wing populist leaders distrust the institutions of liberal democracy because these structures purportedly stand between them and the will of the people. They criticize mainstream politicians for an alleged lack of interest in the problems of ordinary citizens and then make unrealistic promises to solve those problems. Flouting the rule of law and explicitly rejecting the values of liberal democracy are other common tactics among right-wing populists and their followers.

---

[22] Daniele Albertazzi and Duncan McDonnell, "Introduction: The Sceptre and the Spectre," in *Twenty-First Century Populism: The Spectre of Western European Democracy* (New York: Palgrave Macmillan, 2008), 1–11.

[23] Bugaric, "Two Faces."

[24] Mudde, "Populist Zeitgeist"; Margaret Canovan, "Taking Politics to the People: Populism as the Ideology of Democracy," in *Democracies and the Populist Challenge*, ed. Yves Mény and Yves Surel (Palgrave Macmillan, 2002), 25–44; Jan-Werner Müller, *What Is Populism?* (Philadelphia: University of Pennsylvania Press, 2016); Paul A. Taggart, *The New Populism and the New Politics* (London, UK: Palgrave Macmillan, 1996).

[25] Erica Meijers, "Introduction," in *Populism in Europe*, ed. Erica Meijers (Luxembourg: Green European Foundation, 2017), pp. 5, 11–12.

6 SAHAR F. AZIZ AND JOHN L. ESPOSITO

Global Islamophobia in an Era of Populism explores the relationship between two global phenomena rising concurrently: Islamophobia and right-wing populism. The case studies of ten countries across three continents—North America, Europe, and Asia—demonstrate a troubling trend: right-wing politicians, buttressed by civil society groups and conservative media outlets, deploy Islamophobia to intensify the majority ethnic populations' fears of losing power and wealth.

Whether Islamophobic narratives seek to recruit White Christians in the United States and western Europe, Hindus in India, Burmese in Myanmar, or Han people in China, the messaging is the same: Muslims are a threat to the nation's domestic security. Public debates about political violence, social divisions, or economic problems consistently point to Muslims as the scapegoats. They are supposedly conspiring to impose shariah law, planning terrorist attacks, or stealing jobs from the majority group claiming superiority in the nation.[26] Consequently, Muslim minorities across the world are experiencing myriad forms of discrimination by their governments as well as individuals acting on anti-Muslim prejudice.

While the extent of redress available to Muslims varies depending on the nation's government and legal system, Islamophobia is steadily rising globally across the regions studied here. Like any comparative study, this book illuminates both the similarities and differences in the origins and manifestations of Islamophobia. Each chapter provides a context-specific analysis of a nation's historical relationship with Muslims, treatment of immigrants, and commitments (or not) to ethnic and religious pluralism. The book's final chapter, by former South African Ambassador Ibrahim Rasool, is a warning call based on lessons learned from the nation with the longest lasting apartheid system in history.

White Christian Nationalism and Islamophobia in the United States

Among the ten countries studied, the United States stands out as largely comprising immigrants and their progeny. The first wave of European immigrants established a settler-colonial society that nearly exterminated the native population and imported millions of enslaved Africans to build the nation.[27] The legacies of slavery and settler colonialism continue to collectively

---

[26] Cyra Akila Choudhury, "Racecraft and Identity in the Emergence of Islam as a Race" (Legal Studies Research Paper No. 22–02, Florida International University, 2022).

[27] Kiana Cox and Christine Tamir, "Family History, Slavery and Knowledge of Black History" (Race Is Central to Identity for Black Americans and Affects How They Connect with Each Other series) Pew Research Center, April 14, 2022, https://www.pewresearch.org/race-ethnicity/2022/04/14/black-americans-family-history-slavery-and-knowledge-of-black-history/; "Fact Sheet: American

INTRODUCTION 7

disadvantage African Americans and Native American communities, which currently compose 15 percent of the population.[28]

Paradoxically, this "nation of immigrants" has practiced systemic xenophobia against newcomers since its founding. The severity of xenophobia against immigrants correlates to the similarity of their religions, cultures, and skin color to the descendants of the first wave of northwest European, Protestant immigrants. The more different the immigrants than the White Protestant settlers, the worse they were treated. Each wave of immigration from non-European or non-Protestant countries, therefore, was met with a violent backlash of White Protestant nativism. Thus, racism against Asian, Latine, Jewish, and Catholic immigrants is a staple of American history.[29] As such, Islamophobia is a continuation of American xenophobia and racism against non-Whites.

But post-9/11 Islamophobia differs from typical American xenophobia in important ways. Saher Selod and Asma Uddin's chapters demonstrate the pervasive and systematic forms of American Islamophobia during the past twenty years. For the first time in American history, Muslims are treated as the most dangerous domestic and foreign threat to the American polity. If President George W. Bush's and President Barack Obama's policies did not make this clear, then the explicitly Islamophobic discourse of President Donald Trump confirmed it.[30] Contemporary Islamophobia corroborates Joseph Massad's argument: Islam has long been an enemy trope against which Western civilization is elevated as superior.[31]

Notably, the most religious White Americans are often also the most antagonistic toward Muslims. As Asma Uddin notes, "[a] 2017 Pew poll found that two-thirds of white evangelicals believe that Islam is not part of mainstream American society and that it encourages violence more than other faiths do. Compared to 44 percent of Americans overall, 72 percent of white evangelicals see a natural

---

Indians and Alaska Natives—by the Numbers," Administration for Native Americans, accessed January 2, 2023, https://www.acf.hhs.gov/ana/fact-sheet/american-indians-and-alaska-natives-numbers#:~:text=There%20are%205.2%20million%20American,Indian%20or%20Alaska%20Native%20residents.

[28] Natsu Saito Taylor, *Settler Colonialism, Race and the Law: Why Structural Racism Persists* (New York: New York University Press, 2018); "Fact Sheet: American Indians"; "Quick Facts: United States," US Census Bureau, accessed January 8, 2023, https://www.census.gov/quickfacts/fact/table/US/PST045221.

[29] Aziz, *Racial Muslim*.

[30] Asma T. Uddin, "The Politics of Vulnerability: Today's Threat to American Muslims' Religious Freedom," ch. 3 in this volume; Sahar F. Aziz, "A Muslim Registry: The Precursor to Internment?," *Brigham Young University Law Review* 2017, no. 4 (2017): pp. 779–838; Sahar F. Aziz, "Caught in a Preventive Paradigm: Selective Counterterrorism in a Post-9/11 America," *Gonzaga Law Review* 47, no. 2 (2011): pp. 429–92.

[31] Joseph Massad, "The Price of Recognition: The One Islam and the Many," ch. 2 in this volume. .

conflict between Islam and democracy."[32] About half of these evangelicals subscribe to Christian nationalism, and thus pursue this political agenda through self-identity, certain interpretations of US history, "sacred symbols, cherished values, and public policies."[33] Muslims (and other non-Christians) pose a threat to their ethnonationalist vision of America.[34]

Compounding Christian-nationalist fears is the fast-approaching point when Whites will no longer be the majority race. Uddin notes, "[T]he majority of Americans under the age of sixteen are nonwhite and have been since the middle of 2020. Pew has found that whites generally will become a minority by 2055; the US Census says that will happen even sooner, in 2044."[35] These seismic demographic shifts will redraw the lines of in-group identity in ways yet unknown. In one scenario, America could become a minority-controlled nation should White, Judeo-Christian identity retain its group dominance. In the alternative, Whiteness could be socially reconstructed to include light-skinned Latines (the largest non-European racial category) and mixed-race Americans as a means of preserving the majority status necessary for retaining political and social dominance.[36]

Informing White Christian nationalists as well as the American intelligentsia are the works of orientalist scholars Samuel Huntington and Bernard Lewis. Huntington and Lewis's influential work argues that in Orientalist notions of Muslims, "Islam is monolithic as well as a static and unchanging culture that is defined by its antiquated ideas, making it the opposite of cultures that are defined by progress and modernity, like the 'West.'"[37] As a result, "modernity is a racialized concept that only Western and European cultures can achieve."[38]

---

[32] Uddin, "Politics," ch. 3 in this volume. In this passage, Uddin cites Michael Lipka, "Muslims and Islam: Key Findings in the US and around the World," Pew Research Center, August 9, 2017, https://www.pewresearch.org/fact-tank/2017/08/09/muslims-and-islam-key-findings-in-the-u-s-and-around-the-world/; Emma Green, "How Much Discrimination Do Muslims Face in America?," *The Atlantic*, July 26, 2017, https://www.theatlantic.com/politics/archive/2017/07/american-musl ims-trump/534879/); Eric L. McDaniel, Irfan Nooruddin, and Allyson F. Shortle, *The Everyday Crusade: Christian Nationalism in American Politics* (Cambridge: Cambridge University Press, 2022).

[33] Andrew Whitehead and Samuel Perry, *Taking America Back for God: Christian Nationalism in the United States* (Oxford: Oxford University Press, 2020), p. 78; quoted in Uddin, "Politics," ch. 3 in this volume.

[34] Selod, "Islamophobia," ch. 4 in this volume.

[35] Uddin, "Politics," ch. 3 in this volume. Uddin cites Mike Schneider, "Census Shows White Decline, Nonwhite Majority among Youngest," Associated Press, June 25, 2020, https://apnews. com/a3600edf620ccf2759080d00f154c069; "Modern Immigration Wave Brings 59 Million to US, Driving Population Growth and Change through 2065," Pew Research Center, September 28, 2015, https://www.pewresearch.org/hispanic/2015/09/28/modern-immigration-wave-brings-59-million-to-u-s-driving-population-growth-and-change-through-2065/; "Projecting Majority-Minority," US Census Bureau, 2014, https://www.census.gov/content/dam/Census/newsroom/releases/2015/cb15-tps16_graphic.pdf.

[36] Richard Alba, *The Great Demographic Illusion: Majority, Minority, and the Expanding American Mainstream* (Princeton, NJ: Princeton University Press, 2020).

[37] Selod, "Islamophobia," ch. 4 in this volume.

[38] Selod, "Islamophobia," ch. 4 in this volume.

INTRODUCTION 9

Saher Selod notes, "Lewis's scholarship on 'Islamic' cultures was so influential on the foreign policy of the administration of President George W. Bush and Vice President Dick Cheney that he served as an advisor during the Iraq War."[39]

Domestically, Muslims individually and collectively suffered from Islamophobic discrimination and violence. For example, an organized right-wing campaign attacked Keith Ellison, the first Muslim elected to Congress in 2006. Among the various Islamophobic messages circulated was a call not to vote for a Muslim because Islam is an ideology that is inherently violent.[40] Mosques across the country were also attacked, notwithstanding many right-wing politicians' proclaimed commitments to religious freedom. Islamophobic politicians unabashedly argued that mosques trained terrorists, oppressed Muslim women, and threatened domestic Christian hegemony.[41] The anti-Islam hysteria went as far as prompting state legislatures across the country to consider anti-Sharia bills on the grounds that Muslims were secretly plotting to impose Islamic law in the United States.[42]

The same people fomenting hate against Muslims were also peddling anti-Black racism in the anti-Obama birther movement. Deeply rooted racism against African Americans converged with anti-Muslim racism to fuel a right-wing crusade to oust the first African American President.[43] Alleging that Barack Obama was a secret Muslim born outside the United States, the birthers (tellingly led by Donald Trump) exploited the political acceptability of Islamophobia to engage in thinly veiled anti-Black racism. Consequently, Islamophobia in America cannot be understood outside of the context of America's history of xenophobia against immigrants and of anti-Black racism. The same context-specific analysis applies to Europe, where animus toward Muslims dates back centuries.[44]

Xenophobia and Islamophobia in Europe

It is no coincidence that European right-wing populists proclaim it their mission to "protect the identity of the 'Christian Western civilization' by closing borders and attacking cultural, ethnic and religious minorities."[45] The juxtaposition of Europe as civilized against the supposedly barbaric Middle East and North

---

[39] Selod, "Islamophobia," ch. 4 in this volume. Here, Selod cites Douglas Martin, "Bernard Lewis, Influential Scholar of Islam, Is Dead at 101," The New York Times, May 21, 2018, https://www.nytimes.com/2018/05/21/obituaries/bernard-lewis-islam-scholar-dies.html.

[40] Selod, "Islamophobia," ch. 4 in this volume.

[41] Selod, "Islamophobia," ch. 4 in this volume.

[42] Selod, "Islamophobia," ch. 4 in this volume.

[43] Selod, "Islamophobia," ch. 4 in this volume.

[44] Massad, "Price," ch. 2 in this volume.

[45] Meijers, "Introduction," p. 5.

Africa is a narrative that for centuries legitimized colonizing the region. That the Oriental Muslim has served as the quintessential foil against which Western liberalism is constructed makes Muslims in Europe perennially vulnerable to permanent marginalization and scapegoating for domestic grievances.[46]

Islamophobia in Europe is also linked to economics. When European governments enacted austerity measures as part of neoliberal structural reforms, citizens' economic grievances were leveraged by right-wing parties' challenges to incumbents. Neoliberal economic policies coupled with fiscal austerity have contributed to economic stagnation, unemployment, and poverty. Right-wing populists thus strategically exploit the consequent disaffection to call for the dissolution of the EU. Lacking an alternative economic plan, the political right misdirects public angst to collectively blame immigrants, especially Muslims.

While all non-European immigrants were targets of right-wing politicians before 9/11, European xenophobia has been directed almost exclusively at Muslims. What was once ethnonationalist has become an ethno-religious threat perception. The Islamophobia strategy has proven wildly successful, as evidenced by right-wing populist parties' alarmingly rapid growth.[47] Contemporary right-wing populists portray cultural tolerance, migration, multiculturalism, religious neutrality, and pluralism as threats to the interests and livelihoods of the White Christian majority.[48] Even voters who do not regard themselves as right-wing still support Marine Le Pen's Nationalist Front Party in France or Jörg Haider's Freedom Party in Austria, because of a shared sense of racial fear among White Christians.[49]

European Islamophobia's narratives mirror those in North America: Islam is incompatible with an imagined homogeneity of White Christian values. No distinction is made between the tiny percentage of Muslims engaging in terrorism and the tens of millions of ordinary, law-abiding Muslims. Indeed, the latter are purportedly Trojan horses waiting to invade Western nations from within. As Farid Hafez, Marwan Mohammed, and Ivan Kalmar explain, populist right-wing parties define their electoral strategy by attacking Muslims and Islam as the scapegoats for the nation's economic problems. This translates

---

[46] Massad, "Price," ch. 2 in this volume.

[47] Enes Bayrakli and Farid Hafez, eds., *European Islamophobia Report 2021* (Vienna, Austria: Leopold Weiss Institute, 2022), https://islamophobiareport.com/en/.

[48] Hafez, "Postcolonialism," ch. 5 in this volume; Mobashra Tazamal, "Islamophobia: How the Far Right Went Mainstream in Britain," ch. 6 in this volume; Marwan Mohammed, "France's Islamophobic Bloc and the 'Mainstreamization' of the Far Right," ch. 7 in this volume; Ivan Kalmar, "Islamophobia without Muslims? Not Only in Eastern Europe," ch. 8 in this volume; Sahar F. Aziz and Sarah Calderone, "Islamophobia in Russia: Ethnicity, Migration, and National Security," ch. 9 in this volume; John Farmer and Ava Majlesi, "Muslim Life in Belgium: In Search of a *Vivre ensemble*," ch. 10 in this volume.

[49] Hafez, "Postcolonialism," ch. 5 in this volume; Mohammed, "France's Islamophobic Bloc," ch. 7 in this volume.

INTRODUCTION 11

politically into Islamophobic populist parties' promises to shut down mosques and Islamic schools, ban the hijab and halal food, and bar Muslims from entering their countries. Moreover, populists attack mainstream incumbent liberal politicians who support cultural tolerance and multiculturalism as part of the corrupt elite oppressing the ordinary (non-Muslim, White) native-born citizens. Islamophobia is the right-wing populist anti-paradigm.[50]

The chapters examining Islamophobia in Europe reveal how each nation's distinct history shapes ethnonationalist populism. Germany's colonial practices in southwest Africa, for example, buttresses its Nazi past to sustain racist politics, even if marginalized. Farid Hafez deftly explains how German tensions arising from reunification and anti-immigrant sentiment converged after 2001 to mainstream Islamophobia, despite the nation's decades-long attempts to combat racism after the Holocaust. Hafez highlights that right-wing populists promote the "notion of an imagined Judeo-Christian tradition that excludes the third-largest religion from German society, with Muslims portrayed as unwilling fit into society (*integrationsunwillig*). Islamism was used primarily in connection to extremism as a security threat."[51] Media and politics reproduced a discourse that portrayed immigration as a threat to German society and, more specifically, Muslims as a threat to national security especially after 9/11.[52]

As a result, polls show that in 2019, "50 percent of the population from the former west Germany, and 57 percent of those from the former east Germany believe that Islam poses a threat to them."[53] Another poll found "42 percent of Germans from the former west Germany and 51 percent from the former east Germany agree with the statement that Muslims should be prohibited from immigrating to Germany."[54] But the anti-Muslim prejudice is not limited to Germany. Right-wing political parties in other European countries (such as the Netherlands, France, Austria, and Belgium) that infrequently cooperated in the

---

[50] Cas Mudde and Cristobal Rovira Kaltwasser, *Populism: A Very Short Introduction* (Oxford: Oxford University Press, 2017).

[51] Hafez, "Postcolonialism," ch. 5 in this volume. Here, Hafez cites Farid Hafez, "Islamophobie und die deutschen Bundestagsparteien: Eine Analyse vom 27. Oktober 2009 bis 9. Juni 2011" ["Islamophobia and the German Parliamentary Parties: An Analysis from October 27, 2009, to June 9, 2011"], in *Verhärtete Fronten: Der schwere Weg zu einer vernünftigen Islamkritik* [*Hardened Fronts: The Hard Way to a Reasonable Criticism of Islam*], ed. Thorsten Gerald Schneiders (Wiesbaden, Germany: Springer, 2012).

[52] Hafez, "Postcolonialism," ch. 5 in this volume.

[53] Hafez, "Postcolonialism," ch. 5 in this volume. Hafez here cites Gert Pickel, *Weltanschauliche Vielfalt und Demokratie: Wie sich religiöse Pluralität auf die politische Kultur auswirkt* [*Ideological Diversity and Democracy: How Religious Plurality Affects Political Culture*] (Gütersloh, Germany: Bertelsmann Stiftung, 2019), https://www.bertelsmann-stiftung.de/fileadmin/files/BSt/Publikationen/GrauePublikationen/Religionsmonitor_Vielfalt_und_Demokratie_7_2019.pdf.

[54] Hafez, "Postcolonialism," ch. 5 in this volume. In this passage, Hafez cites Oliver Decker and Elmar Brähler, *Flucht ins Autoritäre: Rechtsextreme Dynamiken in der Mitte der Gesellschaft* [*Flight into Authoritarianism: Right-Wing Extremist Dynamics in the Middle of Society*] (Gießen, Germany: Psychosozial-Verlag, 2018).

past are now united under the banner of fighting alleged Islamization of their societies.[55]

Mobashra Tazamal explains the relationship between Islamophobia and right-wing populist groups in Britain (where Muslims are 6.5 percent of the population) during the historic Brexit debates.[56] After growing opposition to the EU, a sentiment shared across conservatives in Europe, Britons put the issue to a referendum. What should have been a debate over political sovereignty and economic policy turned into a boon for ethno-religious populists. Tazamal highlights the role of British politician Nigel Farage, head of the right-wing United Kingdom Independence Party (UKIP), in the Brexit campaign.[57] In leading Leave.EU, Farage "deployed populist tactics by playing on perceived grievances among the white working class. The campaign put immigration at the heart of its messaging, claiming that it put a strain on jobs and public services."[58] Tazamal notes that only ten days before the Brexit vote, the UKIP distributed "the infamous Breaking Point poster . . . showing a long queue of refugees, primarily people of color, with the slogan 'Breaking point: The EU has failed us all' and subheading 'We must break free of the EU and take back control of our borders.'"[59] Farage went even further to blame refugees for all violence in Europe and "insinuated that those fleeing persecution, bombs, and mass violence were likely to be 'jihadi terrorists' rather than refugees."[60]

The Islamophobic strategy was so successful that a 2017 study found "psychological predictors of xenophobia were strongly linked with voting to leave the EU and support for the outcome of the referendum."[61] Likewise, a 2018 poll by "Hope Not Hate found that almost half of Conservative voters (47 percent) and

---

[55] Farid Hafez, "Shifting Borders: Islamophobia as Common Ground for Building Pan-European Right-Wing Unity," *Patterns of Prejudice*, 48, no. 5 (2014): pp. 479–99.

[56] Aamna Mohdin, "Census Says 39% of Muslims Live in Most Deprived Areas of England and Wales," *The Guardian*, November 30, 2022, https://www.theguardian.com/world/2022/nov/30/census-says-39-of-muslims-live-in-most-deprived-areas-of-england-and-wales.

[57] "Factsheet: UKIP," Bridge Initiative, January 7, 2019, https://bridge.georgetown.edu/research/factsheet-ukip/.

[58] Tazamal, "Islamophobia," ch. 6 in this volume. Tazamal here cites Adam Lusher, "EU Immigrants Help Create Jobs, Not Take Them, Study Claims," *Independent*, June 20, 2016, https://www.independent.co.uk/news/uk/politics/eu-referendum-immigration-immigrants-jobs-brexit-remain-what-happens-unemployment-a7091566.html.

[59] Tazamal, "Islamophobia," ch. 6 in this volume.

[60] Tazamal, "Islamophobia," ch. 6 in this volume. Here, Tazamal cites Rowena Mason and Heather Stewart, "Nigel Farage Anti-Migrant Poster Reported to Police," *The Guardian*, June 16, 2016, https://www.theguardian.com/politics/2016/jun/16/nigel-farage-defends-ukip-breaking-point-poster-queue-of-migrants.

[61] Agnieszka Golec de Zavala, Rita Guerra, and Claudia Simão, "The Relationship between the Brexit Vote and Individual Predictors of Prejudice: Collective Narcissism, Right Wing Authoritarianism, Social Dominance Orientation," *Frontiers Psychology*, November 27, 2017, https://www.frontiersin.org/articles/10.3389/fpsyg.2017.02023/full#h5; Josh Gabbatiss, "Brexit Strongly Linked to Xenophobia, Scientists Conclude," *Independent*, November 27, 2017, https://www.independent.co.uk/news/science/brexit-prejudice-scientists-link-foreigners-immigrants-racism-xenophobia-leave-eu-a8078586.html; quoted in Tazamal, "Islamophobia," ch. 6 in this volume.

INTRODUCTION   13

those who voted to leave the EU (49 percent) believed that Islam was a threat to the British way of life."[62] Tazamal's chapter connects the rising xenophobia in Britain to hate crimes, which increased by 57 percent in the week following the Brexit vote while cases of religious and racially motivated hate crimes increased by 23 percent in the subsequent year.[63]

Concurrently, Islamophobia has been on the rise in France but under a different political narrative. France's history of colonization in North Africa made it uniquely antagonistic toward Muslims. Even though Muslims of North African descent are France's largest religious and ethnic minority, Marwan Mohammed argues that the very presence of Muslims on French soil is perceived as a problem by both the political right and left in what is commonly termed the *Muslim problem*.[64] Mohammed concludes that "France is one of the Western democracies that goes the furthest in developing laws and institutional arrangements for the control, discipline, and legal discrimination of Muslim populations, limiting the legal means to fight against Islamophobia."[65] He highlights a key difference in France as compared to other European countries: "Rather than describe the tension between an immutable, white, and Catholic France and an unassimilable, nonwhite, and non-European population, [Islamophobic discourse] claimed to defend the 'Republic' and 'secularism' besieged by 'Islamism.'"[66] Mohammed's nuanced analysis reveals the connection between Islamophobia among the left and right in France. For example, the "Great Replacement" conspiracy theories of the right wing are not much different from the "small-replacement" theories of the French left, which both center on anti-Muslim racism, albeit for different reasons.

But even in European countries with few Muslims, Islamophobia is still prevalent. Ivan Kalmar's chapter perceptively demonstrates the salience of Islamophobia in Poland, the Czech Republic, Slovakia, and Hungary. The Pew Research Center finds that "Muslims made up less than 0.1 percent of the

---

[62] Tazamal, "Islamophobia," ch. 6 in this volume. Here, Tazamal cites Frances Perraudin, "Third of Britons Believe Islam Threatens British Way of Life, Says Report," *The Guardian*, February 17, 2019, https://www.theguardian.com/world/2019/feb/17/third-of-britons-believe-islam-threatens-british-way-of-life-says-report.

[63] "Post Brexit, Post Trump Islamophobia," Muslim Engagement and Development, October 2017, https://www.mend.org.uk/wp-content/uploads/2017/10/Post-Brexit-Post-Trump-Islamopho bia.pdf; May Bulman, "Brexit Vote Sees Highest Spike in Religious and Racial Hate Crimes Ever Recorded," *Independent*, July 10, 2017, https://www.independent.co.uk/news/uk/home-news/racist-hate-crimes-surge-record-high-after-brexit-vote-new-figures-reveal-a7829551.html.

[64] Mohammed, "France's Islamophobic Bloc," ch. 7 in this volume. Mohammed here cites Joseph Gusfield, *La Culture des problèmes publics: L'Alcool au volant; la production d'un ordre symbolique* [*The Culture of Public Problems: Drinking and Driving; the Production of a Symbolic Order*] (Paris: Economica, 2009).

[65] Mohammed, "France's Islamophobic Bloc," ch. 7 in this volume.

[66] Mohammed, "France's Islamophobic Bloc," ch. 7 in this volume. Mohammed here cites Abdellali Hajjat and Marwan Mohammed, *Islamophobie: Comment les élites fabriquent le "problème musulman"* [*How the Elites Construct the "Muslim Problem"*] (Paris: La Découverte, 2013), ch. 3.

population in Poland, 0.1 percent in Slovakia, 0.2 percent in the Czech Republic, and 0.4 percent in Hungary in 2016."[67] Kalmar argues that while the Syrian war that brought more than a million refugees to Europe through land and sea triggered overt Islamophobic racism, the explanation for it is more complex.[68] The phenomena of *Islamophobia without Muslims* is the consequence of *"peripherality*, as it manifests itself in the current stage of capitalist society in the EU and elsewhere. The frustrations and insecurities of peripheral areas and groups in the west have found a misdirected outlet in Islamophobia. East central Europe is one of these peripheral areas, but it is not the only one."[69]

According to Kalmar's theory, geographic and class peripherality within the EU paradoxically correlates with Islamophobia. Hence, countries most harmed by the rise of the neoliberal order, because of their peripherality from the centers of power in Europe, may express their grievances through Islamophobia, among other forms. This is facilitated by eastern central European countries' "close relationship to antisemitism [that] makes it possible to tap into the affective and rhetorical reservoir also of anti-Judaism."[70] Indeed, Kalmar points out that the racialization of Muslims in European Islamophobic discourse is disturbingly similar to the racialization of Jews during World War II.[71]

In their analysis of Islamophobia in Belgium, John Farmer and Ava Majlesi identify the most pressing challenge facing Muslims: police abuse. Segregated into ghettos, the mostly low-income Muslim communities are over-policed as suspected terrorists. The Belgian populists who leveraged the GWOT to perpetuate Islamophobia, as did their counterparts across Europe and North America, gained a significant following the decade prior to 9/11. The far-right party now known as the Flemish Interest Party began its rise in 1991, when it won 6.6 percent of the vote in the national elections.[72] Farmer and Majlesi note that the party's popularity rose with its anti-immigrant calls for "abolishing 'multicultural indoctrination' in schools, setting up a 'foreigners' police' charged with tracking down illegal immigrants in Belgium, and a series of limitations on the rights of foreigners in the country."[73]

---

[67] Kalmar, "Islamophobia," ch. 8 in this volume. Here, Kalmar cites Conrad Hackett, Phillip Connor, Marcin Stonawski, and Michaela Potančoková, "Europe's Growing Muslim Population," Pew Research Center, November 29, 2017, https://www.pewforum.org/2017/11/29/europes-growing-muslim-population/pf_11-29-17_muslims-update-20/.

[68] Kalmar, "Islamophobia," ch. 8 in this volume.

[69] Kalmar, "Islamophobia," ch. 8 in this volume (emphasis in original).

[70] Kalmar, "Islamophobia," ch. 8 in this volume. In this passage, Kalmar cites Ivan Kalmar, *Early Orientalism: Imagined Islam and the Notion of Sublime Power* (New York: Routledge, 2014); Ivan Kalmar, "Orientalism," in *Key Concepts in the Study of Antisemitism*, ed. Sol Goldberg, Scott Ury, and Kalman Weiser (Cham, Switzerland: Palgrave, 2020), pp. 187–99.

[71] Kalmar, "Islamophobia," ch. 8 in this volume.

[72] Farmer and Majlesi, "Muslim Life," ch. 10 in this volume.

[73] Laurens Cerulus, "Inside the Far Right's Flemish Victory," *Politico*, May 27, 2019, https://www.politico.eu/article/inside-the-far-rights-flemish-victory/; quoted in Farmer and Majlesi, "Muslim Life," ch. 10 in this volume.

INTRODUCTION 15

Over time, what were once the fringe ideas of a far-right-wing party moved into the mainstream, with support in the highest levels of Belgian government.[74] By 2020, Belgium experienced "'some of the largest decreases in tolerant attitudes,' with its score falling by 1.33 index points" in the Gallup Migrant Acceptance Index.[75]

Farmer and Majlesi's analysis also shows how government structures make Belgium uniquely vulnerable to the mainstreaming of right-wing populism. Specifically, the nation's tripartite federalist structure between French-, German-, and Flemish-speaking regions leaves little room for others to belong. Despite living in Belgium for multiple generations, Belgian Muslims are relegated to being perpetual outsiders. This makes them especially vulnerable to collective punishment when an individual Muslim commits a terrorist act. Moreover, laws that circumscribe religious freedoms, such as prohibiting women from wearing the headscarf, only reinforce Muslim communities' outsider status. The combination of over-policing, political vilification, and the denial of full religious-freedom rights are products of the racialization of Muslim identity as dangerous and permanently foreign—an Islamophobic stereotype also afflicting Muslim minorities in Asia.

Hindu, Han, and Burmese Supremacy in Asia

South Asia is home to nearly 600 million Muslims.[76] Indeed, the three most populous Muslim-majority countries are in Asia: Indonesia (280 million), Pakistan (238 million), and Bangladesh (172 million).[77] In India, although Muslims are only 13 percent of the population of 1.4 billion, they are the third-largest Muslim population living in a single state, at 200 million people.[78] Despite having lived in India for multiple generations, Indian Muslims face varying forms and degrees

---

[74] Farmer and Majlesi, "Muslim Life," ch. 10 in this volume.

[75] Farmer and Majlesi, "Muslim Life," ch. 10 in this volume. Here, Farmer and Majlesi cite Alex Berry, "Anti-Immigrant Attitudes Rise Worldwide: Poll," *Deutsche Welle*, September 23, 2020, https://www.dw.com/en/anti-immigrant-attitudes-rise-worldwide-poll/a-55024481; Neli Esipova, Julie Ray, and Anita Pugliese, "World Grows Less Accepting of Migrants," Gallup, September 23, 2020, https://news.gallup.com/poll/320678/world-grows-less-accepting-migrants.aspx.

[76] "Muslim Population by Country 2023," World Population Review, accessed January 4, 2023, https://worldpopulationreview.com/country-rankings/muslim-population-by-country.

[77] "Muslim Population by Country 2023"; "Indonesia Population (Live)," Worldometers.info, accessed January 4, 2023, https://www.worldometers.info/world-population/indonesia-population/; "Pakistan Population 2023 (Live)," World Population Review, accessed January 4, 2023, https://worldpopulationreview.com/countries/pakistan-population; "Bangladesh Population 2023 (Live)," World Population Review, accessed January 4, 2023, https://worldpopulationreview.com/countries/bangladesh-population.

[78] "India Population 2023 (Live)," World Population Review, accessed January 4, 2023, https://worldpopulationreview.com/countries/india-population.

16 SAHAR F. AZIZ AND JOHN L. ESPOSITO

of oppression. To be sure, the civil war after India obtained independence from Britain unleashed violence against both Hindus and Muslims who were forcibly relocated to present-day Pakistan, Bangladesh, and India. But Muslims in India increasingly experienced sectarian violence by a Hindu majority that treated them as a fifth column that was presumptively loyal to Pakistan.

While the complex origins of Islamophobia intersect with caste, class, and ethnicity in India, the political ideology of Hindutva has engendered a right-wing populist movement centered on Hindu supremacy. Audrey Truschke's cogent analysis demonstrates that "a consistent feature of Hindutva ideologues is the treatment of Muslims as their primary enemy."[79] As a result, "[m]any Hindutva discussions and writings cast Muslims as 'internal threats' and blood-thirsty conquerors, from Savarkar to Indian propaganda regarding the spread of COVID-19."[80] Truschke explains how this political movement that inspired the killer of Mahatma Gandhi is now the same ideology of the Bharatiya Janata Party (BJP)—the Hindu-nationalist party of Indian Prime Minister Narendra Modi.[81]

Since taking control of India's central government in 2014, the BJP has "accelerated [its] agenda to transform the constitutionally secular nation of India into an ethnonationalist state intolerant of religious minorities."[82] Truschke's chapter shows the danger posed to Indian Muslims by Hindutva by examining in depth three major events: the 2019 state policy changes regarding Kashmir, the late-2019 Citizenship Amendment Act, and the February 2020 Delhi riots.[83] In each event, the BJP-controlled Indian government exercised power to further Muslims' status as second-class citizens through laws, social policies, and a failure to hold accountable perpetrators of pogroms against Muslims. Meanwhile, then US President Donald Trump embraced Narendra Modi's policies, further evincing the transnationality of Islamophobia.

Supplementing Truschke's focus on human rights and political inequality, Stuti Govil and D. Asher Ghertner's chapter highlights an under-researched consequence of Islamophobia: "a spatial project of material denial, infrastructural disconnect, municipal exclusion, and spatial relegation."[84] Specifically, the BJP and

---

[79] Truschke, "Displacing," ch. 11 in this volume. See Shakuntala Banaji and Ram Bhat, "How Anti-Muslim Disinformation Campaigns in India Have Surged during COVID-19," LSE COVID-19 Blog, September 30, 2020, https://blogs.lse.ac.uk/covid19/2020/09/30/how-anti-muslim-disinfo rmation-campaigns-in-india-have-surged-during-covid-19/; Harsh Mander, "The Coronavirus Has Morphed into an Anti-Muslim Virus," Wire, April 13, 2020, https://thewire.in/communalism/coro navirus-anti-muslim-propaganda-india.

[80] Truschke, "Displacing," ch. 11 in this volume. Truschke here cites Christophe Jaffrelot, ed., Hindu Nationalism: A Reader (Princeton, NJ: Princeton University Press, 2007), p. 97.

[81] Truschke, "Displacing," ch. 11 in this volume.

[82] Truschke, "Displacing," ch. 11 in this volume.

[83] Truschke, "Displacing," ch. 11 in this volume.

[84] Stuti Govil and D. Asher Ghertner, "Contesting the Spatialization of Islamophobia in Urban India," ch. 12 in this volume. Here, Govil and Ghertner cite Nikhil Anand, "Municipal Disconnect: On Abject Water and Its Urban Infrastructures," Ethnography 13, no. 4 (2012): pp. 487–509.

INTRODUCTION 17

its supporters are harming "the everyday lived experience of Muslims struggling to access clean water and safe neighborhoods and to enjoy residential tenure security, economic facilities, and other basic needs."[85] Govil and Ghertner's examination of urban citizenship in India brings to light Muslim ghettoization and infrastructural neglect—an adverse consequence of systemic racism wherever it operates.[86] They argue that "Islamophobia as spatial practice as much as political discourse helps make evident the spatial predicates of Islamophobia within a longer history of Muslim ghettoization that predates the national rise of the BJP and the Babri Masjid demolition as well as the global, post-War-on-Terror discourse of 'Muslim terror' that often frames how Islamophobia is understood in South Asia and beyond."[87]

Khaled Beydoun examines another Muslim minority native to the land: the Uyghurs of the Xinyang province in northwest China. After being ruled by various dynasties for centuries, the Uyghurs were absorbed into the Republic of China when it was established in 1912. During the Chinese civil war in 1944, the Uyghur established the East Turkestan Republic, an event that has since caused the Chinese Communist Party to suspect Uyghurs as disloyal subversives.[88]

The independent Uyghur nation-state lasted only four years; in 1949, China annexed and renamed it *Xinjiang*, which means "new frontier" in Mandarin.[89]

Of Turkic ethnic origins, the Uyghurs' physical features are noticeably distinct from the Han majority. Their Muslim identity and Islamic practices also distinguish them in a predominantly Buddhist country. Beydoun notes that Uyghurs' claims of indigeneity to Xinjian threaten China's racial project to create a monolithic Chinese identity centered on Han identity. Toward that end, "[a] leading Chinese official declared at a United Nations Permanent Forum on Indigenous Issues hearing that 'China has no indigenous peoples.'"[90] Beydoun argues that the "Sinicization campaign is an 'inherently imperial project' seeking to suppress

---

[85] Govil and Ghertner, "Contesting," ch. 12 in this volume.

[86] Govil and Ghertner, "Contesting," ch. 12 in this volume. In the United States, anti-Black systemic racism also produces impoverished Black ghettos, infrastructure neglect, and mass incarceration. See Sheryll Cashin, *White Space, Black Hood: Opportunity Hoarding and Segregation in the Age of Inequality* (Boston, MA: Beacon Press, 2021).

[87] Govil and Ghertner, "Contesting," ch. 12 in this volume. Govil and Ghertner here cite Andrew Shryock, ed. *Islamophobia/Islamophilia: Beyond the Politics of Enemy and Friend* (Bloomington: Indian University Press, 2010).

[88] Beydoun, "(Un)Made," ch. 13 in this volume.

[89] Beydoun, "(Un)Made," ch. 13 in this volume. Here, Beydoun cites Sean Roberts, *The War on Uyghurs: China's Internal Campaign against a Muslim Minority* (Princeton, NJ: Princeton University Press, 2020), pp.126–27.

[90] Beydoun, "(Un)Made," ch. 13 in this volume. In this passage, Beydoun quotes "Statement by Counsellor Yao Shaojun of the Chinese Delegation at the 15th Session of the Permanent Forum on Indigenous Issues," Permanent Mission of the People's Republic of China to the United Nations, May 10, 2016, https://www.mfa.gov.cn/ce/ceun/eng/chinaandun/socialhr/3rdcommittee/t1308351.htm.

every manifestation of Uyghur identity and, most forcefully, to punish overtly political activity."[91]

The GWOT provided the ideal political cover for intensifying the Chinese government's decades-long attempts to forcibly assimilate Uyghurs. In October 2001, President Jiang Zemin met with President Bush to collaborate on counterterrorism, leading Bush to announce, "We have a common understanding of the magnitude of the threat posed by international terrorism."[92] As the United States targeted Middle Eastern and South Asian Muslim communities in the United States, the Chinese government aggressively cracked down on Uyghurs in Xinjiang.

The eleven million Uyghurs in China are subjected to mass surveillance, coercive cultural assimilation, and suspicion of subversion. All the while, the government is incentivizing, or in some cases forcing, Han Chinese to move to Xinjiang as part of the racial project of Sinicization. Beydoun's chapter explains the devastating consequences of China's unabashedly named Strike Hard campaign against Uyghurs. The destruction of mosques, arbitrary arrests, and the mass detention of one million people in concentration camps were all justified as necessary to preserve national security.[93] But no amount of politicking can cover up what human rights organizations condemn as ethnic genocide.[94]

Simultaneously, another Muslim minority is experiencing genocide in Myanmar. Ronan Lee provides a harrowing description of the brutality and violence experienced by the Rohingya. The Rohingya's Muslim identity marks them as inferior and outsiders to Myanmar's majority religion of Theravada Buddhism, despite their being native to the Rakhana region of the country.[95] For four decades, the ruling junta deployed law and power to oppress the Rohingya. Lee jarringly concludes, "Rohingya found themselves trapped in an apartheid state, and despite centuries of ancestry and uncontroversial post-independence recognition as part of the country's political fabric, they were excluded from the government's list of Indigenous groups, were well along on a path to collective statelessness, and increasingly regarded by the majority of Myanmar's population as foreigners."[96]

---

[91] Beydoun, "(Un)Made," ch. 13 in this volume. Here, Beydoun cites Michael Clarke, "China and the Uyghurs: The 'Palestinianization' of Xinjiang?," *Middle East Policy* 22 (2015): pp. 127, 128.

[92] Robin Wright and Edwin Chin, "Bush Says China Backs War on Terror," *Los Angeles Times*, October 18, 2001, https://www.latimes.com/la-101901bush-story.html; quoted in Beydoun, "(Un)Made," ch. 13 in this volume.

[93] Beydoun, "(Un)Made," ch. 13 in this volume; "OHCHR Assessment of Human Rights Concerns in the Xinjiang Uyghur Autonomous Region, People's Republic of China," United Nations Office of the High Commissioner for Human Rights, August 31, 2022, https://www.ohchr.org/sites/default/files/documents/countries/2022-08-31/22-08-31-final-assesment.pdf.

[94] "OHCHR Assessment."

[95] Ronan Lee, "Islamophobia and Genocide: Myanmar's Rohingya Genocide," ch. 14 in this volume.

[96] Lee, "Islamophobia," ch. 14 in this volume.

INTRODUCTION   19

Deep-seated anti-Muslim bigotry became fertile ground for the ethnic cleansing fueled by prominent Buddhist nationalists actively using social media to encourage religious and ethnic discord targeting Rohingya. Lee notes how Buddhist nationalists use language similar to the Western right-wing populists' Great Replacement theory to warn against an Islamic takeover of Myanmar, notwithstanding that 90 percent of the population is Buddhist.[97] Buddhist nationalists also point to Donald Trump's explicit Islamophobia as validation of their genocidal aims. An influential Buddhist monk proudly declared, "The World singled us out as narrow-minded. But as people from the country that is the grandfather of democracy and human rights elected Donald Trump, who is similar to me in prioritizing nationalism, there will be less finger-pointing from the international community."[98]

Conclusion

When the United States experienced the largest foreign terrorist attack on its soil, President Bush did not mince words. "Over time it's going to be important for nations to know they will be held accountable for inactivity," he said. "You're either with us or against us in the fight against terror."[99] While some countries responded with good-faith attempts to combat legitimate terrorism, autocrats recognized this golden opportunity to crack down on dissidents, political opponents, or insufficiently compliant minorities. In democratic states, liberals and conservatives alike adapted the mantras of Islamophobia to compete for the votes of a fear-stricken public. Right-wing groups also found Islamophobia a salient political platform for pursuing a broader anti-immigrant, anti-EU, or ethnic-supremacist agenda. Put simply, the GWOT legitimated hateful discourse that in turn justified racist state practices against Muslims across the world, albeit to different degrees and in various forms.

Accordingly, each chapter in this volume sounds the alarm about fractured, divided societies. Unprecedented internationalization of social movements, economies, and politics are leveraged by right-wing populists as force multipliers for Islamophobia. In examining origins and manifestations of global Islamophobia, each scholar in this volume offers a nuanced, context-specific analysis grounded in case studies. It will be up to policy-makers,

---

[97] Lee, "Islamophobia," ch. 14 in this volume.

[98] Associated Press, "Anti-Muslim Buddhist Monk in Myanmar: Trump 'Similar to Me,'" Voice of America, November 17, 2016, https://www.voanews.com/a/ap-anti-muslim-buddhist-monk-in-myanmar-trump-similar-to-me/3602121.html; quoted in Lee, "Islamophobia," ch. 14 in this volume.

[99] "'You Are Either with Us or against Us," CNN, November 6, 2001, https://edition.cnn.com/2001/US/11/06/gen.attack.on.terror/.

elected officials, and citizens of the nations discussed herein to decide what kind of country they want: a racist, fractured society controlled by right-wing populists or a pluralist, cohesive society thriving from its diversity. Whatever the path chosen, confronting the transnational nature of Islamophobia cannot be avoided.

PART I
ISLAMOPHOBIA IN NORTH AMERICA

Race, Religion, and Citizenship

2

The Price of Recognition

The One Islam and the Many

Joseph Massad*

In the last three decades, critics of Western multiculturalism and the quest for "diversity" have established that these concepts are both underwritten by the demands of neoliberal transnational capitalism and part of an important "public relations" move to win the consent both of the elites of the Third World and of metropolitan ethnic minorities for the exponential transfer of money from the large majority of the world's poor to a tiny minority of the world's rich.[1] This chapter argues that multiculturalism, calls for diversity, and tolerance of difference are in fact the new racism, both within Europe and North America and on a global scale. The 1980s neologism *postcolonial*, which quickly began to serve the needs of Third World and diasporic metropolitan elites, becomes, as one critic put it, "as much a strategy of differentiating oneself from the racial underclass as it is to speak in its name."[2] This argument is not new; Marxist critics of right-wing variants of dependency theory, a sort of precursor to the "postcolonial," had argued back in the mid-1970s that it was an apology for national capital rather than a subversion of international capitalism or a defense of its impoverished victims globally.[3]

---

* The author delivered earlier versions of this chapter as lectures at the Andrew W. Melon Foundation Colloquium on Difference, Diversity, and Social Inclusion, Haarlem, The Netherlands, June 6, 2017; the University of Texas at Austin, sponsored by the Department of English, Islamic Studies Program by and the Institute for Asian-American Studies, September 28, 2017; the Department of Modern Languages and Literatures and the Department of Religious Studies at the University of Miami, February 12, 2018; and as a keynote address at the Istanbul Biennale, September 15, 2017.

[1] Gayatri Chakravorty Spivak, *A Critique of Postcolonial Reason*, (Cambridge, MA: Harvard University Press, 1999), p. 397.

[2] Spivak, *Critique*, p. 358.

[3] See Ernesto Laclau, "Feudalism and Capitalism in Latin America," *New Left Review* 1, no. 67 (May–June 1971): pp. 19–38.

Joseph Massad, *The Price of Recognition* In: *Global Islamophobia and the Rise of Populism.* Edited by: Sahar F. Aziz and John L. Esposito, Oxford University Press. © Oxford University Press 2024.
DOI: 10.1093/oso/9780197648995.003.0002

Difference Concepts

As for the more fashionable concepts of *diversity* and *difference* that are claimed to be the contemporary successors to a failed multiculturalism, illiberal critics have recognized them early on as capitalist strategies to maintain the centrality of northwestern European and North American whiteness as a liberal formation and as part of capital's free movement. Diversifying such whiteness in our neoliberal age, American political scientist Adolph Reed Jr. posits, had amounted to nothing more than a call for the diversification of the 1 percent who rule the United States and Europe, so that they would include within their ranks 50 percent women, an appropriate percentage of Africans and African Americans, of Latinos, as well as "whatever the appropriate proportions" of gays and lesbians.[4] Reed added that when such diversity is accomplished, it is depicted as amounting to the achievement of social justice.[5]

As for the recognition of difference, proponents also showed that it is a "difference" from Europe as the central "self" of American national identity—which is always already white—or European-Continental identity, meaning northwestern Christian Europe. Frustrated by US President Donald Trump's refusal to uphold the politics of the *elite front* that grouped the capitalist states of Europe and its settler colonies in the Americas and Oceania since World War II, German Chancellor Angela Merkel insisted in May 2017 in the name of Europe, not even in the name of a European Germany, that "we must fight for our own future and our fate ourselves as Europeans."[6] Never mind that millions of people in Germany today do not hail from Europe but from Turkey, a country that Merkel insists should never become part of Europe.[7]

In Germany, as elsewhere in Europe and North America, recognizing "cultural difference" has its limitations, such that the cultures that can be recognized and tolerated are those that are assimilable to what white Europe and white America imagine to be their liberal culture of the European Enlightenment; multicultural recognition is paradoxically limited to what is assimilable. What is noteworthy in this struggle is the essentialist trait attributed to European and Euro-American culture as the unchanging constant liberal culture of the European Enlightenment, which must be contrasted with the anti-essentialist

---

[4] Adolph Reed Jr., "From Jenner to Dolezal: One Trans Good, the Other Not So Much," Common Dreams, June 15, 2015, https://www.commondreams.org/views/2015/06/15/jenner-dolezal-one-trans-good-other-not-so-much.

[5] Reed, "From Jenner to Dolezal."

[6] Emma Stefansky, "Angela Merkel Says Europe Can No Longer Completely Depend on the US and UK following Trump's Visit," *Vanity Fair*, May 28, 2017, https://www.vanityfair.com/news/2017/05/angela-merkel-speech-after-trump-visit.

[7] "German Opposition to Turkey's EU Membership Rises: Poll," *Reuters*, May 27, 2014, https://www.reuters.com/article/us-germany-turkey-poll/german-opposition-to-turkeys-eu-membership-rises-poll-idUSKBN0E71JQ20140527.

notion of illiberal European and non-European cultures that are seen as malleable and capable of, or coercible into, change to approximations of this liberal European culture. Thus, the premise of the call for diversity and multiculturalism is a demand that all must recognize that only white liberal European culture is a constant and referent by which all difference must be measured and overcome. Europe is the telos that all other cultures must strive to reach. Resistance to reach the telos of liberal European Enlightenment culture is grounds for the refusal to recognize or tolerate the resistors, based on attributing to their cultures an essentialist character of constancy, not unlike the one liberal Europeans uniquely attribute to themselves.

Difference here emerges as two pronged: on one hand, difference means that unlike liberal European culture, which need not change or transform itself, all other cultures must transform themselves and become the same as liberal European culture. On the other hand, difference means or collapses into sameness, such that only those cultures that become the same as white liberal European culture will be recognized and tolerated. As for illiberal forms of white culture identified in the United States with support for Donald Trump, the recent liberal calls for their suppression by media, civil society, and state bureaucracy have become the order of the day in Trump's and post-Trump America. The recent victory of illiberal right-wing candidates in German elections has also witnessed much liberal intolerance of the right-wing's opposition to diversity in immigration policy.[8]

Finally, we get to the more recent concept of *social inclusion*, which, based on the above, essentially means recognition by European and American official whiteness of *sameness* in others as a form of tolerable *otherness* that is essentially the same, and including this otherness in what is tolerable within "European" and "American" society.

All four ideologically charged terms—*multiculturalism*, *diversity*, *difference*, and *social inclusion*—turn out to be synonyms and variations on the same theme that can be summarized in the readiness of liberal European and white Americans who uphold them to *recognize* only a form of otherness that strives to become the same as Europe. This approach also seems to be one that not only liberal proponents but also conservative opponents of multiculturalism and diversity agree on, especially in the case of what they call *Islam*. Namely, European and white American recognition of Islam would effectively mean recognition of a "culture" that is the *other* of European liberalism and that refuses to assimilate into it.

---

[8] Jon Stone, "German Elections: Far Right Wins MPs for First Time in Half a Century," *Independent*, September 24, 2017, https://www.independent.co.uk/news/world/politics/german-election-results-exit-poll-2017-live-latest-afd-mps-merkel-alternative-a7964796.html.

The stakes are so high that even a critic of multiculturalism and diversity discourses such as Gayatri Chakravorty Spivak, who views these concepts as tools of international capital and white racism, insists that given that the alternative to liberal multiculturalism is white supremacy, "we [presumably meaning socialists, anti-imperialists, and anti-racists] have to claim some alliance with it."[9] But do "we" actually have to? Spivak's positing white supremacy as an antonym of multiculturalism and diversity is a gross misreading and misidentification of the central issue of contention between these two seemingly opposing discourses.

Price of Recognition

What is the price to be paid for this recognition, and who has to pay it? The price of recognition has been debated in recent scholarship, with a focus on law as the code through which white liberal multiculturalism and calls for diversity recognize alterity.

By forcing difference from whiteness to account for itself in European liberal juridical codes, law becomes the basis for the white liberal state's recognition. In the process, what gets recognized is a set of non-repugnant and tolerable differences, whereas those recognized along with their culture remain under supervision and suspicion lest they deviate from the terms of their tolerability. This is partially the point that Elizabeth Povinelli raises in her important work on Australian indigeneity and the white liberal settler state.[10]

Relatedly, Patchen Markell understands the politics of recognition as a politics of asserting sovereignty by the individual or the group as well as by the state.[11] But as recognition has always been relational, at least since the foundational Hegelian master-and-slave dialectic, the subordination of the slave to the master in the dialectic is the outcome of the master's need for the slave to recognize the master's sovereign power and the slave's acknowledgment of her own lack of power, or non-sovereignty, on the basis of which she surrenders to the master. State recognition therefore solidifies the state's sovereignty through the very terms of recognition it offers to the group, which is now bound by those terms that serve the white liberal multicultural state's needs. This process is carried out through subordinating the identity of those recognized in the vision of multiculturalism and

---

[9] Spivak, *Critique*, p. 396; Gayatri Chakravorty Spivak, *An Aesthetic Education in the Era of Globalization* (Cambridge, MA: Harvard University Press, 2013), p. 142.

[10] See Elizabeth A. Povinelli, *The Cunning of Recognition, Indigenous Alterities and the Making of Australian Multiculturalism* (Durham, NC: Duke University Press, 2002).

[11] Patchen Markell, *Bound by Recognition* (Princeton, NJ: Princeton University Press, 2003).

diversity of the white liberal state itself. The 1989 French *l'affaire du foulard* ("the head-scarf affair") is presented as evidence of this process.[12]

Western liberal subjects' insistence on universalizing their culture and values is not simply a matter of refusing to recognize those who are not liberal European subjects but a realization that their Western liberal subjectivity hinges on eliminating the ontological life of those who resist. As Markell puts it,

> [R]elations of social and political subordination ... [should be viewed] not as systematic failures by some people to recognize others' identities, but as ways of patterning and arranging the world that allow some people and groups to enjoy a semblance of sovereign agency at others' expense.[13]

This approach applies to the context of the discourse on Muslims inside and outside Europe and North America, which is often a discourse on Islam itself rather than about Muslim communities and societies.[14] A number of scholars of religion agree that the development of the multiple significations of Islam after the colonial encounter was greatly conditioned by it.

American Middle East specialist Leonard Binder sketches Western imperial liberalism's efforts at converting Islam into a form that such liberalism can accept and explicitly tells Muslims what the price of recognition by whiteness will be. Binder asserts that

> from the time of the Napoleonic invasion, from the time of the Janissaries, from the time of the Sepoy mutiny, at least, the West has been trying to tell Islam what must be the price of progress in the coin of tradition which is to be surrendered. And from those times, despite the increasing numbers of responsive Muslims, there remains a substantial number that steadfastly argue that it is possible to progress without paying such a heavy cultural price.[15]

In response to Binder, Talal Asad maintains that it is

> no incidental detail that each of the "tellings" cited by [Binder]—when traditional authority was successfully attacked in the name of rationalism and progress—was at the same time an act of violence. In each of them, Western political, economic, and ideological power increased its hold over non-European peoples. That power, unleashed in Enlightenment Europe, continues

---

[12] See Joan Scott, *The Politics of the Veil* (Princeton, NJ: Princeton University Press, 2010).

[13] Markell, *Bound*, p. 5.

[14] The following discussion on Islam and Muslims is based on the author's book. See Joseph A. Massad, *Islam in Liberalism* (Chicago: University of Chicago Press, 2015).

[15] Leonard Binder, *Islamic Liberalism* (Chicago: University of Chicago Press, 1988), p. 293.

28 JOSEPH MASSAD

to restructure the lives of non-European peoples, often through the agency of non-Europeans themselves. And if "Islamic fundamentalism" is a response to that power, then certainly so, even more thoroughly, are the intellectual currents called "modernist Islam" (which is concerned to adapt theology to the models of Christian modernism) and "Muslim secularism" (which [is] preoccupied less with theology than with separating religion from politics in national life). And so, too, are the progressivist movements in literature and the arts, in politics and law, that have arisen in Muslim societies.[16]

Here, Asad precisely points out that the price had already been paid in the transformation of Muslim societies through their responses to and encounters with European capitalist imperialism.

One Islam and the Many

If modernist Islam, or Muslim progressivist movements—indeed, if liberal Muslim politics and a class of liberal intelligentsia in Muslim-majority countries—emerged as an outcome of European imperialism, European colonial liberals initially saw and welcomed them as being opposed to "Islam." Only fundamentalist forms of Islam were considered by white European and Euro-American liberals and conservatives as reflecting true "Islam," a position that is espoused today by white supremacists, right-wing Islamophobes, and some Islamists.[17] The more ingenious move by liberal multiculturalism and calls for diversity in the last two decades, however, has been the multiplication of Islam as Islams. As a result, white liberal multiculturalism and calls for diversity are open to all those other liberal- and European-like Islams and are only opposed to the Islam of the Islamists, which they cannot tolerate; here comes the one Islam and the many.

The price of recognition in this case is the claim to recognize the many and to disavow the one, which problematically seems to outnumber and outweigh the many and to implicate them with it. This is especially the case as relates to the central attributes that multiculturalism considers part of liberal European culture—namely, democracy and secularism, which are absent in the one Islam.

In this context, French philosopher Jacques Derrida announced that unlike Christianity or Judaism, or a "mixed religious culture,"

---

[16] Talal Asad, *Genealogies of Religion* (Baltimore, MD: John Hopkins Press, 1993), pp. 228–29.
[17] Massad, *Islam in Liberalism.*

THE PRICE OF RECOGNITION 29

Islam, or a certain Islam, would thus be the only religious or theocratic culture [worldwide] that can still, in fact or in principle, inspire and declare any resistance to democracy. If it does not actually resist what might be called a real or actual democratization, one whose reality may be more or less contested, it can at least resist the democratic principle, claim, or allegation, the legacy and the old name of "democracy."[18]

Derrida adds that

this Islam, this particular one and not Islam in general (if such a thing exists), would represent the only religious culture that would have resisted up until now a European (that is, Greco-Christian and globalatinizing) process of secularization, and thus of democratization, and thus, in the strict sense, of politicization.[19]

While Saudi Arabia is the only "spectacular" example that Derrida cites when he speaks of "Islam," or of "a certain Islam"—Saudi Arabia has a population of 28 million people out of 1.2 billion Muslims worldwide—it is this "Islam" that he wants to privilege against all the other Islams, whose existence he implies by way of alibi. Indeed, he is interested in producing a new democratic Islam, and as a missionary of Judeo-Christian democracy—he names Christian countries and the Jewish settler-colony as democracies or at least as claimants to democracy— Derrida elaborates on the necessary missionary tasks and responsibilities of Judeo-Christians toward Muslims:

For whoever, by hypothesis, considers him- or herself a friend of democracy in the world and not only in his or her own country[,] . . . the task would consist in doing everything possible to join forces with all those who, and first of all in the Islamic world, fight not only for the secularization of the political (however ambiguous this secularization remains), for the emergence of a laic subjectivity, but also for an interpretation of the Koranic heritage that privileges, from the inside as it were, the democratic virtualities that are probably not any more apparent and readable at first glance, and readable under this name, than they were in the Old and New Testaments.[20]

Derrida discusses much of this under the heading "the other of democracy," which Islam has come to occupy and which he constitutes as "a certain

[18] Jacques Derrida, *Rogues: Two Essays on Reason* (Palo Alto, CA: Stanford University Press, 2005), p. 29.
[19] Derrida, *Rogues*, p. 31.
[20] Derrida, *Rogues*, p. 31.

30 JOSEPH MASSAD

Arab and Islamic world" that is also an "an Arab and Islamic exception."[21] Note that Derrida's interest in "the other of democracy" never shifts to who "the self of democracy" is, which he takes for granted, presumably as Christianity, Protestantism, the Judeo-Christian, Europe, the United States, and liberalism. When speaking of Islam, evidently, even the critical Derrida becomes like many European and US liberals in considering the culture of liberal European democracy the referent and the telos to which Islam, or a certain Islam, must strive. But Derrida is illustrative of the rest.

Immigration, Europeanness, and Demography

The debate on immigrants in western Europe, especially on Muslim immigrants and citizens, whether in the Netherlands, Germany, France, Sweden, Italy, or the United Kingdom, has been part of the campaign of assimilation of Muslims into specific European nationness—Germanness, Frenchness, Dutchness, etc.—as authentic, stable, and one to which all immigrants must adhere. What remains unquestioned is whether Europeanness—or more specifically, Dutchness, and Frenchness, and Germanness—should transform both themselves and what they consider to be their European cultures in light of the millions of Dutch, French, or German citizens who are not of European origins and relate to the past and present of Europe and its purported culture very differently. Would liberal white Dutch citizens, for example, consider their call for diversity and multiculturalism to become one of transforming their own culture to be compatible with the cultures of Dutch citizens of African, Indonesian, Turkish, or Arab origins? Would white French proponents of assimilation or *intégration* consider integrating what they consider to be French European laic culture into the culture of French citizens of Southeast Asian and African origins, Muslims and otherwise? These questions are unthinkable and, even if thinkable, sound unreasonable or even absurd in the context of the assumption that European liberal culture is the referent and the telos toward which all other cultures must strive. These questions would be reasonable only if that assumption were abandoned.

There may also be the objection of demography. White liberal Americans continue to assume that, as English-speaking whites are a demographic majority in the United States, all non-English-speaking immigrants must assimilate into their culture. What this assumption ignores, however, is the flexibility and malleability of the legal and social category of whiteness—read *Englishness*—in

---

[21] Derrida, *Rogues*, pp. 28, 41. For an important critique of Derrida, see Anne Norton, "On the Muslim Question," in *Democracy, Religious Pluralism and the Liberal Dilemma of Accommodation*, Studies in Global Justice 7, ed. Monica Mookherjee (New York: Springer Link, 2011): pp. 65–75.

THE PRICE OF RECOGNITION   31

the United States. As historical studies have demonstrated, many of those considered socially or legally white today in the United States were not always so before World War I, World War II, or even the 1960s; these groups include Italian Americans, Irish Americans, Hungarian Americans, Greek Americans, let alone Arab Americans and Indian Americans.[22]

Many in the United States today worry that white people will become a minority in the country before midcentury.[23] While those concerned about whites becoming a minority understand that this is not an assured outcome, as many children of minorities today may become white in the interim and therefore guarantee white demographic supremacy in the country, what they ignore is that by a World War I definition of whiteness, whites have already been a minority in the United States for several decades.[24] Since assimilable nonwhites have become white in the United States by agreeing to surrender their languages and many aspects of their cultures and traditions as the price of being recognized as whites, this process led to the expansion of the ranks of whiteness. Native Americans, African Americans, and a majority of Hispanic Americans and Asian Americans remain outside that category whose very existence hinges on their exclusion by definition—although in the case of Asian Americans, assimilation into honorary whiteness is debated as a possibility.[25]

It is noteworthy in this context to point out that American Jews had been legally, though not socially, racialized as part of white people since the foundation of the US republic, though they continued to suffer from religious discrimination as Jews and ethnic-based social discrimination, but not political discrimination, as "Semites."[26] Since the late 1950s, and certainly by the 1960s, Jews were accepted as white people, to the point of being thoroughly de-Semitized, in addition to the annexation of their religion to Christianity through the invention of the "Judeo-Christian."[27] More recently though, there has been a renewed attempt

---

[22] On Arab Americans, see Joseph Massad, "Palestinians and the Limits of Racialized Discourse," in *The Persistence of the Palestinian Question: Essays on Zionism and the Palestinians*, ed. Joseph A. Massad (London: Routledge, 2006), p. 93.

[23] Evan Horowitz, "When Will Minorities Be the Majority," *The Boston Globe*, February 26, 2016, https://www.bostonglobe.com/news/politics/2016/02/26/when-will-minorities-majority/9v5m1Jj 8hdGcXvpXtbQT5I/story.html; Sahar F. Aziz, *The Racial Muslim: When Racism Quashes Religious Freedom* (Berkeley: University of California Press, 2021).

[24] On the malleability of legal whiteness in the United States, see Michael Omi and Howard Winant, *Racial Formation in the United States: From the 1960s to the 1980s* (New York: Routledge and Kegan Paul, 1986); Matthew Frye Jacobson, *Whiteness of a Different Color: European Immigrants and the Alchemy of Race* (Cambridge, MA: Harvard University Press, 1998); Ian Haney-Lopéz, *White by Law: The Legal Construction of Race* (New York: New York University Press, 1996); Aziz, *Racial Muslim*.

[25] On "honorary" whiteness, see Massad, "Palestinians," pp. 79–95.

[26] See Joseph Massad, "Forget Semitism!," in *Islam in Liberalism* (Chicago: University of Chicago Press, 2015), pp. 312–41; Aziz, *Racial Muslim*.

[27] See Massad, *Islam in Liberalism*, pp. 29–30.

32   JOSEPH MASSAD

to re-racialize Jews by Israel and Zionism but as a race among other white races, though one with unique genetic markers.

A few years ago, Israeli newspapers reported that "[a] group of experts on genetics and Halacha (Jewish religious law), who are studying the so-called 'Jewish gene,' are claiming that the gene can help prove one's 'Jewishness' in line with Jewish religious law," eliminating the need for the arduous process of conversion to Judaism by those whose Jewishness cannot be ascertained.[28] Muslim Americans and Muslim Europeans, however, who had not been racialized historically, given their multiple geographic origins (Asia, Africa, Europe), have become increasingly Semitized and racialized alongside Arabs, who were the only group of Muslims and Christians who had been considered Semites until recently.[29] However, if Muslim Americans and Muslim Europeans were cast outside whiteness based on the notion of the one Islam, the multicultural and diversity moves seek to bring them back through the notion of the many.

US Pluralization of Islam

With these entrenched notions as background, the United States began to waver on Samuel P. Huntington's conservative notion of the "clash of civilizations" and adopted a new project of pluralizing the one Islam identified by Huntington and his culturalist predecessors while maintaining Christianity as a singular referent.[30] This pluralization of Islam, as Islams, allowed the United States to support the emergence of a new "Islam"—a liberal form that is more in tune with US imperial designs and that would approximate modern Western notions of religions and religious subjectivities, as well as Western liberal citizenship, so as not to be incompatible with the rhetoric of democracy. Simultaneously, it permits the United States to wage war against that other Islam that continues to resist the Western (neo)liberal order while allying itself with and weaponizing so-called Jihadist versions of it (e.g., the Mujahidin, Al-Qaida, and ISIS) when the imperial need arises, as it did in Afghanistan in the 1980s and in Syria and Iraq in the last decade. The very suspension of certain citizenship rights of Muslims as individuals and communities in Europe and the United States or the redefinition of citizenship as a secular-Christian European liberal norm that should be imposed on Muslims is essentially a reinforcement of the understanding of citizenship as a Western value that is in opposition to Muslim

[28] Elisha Ben Kimon, "Can Jewishness Be Proven with a Simple Saliva Test?," *Ynet News*, May 28, 2017, http://www.ynetnews.com/articles/0,7340,L-4968443,00.html.

[29] Massad, "Forget Semitism!," pp. 312–34.

[30] Samuel P. Huntington, *The Clash of Civilizations and the Remaking of the World Order* (New York: Simon & Schuster, 1996).

THE PRICE OF RECOGNITION   33

tradition and corrupted in the hands of Muslims and must be withdrawn from them or imposed on them as a Western construct depending on their adherence to the one Islam or the many.

To this end, the United States embarked on a new project once the new millennium started and in the shadow of the September 11, 2001, attacks: one of "reforming" the "culture" of "Islam." This project was not unlike American cultural policies since the dawn of the Cold War, except that it now had a broader cultural and religious focus on Islam than the more specific ideological focus it had before on Communism, which also failed to foster liberal citizenship.[31] The new project, like the previous one, would involve major wars but have a much larger budget, in the trillions of dollars, aiming not only to destroy existing regimes, religions, and ideologies but also, and equally important, to produce new ones compatible with a multicultural vision of diversity, social inclusion, and tolerance.

In a 2003 report, the National Security Research Division of the Rand Corporation identified which Islams were necessary for the United States to produce. The report summarized its goal at the outset:

> Islam is an important religion with enormous political and societal influence; it inspires a variety of ideologies and political actions, some of which are dangerous to global stability; and it therefore seems sensible to foster the strains within it that call for a more moderate, democratic, peaceful, and tolerant social order. The question is how best to do this.[32]

The report recognizes that "it is no easy matter [for Americans] to transform a major world religion. If 'nation-building' is a daunting task, 'religion-building' is immeasurably more perilous and complex."[33] The report is clear that while there has been and is room for different kinds of rapprochements with Muslim "fundamentalists" and "traditionalists", it is the "modernists" whose "vision matches our own. Of all the groups, this one is most congenial to the values and the spirit of modern democratic society."[34]

---

[31] See Frances Stoner Saunders, *The Cultural Cold War: The CIA and the World of Arts and Letters* (New York: New Press, 2001). On the CIA production and funding of "culture" in the Arab world, see Timothy Mitchell, "The Middle East in the Past and Future of Social Science," in *The Politics of Knowledge: Area Studies and the Discipline*, ed. David Szanton (Berkeley, CA: GAIA Books, 2003), pp. 9–12.

[32] Cheryl Benard, *Civil Democratic Islam: Partners, Resources, and Strategies* (Santa Monica, CA: Rand, 2003), p. 1. For an important discussion of the report, see also Saba Mahmood, "Secularism, Hermeneutics, and Empire: The Politics of Islamic Reformation," *Public Culture* 18, no. 2 (2006).

[33] Benard, *Civil Democratic Islam*, p. 3.

[34] Benard, *Civil Democratic Islam*, p. 37.

34   JOSEPH MASSAD

This view is hardly only that of US imperial strategists, but as Saba Mahmood has astutely noted,

> [I]t has become de rigueur for leftists and liberals alike to link the fate of democracy in the Muslim world with the institutionalization of secularism both as a political doctrine and as a political ethic. This coupling is now broadly echoed within the discourse emanating from the US State Department, particularly its programmatic efforts to reshape and transform "Islam from within."[35]

With this in-mind, Mahmood suggests that "the political solution that secularism proffers . . . lies not so much in tolerating difference and diversity but in remaking certain kinds of religious subjectivities (even if this requires the use of violence) so as to render them compliant with liberal political rule."[36] What we see emerge then is a secular religion, or perhaps even a secular fundamentalism, that seeks to overthrow Islamic "fundamentalism" in its embrace of its own progressive values that are fighting the "reactionary" values of "fundamentalist Islam."[37]

This agenda of multiplying Islam is shared in France by the popular media and academic psychoanalyst Fethi Benslama who explains that the many "Islams" he identifies are diverse, various, and sometimes unconnected, even though they may all hide "behind" the singular name *Islam*.[38] Benslama, a Frenchman of Tunisian origins, understands the attempt to homogenize Islams into Islam as not only an Islamist project but also a European attempt to deal with the rise of many "Islamist" movements in different geographic and social contexts.[39]

The problem with the multiplicity of Islam as Islams, however, is something Benslama and others do not explain adequately, if at all. If Islam should always be seen as plural and multiple, in the form of Islams, and never in the singular form, then what are "Islams" a plural of, what are they multiples of? Since this plurality refers to the signifier and the signified, proponents of the many Islams do not elaborate on whether the signifieds have anything in common other than the signifier. If both signifiers and signifieds are plural, would this mean that the term *Islam* is actually and simply a homonym, which in itself is what creates the confusion for religious Muslims and for European multiculturalists and their opponents?

Still, however, the notion of Islam as plural, as Islams, does not solve the problem that liberal multipliers of Islam wish to solve—namely, that Islam in

---

[35] Mahmood, "Secularism," p. 323.
[36] Mahmood, "Secularism," p. 328.
[37] See Talal Asad, *Formations of the Secular* (Stanford, CA: Stanford University Press, 2003).
[38] Fethi Benslama, *La Psychanalyse à l'épreuve de l'Islam* (Paris: Flammarion, 2002), p. 23.
[39] Benslama, *La Psychanalyse*, p. 23.

its entirety and in all its forms had come to constitute the other of European liberal Enlightenment culture. Were one to accept the contention that there may be varieties of Islams that are compatible with European liberal culture, one of those that is not compatible would still be singled out as its other, and that is the one Islam that European liberalism and its multicultural and diversity project contest and want to eliminate. This dilemma brings us back to the same troubling question with which we began: must those of us who oppose liberal multiculturalism and calls for diversity on anti-racist, anti-imperialist, and anti-neoliberal grounds "claim some alliance" with them, as Spivak insists?

Conclusion

Multiculturalism, calls for diversity, tolerance of difference, and social inclusion turn out to share the same white-supremacist notion that insists that European liberal Enlightenment culture is the superior culture and Europe's gift to the world, which the rest of the world can receive graciously or be coerced to accept as the price of recognition. As such, how different are they from conservative and white-supremacist calls that insist that European liberal Enlightenment culture is the most superior culture on the planet and should remain the exclusive property of true white Europeans in Europe and its settler-colonies rather than be universalized?

Both liberal proponents of multiculturalism and calls for diversity and their conservative, openly white-supremacist opponents aim at establishing the dominance of northwest European culture and white US capital globally through neoliberal financialization. The former do so through the cultural instrument of universalizing a static notion of liberal European Enlightenment culture by suasion or force, and the latter insist on not universalizing it as a way of imposing its economic control of the globe by suasion with those who recognize its superior military and financial power, or by the use of force against all those who stand in its way.

As multiculturalism and calls for diversity prove to be equally committed to white supremacy, if in a latent form, as their openly and manifestly white-supremacist opponents, those who oppose racism and the depredations of international capital need not be forced to choose between the two, let alone claim some alliance with either of them. Their task and duty is to resist and oppose them with equal force.

3

The Politics of Vulnerability: Today's Threat to American Muslims' Religious Freedom

Asma T. Uddin

Donald Trump's presidency may have come to a close, but the forces that elected him and continue to trumpet Trumpism are still very much influential. Throughout his term, diverse commentators analyzed Trump through the lens of the now infamous 81 percent of white evangelicals who helped elect him and who supported him either silently or vociferously throughout much of his term.[1]

Islamophobia was and is a key element of this phenomenon. Throughout Trump's 2016 campaign, he evoked the Muslim bogeyman, proposing everything from a Muslim registry to surveilling mosques and banning Muslims from the country.[2] He was appealing to his base of conservative populists, and white evangelicals in particular. Immediately after the 2016 US presidential election, a study on the role of religion in US populism found that, across all religious groups, white evangelicals scored highest for "conservative populism."[3] They asserted their populism as a way of defending their "ethnic identity" and exhibited "anti-immigrant sentiment, nativism, 'white power' ideologies, and Islamophobia."[4]

Once elected, Trump continued his Islamophobic rhetoric and policies with the unwavering support of these same evangelicals. One set of polls measured Americans' approval of Trump's Executive Order No. 13769, which temporarily blocked individuals from seven majority-Muslim countries from entering

---

[1] See, for example, Myriam Renaud, "Why White Evangelicals Stuck with Trump," University of Chicago Divinity School, February 11, 2021, https://divinity.uchicago.edu/sightings/articles/why-white-evangelicals-stuck-trump; Sarah Pulliam Bailey, "White Evangelicals Voted Overwhelmingly for Donald Trump, Exit Polls Show," *The Washington Post*, November 9, 2016, https://www.washingtonpost.com/news/acts-of-faith/wp/2016/11/09/exit-polls-show-white-evangelicals-voted-overwhelmingly-for-donald-trump/.

[2] Sahar F. Aziz, "A Muslim Registry: The Precursor to Internment?" *BYU Law Review* 2017, no. 4 (2017): pp. 779–838.

[3] James L. Guth, "Are White Evangelicals Populists? The View from the 2016 American National Election Study," *Review of Faith and International Affairs* 17, no. 3 (2019): pp. 20–35.

[4] Guth, "Are White Evangelicals Populists?"

Asma T. Uddin, *The Politics of Vulnerability: Today's Threat to American Muslims' Religious Freedom* In: *Global Islamophobia and the Rise of Populism*. Edited by: Sahar F. Aziz and John L. Esposito, Oxford University Press.
© Oxford University Press 2024. DOI: 10.1093/oso/9780197648995.003.0003

THE POLITICS OF VULNERABILITY   37

the United States. Pew Research found that 76 percent of white evangelicals supported the ban,[5] and the Public Religion Research Institute (PRRI) revealed that white evangelicals, in supporting the ban, stood apart from all other religious groups, including Catholics, mainline Protestants, and religious minorities.[6] The numbers of white evangelicals supporting the ban even increased from when candidate Trump first announced the ban on the campaign trail: 55 percent supported it during the election, and 61 percent supported it when it was implemented.[7] For every other religious group, the trend was in the opposite direction.[8]

Pieces like *The Christian Science Monitor*'s "Why Evangelicals Are Trump's Strongest Travel-Ban Supporters" and *Christianity Today*'s "Most White Evangelicals Don't Believe Muslims Belong in America" noted that white evangelicals do not just think Muslim immigrants are the problem—they also think American Muslims, and Islam generally, pose a threat to America's Christian identity.[9] A 2017 Pew poll found that two-thirds of white evangelicals believe that Islam is not part of mainstream American society and that it encourages violence more than other faiths do.[10] Compared to 44 percent of Americans overall, 72 percent of white evangelicals see a natural conflict between Islam and democracy.[11] According to a 2017 Baylor University survey, 52 percent of white evangelicals believe that Muslims want to limit their freedom.[12]

In 2018, the Institute for Social Policy and Understanding's (ISPU) Islamophobia Index found that while the majority of Americans (66 percent) agree that "the negative things politicians say regarding Muslims is harmful to our country," white evangelicals were the group least likely to agree with this

[5] Gregory A. Smith, "Most White Evangelicals Approve of Trump Travel Prohibition and Express Concerns about Extremism," Pew Research Center, February 27, 2017, https://www.pewresearch.org/fact-tank/2017/02/27/most-white-evangelicals-approve-of-trump-travel-prohibition-and-express-concerns-about-extremism/.

[6] Daniel Cox and Robert P. Jones, "47% of the Country Say Trump Has Violated the Constitution, but Few Support Impeachment," PRRI, February 24, 2017, https://www.prri.org/research/poll-trump-impeachment-constitution-partisanship-muslim-ban/.

[7] Cox and Jones, "47% of the Country."

[8] Cox and Jones, "47% of the Country."

[9] Harry Bruinius, "Why Evangelicals Are Trump's Strongest Travel-Ban Supporters," *The Christian Science Monitor*, March 3, 2017, https://www.csmonitor.com/USA/Politics/2017/0303/Why-Evangelicals-are-Trump-s-strongest-travel-ban-supporters; Kate Shellnut, "Most White Evangelicals Don't Believe Muslims Belong in America," *Christianity Today*, July 26, 2017, https://www.christianitytoday.com/news/2017/july/pew-how-white-evangelicals-view-us-muslims-islam.html.

[10] Michael Lipka, "Muslims and Islam: Key Findings in the US and around the World," Pew Research Center, August 9, 2017, https://www.pewresearch.org/fact-tank/2017/08/09/muslims-and-islam-key-findings-in-the-u-s-and-around-the-world/.

[11] Emma Green, "How Much Discrimination Do Muslims Face in America?" *The Atlantic*, July 26, 2017, https://www.theatlantic.com/politics/archive/2017/07/american-muslims-trump/534879/.

[12] Julie Zauzmer and Michelle Boorstein, "Evangelicals Fear Muslims, Atheists Fear Christians: New Poll Shows How Americans Mistrust One Another," *The Washington Post*, September 7, 2017, https://www.washingtonpost.com/news/acts-of-faith/wp/2017/09/07/evangelicals-fear-muslims-atheists-fear-christians-how-americans-mistrust-each-other/.

statement.[13] In 2019, ISPU found that "white Evangelicals score the highest on the Islamophobia Index with as many as 44% holding unfavorable opinions about Muslims, which is twice as many as those who hold favorable opinions (20%)."[14]

What might explain the evangelical animosity toward Muslims? Islamophobia is a complex matter, with elements of racialization and securitization.[15] Racialization is the stereotyping by white Americans of Muslims as homogenously "brown" and "Arab" instead of the as ethnically diverse group that they are.[16] The racialization of Muslims often begets racism because of the perceived negative attributes of this brownness.[17] Securitization refers to the impact of the 9/11 attacks on perceptions of Muslims as both internal and external security threats.[18]

These and other factors are important to parse, but this chapter takes a different tack. It assesses the role of populist sentiment as expressed through political tribalism. It seeks to draw attention to the heretofore under-evaluated elements of group dynamics and social psychology in anti-Muslim discrimination.

A Note on Christian Nationalism

Before delving into the social psychology of conservative white evangelical populism, it is important to distinguish this group from Christian nationalists, who are motivated more by distinct political goals and less by the group dynamics analyzed in this chapter.

Sociologists Andrew Whitehead and Samuel Perry define Christian nationalism as "a cultural framework—a collection of myths, traditions, symbols, narratives, and value systems—that idealizes and advocates a fusion of Christianity with American civic life."[19] The *Christianity* of Christian nationalism is not just about religion; it also "includes assumptions of nativism, white supremacy, patriarchy, and heteronormativity, along with divine sanction for

---

[13] Youssef Chouhoud and Dalia Mogahed, "American Muslim Poll 2018: Full Report," ISPU, April 30, 2018, https://www.ispu.org/american-muslim-poll-2018-full-report/.

[14] Dalia Mogahed, "American Muslim Poll 2019: Predicting and Preventing Islamophobia," ISPU, May 1, 2019, https://www.ispu.org/american-muslim-poll-2019-predicting-and-preventing-islam ophobia/.

[15] Allyson F. Shortle and Ronald Keith Gaddie, "Religious Nationalism and Perceptions of Muslims and Islam," *Politics and Religion* 8 (2015): p. 437.

[16] Shortle and Gaddie, "Religious Nationalism," p. 437.

[17] Sahar F. Aziz, *The Racial Muslim: When Racism Quashes Religious Freedom* (Berkeley: University of California Press, 2021).

[18] Shortle and Gaddie, "Religious Nationalism," p. 437.

[19] Andrew Whitehead and Samuel Perry, *Taking America Back for God: Christian Nationalism in the United States* (Oxford: Oxford University Press, 2020) (emphasis in original), p. 10.

THE POLITICS OF VULNERABILITY 39

authoritarian control and militarism."[20] It is centered on America as a Christian nation and seeks to preserve that Christian character through self-identity, interpretations of US history, "sacred symbols, cherished values, and public policies."[21]

Importantly, Christian nationalism is not the same thing as racism. We cannot say, for instance, that "Christian nationalism is really just about racism."[22] One can be a member of a racial minority and hold certain nationalist beliefs, leading one to adopt a racial justice orientation. What matters, Whitehead and Perry write, is the "*intersection* of race and Christian nationalism."[23]

Christian nationalism is also distinct from the theological tradition known as evangelicalism, which requires a belief in biblical inerrancy and the importance of evangelism, or sharing the Christian faith with others. While "[r]oughly half of evangelicals . . . embrace Christian nationalism to some degree," Christian nationalism "should not be thought of as synonymous with 'evangelicalism' or even 'white evangelicalism.' . . . Stated simply: being an evangelical, or even a white evangelical as pollsters often define that category, tells us almost nothing about a person's social attitudes or behavior once Christian nationalism has been considered."[24]

Researchers Allyson F. Shortle and Ronald Keith Gaddie agree that white evangelicalism and Christian nationalism are not one and the same, but they do intersect.[25] Studies on religion in political behavior often start with the three B's: religious belonging, belief, and behavior. Belonging is about religious affiliation, belief is about religious worldview, and behavior is about religious practice.[26] Shortle and Gaddie's study found that "evangelical belonging plays a secondary role in shaping out-group attitudes, while the belief that America is a divinely inspired nation lends a superior explanation of prejudicial attitudes in America."[27]

The distinction is often one of goals: political versus religious goals. Even appeals to a "Christian nation" are fundamentally different depending on whether the appeal is to a Christian nation as a *religious* goal versus a *political* goal. The first goal is that of a set of people who want to mobilize religious action and influence American society with their pious Christian example. The second goal is that of a set who want to define the parameters of what America is and who true

---

[20] Whitehead and Perry, *Taking America Back*, p. 10.
[21] Whitehead and Perry, *Taking America Back*, p. 78.
[22] Whitehead and Perry, *Taking America Back*, p. 19.
[23] Whitehead and Perry, *Taking America Back*, p. 19.
[24] Whitehead and Perry, *Taking America Back*, p. 20.
[25] Shortle and Gaddie, "Religious Nationalism."
[26] Shortle and Gaddie, "Religious Nationalism," p. 436.
[27] Shortle and Gaddie, "Religious Nationalism," p. 440.

Americans are. For example, one prominent Christian nationalist has said, "God will curse the nation that sanctions . . . [a] culture of diversity."[28]

This chapter will focus on the former set—conservative Christians with religious goals—that is, non-nationalist conservative white evangelicals.

Group Identity and Intergroup Bias

I once asked a roundtable of people who work on religious engagement programs and religious freedom advocacy whether political tribalism drives anti-Muslim hostility among white evangelicals. They responded, "Definitely. Everything is tribal nowadays. Muslims are part of a different religious tribe and inasmuch as they align with progressives, a different political tribe also," and "Yes. [Conservative white evangelicals] believe Democrats are trying to encourage Muslim immigration because it will help them de-Christianize America."[29]

To understand this dynamic, it is helpful to have a basic understanding of group identity. Much of what we know about group dynamics is based on a series of experiments conducted by social psychologist Henri Tajfel in the 1970s.[30] In one study, he took sixty-four boys from the same school; the boys all knew each other and already had a sense of community.[31] First, the researchers told the boys they wanted to test visual judgment. The boys were shown clusters of dots and had to estimate how many dots they saw. After the researchers tallied (or pretended to tally) the results, the researchers told the boys they were dividing them into groups: one group included boys who had guessed a high number of dots on the visual judgment test and one included those who had guessed low. In reality, the researchers divided the group randomly; their purpose was only to test what happened next.[32]

The researchers then gave the two groups some money and asked them to distribute it to other boys in the study. The boys could not keep any money for themselves; they had to give it to the others, but they chose how they would allocate the money, and they knew if it went to members of their own group or the out-group.[33] What Tajfel learned from the study shocked him about the power of

---

[28] Robert Jeffress, *Twilight's Last Gleaming: How America's Last Days Can Be Your Best Days* (New York: Worthy Books, 2012).

[29] "Politics of Vulnerability" (roundtable Participants: Andrew Lewis, Aneelah Afzali, Christy Vines, Dalia Mogahed, Jenan Mohajir, Justin Giboney, Mahan Mirza, Majid Al Sayegh, Michal Muelenberg, Mark Hamilton, Sherif Azami, Sohaib Sultan, Terry Kyllo, Travis Wussow, Omar Suleiman, Kevin Singer, Matthew Kaemingyk, Amar Peterman, Jihad Turk, Saeed Khan, Vanita Snow, Mike Tolhurst, Aspen Institute Inclusive America Project's Politics of Vulnerability Meeting, Washington, DC, March 2–3, 2020).

[30] Ezra Klein, *Why We're Polarized* (New York: Avid Reader Press, 2020).

[31] Klein, *Why We're Polarized.*

[32] Klein, *Why We're Polarized.*

[33] Klein, *Why We're Polarized.*

THE POLITICS OF VULNERABILITY   41

group identity: most of the boys in each group gave money to their own group members instead of to the out-group. The boys had been divided on the basis of completely meaningless criteria, but they still chose their own group over the other one.[34] There was no substantive benefit to choosing their own group, but they still did so because of the powerful pull of group identity.[35]

In a second study, Tajfel changed the setup so that when the boys were allocating money, they had to choose between maximizing their own amount of money and maximizing how much more their group got compared to the out-group.[36] The boys chose the former; they were okay with giving their own group less as long as they had significantly more money than the out-group.[37]

As a series of subsequent experiments by Tajfel and others confirmed, people exhibit discriminatory intergroup behavior in a way that created the biggest gap between their group and the out-group: "Far from the money being the prime motivator, 'it is the winning that seems more important to them.'"[38]

Intergroup Bias and US Partisanship

Our allegiance to our political tribes is no different than the usual dynamic of group loyalty and intergroup bias. Elections are pure team rivalry. What is worse, however, is that in our present political climate, these group rivalries pose ever more serious implications because of what Lilliana Mason in *Uncivil Agreement: How Politics Became Our Identity* calls the emergence of "mega-identities":

> A single vote can now indicate a person's partisan preference *as well as* his or her religion, race, ethnicity, gender, neighborhood, and favorite grocery store. This is no longer a single social identity. Partisanship can now be thought of as a mega-identity, with all the psychological and behavioral magnifications that implies.[39]

The difference between what we typically understand as partisan preferences and Mason's "mega-identity" concept is the difference between sorting and polarizing. The first is issue-based polarization: we cluster together based on our policy opinions. The second is identity-based polarization: we cluster together

[34] Klein, *Why We're Polarized.*
[35] Klein, *Why We're Polarized.*
[36] Klein, *Why We're Polarized.*
[37] Klein, *Why We're Polarized.*
[38] Klein, *Why We're Polarized,* 55.
[39] Lilliana Mason, *Uncivil Agreement: How Politics Became Our Identity* (Chicago: University of Chicago Press, 2018), 14.

based on political identities and those political identities polarize our other identities. Issue conflicts are just one of many expressions of that hostility.[40]

In this ever-widening circle of partisan preferences, almost nothing is apolitical anymore. Consider a 2004 advertisement by the Club for Growth, a conservative group that advocates for lower taxes and deregulation, against then presidential candidate Howard Dean.[41] The ad featured someone asking an older white couple what they think of Dean's plan, and the man responded, " 'I think Howard Dean should take his tax-hiking, government-expanding, latte-drinking, sushi-eating, Volvo-driving, *New York Times*–reading—.' His wife cuts in, 'Body-piercing, Hollywood-loving, left-wing freak show back to Vermont, where it belongs.' "[42] Each of these traits reinforces a particular mega-identity, and when each of the traits is activated—for example, by visual referents in an ad—all of them are activated.

Something similar appears to be at work when it comes to Muslims and liberals. Eboo Patel hints at this in *Out of Many Faiths: Religious Diversity and the American Promise*, in which he notes that Muslims are given platforms by outlets like *The New York Times*, National Public Radio (NPR), CNN, and *The New Yorker*.[43] These outlets are

> associated with urban, multicultural, progressive Whole Foods America; not so much white, rural, conservative Cracker Barrel America. One gets the sense that if Trump's America insists on casting Muslims as villains . . . then Barack Obama's America will respond by promoting Muslims whom they consider heroes. . . . Muslims, in other words, have become a totem in the current chapter of the American culture wars, a symbol that signals, above all, a tribal belonging (Trump/red/rural/evangelical/Cracker Barrel versus Obama/blue/urban/secular/Whole Foods), with each tribe doing its best to foist on the category "Muslim" its preferred set of characteristics.[44]

In other words, Muslims—and especially liberal advocacy on behalf of Muslims—are traits of the liberal mega-identity, and opposition to Muslims is a trait of the conservative mega-identity. What happens when American Muslims get lumped into a liberal mega-identity—that is, defined by conservatives as anti-Christian and anti-America? Muslims take on those traits, too.

[40] Klein, *Why We're Polarized*, 32–33.
[41] Klein, *Why We're Polarized*.
[42] Klein, *Why We're Polarized*, 69.
[43] Eboo Patel, *Out of Many Faiths: Religious Diversity and the American Promise* (Princeton, NJ: Princeton University Press, 2018).
[44] Patel, *Out of Many Faiths*.

According to Mason, the psychological implications are very dangerous.[45] When our racial, religious, and other identities are wrapped up with our political party, and if our party loses an election or some other partisan battle, the psychological impact is much worse.[46] It is like we lost the competition between racial and religious groups, too. It makes us feel threatened, and when we feel threatened, we lash out against the out-group.

This dynamic is particularly relevant now, when many white Christian conservatives are feeling under siege.[47] While in-group favoritism does not always result in out-group bias, in the religious context, tribalism *has* resulted in out-group hostility—and Muslims are one of the primary targets of this hostility.

Perceptions of threat are part of the reason why. Oxford political scientists Miles Hewstone, Mark Rubin, and Hazel Willis write, "[T]he constraints normally in place, which limit intergroup bias to in-group favoritism, are lifted when out-groups are associated with stronger emotions."[48] Stronger emotions include feeling like the out-group is moving against you as a member of the in-group because "an out-group seen as threatening may elicit fear and hostile actions."[49] Whereas *high-status* groups, meaning those that are a numerical majority and have power, do not feel threatened by minorities when the status gap is very wide, they are more likely to feel threatened when the status gap is closing.[50]

Perceptions of Threat: The End of White Christian America

There are multiple demographic trends contributing to white evangelicals' perception of threat. First, and for the first time in US history, white racial dominance is on the decline. In 1965, white Americans constituted 84 percent of the US population.[51] Since then, there has been an influx of immigrants, with nearly fifty-nine million arriving in the last fifty years alone.[52] Between 1965 and 2015, the American Asian population grew from 1.3 million to eighteen million, and the Hispanic population went from eight million to almost fifty-seven million.[53]

[45] Mason, *Uncivil Agreement*.

[46] "Lilliana Mason on Uncivil Agreement," YouTube, May 1, 2020, https://www.youtube.com/watch?v=TC4SQ9oasnU.

[47] Robert P. Jones, *The End of White Christian America* (New York: Simon and Schuster, 2016).

[48] Miles Hewstone, Mark Rubin, and Hazel Willis, "Intergroup Bias," *Annual Review of Psychology* 53, no.1 (2002): p. 579.

[49] Hewstone, Rubin, and Willis, "Intergroup Bias," p. 580.

[50] Hewstone, Rubin, and Willis, "Intergroup Bias," p. 585.

[51] "Modern Immigration Wave Brings 59 Million to US, Driving Population Growth and Change through 2065," Pew Research Center, September 28, 2015, https://www.pewresearch.org/hispanic/2015/09/28/modern-immigration-wave-brings-59-million-to-u-s-driving-population-growth-and-change-through-2065/.

[52] "Modern Immigration Wave."

[53] "Modern Immigration Wave."

America's complexion is "browning," and in several states—including America's most populous ones, Texas and California—whites are already a minority.[54] NPR reported in 2016 that nonwhite babies now outnumber non-Hispanic white babies.[55] The majority of Americans under the age of sixteen are nonwhite and have been since the middle of 2020.[56] Pew has found that whites generally will become a minority by 2055;[57] the US census says that will happen even sooner, in 2044.[58]

Second, and also for the first time in US history, white Protestant Christians are a minority in America. A 2017 PRRI study found that white Protestant Christians constitute only 43 percent of the US population.[59] Robert Jones, the founder of PRRI, calls it the "end of White Christian America."[60] To understand the gravity of the shift, consider that in 1976, eight in ten Americans were white Christians, and 55 percent of Americans were white Protestants.[61] In 1996, white Christians still made up two-thirds of the population. Today, they do not even constitute a majority.[62] Among these white Protestants, white evangelicals have also seen a precipitous drop. In the 1990s, white evangelicals constituted 27 percent of the US population; today it is somewhere between 17 and 13 percent.[63]

Third, the demise of white Protestant America has brought with it an end to "the cultural and institutional world built primarily by white Protestants that dominated American culture until the last decade."[64] Not only is Christianity declining but so is religion overall. An increasing number of Americans are religiously unaffiliated (the so-called nones), and in 2019, the percentage of nones became roughly the same as the percentage of evangelicals or Catholics.[65] By

---

[54] William H. Frey, "Less Than Half of US Children under 15 Are White, Census Shows," Brookings Institution, June 24, 2019, https://www.brookings.edu/research/less-than-half-of-us-children-under-15-are-white-census-shows/.

[55] Kendra Yoshinaga, "Babies of Color Are Now the Majority, Census Says," NPR, July 1, 2016, https://www.npr.org/sections/ed/2016/07/01/484325664/babies-of-color-are-now-the-majority-census-says.

[56] Mike Schneider, "Census Shows White Decline, Nonwhite Majority among Youngest," Associated Press, June 25, 2020, https://apnews.com/a3600edf620ccf2759080d00f154c069.

[57] "Modern Immigration Wave."

[58] "Projecting Majority-Minority," US Census Bureau, 2014, https://www.census.gov/content/dam/Census/newsroom/releases/2015/cb15-tps16_graphic.pdf.

[59] Daniel Cox and Robert P. Jones, "America's Changing Religious Identity," PRRI, September 6, 2017, https://www.prri.org/research/american-religious-landscape-christian-religiously-unaffiliated/.

[60] Jones, *End*.

[61] Jones, *End*.

[62] Jones, *End*.

[63] Harriet Sherwood, "'Toxic Christianity': The Evangelicals Creating Champions for Trump," *The Guardian*, October 21, 2018, https://www.theguardian.com/us-news/2018/oct/21/evangelical-christians-trump-liberty-university-jerry-falwell.

[64] Jones, *End*.

[65] Samuel Smith, "Religious 'Nones' Now as Big as Evangelicals in the US, New Data Shows," *The Christian Post*, March 20, 2019, https://www.christianpost.com/news/religious-nones-now-as-big-as-evangelicals-in-the-us-new-data-shows.html.

THE POLITICS OF VULNERABILITY   45

2016, the nones already constituted the nation's largest religious voting bloc.[66] The massive shift signaled growing discontent with organized religion generally. Altogether, Jones says, this shift has precipitated an "internal identity crisis" that has generated tremendous anger, insecurity, and anxiety.[67] Unfortunately, that anger has been directed outward toward a number of minority groups— Muslims included.

Perceptions of Threat in Europe and Its Impact on American Dynamics

This phenomenon is not unique to American conservatives. In fact, it is emblematic of conservatives throughout Europe and is at the root of populism in those countries. From Marine Le Pen's National Rally in France to Matteo Salvini's Five Star Movement in Italy and Viktor Orbán's Fidesz in Hungary, populist leaders and their parties are becoming increasingly prominent, and scholars say that political and cultural vulnerabilities are a significant reason why.

The popular conception of populism on the political Left is that it is driven by some combination of factors such as racism, short-lived backlash to immigrants, "the system," and economic scarcity.[68] But politics professor Matthew Goodwin writes that, although these factors play a role, their influence in the debate is "wholly disproportionate to their significance, and they distract from dealing with the actual grievances that are fueling populism."[69] Goodwin writes, "Today's thinkers, writers and groups on the left have subscribed to a number of theories [about populism], all of which are incorrect."[70] One of them is the mistaken belief that we can blame it all on racism, "and perhaps even latent public support for fascism."[71] Racism is an important piece of the problem, but outsized focus on it takes attention away from the issues that need to be addressed to bring about real change and healing.

In fact, Goodwin and Eatwell explain that what we really need to look at are "four deep-rooted societal shifts: the 'four Ds,'" which include high levels of

---

[66] Christopher Ingraham, "The Non-Religious Are Now the Country's Largest Religious Voting Bloc." *The Washington Post*, July 14, 2016, https://www.washingtonpost.com/news/wonk/wp/2016/07/14/the-non-religious-are-now-the-countrys-largest-religious-voting-bloc/.

[67] Jones, *End.*

[68] Matthew Goodwin, "National Populism Is Unstoppable—and the Left Still Doesn't Understand It." *The Guardian*, November 8, 2018, https://www.theguardian.com/commentisfree/2018/nov/08/national-populism-immigration-financial-crisis-globalisation.

[69] Goodwin, "National Populism."

[70] Goodwin, "National Populism."

[71] Roger Eatwell and Matthew Goodwin, *National Populism: The Revolt against Liberal Democracy* (New York: Pelican, 2018). https://www.theguardian.com/commentisfree/2018/nov/08/national-populism-immigration-financial-crisis-globalisation

political distrust; "strong and entrenched fears about the perceived destruction of national cultures, ways of life and values, amid unprecedented and rapid rates of immigration and ethnic change"; anxiety about deprivation and the loss of jobs and income; and dealignment, "in which bonds between voters and traditional parties are breaking down."[72]

The second *D*, "strong and entrenched fears about the perceived destruction of national cultures, ways of life and values, amid unprecedented and rapid rates of immigration and ethnic change," is connected to concerns about political correctness. Such "restrictive communicative norms" make people feel like they cannot vocalize their concerns, Goodwin says.[73] What these people want is "cohesive, inclusive communities that share a core skeleton of values."[74] They "aren't looking for a cultural straitjacket," but they do want some core similarities like language and values that are shared by all people.[75] These similarities foster social in-group trust and boost self-esteem for group members, and in many parts of the world, that cohesion is lacking or perceived to be lacking.[76]

Goodwin also points to the pace of change. He writes that it is not true that populists do not want diversity; instead, the problem for them is that diversity has grown exponentially in a short amount of time, and white conservatives are struggling to adapt.[77] The debate is not about "open versus closed"; it is more useful to think of it as a debate between people who are comfortable with fast versus slow change. . . . The research since 2016 shows that one of the key drivers of populism is rapid demographic change in areas that were historically predominantly white and suddenly experienced an injection of diversity."[78] Miriam Juan Torres from More in Common, a nonprofit that studies American polarization, explains it this way:

Below a certain threshold, an influx of immigrants does not seem to strengthen a particular notion of the in-group. It is when immigration is perceived as posing a challenge to the "normative order" that the need to retreat to a narrower definition of that "us" seems to develop.[79]

---

[72] Goodwin, "National Populism."
[73] "Matthew Goodwin and Henry Olsen: National Populism," *Faith Angle*, November 1, 2019, https://faithangle.podbean.com/e/matthew-goodwin-and-henry-olsen-national-populism/.
[74] "Matthew Goodwin and Henry Olsen."
[75] "Matthew Goodwin and Henry Olsen."
[76] "Matthew Goodwin and Henry Olsen."
[77] Goodwin, "National Populism."
[78] "Matthew Goodwin and Henry Olsen."
[79] Caroline Kitchener, "The Trouble with Tribalism," *The Atlantic*, October 17, 2018, https://www.theatlantic.com/membership/archive/2018/10/trouble-tribalism/573307/.

THE POLITICS OF VULNERABILITY   47

The New York Times's podcast *The Daily* highlighted similar trends in its "The Battle for Europe" series, which examines the rise of populism in France, Italy, Poland, and Germany. In each episode, the reporters identify feelings "of being left behind, and of being ignored."[80] In Poland, for example, the populist is "the Polish person who feels that their Catholic values are being sort of fundamentally threatened."[81] In each country examined, the populists reject "the tenets of liberal democracy—capitalism, globalization, the protection of minorities—because in a way, each of these tenets feels like a rejection of [the populists]."[82]

Shadi Hamid describes the defining features of European populism as anti-Muslim and anti-Islam sentiment: attitudes toward Muslims are a "powerful proxy for a long list of primarily cultural issues and grievances, including . . . the decline of Christianity, race, and demographic concerns."[83] The French writer Renaud Camus describes the core concern as "the great replacement"; about Muslims specifically, he "warns grotesquely of a 'genocide by substitution,' the replacement of white French and European order by Muslim hordes in a plot orchestrated by cosmopolitan elite."[84]

Though the American and European situations are importantly distinct, this idea of Muslims as proxies for larger issues is also true of America, as evidenced by, among other things, the centrality of anti-Muslim measures to Trump's 2016 campaign. In particular, many conservative white evangelicals—like conservative Christians generally—are deeply concerned about the status of Christians around the world. In the case of Europe specifically, these Christians are alarmed by Muslim population growth in Europe at a time when Christianity is fast declining.[85] It is not uncommon to hear conservative Christians fretting that the United States will repeat the European trend. The shared concern points to the similar social psychological dynamics, as in the European context, and the need to address those dynamics in order to help resolve anti-Muslim discrimination in the United States.

---

[80] "Part 5: Can Liberal Democracy Survive in Europe," *The New York Times: The Daily*, June 14, 2019, https://www.nytimes.com/2019/06/14/podcasts/the-daily/europe-liberal-democracy-germany.html.

[81] "Part 4: Poland's Culture Wars," *The New York Times: The Daily*, June 13, 2019, https://www.nytimes.com/2019/06/13/podcasts/the-daily/poland-nationalism-democracy.html.

[82] "Part 5: Can Liberal Democracy."

[83] Shadi Hamid, "The Role of Islam in European Populism: How Refugee Flows and Fear of Muslims Drive Right-Wing Support," *Foreign Policy*, February 26, 2019, https://www.brookings.edu/wp-content/uploads/2019/02/FP_20190226_islam_far_right_hamid.pdf.

[84] Roger Cohen, "Trump's Last Stand for White America," *The New York Times*, October 16, 2020, https://www.nytimes.com/2020/10/16/opinion/trump-2020.html?referringSource=articleShare.

[85] Christopher Caldwell, *Reflections on the Revolution in Europe: Immigration, Islam and the West* (New York: Anchor Books, 2010).

Impact on Religious Minorities: Discounting Anti-Muslim Discrimination

There are several theories for why threat leads to bias. One is Tajfel's social identity theory. When a high-status group protects its members, the members feel greater self-esteem.[86] When that status is challenged, members feel depressed and lash out at the threatening out-group.[87] Other studies on two closely-related social psychological traits posit something similar.

Social Dominance Orientation

The first trait is social dominance orientation (SDO), or a desire to want one's group to dominate the out-group; feelings of threat make this tendency worse.[88]

Scholars have tested the connection between SDO and support for Trump. Professors Rogers M. Smith and Desmond King write that a "wide variety of studies, including experimental research, public opinion surveys, analyses of voting statistics, and panel studies show that [Trump's] victim narrative connected powerfully with those with strong attachments to traditionally dominant identities."[89] Political scientist Diana C. Mutz found these trends even among people who in past elections might not have voted for Trump. People who felt their status was threatened experienced an increase in SDO—that is, a desire to dominate the out-group, which in turn led them to "defect to Trump."[90]

Mutz tested this specifically with respect to attitudes toward Muslims. Respondents were asked to what extent Muslims and Christians, among others, were discriminated against in America.[91] She found that people who voted for Trump perceived Christians as experiencing greater discrimination than Muslims did.[92] Other studies have also documented the partisan divide, while not connecting it to SDO specifically, when it comes to attitudes about anti-Muslim discrimination. In 2020, the University of Chicago Divinity School and the Associated Press-NORC Center for Public Affairs Research (AP-NORC) found that while half of Americans believe that American Muslims' religious freedom is threatened at least somewhat, only about three in ten white

---

[86] Hewstone, Rubin, and Willis, "Intergroup Bias."

[87] Hewstone, Rubin, and Willis, "Intergroup Bias."

[88] Diana C. Mutz, "Status Threat, Not Economic Hardship, Explains the 2016 Presidential Vote," *Proceedings of the National Academy of Sciences* 115, no. 19 (May 2018): pp. E4330–E4339.

[89] Rogers M. Smith and Desmond King, "White Protectionism in America," *Perspectives on Politics* 19, no. 2 (2021): pp. 5.

[90] Mutz, "Status Threat."

[91] Mutz, "Status Threat."

[92] Mutz, "Status Threat."

evangelicals in the U.S. said the same.[93] In 2019, Pew found that Democrats and those who lean Democratic "are more likely than Republicans and Republican leaners to say Muslims face at least some discrimination in the US (92% vs. 69%)," while "[a]t the same time, Republicans are much more likely than Democrats to say evangelicals face discrimination (70% vs. 32%)."[94]

In 2017, the Rasmussen Report found that "[f]ifty-six percent (56%) of Democrats . . . believe most Muslims in this country are mistreated, a view shared by only 22% of Republicans."[95] That same year, PRRI found that Democrats were four times as likely to believe that Muslims faced greater discrimination than Christians did.[96] Republicans thought the two groups suffered roughly equally, but among white evangelicals specifically, PRRI found that 57 percent said that anti-Christian discrimination is widespread in the United States, while only 44 percent said the same thing about anti-Muslim discrimination.[97]

Similar to Mutz's findings, there appears to be a correlation between the political climate and perceptions of status threat. Polls from several years or even a year before the 2016 presidential election found that fewer white evangelicals thought they faced more discrimination than Muslims do. A 2013 PRRI survey, for instance, found that 59 percent of white evangelicals thought that Muslims faced more discrimination than evangelicals did; 56 percent responded that way to an October 2016 poll.[98] By February 2017, that number had dropped 12 percentage points.[99]

Authoritarianism

Scholars have separately studied a second social psychological trait called *authoritarianism*, which refers to a personality type that sees the world as black and

---

[93] Elana Schor and Hannah Fingerhut, "Religious Freedom in America: Popular and Polarizing," Associated Press, August 5, 2020, https://apnews.com/article/donald-trump-religion-u-s-news-virus-outbreak-reinventing-faith-535624d93b8ce3d271019200e362b0cf.

[94] David Masci, "Many Americans See Religious Discrimination in US—Especially against Muslims," Pew Research Center, May 17, 2019, https://www.pewresearch.org/fact-tank/2019/05/17/many-americans-see-religious-discrimination-in-u-s-especially-against-muslims/.

[95] "Democrats Think Muslims Worse Off Here Than Christians Are in Muslim World," *Rasmussen Reports*, February 7, 2017, https://www.rasmussenreports.com/public_content/politics/general_p olitics/february_2017/democrats_think_muslims_worse_off_here_than_christians_are_in_musli m_world.

[96] Daniel Cox and Robert P. Jones, "Majority of Americans Oppose Transgender Bathroom Restrictions," PRRI, March 10, 2017, https://www.prri.org/research/lgbt-transgender-bathroom-dis crimination-religious-liberty/.

[97] Cox and Jones, "Majority."

[98] Emma Green, "White Evangelicals Believe They Face More Discrimination Than Muslims," *The Atlantic*, March 10, 2017, https://www.theatlantic.com/politics/archive/2017/03/perceptions-dis crimination-muslims-christians/519135/.

[99] Green, "White Evangelicals."

50 ASMA T. UDDIN

white and society as fragile, and it consequently seeks to impose hierarchy, order, and uniformity.[100]

In a 2011 study, Marc Hetherington and Elizabeth Suhay tested the connection between authoritarianism and perceptions of threat from terrorism and found that people who score high on authoritarianism do not "become more hawkish or less supportive of civil liberties in response to a perceived threat of terrorism"; they hold these positions even in the absence of threat.[101] But people "who are less authoritarian adopt more restrictive and aggressive policy stands when they perceive a threat from terrorism. In other words, many *average Americans* become susceptible to 'authoritarian thinking' when they perceive a grave threat to their safety."[102]

> A similar tendency comes into play when Christians feel threatened about their status in the United States; they begin to acquiesce to the views of Christian nationalists, or those who seek to define America as a Christian nation and to exclude minorities like Muslims from the national fabric. Political scientist Andrew Lewis explained it to me this way:
> Those who are constantly inundated with perspectives that Christianity is threatened (even if they are not necessarily hostile to other religious faiths) are more likely to accommodate Christian nationalist views on their own side. Trying to push back against nationalism from your team and religious discrimination on the other team is a difficult path to follow.[103]

In other words, it is difficult for many non-nationalists to both resist liberals' attacks on their Christian practices and also to resist Christian nationalists' push to privilege Christianity. So they accommodate the rhetoric and tactics of the Christian nationalists, even if they are more open to diverse faiths. Importantly, Lewis says,

> all of this is wrapped up in partisanship, as partisan leaders prime these responses—both out-group intolerance and in-group protection. In some eras, partisans have played homage to protecting Christians from losing ground to secularism or liberals. But now partisans on the Right are increasingly emphasizing both secularism and liberalism, as well as Islam and other foreign religions.[104]

---

[100] Marc J. Hetherington and Elizabeth Suhay, "Authoritarianism, Threat, and Americans' Support for the War on Terror," *American Journal of Political Science* 55, no. 3 (2011): pp. 546–60
[101] Hetherington and Suhay, "Authoritarianism."
[102] Hetherington and Suhay, "Authoritarianism."
[103] Email, May 26, 2020.
[104] Email, May 26, 2020.

THE POLITICS OF VULNERABILITY   51

This trend explains Mutz's findings, too: Trump's deft use of the victim narrative helped attract voters who were experiencing status threat.[105] On the campaign trail, he told them in the clearest terms, "We will have so much winning if I get elected that you may get bored with the winning."[106]

In sum, then, authoritarianism and SDO are triggered by a perceived threat, and people respond by protecting the in-group and excluding the threatening outsider. These dynamics are key to understanding how and why anti-Muslim sentiment is generated.

Impact on Religious Minorities: Opposition to Muslims' Rights

The conflation of the threat from the Left with Muslims extends beyond just rhetorical posturing. The political divides are exacerbated regularly by professional fearmongers who develop far-fetched conspiracy theories and the influential right-wing figures in media and politics who disseminate the theories.[107] Altogether, these efforts result in significant legal challenges to Muslims' religious rights, from building mosques to anti-bullying programs in public schools.[108]

Many of the conspiracy theories originate at the Center for Security Policy (CSP). CSP-funded author Jim Simpson authored two books on the subject: *The Red-Green Axis: Refugees, Immigration and the Agenda to Erase America* and *The Red-Green Axis 2.0: An Existential Threat to America and the World.* The "red" relates to the red of communist flags and implicitly connects the political Left, communism, and socialism. The "green" points to the green often found in the national flags of majority-Muslim countries, as green symbolizes Islam. According to Simpson, this axis of Islam and liberalism endeavors to re-create America and fundamentally alter its culture—a process he calls "civilization jihad."[109]

CSP-funded writer Matthew Vadum discusses a similar theme in *Team Jihad: How Sharia-Supremacists Collaborate with Leftists to Destroy the United States.* Meanwhile, David Horowitz, well known for his anti-Muslim advocacy,

---

[105] Mutz, "Status Threat."

[106] Scott Eric Kaufman, "Donald Trump: If Elected, 'We'll Have So Much Winning, You'll Get Bored with Winning,'" *Salon*, September 9, 2015, https://www.salon.com/2015/09/09/donald_trump_if_elected_well_have_so_much_winning_youll_get_bored_with_winning/.

[107] Wajahat Ali, Eli Clifton, Matthew Duss, Lee Fang, Scott Keyes, and Faiz Shakir, "The Roots of the Islamophobia Network in America," Center for American Progress, August 26, 2011, https://cdn.americanprogress.org/wp-content/uploads/issues/2011/08/pdf/islamophobia.pdf.

[108] For a fuller discussion, see Asma Uddin, *When Islam Is Not a Religion* (New York: Pegasus Books, 2019).

[109] James Simpson, *The Red-Green Axis: Refugees, Immigration and the Agenda to Erase America* (Washington, DC: Center for Security Policy, 2015).

has written *Unholy Alliance: Radical Islam and the American Left*. And Andrew McCarthy, a former assistant US attorney and columnist for the *National Review*, puts forth a similar theory in *The Grand Jihad: How Islam and the Left Sabotage America*.

In all cases, the idea is that the political Left in the United States is working with Muslims to destroy America's Christian character. The fearmongers reason that any attempt by liberals to expand protections or rights for Muslims must be resisted as part of a broader effort to preserve the United States as a Christian nation. Among other things, this impulse has resulted in a nationwide resistance movement to building mosques. Guided by CSP's handbook "Mosques in America: A Guide to Accountable Permit Hearings and Continuing Citizen Oversight," Americans have learned to "express questions and reservations in a manner appropriate to the relevant civic forum's purpose" and to avoid "expressing alarm as hysteria," as that could be "used to characterize the entire oversight effort as racially biased and ignorant."[110] The efforts have born many successes; today, mosque construction is almost always challenged and often delayed by years by these protests.[111]

In the public-school context, Christian advocacy groups like the Freedom of Conscience Defense Fund (FCDF) and American Center for Law and Justice (ACLJ) regularly challenge accommodations for Muslim students in public schools.[112] FCDF has successfully challenged a school district in Washington state that sought to provide a welcoming environment for Muslim students fasting during Ramadan.[113] FCDF is also currently planning a challenge to an anti-bullying program in Minneapolis, which was created in response to complaints about faith-based bullying filed by the city's large Somali Muslim population.[114] And it is investigating a program in Seattle public schools that seeks to better inform students about Islam and its holidays and to create a safer and more welcoming environment for Muslim students.[115]

Meanwhile, with ACLJ's help, parents and students have objected to school lessons on Islam, which is taught in cultural and historical terms alongside other

---

[110] Karen Lugo, *Mosques in America: A Guide to Accountable Permit Hearings and Continuing Citizen Oversight* (Washington, DC: Center for Security Policy, 2016), http://www.centerforsecurit ypolicy.org/wp-content/uploads/2016/12/Mosque_in_America.pdf.

[111] "Nationwide Anti-Mosque Activity," American Civil Liberties Union, May 2018, https://www. aclu.org/issues/national-security/discriminatory-profiling/nationwide-anti-mosque-activity.

[112] "FCDF Sends Letter to Seattle Public Schools Regarding Pro-Muslim Program," FCDF, July 8, 2018, https://www.fcdflegal.org/fcdf-sends-letter-to-seattle-public-schools-regarding-pro-muslim-program/.

[113] "FCDF Sends Letter."

[114] "FCDF Demands Emails from Minneapolis Public Schools Regarding Relationship with CAIR," FCDF, August 17, 2018, https://www.fcdflegal.org/fcdf-demands-emails-from-minneapolis-public-schools-regarding-relationship-with-cair/.

[115] "FCDF Sends Letter."

religions in various social studies courses.[116] In a Georgia case, parents objected to a worksheet that tested students on various Muslim beliefs and, in particular, the fill-in-the-blank sentence "Allah is the [blank] worshipped by Jews & Christians," with the correct answer being "same God."[117] In Maryland, a student challenged another fill-in-the-blank sentence, this one about the Islamic creed; students had to answer that, according to Islam, "[t]here is no god but *Allah* and Muhammad is the *messenger* of Allah."[118] After the complaining student lost her case in the appellate court, she took it to the US Supreme Court, which declined to hear the case in October 2019.[119] In New Jersey, the same fill-in-the-blank sentence, given as homework after students watched a brief cartoon video on the five pillars of Islam, ignited complaints that landed the parents on Fox's *Tucker Carlson Tonight*.[120] The discussion there alleged that the school district "was suppressing discussion about Christianity while proselytizing Islam."[121] In other cases, challenges like this have resulted in everything from textbooks being rewritten to schools being placed in emergency lockdowns because of threats.[122]

State Responses to Islamophobia

Throughout the Trump administration's tenure, professional anti-Muslim agitators like CSP and its founder, Frank Gaffney, moved closer to the halls of power.[123] As Beinart explained in his March 2017 piece "The Denationalization of American Muslims," Washington conservatives used to ridicule Gaffney's claims and stigmatize him for making them.[124] But things changed quickly after Trump's election.

---

[116] Ty Tagami, "Lessons about Religion Stir, and Are Stirred by, Suspicion of Islam," *The Atlanta Journal-Constitution*, October 5, 2015, https://www.ajc.com/news/local-education/lessons-about-religion-stir-and-are-stirred-suspicion-islam/w6nfM7CMxchh1fOantyGZO/.

[117] Tagami, "Lessons."

[118] "Islam in Public School Challenge Rejected by Supreme Court," Bloomberg Law, October 15, 2019, https://news.bloomberglaw.com/us-law-week/islam-in-public-school-challenge-rejected-by-supreme-court.

[119] "Islam in Public School Challenge."

[120] Matt Katz, "Allegations of Islam Indoctrination in Public Schools Spread to New Jersey," WNYC, April 10, 2017, https://www.wnyc.org/story/allegations-islam-indoctrination-public-schools-spread-nj/.

[121] Katz, "Allegations."

[122] Jess Staufenberg, "Arabic Calligraphy Lesson Causes School Security Lockdown in Virginia," *Independent*, December 18, 2015, https://www.independent.co.uk/news/world/americas/arabic-calligraphy-lesson-causes-school-security-lockdown-in-virginia-a6778296.html.

[123] Ali, Clifton, Duss, Fang, Keyes, and Shakir, "Roots."

[124] Peter Beinart, "The Denationalization of American Muslims," *The Atlantic*, March 19, 2017, https://www.theatlantic.com/politics/archive/2017/03/frank-gaffney-donald-trump-and-the-denationalization-of-american-muslims/519954/.

54   ASMA T. UDDIN

In 2003, after Gaffney attacked two Muslim staffers in the George W. Bush White House, anti-tax crusader Grover Norquist banned him from his influential "Wednesday meeting" of conservative activists.[125] In 2011, according to sources close to the organization, the American Conservative Union (ACU) informally barred Gaffney from speaking at CPAC, the ACU's signature event.[126] In 2013, the Bradley Foundation, which had backed the CSP since 1988, cut off funds.[127] That same year, Gaffney lost the *Washington Times* column he had been writing since the late 1990s.[128] As late as December 2015, *The Daily Beast* had declared that "Frank Gaffney has been shunned by pretty much everyone in conservative intellectual circles."[129]

Yet less than eighteen months later, America was led by a president, Donald Trump, who has frequently cited CSP when justifying his policies toward Muslims.[130] Trump's chief strategist, Steve Bannon, has called Gaffney "one of the senior thought leaders and men of action in this whole war against Islamic radical jihad."[131] Trump's Attorney General Jeff Sessions, who has said "Sharia law fundamentally conflicts with our magnificent constitutional order," in 2015 won the CSP's Keeper of the Flame award.[132] Trump's CIA Director Mike Pompeo has appeared on Gaffney's radio program more than twenty-four times since 2013.[133] Sebastian Gorka, who runs a kind of parallel National Security Council inside the White House called the Strategic Initiatives Group, has appeared on Gaffney's radio program eighteen times during that period; he has called sharia "antithetical to the values of this great nation" and recently refused to say whether he considered Islam a religion.[134]

With colleagues and advisors like these, it is no wonder that Trump parrots the Gaffney talking points. Gaffney speaks often of Muslims and Muslim institutions as "Trojan horses."[135] Trump used that precise metaphor in June 2016, the day after the Pulse nightclub shooting, when he said that refugees and immigrants "could be a better, bigger more horrible version than the legendary Trojan horse ever was."[136] He also said his Democratic opponent would be the one to let the Trojan horse in: "Altogether, under the [Hillary] Clinton plan, you'd be admitting

---

[125] Beinart, "Denationalization."
[126] Beinart, "Denationalization."
[127] Beinart, "Denationalization."
[128] Beinart, "Denationalization."
[129] Beinart, "Denationalization."
[130] Beinart, "Denationalization."
[131] Beinart, "Denationalization."
[132] Beinart, "Denationalization."
[133] Beinart, "Denationalization."
[134] Beinart, "Denationalization."
[135] Emily Schultheis, "Donald Trump Warns Refugees Could Be 'Trojan Horse' for US," *CBS News*, June 13, 2016, https://www.cbsnews.com/news/donald-trump-warns-refugees-could-be-trojan-horse-for-u-s/.
[136] Schultheis, "Donald Trump."

THE POLITICS OF VULNERABILITY 55

hundreds of thousands of refugees from the Middle East with no system to vet them or to prevent the radicalization of their children."[137] And he threw in an additional allegation of Muslim deception, claiming that American Muslims knew what the Pulse shooter was planning and did not alert authorities: "They know what's going on. They know that he was bad. . . . But you know what? They didn't turn [him] in."[138]

That Trump not only did not repudiate Gaffney et al.,'s bogus claims but parroted them reflects the state's ready embrace of Islamophobia. Understood in the context of the social psychological drivers of anti-Muslim sentiment—and its overlap with US partisanship—it becomes clear that Islamophobia is a critical means of signaling in-group political solidarity and is cultivated for that very purpose.

Conclusion

America is increasingly becoming consumed with political tribalism. Our political identities have morphed well beyond issue positions to include racial, religious, and other traits, such that an electoral loss for our team exerts tremendous psychological pressure on us. This polarization, coupled with perceptions of threat that heighten social psychological tendencies toward social dominance and authoritarianism, result in concrete harm to religious (and other) minorities. That is, tribalism sets up the dynamics that transform members of the out-group from fellow humans who are entitled to human rights to members of an out-group who must be defeated at all costs, lest our own team loses.

This dynamic is evident in the treatment of Muslims' rights in the United States. Not only is anti-Muslim discrimination minimized by this focus on Christians' own sense of victimhood, but it also manifests in active social, political, and legal challenges to Muslims' religious rights. Devising effective strategies to combat Islamophobia thus requires finding ways to lower perceptions of threat. Many of the same studies that diagnose the problems of social dominance orientation, and authoritarianism, should be mined for concrete strategies for change.

[137] Schultheis, "Donald Trump."
[138] Peter Beinart, "The Attack in Manhattan Poses a Test for Donald Trump," The Atlantic, October 31, 2017, https://www.theatlantic.com/politics/archive/2017/10/the-attack-in-manhattan-poses-a-test-for-donald-trump/544592/.

4

Anti-Muslim Racism and the Rise of Ethnonationalist Populism in the United States

Saher Selod

One of the most shocking moments for Americans was watching what unfolded on live television on January 6, 2021. Congress was set to count electoral votes in a joint session and officially name Joe Biden as the 46th president of the United States. Before the votes could be formally counted, a mob of overwhelmingly white men stormed the US Capitol—many yelling "Hang Mike Pence!"—resulting in the death of five people.[1] For those who witnessed the developments from the comforts of our homes, the events were shocking, but not unbelievable. The last decade has featured a sharp increase in both right-wing and nativist populism in the United States. Many studies have focused on the economic woes and racist underpinnings of the rise of these new factions in the United States.[2] But understudied are the ways that the rise in nativism and populism are also tied to an increase in anti-Muslim racism because of the Global War on Terror.

The rise in populism in the United States has garnered much attention from scholars and journalists. Arlie Hochschild's book *Strangers in their Own Land: Anger and Mourning on the American Right* provided those in search of answers related to what was happening in white working-class America and the growing resentment that culminated in the election of a right-wing populist president.[3] Interviews with individuals in Lake Charles, Louisiana, indeed

---

[1] Martin Pengelly, "Trump Defended Rioters Who Threatened to Hang 'Mike Pence,' Audio Reveals," *The Guardian*, November 12, 2021, https://www.theguardian.com/us-news/2021/nov/12/trump-capitol-attack-rioters-mike-pence.

[2] Bart Bonikowski, "Three Lessons of Contemporary Populism in Europe and the United States," *Brown Journal of World Affairs* 23, no. 1 (Fall–Winter 2016): pp. 9–24; Jeffrey Haynes, "From Huntington to Trump: Twenty-Five Years of the 'Clash of Civilizations,'" *Review of Faith and International Affairs* 17, no. 1 (2019): pp. 11–23; Andrew L. Whitehead, Samuel L. Perry, and Joseph O. Baker, "Make America Christian Again: Christian Nationalism and Voting for Donald Trump in the 2016 Presidential Election," *Sociology of Religion* 79, no. 2 (Summer 2018): pp. 147–71.

[3] Arlie Russell Hochschild, *Strangers in Their Own Land: Anger and Mourning on the American Right* (New York: New Press, 2018).

Saher Selod, *Anti-Muslim Racism and the Rise of Ethnonationalist Populism in the United States* In: *Global Islamophobia and the Rise of Populism*. Edited by: Sahar F. Aziz and John L. Esposito, Oxford University Press.
© Oxford University Press 2024. DOI: 10.1093/oso/9780197648995.003.0004

revealed that many Americans felt left behind in an increasingly diverse society. Focusing on the Tea Party, Hochschild's work has felt particularly relevant for liberals who wanted to understand the outcome of the 2016 presidential election, one that many thought would easily go to the Democratic candidate, Hillary Clinton. The election of Donald J. Trump as the 45th president of the United States shocked many, as he ran on an overtly racist platform. He referred to Mexicans as "rapists" and incited his supporters with a call on the campaign trail to ban and register Muslims.[4] At a town hall in New Hampshire on September 17, 2015, he told the crowd, "We have a *problem* in this country; it's called *Muslims*. We know our current president is one."[5] Almost two months later, after the terrorist attacks in France, including at the Bataclan club, Trump was quoted as saying he would strongly consider shutting down mosques.[6] While these statements got a lot of media attention for their outrageous, overtly racist tone, anti-Muslim sentiments had been lingering in the United States for decades prior to the election of Trump. From the Iran Hostage Crisis in 1979 to 9/11, the social construction of Muslims as a threat to national security and a potential danger to society existed well before September 11, 2001, but has been growing at a rapid pace since the attacks.[7]

An ethnonationalist movement was brewing in the United States that mobilized around the threat of Islam taking over. Trump played a role in this movement, profiting from it by stoking the anger and hatred toward Muslims already existing among ethnonationalist populists. While the economic woes that scholars like Hochschild emphasize are important to uncover, the role of anti-Muslim racism in the rise of this ethnonationalism should not be minimized. This chapter examines how politicians and Islamophobic activists have been promoting anti-Muslim sentiments since 9/11. The rise in anti-Muslim racism is important in understanding the rise in right-wing and ethnonationalist populism.

---

[4] Mary Romero, "Trump's Immigration Attacks, in Brief," *Contexts* 17, no. 1 (2018): pp. 34–41.

[5] Jenna Johnson and Abigail Hauslohner, "'I Think Islam Hates Us': A Timeline of Trump's Comments about Islam and Muslims," *The Washington Post*, May 20, 2017, https://www.washingtonpost.com/news/post-politics/wp/2017/05/20/i-think-islam-hates-us-a-timeline-of-trumps-comments-about-islam-and-muslims/ (emphasis added).

[6] Johnson and Hauslohner, "'I Think.'"

[7] Sahar F. Aziz, *The Racial Muslim: When Racism Quashes Religious Freedom* (Berkeley: University of California Press, 2021); Louis A. Cainkar, *Homeland Insecurity: The Arab American and Muslim American Experience After 9/11* (New York: Russell Sage Foundation, 2009); Erik Love, *Islamophobia and Racism in America* (New York: New York University Press, 2017); Nazita Lajevardi, *Outsiders at Home: The Politics of American Islamophobia* (Cambridge: Cambridge University Press, 2020); Edward W. Said, *Orientalism* (New York: Vintage, 1979); Saher Selod, *Forever Suspect: Racialized Surveillance of Muslim Americans in the War on Terror* (New Brunswick, NJ: Rutgers University Press, 2018).

Populism and Ethnonationalism

When people hear the term *populism*, particularly in the current context, they may think that anyone who espouses populist views must also be xenophobic and racist. This makes sense given that since the election of President Barack Obama, a form of populism that is also anti-immigrant and anti-Muslim has undoubtedly grown.[8] But populism has a long history in the United States and is not always embraced by xenophobes. Bonikowski defines *populism* as "a form of politics predicated on the moral vilification of elites and the veneration of ordinary people, who are seen as the sole legitimate source of political power."[9] This definition enables a critique of those in power by all political factions of the country for being elitist and not having the people's interests at heart. This attitude can be seen in a populist left movement in the United States that is reflected in Bernie Sanders and his supporters.[10] This group's critique of the elite is an economic one that does not appear to have the anti-immigrant and xenophobic flavor of right-wing populism.

The election of President Trump sheds light on a populist strain growing in the United States that is also nativist and xenophobic, revealing the impact of a growing nationalist ideology tied to misogyny and racism against Muslims. The rise in nationalism in the United States is partially the result of the wars in Iraq and Afghanistan since 9/11. Ethnonationalism, compared to nationalism, emphasizes an exclusionary aspect, in which the nation is seen as under threat of immigrants and other groups.[11] Ethnonationalism is based on the idea that the nation is being taken over by foreigners and that the country is losing its original characteristics, which are seen as predominantly white and Christian. Scholars found that in Trump's election, Christian nationalism played a role with supporters who viewed him as returning the United States to its Christian roots.[12] The rise in populist ideologies must be understood within the context of the growing racialization of Muslims because of the Global War on Terror.

---

[8] Bart Bonikowski, "Trump's Populism: The Mobilization of Nationalist Cleavages and the Future of US Democracy," in *When Democracy Trumps Populism: European and Latin America Lessons for the United States*, ed. Kurt Weyland and Raúl L. Madrid (Cambridge: Cambridge University Press, 2019), pp. 110–31.

[9] Bart Bonikowski, "Ethno-Nationalist Populism and the Mobilization of Collective Resentment," *British Journal of Sociology* 68, no. 1 (2017): p. 184.

[10] Bonikowski, "Ethno-Nationalist Populism," pp. 181–213.

[11] Bart Bonikowski, "Ethno-Nationalist Populism"; Laura Cervi, "Exclusionary Populism and Islamophobia: A Comparative Analysis of Italy and Spain," *Religions* 11, no. 10 (2020): p. 516.

[12] Whitehead, Perry, and Baker, "Make America Christian."

Clash of Civilizations and Anti-Muslim Racism

Anti-Muslim sentiments did not begin with the attacks of September 11, 2001, but has a long history that dates back for centuries. In 1979, Edward Said showed in his book *Orientalism* that Arabs and Muslims have historically been portrayed as barbaric, misogynist, anti-modern, and uncivilized.[13] He identified this orientalist ideology in European artwork, literature, and scholarship from the 18th and 19th centuries, revealing how this construction of knowledge of the "Muslim world" was used to justify colonizing Arab countries. In his later years, he debated with American scholars Samuel Huntington and Bernard Lewis, who perpetuated the idea that Muslims were culturally incapable of valuing democracy and modernity. Samuel Huntington made the argument in his article "The Clash of Civilizations?" that as the Cold War was waning, the West's next major conflict would be with Islamic cultures.[14] This argument is riddled with cultural racism because it views Islam as an inherently antiquated culture and, consequently, nation-states that are predominantly Muslim as similarly antiquated.[15]

The pitting of Islamic civilizations against the West has not come to fruition. In fact, Muslim-majority countries are not unified by their religious identity and behave in their own economic and political interests. A prime example is how former Pakistani Prime Minister Imran Khan has deflected questions about the treatment of Uyghur Muslims by Chinese President Xi Jinping when asked about Pakistan's relationship with China. For Pakistan, a country that is heavily in debt, the abuses of Muslims in China are not an impediment to financial reliance.[16] There is no unified Islamic bloc, even though the idea that Muslims are a monolithic group is a common stereotype.

The demonization of Islam as an inherently violent religion can also be seen in Bernard Lewis's article "The Roots of Muslim Rage."[17] Lewis argues in this piece that there is a tendency for Muslim men toward rage and violence. He writes that this anger stems from Western influences in Muslim countries, which include the liberation of women. According to Lewis, as women gain more rights, Muslim men become enraged and tend toward violence. These notions that Muslims are inherently violent or angry and culturally antithetical to modernity or Democratic values are forms of cultural racism. They are orientalist at their very core because they promote the idea that Islam is monolithic as well as a static and unchanging culture that is defined by its antiquated ideas, making

[13] Edward W. Said, *Orientalism* (New York: Vintage, 1979).
[14] Samuel P. Huntington, "The Clash of Civilizations?," *Foreign Affairs* 72, no. 3 (1993): p. 22.
[15] Huntington, "Clash," p. 22.
[16] "Pakistan's Khan Backs China on Uighurs, Praises One-Party System," *Al Jazeera*, July 2, 2021, https://www.aljazeera.com/news/2021/7/2/pakistan-imran-khan-china-uighurs.
[17] Bernard Lewis, "The Roots of Muslim Rage," *Atlantic Monthly*, September 1990, http://tony-silva.com/download/muslimrage-atlantic.pdf.

60 SAHER SELOD

it the opposite of cultures that are defined by progress and modernity, like the "West." Based on this argument, modernity is a racialized concept that only Western and European cultures can achieve.[18]

Both Lewis and Huntington pushed a portrait of Islam that was not only inaccurate but also demonizing. Their influence went beyond the academy and crept into foreign policy. Lewis's scholarship on "Islamic" cultures was so influential on the foreign policy of the administration of President George W. Bush and Vice President Dick Cheney that he advised both prior to the Iraq War after 9/11.[19] American orientalism was in full swing both globally and domestically because of 9/11, resulting in the institutionalization of discrimination against Muslims.[20] The years that followed 9/11, including the political rhetoric from the Bush administration, the rise of the Tea Party, the Ground Zero mosque controversy, and the anti-sharia bill movement reflect the growth of an ethnonationalism that is tied to the racialization of Muslims.

Bush and the Global War on Terror

On October 7, 2001, the United States along with the United Kingdom began Operation Enduring Freedom, which involved the military invasion of Afghanistan in response to the terrorist attacks of September 11, 2001. President Bush demanded that the Taliban hand over Osama bin Laden to the United States for orchestrating the attack. This request was denied, and a twenty-year military campaign in Afghanistan began.[21] The terrorist attacks on September 11, 2001, resulted in a boost to President Bush's popularity, which had been suffering from a contested election. The country suddenly rallied around Bush, with 60 percent of Americans expressing trust in the government, which had not been seen in decades.[22] Although this confidence in government eventually dropped, terrorism would become a major talking point and campaign issue for politicians in the decades to come. The political rhetoric reveals how a growing nationalist identity was tied to protecting the country from another terrorist attack. According to a Pew Research Center report, after the terrorist attacks,

[18] José Itzigsohn and Karida L. Brown, *Sociology of W. E. B. Du Bois* (New York: New York University Press, 2020).

[19] Douglas Martin, "Bernard Lewis, Influential Scholar of Islam, Is Dead at 101," *The New York Times*, May 21, 2018, https://www.nytimes.com/2018/05/21/obituaries/bernard-lewis-islam-scho lar-dies.html.

[20] Aziz, *Racial Muslim*.

[21] "The Global War on Terrorism: The First 100 Days," US Department of State Archives, January 20, 2009, https://2001-2009.state.gov/s/ct/rls/wh/6947.htm.

[22] Hannah Hartig and Carroll Doherty, "Two Decades Later, the Enduring Legacy of 9/11," Pew Research Center, August 9, 2021, https://www.pewresearch.org/politics/2021/09/02/two-decades-later-the-enduring-legacy-of-9-11/.

patriotic sentiment surged in the United States, with 79 percent of American adults claiming that they had displayed an American flag.[23] This increased patriotism was tied to politicians' construction of an enemy that targeted Americans out of hatred for freedom, democracy, and even women.

On September 20, 2001, President Bush gave an address to the nation about the terrorist attacks. Bush's speech provides examples of this framing of terrorists. In this speech he categorized Muslims in two camps: there are "good" Muslims and "bad" ones. The terrorists exemplify the "bad" ones who have hijacked the religion to commit acts of violence:

Al Qaeda is to terror what the Mafia is to crime. But its goal is not making money, its goal is remaking the world and imposing its radical beliefs on people everywhere.

The terrorists practice a fringe form of Islamic extremism that has been rejected by Muslim scholars and the vast majority of Muslim clerics[,] a fringe movement that perverts the peaceful teachings of Islam.[24]

Here, Bush distinguished between the type of Islam that the terrorist practices versus peaceful Muslims. And while this may appear to be a positive framing in that it acknowledges that there are peaceful Muslims in the world, it still equates Islam with violence, as the speech framed the motivation for the attacks as imposing radical beliefs on the world. By stripping the terrorists of any political or socioeconomic motivations, they are viewed as irrational actors whose sole purpose is to dominate.[25] Thus, radical and extremist viewpoints are the threat.

The speech also framed the terrorist attacks as an attack of civilization. The United States is marked by civilization, and a threat to the United States is a threat to any civilization globally:

This is not, however, just America's fight. And what is at stake is not just America's freedom.

This is the world's fight. This is civilization's fight. This is the fight of all who believe in progress and pluralism, tolerance, and freedom.

We ask every nation to join us. We will ask and we will need the help of police forces, intelligence service and banking systems around the world. The United States is grateful that many nations and many international organizations

---

[23] Hartig and Doherty, "Two Decades."

[24] "Text: President Bush Addresses the Nation," *The Washington Post*, September 20, 2011, https://www.washingtonpost.com/wp-srv/nation/specials/attacked/transcripts/bushaddress_092001.html.

[25] Lisa Stampnitzky, *Disciplining Terror: How Experts Invented "Terrorism"* (Cambridge: Cambridge University Press, 2013).

have already responded with sympathy and with support—nations from Latin America to Asia to Africa to Europe to the Islamic world.[26]

The terms *civilization* and the *Islamic world* are eerily reminiscent of Samuel Huntington's work on "The Clash of Civilizations?" Bush referenced the continents of Latin America, Asia, Africa, and Europe; however, he reduced Arab countries to the "Islamic world." Huntington argued that the next major conflict would be between the "West" and the "Islamic world."[27] Here, Bush appealed to similar ideas that the military invasion of Afghanistan is about protecting a civilized culture from forces—radical Islamic terrorism—that want to destroy democracy and modernity. The equation of the United States with "civilization" produces boundaries that situate the United States as enlightened, modern, and progressive; therefore, an attack on the United States is an attack on democratic values. Modernity and progress are Western characteristics, while violence and destruction are associated with Islamic cultures.

Furthermore, Bush implied the idea that Muslims are not part of American "civilization" and thus are outsiders. At the same time as stating that not all Muslims are bad, he repeatedly associated Islam with terror and brought up its distinction from American ideals. This association of Islam as inherently incompatible with American values and culture became mobilizing rhetoric for right-wing groups and politicians.

The Rise in the Tea Party and Anti-Muslim Racism

The Tea Party initially formed in 2009 in response to a desire to limit the government's role in Americans' lives by lowering taxes and reducing government spending. It was originally a movement of mostly white, middle-class men who leaned Republican and opposed Obama's economic policies.[28] The movement's name is credited to an outburst on the Chicago Merchant Exchange by CNBC reporter Rick Santelli about Obama's mortgage bailout. Santelli called on people to join him at the "Chicago Tea Party"; shortly after this outburst, "Tea Party" protests were held in a dozen cities across the country.[29]

Opposition to Obama's stimulus package and the Affordable Care Act mobilized the rise of the Tea Party, but the resistance to these government

---

[26] "Text: President Bush."

[27] "Text: President Bush."

[28] Vanessa Williamson, Theda Skocpol, and John Coggin, "The Tea Party and the Remaking of Republican Conservatism," *Perspectives on Politics* 9, no. 1 (2011): pp. 25–43.

[29] Jeff Cox, "5 Years Later Rick Santelli 'Tea Party' Rant Revisited," *CNBC*, February 24, 2014, https://www.cnbc.com/2014/02/24/5-years-later-rick-santelli-tea-party-rant-revisited.html.

programs aligns with racist ideologies about who deserves government assistance.[30] One study showed how racial resentment was a characteristic of many individuals who identified as Tea Party members.[31] Thus, the notion that some members did not harbor racist viewpoints and were only concerned with taxes and economic programs fails to account for the long history of how welfare programs have historically been framed and targeted as giving unfair handouts to African Americans.

Even though there was a racial tenor to the original Tea Party members, various factions grew that espoused overt racist, nativist, and Islamophobic ideologies. The Tea Party Patriots, Tea Party Nation, and the Southern Tea Party are just a few examples of the various groups that formed. The Southern Tea Party, for example, can be differentiated from other Tea Party groups for its openly racist sentiments and particularly its anti-Obama focus.[32] The anti-Obama racism of Southern Tea Party members is most notable in the signage brought to their protests.[33] In addition to racial slurs, the signs included racist messages saying, among other things, that Obama should go back to Kenya, as well as Islamophobic rhetoric because of the rumors that he is secretly a Muslim. The increasingly Islamophobic rhetoric of Tea Party politicians or politicians courting Tea Partiers revealed that espousing anti-Muslim rhetoric was politically advantageous.[34]

The targeting of Keith Ellison, an African American Muslim, is another example of how some Tea Partiers viewed Muslims as incapable of being American. Ellison, a Democrat, was the first Muslim elected to Congress in 2006. Ellison faced a series of attacks because of his religious identity. Judson Phillips, the leader of the Tea Party Nation, tried to mobilize voters against Ellison. Phillips sent out an email to voters in Minnesota encouraging them not to re-elect Muslim Congressman Keith Ellison and accusing him of supporting terrorism:

> There are a lot of liberals who need to be retired this year, but there are few I can think of more deserving than Keith Ellison. Ellison is one of the most radical members of congress. He has a ZERO rating from the American Conservative Union. He is the only Muslim member of congress. He supports the Counsel for

[30] Adolphus G. Belk, "Fire on the Right: The Tea Party vs. Barack Obama," *Souls* 14, nos. 1–2 (2012): pp. 77–87.

[31] Daniel Tope, Justin Pickett, and Ted Chiricos, "Anti-Minority Attitudes and Tea Party Movement Membership," *Social Science Research* 51 (2014): pp. 322–37.

[32] Angie Maxwell and T. Wayne Parent, "The Obama Trigger: Presidential Approval and Tea Party Membership," *Social Science Quarterly* 93, no. 5 (2012): pp. 1384–401.

[33] Angie Maxwell, "How Southern Racism Found a Home in the Tea Party," *Vox*, July 7, 2016, https://www.vox.com/2016/7/7/12118872/southern-racism-tea-party-trump.

[34] Ashley Jardina and LaFleur Stephens-Dougan, "The Electoral Consequences of Anti-Muslim Prejudice," *Electoral Studies* 72 (August 2021).

American Islamic Relations, HAMAS and has helped congress send millions of tax [*sic*] to terrorists in Gaza.[35]

The association of Ellison with terrorism and radicalization reflects how American Muslims were portrayed as not only a danger to American society but also a threat to democracy. While Phillips was quoted as saying that Muslims should be able to run for office because the Constitution allows it, he also stated he would not vote for Muslims because they believe in an ideology that is inherently violent.[36] This type of rhetoric that portrays Muslims as radicalized, violent, and potentially invading the American landscape was also used to justify a protest campaign against the building of mosques in the United States.

Ground Zero Mosque Controversy

One of the ways Muslims have been made to feel like outsiders in the United States is through the protest of mosques being built. One study showed that in areas where there was organizing against building of mosques, Tea Party activists joined the cause.[37] In 2010, the Ground Zero mosque controversy brought these protests onto the national stage. Sarah Palin, candidate for vice president as John McCain's running mate, tweeted that Muslims should not build a mosque in New York City at what was referred to as Ground Zero, where the World Trade Centers were once located; she wrote, "Peaceful Muslims, pls refudiate."[38] While some mocked her misuse of the English language, it garnered an astounding amount of media attention and impact.

In reality, an Islamic center referred to as Park51—not a mosque—was to be built blocks away from the site of the terrorist attacks. But Islamophobic activist Pamela Geller started a campaign protesting its construction on the premise that the mosque represented the threat of the Islamization of America.[39] Ground Zero

---

[35] Nick Wing, "Tea Party Founder Judson Phillips Admits He Has a 'Real Problem' with Isla," *Huffington Post*, October 28, 2010, https://www.huffpost.com/entry/judson-phillips-tea-party-isl am_n_775260.

[36] Justin Elliott, "Tea Party Nation Founder: I Have a Real Problem with Islam," *Salon*, October 27, 2010, https://www.salon.com/2010/10/27/judson_phillilps_on_islam/.

[37] Nadia Marzouki, "Islamophobia and the Tea Party," *Mint*, November 26, 2016, https://www.livemint.com/Sundayapp/SBohvTng6N7LZVluMQ1LHI/Islamophobia-and-the-Tea-Party.html.

[38] Tim Murphy, "The Fight over Ground Zero Mosque Was a Grim Preview of the Trump Era," *Mother Jones*, September 9, 2021, https://www.motherjones.com/politics/2021/09/september-11-ground-zero-mosque-trump/.

[39] CNN Wire Staff, "Protesters Descend on Ground Zero for Anti-Mosque Demonstration," CNN, June 7, 2010, http://www.cnn.com/2010/US/06/06/new.york.ground.zero.mosque/index.html.

mosque protests began to pop up in campaign election ads to garner support for some Republican candidates. Rick Scott, for example, ran an ad in which he referred to the mosque as "Obama's mosque."[40] Renee Ellmers used the Ground Zero controversy in a campaign ad against Democratic incumbent Bob Ethridge for North Carolina's 2nd congressional district.[41] The ad began with what appeared to be orientalist paintings of Arabs, with a man narrating, "After the Muslims conquered Jerusalem, Cordoba and Constantinople, they built victory mosques and now they want to build a mosque by Ground Zero."[42] The campaign ad accused Ethridge of remaining silent on the issue, while Ellmers opposed the building of what he referred to as a "victory mosque," referencing 9/11. Endorsed by Sarah Palin and using these Islamophobic tactics, Ellmers won the election in 2010. But perhaps one of the most offensive statements about the mosque came from former Tea Party Express leader Mark Williams. The comments he made, which were shared in a blog post for *The Atlantic* about the Tea Party, were some of the most egregious at the time:

> The animals of allah for whom any day is a great day for a massacre are drooling over the positive response that they are getting from New York City officials over a proposal to build a 13 story monument to the 9/11 Muslims who hijacked those 4 airliners. The monument would consist of a Mosque for the worship of their monkey-god and a "cultural center" for to propagandize for the extermination of all things not approved by their cult.[43]

Williams also referred to Obama as an "Indonesian Muslim turned welfare thug."[44] Opposition to the building of mosques did not start in 2010, but the Ground Zero controversy ignited the anti-mosque movement around the country. The American Civil Liberties Union (ACLU) created a map that shows protests against the building of these mosques has increased drastically since 2010.[45] While some of the reasons offered are traffic and noise concerns rather than the Islamization of America, the campaign reflects the ways in which Islam

---

[40] David Gura, "Republican Gubernatorial Candidate Cuts First 'Ground Zero Mosque' Political Ad," NPR: The Two Way, August 17, 2010, https://www.npr.org/sections/thetwo-way/2010/08/17/129252480/republican-gubernatorial-candidate-cuts-first-ground-zero-mosque-political-ad.

[41] Murphy, "Fight."

[42] Murphy, "Fight."

[43] Chris Good, "Take a Ride on the Tea Party Express," *The Atlantic*, June 18, 2010, https://www.theatlantic.com/politics/archive/2010/06/mark-williams-steps-aside-as-chairman-of-tea-party-express/58402/.

[44] Chris Good, "Mark Williams Steps Aside as Chairman of Tea Party Express," *The Atlantic*, June 18, 2010, https://www.theatlantic.com/politics/archive/2010/06/mark-williams-steps-aside-as-chairman-of-tea-party-express/58402/.

[45] "Nationwide Anti-Mosque Activity," ACLU, January 2022, https://www.aclu.org/issues/national-security/discriminatory-profiling/nationwide-anti-mosque-activity.

Anti-Sharia Bills

At the same time when there were protests of the Ground Zero mosques, there was another movement developing around so-called anti-sharia bills throughout the country. David Yerushalmi, a cofounder of the American Freedom Law Center and a member of the Center for Security Policy (CSP), conceived of the anti-sharia movement.[46] Since 2010, various lawmakers around the country have introduced anti-sharia bills. The bills are meant to prevent judges from allowing Islamic law to influence their rulings. The CSP produced these bills, which have been introduced in forty-seven states.[47] A *USA Today* report uncovered how these anti-sharia bills introduced in different states have exactly the same language, making them copycat laws.[48] Using a computer algorithm to detect similarities in language, investigators were able to trace these laws back to the CSP. While many of them have not been enacted, fourteen of them have successfully become law. The architects of the bills were careful not to use the term *sharia* in the bills, instead referring to "foreign laws." According to the report, once legislators introduced the bills, Islamophobic organizations like ACT for America would campaign for citizens to show up to support these bills.

In 2018, Idaho State Representative Eric Redman's anti-sharia bill, HB 419, passed with a vote of 44–24 in the Idaho House of Representatives.[49] Redman acknowledged that no Idaho judge had ruled on foreign laws to date but stated that the bill was preventative. He relied on a ruling by a New Jersey judge who did not favor a protection order for an abused Muslim woman because her husband used religion to justify the abuse.[50] This ruling, which was determined invalid and overturned, has been repeatedly used as justification for passing these "anti-sharia" bills. Even though the US Constitution explicitly states that the use of any foreign law is not permitted in courts and the American Bar Association has

---

[46] Andrea Elliott, "The Man behind the Anti-Shariah Movement," *The New York Times*, July 30, 2011, https://www.nytimes.com/2011/07/31/us/31shariah.html?_r=0.

[47] Mark Olalde and Dustin Gardiner, "The Network behind State Bills 'Countering' Sharia Law and Terrorism," Center for Public Integrity, July 18, 2019, https://publicintegrity.org/politics/state-politics/copy-paste-legislate/many-state-bills-one-source-behind-the-push-to-ban-sharia-law/.

[48] Olalde and Gardiner, "Network."

[49] Betsy Russell, "House Passes Anti-Sharia Law Bill, 44–24," *Eyes on Boise*, February 20, 2018, https://www.spokesman.com/blogs/boise/2018/feb/20/house-passes-anti-sharia-law-bill-44-24/.

[50] Russell, "House."

RISE OF ETHNONATIONALIST POPULISM   67

denounced the introduction of these "anti-sharia" bills, they continue to make their way into legislators' hands.[51]

Yerushalmi has stated that the ultimate purpose of these bills is to create some type of "friction" and to get people thinking about sharia laws infiltrating the United States.[52] This fearmongering around Muslims invading the United States and turning it into an Islamic state has had a significant impact. The increasing number of politicians introducing the laws demonstrates that it is an issue supported by voters, especially as groups like ACT for America encourage people to mobilize around it. Indeed, the role of anti-Muslim organizations in controlling the narrative about Muslims in the United States should not be underestimated. According to a study by Christopher Bail, Islamophobic organizations like ACT for America have been successful in controlling media narratives with press releases that demonize Muslims and perpetuate myths about them.[53] Through plagiarism-identification software, Bail was able to match the language in the press releases to media coverage of Muslims.[54] Islamophobic organizations have thus played a significant role in the rise of ethnonationalism, spreading misinformation about Muslims trying to invade and take over the United States.

The Birther Movement and "Obama Is a Muslim"

Like the anti-sharia bill movement and the Ground Zero mosque controversy, the birther movement has contributed to partisan politics in the United States. The basic premise of this movement is that President Obama was not born in the United States but in Kenya and therefore not an American citizen and ineligible to be president. These rumors stemmed from a mistake by Obama's literary agent that misidentified his birthplace on a document that was only meant to be circulated within the publishing industry. The literary agent who made the error came out publicly to address how this happened, noting it was not based on any information coming from Obama himself; nevertheless, Obama produced evidence—his actual birth certificate—showing that he was born in the United States and a US citizen.[55]

---

[51] Swathi Shanmugasundaram, "Anti-Sharia Law Bills in the United States," ACLU, February 5, 2018, https://www.splcenter.org/hatewatch/2018/02/05/anti-sharia-law-bills-united-states.

[52] Elliott, "Man."

[53] Christopher Bail, *Terrified: How Anti-Muslim Fringe Organizations Became Mainstream* (Princeton, NJ: Princeton University Press, 2014).

[54] Bail, *Terrified.*

[55] "Obama Birther Rumors Debunked as Literary Agent Clarifies Mistake," *Huffington Post*, May 17, 2012, https://www.huffpost.com/entry/obama-birthers_n_1526222.

68 SAHER SELOD

Regardless of the proof he provided, the birther movement took off and continues to influence American voters. High-profile politicians like Newt Gingrich and Donald Trump in media interviews also perpetuated the idea that Obama was not a citizen.[56] Prior to campaigning for president, Trump made several comments questioning Obama's birth certificate, even after other Republican politicians eventually recognized his American citizen. For example, former Republican US representative of Minnesota, Michele Bachman, who once questioned Obama's birthplace, eventually accepted the validity of his birth certificate and stated that the issue should be put to rest.[57] Yet Trump perpetuated this rumor in media interviews, like on *The Laura Ingraham Show*:

> He doesn't have a birth certificate, or if he does, there's something on that certificate that is very bad for him. Now, somebody told me—and I have no idea if this is bad for him or not, but perhaps it would be—that where it says "religion," it might have "Muslim." And if you're a Muslim, you don't change your religion, by the way.[58]

Trump stated later that he was proud to be a birther, something that others were afraid to admit. Although Trump eventually backed down from this claim in 2016 and acknowledged that Obama was born in the United States, these types of statements from politicians and Islamophobic activists played into the rising ethnonationalist fervor.[59] One study showed that whites who tended to believe the birther movement were those who held strong racial animus.[60] Even with the birther movement dying down, polling data showed that in 2017, 31 percent of Americans still believed that Obama may not have been born in the United States.[61] The traction that the birther movement gained reflects growing anti-Black and anti-immigrant sentiments in the United States. The anti-Muslim aspect of the birther movement came at a time when racism toward Muslims was peaking, seen in anti-sharia bills and the Ground Zero mosque controversy, and similarly played a significant role in the rise in ethnonationalist populism.

The misidentification of Obama as a Muslim reveals the level of anti-Muslim racism in the United States. While campaigning for president in 2008,

---

[56] Adam Serwer, "Birtherism of a Nation," *The Atlantic*, May 13, 2020, https://www.theatlantic.com/ideas/archive/2020/05/birtherism-and-trump/610978/.

[57] Maggie Haberman, "Bachmann: Birther Issue Settled," *Politico*, April 20, 2011, https://www.politico.com/story/2011/04/bachmann-birther-issue-settled-053468.

[58] Gregory Krieg, "14 of Trump's Most Outrageous 'Birther' Claims-Half from After 9/11," CNN, September 16, 2016, https://www.cnn.com/2016/09/09/politics/donald-trump-birther/index.html.

[59] "Donald Trump Admits President Obama Was Born in the US," BBC, September 16, 2016, https://www.bbc.com/news/av/world-us-canada-37389180.

[60] Ashley Jardina and Michael Traugott, "The Genesis of the Birther Rumor: Partisanship, Racial Attitudes, and Political Knowledge," *Journal of Race, Ethnicity, and Politics* 4, no. 1 (2019): pp. 60–80.

[61] Jardina and Traugott, "Genesis."

RISE OF ETHNONATIONALIST POPULISM 69

Senator John McCain was questioned by an older white woman at a town hall in Minnesota. The woman stood up, grabbed the microphone, and began by expressing her distrust in Obama, to which McCain nodded approvingly, but when she continued and stated that "he is an Arab," McCain quickly shook his head in disapproval, grabbed the microphone and said, "No ma'am. He is a decent family man, citizen that I just happen to have disagreements with."[62] McCain's response was followed by boos from the audience. The notion that Obama was an Arab can be seen as a substitute for the idea that he is a Muslim, as Americans often conflate the idea that Arabs are Muslims and Muslims are Arabs.[63]

The birther movement, in its focus on Obama's citizenship, explicitly drew questions about his religious identity, as exemplified in Trump's statements above. Rumors that he was not born in the United States were compounded with the idea that he was also not a Christian. While Democratic competitors initially engaged with this rumor in order to beat him in the elections, they eventually dropped this tactic. The rumor has continuously been perpetuated in conservative media and by Republican politicians since 2010.[64] According to a study, conservative websites initially spread the rumor, which was then picked up through blogs and emails.[65] And while mainstream media described it as a lie, its continual coverage contributed to the perpetuation of the rumor.

Politicians also kept the rumor afloat to woo potential voters. When Republican Wisconsin Governor Scott Walker was eyeing a presidential run in 2016, he was asked in an interview if he thought President Obama was a Christian, to which he responded, "I don't know."[66] Although he did not state that Obama was a Muslim, his uncertain answer was enough to demonstrate doubt as to whether he was a Christian. According to a CNN/ORC poll taken in 2015, 29 percent of Americans believed that Obama is a Muslim, alongside 43 percent of Republicans.[67] These figures represent an increase from a Public Religion Research Institute (PRRI) poll taken in 2012, which showed that 16 percent

---

[62] Emily Stewart, "Watch John McCain Defend Barack Obama against a Racist Voter in 2008," *Vox*, September 1, 2018, https://www.vox.com/policy-and-politics/2018/8/25/17782572/john-mccain-barack-obama-statement-2008-video.

[63] Selod, *Forever Suspect*.

[64] Geoffrey C. Layman, Kerem Ozan Kalkan, and John C. Green, "A Muslim President? Misperceptions of Barack Obama's Faith in the 2008 Presidential Campaign," *Journal for the Scientific Study of Religion* 53, no. 3 (2014): pp 534–55.

[65] Barry A. Hollander, "Persistence in the Perception of Barack Obama as a Muslim in the 2008 Presidential Campaign," *Journal of Media and Religion* 9, no. 2 (2010): pp. 55–66.

[66] Adam Howard, "Scott Walker: 'I Don't Know' If Obama Is Christian," MSNBC, February 21, 2015, https://www.msnbc.com/msnbc/scott-walker-i-dont-know-if-obama-christian-msna535201.

[67] Jennifer Agiesta, "Misperceptions Persist about Obama's Faith, but Aren't So Widespread," CNN, September 14, 2015, https://www.cnn.com/2015/09/13/politics/barack-obama-religion-christian-misperceptions/index.html.

70   SAHER SELOD

of Americans believed that Obama is a Muslim.[68] Another study found that Christian conservatives were likely to believe that Obama is not a Muslim.[69]

Marking Obama as a Muslim was a tactic used by politicians to de-Americanize him, as Islam and Muslims are viewed as inherently un-American.[70] The rumor is yet another example of the ways that racist attitudes toward Muslims contributes to an ethnonationalist populism based on fears of Islam invading the nation. Because of this, Muslims are treated with suspicion and distrust and their surveillance justified. Representative Peter King, the former Homeland Security Committee chair, capitalized on these attempts to situate Islam and Muslims as a potential threat to America by holding congressional hearings on the radicalization of Muslims in 2011.[71] Contextualizing the ways in which the Muslim threat has been perpetuated since 9/11, the rise of Trump as an ethnonationalist populist president is not surprising.

Conclusion: The Ascendancy of Trump and the Future

As shown in this chapter, when Donald Trump ran for president, he was able to appease a rising nationalistic and xenophobic demographic of the population through his anti-Muslim, anti-immigrant, and antigovernment rhetoric.[72] The rise of the Tea Party, the Ground Zero mosque controversy, and the birther movement in the decade after 9/11 coalesced in such a way that the idea of banning Muslims from entering this country was not far-fetched rhetoric for many conservatives.[73] Trump himself participated in the birther conspiracy, thus aligning his Islamophobic rhetoric with a rising ethnonationalist sentiments.

In an interview on MSNBC, in response to the coordinated terrorist attacks at several locations in Paris including the Bataclan theater, Trump stated that he would surveil mosques in the United States. When asked what he would do to protect US citizens from terrorism he responded with, "You are going to have to watch and study the mosques, because a lot of talk is going on at the mosques."[74]

---

[68] Cristina Stanojevich, "Attitude's about Obama's Religious Beliefs," PRRI, September 6, 2012, https://www.prri.org/spotlight/graphic-of-the-week-attitudes-about-obamas-religious-beliefs/.

[69] Hollander, "Persistence."

[70] Aziz, *Racial Muslim*; Lajevardi, *Outsiders*; Layman, Kalkan, and Green, "Muslim President"; Selod, *Forever Suspect*.

[71] Sheryl Gay Stolberg and Laura Goodstein, "Domestic Terrorism Hearing Opens with Contrasting Views on Dangers," *The New York Times*, March 10, 2011, https://www.nytimes.com/2011/03/11/us/politics/11king.html.

[72] Bonikowski, "Trump's Populism."

[73] Nash Jenkins, "Republicans Are Thrilled with the Supreme Court's Decision Upholding Trump's Travel Ban," *Time*, June 26, 2018, https://time.com/5322856/trump-travel-ban-republicans/.

[74] "Trump: We Must Watch and Study Mosques," MSNBC: Morning Joe, November 16, 2015, https://www.msnbc.com/morning-joe/watch/trump-we-must-watch-and-study-mosques-56756 3331864.

He went on to state that there was great surveillance of the mosques in New York City, referring to the New York Police Department (NYPD) surveillance program that monitored mosques and Muslim student organizations on college campuses. The program ended with a lawsuit in which Muslims claimed that they were religiously profiled. The NYPD admitted that no intelligence had been obtained through the program.[75] The program was subsequently dismantled, yet Trump insinuated that he would invest in such problematic surveillance programs as president. Trump's ascendancy to the presidency must be understood within the context of a rising ethnonationalist fervor that views immigrants and Muslims as not only outside of an American identity but as a threat to it. Thus, it is not surprising that Trump's rhetoric became increasingly more toxic toward Muslims as the campaign continued; he advocated for registering Muslims and even banning them from coming to the United States.[76]

Anti-Muslim prejudice plays a role in white voters' presidential choice.[77] The continued racialization of Muslims results in their sustained presence in the minds of voters as a potential threat, influencing voting patterns.[78] When Trump became president, he surrounded himself with several individuals who were viewed by many as fringe Islamophobic activists. Frank Gaffney, one of the architects behind the anti-sharia bill movement, was suspected of being one of his advisors.[79] Stephen Miller and Steve Bannon, Trump's former advisor and White House chief strategist, respectively, were both proponents of an ethnonationalist view of America. Miller was responsible for the harsh anti-immigration policies under Trump, and Bannon was the cofounder of *Breitbart*, which has pushed Muslim conspiracy theories. Trump's presidency in many ways legitimized an ethnonationalist agenda that is partially driven by animosity toward Muslims. While many hoped there would be a return to normalcy after he left office, his presidency should instead serve as a warning that ethnonationalist populism will not go away anytime soon but has gained true political momentum.[80]

As ethnonationalist populism and anti-Muslim racism endures, however, there has also been a counter to this overt anti-Muslim racism. In 2020, a record number of Muslim candidates ran for office and won their elections. According to a report by the Council for American Islamic Relations (CAIR), Jetpac, and MPower Change, 181 Muslims ran for local, state, and federal elections, with

---

[75] "Trump: We Must Watch."

[76] Dara Lind, "Donald Trump's Proposed 'Muslim Registry,' Explained," *Vox*, November 16, 2016, https://www.vox.com/policy-and-politics/2016/11/16/13649764/trump-muslim-register-database.

[77] Jardina and Stephens-Dougan, "Electoral Consequences."

[78] Jardina and Stephens-Dougan, "Electoral Consequences."

[79] Michael Crowley, "Gaffney Denies NYT, WSJ Reports That He Is a Trump Adviser," *Politico*, November 16, 2016, https://www.politico.com/blogs/donald-trump-administration/2016/11/gaffney-denies-nyt-wsj-reports-that-hes-a-trump-adviser-231504.

[80] Bonikowski, "Trump's Populism."

44 percent winning their elections.[81] This number is impressive given the history of anti-Muslim racism that Muslim politicians previously and continually face. As such, it appears that the rise in xenophobic and racist ethnonationalism is being met with strong political engagement by Muslims in the United States. The role that anti-Muslim racism will continue to play in politics is yet to be seen. On December 14, 2021, US Representative Ilhan Omar, a Democrat from Minnesota, helped pass a bill called the Combatting International Islamophobia Act in the US House of Representatives, with 219 votes for it and 212 votes against.[82] This act creates a special task force to investigate rising racism toward Muslims in the United States, something that has been ignored for far too long. Thus, there is a small sliver of hope that some movement is being made to combat the anti-Muslim racism that has been largely ignored over the last twenty years, even as this ethnonationalist populism continues to rise.

[81] Ibrahim Hooper, "CAIR, Jetpac, MPower Change Release Groundbreaking Report on American Muslim Candidates in 2020 Election Cycle," CAIR, March 15, 2021, https://www.cair.com/press_r eleases/cair-jetpac-mpower-change-release-groundbreaking-report-on-american-muslim-candida tes-in-2020-election-cycle/.

[82] Felicia Sonmez and Anjuman Ali, "House Votes for Legislation to Combat Islamophobia Abroad After Republican Falsely Accuses Rep. Omar of Being 'Affiliated' with Terrorist Organizations," *The Washington Post*, December 14, 2021, https://www.washingtonpost.com/politics/islamophobia-omar-house-democrats/2021/12/14/dc2beda4-5c61-11ec-8665-aed48580f911_story.html.

PART II
ISLAMOPHOBIA IN EUROPE
Xenophobia, Anti-Semitism, and Nationalism

5

Postcolonialism, Post–National Socialism, German Reunification, and the Rise of the Far Right

Making Sense of Islamophobia in Germany

Farid Hafez

At the heart of this book are two significant questions. On one hand, it seeks to understand the various factors—political, social, economic, and historical—that explain the rise in Islamophobia over the past two decades.[1] On the other hand, it interrogates how this growth is related to the rise in right-wing populism in each respective country. To understand Islamophobia in Germany today, one must consider that Islamophobia far predates Germany itself and can be found even further back than the German Empire, starting with the Kaiserreich in 1871.[2] If the rise of Islamophobia is connected to more than just the rise of right-wing populism, the German case is especially intriguing.

In contrast to most other western European countries, postwar Germany has been perceived as an exceptional case because it had no right-wing parties represented in its national parliament until 2017.[3] While right-wing political parties existed before 2017 and had slight impact on other parties' policymaking from the late 1980s onward, they were not able to serve as legitimate parties in western Germany, where there was a public consensus in the

---

[1] According to a decolonial reading, Islamophobia is defined as the expansion of a global racial order, the basis of which had been laid in 1492. For a decolonial reading of Islamophobia, see Ramón Grosfoguel, "Epistemic Islamophobia and Colonial Social Sciences," *Human Architecture: Journal of the Sociology of Self-Knowledge* 8, no. 2 (2010): pp. 29–38. In this case, Islamophobia is part and parcel of the global world order emanating from centers of power that even shape the Muslim world. See Enes Bayraklı and Farid Hafez, eds., *Islamophobia in Muslim Majority Societies* (New York: Routledge, 2019).

[2] Iman Attia, *Orient- und IslamBilder: Interdisziplinäre Beiträge zu Orientalismus und antimuslimischem Rassismus* [*Orient and Islam Images: Interdisciplinary Contributions to Orientalism and Anti-Muslim Racism*] (Münster: Unrast-Verlag, 2007).

[3] Uwe Backes and Cas Mudde, "Germany: Extremism without Successful Parties," *Parliamentary Affairs* 53, no. 3 (2000): pp. 457–68.

Farid Hafez, *Postcolonialism, Post–National Socialism, German Reunification, and the Rise of the Far Right* In: *Global Islamophobia and the Rise of Populism*. Edited by: Sahar F. Aziz and John L. Esposito, Oxford University Press. © Oxford University Press 2024. DOI: 10.1093/oso/9780197648995.003.0005

76 FARID HAFEZ

post-Nazi era that did not welcome any re-engagement in latter-day National Socialist activities.[4] In the socialist republic of East Germany, which was a de facto one-party state under the Socialist Unity Party of Germany (SED), antifascism was formally embraced as part of the official state's ideology. But with German reunification in 1989–90, questions about identity came to the forefront. Right-wing populist movements and parties saw this as an opportunity to expand their base.

The rise of Islamophobia, especially as a structural form of racism,[5] must be viewed from a longer range historical perspective. The problem of Islamophobia in the German case should be viewed in relation to the country's history of Nazi rule and beyond, going as far back as the brief German colonial era of the Kaiserreich, which in many ways laid the groundwork for the Nazi regime.[6] Denazification was never comprehensively completed, and postwar German bureaucracy and government agencies retained ex-Nazis among their ranks. Future German bureaucrats and government officials relied on ex-Nazis.[7] Also, the intelligence services of the Allied forces, including the United States and Britain, relied on ex-Nazis as informants and sources.[8]

Accordingly, this chapter will first explore the historical legacy of racial thought in Germany. In doing so, it demonstrates how postcolonialism, post-Nazism, and German reunification following the Cold War era are important factors for understanding the context in which right-wing populism relates to the increasing relevance of Islamophobia in Germany since 9/11. It will then discuss the late arrival of right-wing populism to German party politics. Islamophobia as a state praxis is a hegemonic idea across center-left and center-right political camps, and a force fueling right-wing terrorism. After covering the role of the Alternative for Germany (AfD) party in international right-wing networks, the chapter ends with evaluating how the German state is reacting to the rise in Islamophobia.

---

[4] Nicole Berbuir, Marcel Lewandowsky, and Jasmin Siri, "The AfD and Its Sympathisers: Finally a Right-Wing Populist Movement in Germany?," *German Politics* 24, no. 2 (2015): pp. 154–78.

[5] Understanding Islamophobia or anti-Muslim racism (which this author equates) as structural means going beyond the individual as well as the institution. For John Powell, "Structural racism or racialization emphasizes the interaction of multiple institutions in an ongoing process of producing racialized outcomes." See John A. Powell, "Structural Racism: Building upon the Insights of John Calmore," *North Carolina Law Review* 86, no. 3 (March 2008): pp. 791–816.

[6] Eric Ames, Marcia Klotz, and Lora Wildenthal, eds., *Germany's Colonial Pasts* (Lincoln: University of Nebraska Press, 2005).

[7] Stephen Tyas, "Smoke and Mirrors: The German Foreign Intelligence Service's Release of Names of Former Nazi Employees," *Holocaust and Genocide Studies* 25, no. 2 (2011): pp. 290–99.

[8] Luke Daly-Groves, "Control Not Morality? Explaining the Selective Employment of Nazi War Criminals by British and American Intelligence Agencies in Occupied Germany," *Intelligence and National Security* 35, no. 3 (2020): pp. 331–49.

The Roots of Islamophobia in Germany: Postcolonialism, Post-Nazism, German Reunification

Contemporary Islamophobia on the political right did not originate with the emergence of AfD, the first successful right-wing political party in Germany since World War II. Rather, the endeavor to analyze and confront anti-Muslim racism is embedded in the much larger contexts of both Germany's history of colonialism and Nazism and the global implications of the Soviet collapse alongside Germany's reunification.

First, when it comes to colonialism and racism in Germany, one encounters a denial of the existence of racism, owing in large part to the historical and scholarly neglect of racism in Germany from the colonial period of German South West Africa to the present.[9] While the German Kaiserreich was, formally speaking, a latecomer to the project of colonialism, only acquiring colonies in the mid-1880s and officially occupying territory for thirty years,[10] by the late 1890s, Germany had already amassed the world's fourth-largest colonial empire after Britain, France, and the Netherlands.[11]

The colonial experience had its impact on German society. The arts and popular culture, trade and migration regimes, knowledge production, and especially anthropology and geography were deeply connected to the German colonial project. Key ideological notions like race,[12] which would take a formative role in the coming years, especially informing the Nazi regime, were developed during the era of colonialism.[13]

Some scholars have also traced the origins of the Nazis' genocidal politics to the brutal colonial wars in Africa.[14] Nevertheless, the German public has been quite ignorant about the history of German colonialism, something the German

---

[9] Fatima El-Tayeb, "'Blood Is a Very Special Juice': Racialized Bodies and Citizenship in Twentieth-Century Germany," *International Review of Social History* 44 (1999): pp. 149–69.

[10] Britta Schilling, "German Postcolonialism in Four Dimensions: A Historical Perspective," *Postcolonial Studies* 18, no. 4 (2015): pp. 427–39.

[11] Sebastian Conrad, *German Colonialism: A Short History* (Cambridge: Cambridge University Press, 2012), p. 3.

[12] Ulrike Hamann, *Prekäre koloniale Ordnung: Rassistische Konjunkturen im Widerspruch; Deutsches Kolonialregime 1884–1914* [*Precarious Colonial Order: Racist Conjunctures in Contradiction; the German Colonial Regime 1884–1914*] (Bielefeld, Germany: Transcript Verlag, 2015).

[13] Pascal Grosse, "What Does German Colonialism Have to Do with National Socialism? A Conceptual Framework," in *Germany's Colonial Pasts*, ed. Eric Ames, Marcia Klotz, and Lora Wildenthal (Lincoln: University of Nebraska Press, 2005), pp. 115–34.

[14] Jürgen Zimmerer, "The Birth of the Ostland out of the Spirit of Colonialism: A Postcolonial Perspective on the Nazi Policy of Conquest and Extermination," *Patterns of Prejudice* 39, no. 2 (2005): pp. 197–219; Benjamin Madley, "From Africa to Auschwitz: How German South West Africa Incubated Ideas and Methods Adopted and Developed by the Nazis in Eastern Europe," *European History Quarterly* 35, no. 3 (2005): pp. 429–64; Thomas Kühne, "Colonialism and the Holocaust: Continuities, Causations, and Complexities," *Journal of Genocide Research* 15, no. 3 (2013): pp. 339–62.

78   FARID HAFEZ

historian Jürgen Zimmerer has referred to as "Germans' colonial amnesia."[15] Within this context, German scholar Fatima El-Tayeb argues that Europe, and especially Germany, largely

> continues to imagine itself as an autonomous entity . . . untouched by "race matters[,]". . . a color-blind continent in which difference is marked along lines of nationality and ethnicity. Others are routinely ascribed a position outside the nation, allowing the externalization and thus silencing of a debate on the legacy of racism and colonialism.[16]

She further claims that this can be achieved by excluding colonialism, which leads to the externalization of its postcolonial populations, from the list of key events that have shaped contemporary Europe.[17] This, among other factors, makes the Muslim embody the position of religious and cultural rival to Christianity and situates enlightened Europe opposite the African migrant, who is Europe's external other.

Second, the history of German *völkisch* anti-Semitism, which led to the annihilation of six million Jews in the Holocaust, initially resulted in a denial of guilt. This response later led to depoliticization through the creation of a culture of remembrance in which *völkisch* anti-Semitism was framed as an isolated phenomenon, without engaging in critical reflection on contemporary racism in Germany, what historian Astrid Messerschmidt termed the "post-Nazi" era

---

[15] Jürgen Zimmerer, "Kolonialismus und kollektive Identität: Erinnerungsorte der deutschen Kolonialgeschichte" ["Colonialism and Collective Identity: Places of Memory in German Colonial History"], in *Kein Platz an der Sonne: Erinnerungsorte der deutschen Kolonialgeschichte* [*No Place under the Sun: Places of Remembrance of German Colonial History*], ed. Jürgen Zimmerer (Bonn, Germany: Bundeszentrale für Politische Bildung, 2013), p. 9. Only in the late 1960s, Germans started to reflect critically on their colonial past, inspired by the global process of decolonization; the challenge put forth by historians of the German Democratic Republic, which had a more critical perspective on imperialism; as well as the scholarship of American historians and studies conducted by scholars from the independent, postcolonial African states. The decades before were characterized by an official writing of history by former colonialists, who attempted to present Germany as a benevolent empire. One example is former German East African Governor Heinrich Schnee's *Deutsches Kolonial-Lexikon* [*German Colonial Lexicon*], which was designed around defending the international claim that crime and violence ruled German colonies. For Schnee, this was a *Kolonialschuldluege*, or "colonial guilt lie." See Conrad, *German Colonialism*, pp. 6–8. More recently, the Herero of Namibia launched claims for reparations from Germany, bringing the colonial past back into the agenda for German society. During the worldwide Black Lives Matter rallies, sparked by the murder of George Floyd in May 2020, statues of German colonizers were torn down, and debates about renaming institutions and streets referring to the colonial past reemerged in daily politics. See Christoph Hasselbach, "Germany's Colonial Era Brought to Light Amid Global Protest," *Deutsche Welle*, June 22, 2020, https://www.dw.com/en/germanys-colonial-era-brought-to-light-amid-global-protest/a-53898330.

[16] Fatima El-Tayeb, "'The Birth of a European Public': Migration, Postnationality, and Race in the Uniting of Europe," *American Quarterly* 60, no. 3 (2008): p. 658.

[17] Fatima El-Tayeb, "'Birth,'" p. 658.

in Germany.[18] In this context, many scholars in Germany and elsewhere have pointed to the commonalities between anti-Semitism and Islamophobia.[19] For instance, while Jews were alleged to be building a separate state within the German nation-state, Muslims today are seen as creating so-called parallel societies.[20] While Jews, whose allegiance was assumed be to a global Jewish community, were believed to be the enemies of the German nation-state, Muslims today are perceived as first and foremost loyal to the ummah, or global Muslim community, rather than the German nation or European supranation.[21]

The third important factor that has shaped German debates about identity and in turn affected the othering of Muslims was the fall of the Berlin Wall in November 1989. The subsequent political unification of the two German states, which was completed on October 3, 1990, implied a deeper transformation. In social and cultural terms, questions of national identity were also raised. Germany only recognized in 2005 that it had become a country of immigration, although low-paid *Gastarbeiter*, or guest workers from Turkey and other countries had been invited since the 1960s to rebuild the economy.[22] The old citizenship regime that determined rights along the lines of blood or race was modified with a new approach—from *ius sanguis* to some *ius soli*—that allowed for greater integration.[23] Nationalist approaches in these debates have nevertheless been perennial.

Meanwhile, the Soviet collapse and apparent victory of the free world under US leadership affected the debates in Germany. Germany, which was rebuilt with the help of the American Marshall Plan,[24] became a significant ally for former President George W. Bush's "War on Terror" and subsequently initiated surveillance techniques on its own domestic Muslim population.[25] Following the

---

[18] Astrid Messerschmidt, "Rassismusthematisierungen in den Nachwirkungen des Nationalsozialismus und seiner Aufarbeitung" ["Issues of Racism in the Aftermath of National Socialism and Its Coming to Terms"], in *Rassismuskritik und Widerstandsformen*, ed. Karim Fereidooni and Meral El (Wiesbaden, Germany: Springer VS, 2017), pp. 855–67.

[19] For an overview, see Farid Hafez, "Comparing Anti-Semitism and Islamophobia: The State of the Field," *Islamophobia Studies Journal* 3 (2016); Anna Esther Younes, *Race, Colonialism and the Figure of the Jew in a New Germany* (dissertation, Graduate Institute of International and Development Studies, 2016).

[20] This phenomenon is called the "Muslim ghetto" in other European countries.

[21] Armin Langer, "'Judaism Is Not a Religion, but a Political Organization': German Jews under Suspicion in the Age of Enlightenment and Parallels to Contemporary Islamophobic Discourses," *Islamophobia Studies Yearbook*, vol. 11 (Vienna: New Academic Press, 2020), pp. 91–110.

[22] Cüneyt Dinç, "Gastarbeiter in Germany," *The Wiley Blackwell Encyclopedia of Race, Ethnicity, and Nationalism*, ed. John Stone et al. (Hoboken, NJ: John Wiley, 2016), 1–4.

[23] Friedrich Heckmann, *From Ethnic Nation to Universalistic Immigrant Integration: Germany* (Oldenburg, Germany: De Gruyter, 2016).

[24] Gerd Hardach, "The Marshall Plan in Germany, 1948–1952," *Journal of European Economic History* 16, no. 3 (1987): pp. 433–85.

[25] Werner Schiffauer, "Suspect Subjects: Muslim Migrants and the Security Agencies in Germany," in *The Social Life of Anti-Terrorist Laws: The War on Terror and the Classification of the "Dangerous Other*," ed. Julia Eckert (Bielefeld, Germany: Transcript, 2008), pp. 55–78.

80 FARID HAFEZ

attacks on September 11, 2001, a politicization of Islam that went hand in hand with increasing negative attitudes vis-à-vis Islam and Muslims could also be observed in Germany.[26]

Belated Right-Wing Populism?

One might assume that against this backdrop, Muslims would also have been targeted quite early by political parties, especially from the right. However, this did not occur, as Islam was not yet a salient political issue and right-wing parties were not yet successful on a national level. As Michael Minkenberg and Malisa Zobel remind us, one must always consider three factors when looking at right-wing populism in Germany in a historical perspective.[27] First, there have always been active radical-right subcultures and movements with violent tendencies. But they have been quite marginal in number and unrepresented in parliament. Second, Germany's federally elected upper legislative chamber assigns importance to regional parliaments at the *Länder*, or state, level, which in turn makes regional politics more relevant. The mobilization against Muslims has long been triggered primarily by national debates, not regional ones. Third, East-West differences increased following the reunification of Germany.

Several right-wing parties existed prior to the reunification but did not succeed on a national level. These include the Nationaldemokratische Partei Deutschlands, or National Democratic Party of Germany (NPD), which was founded in 1964; the Deutsche Volksunion, or German Volk Union (DVU), which was founded in 1971 and participated in the 1987 elections; and the Republikaner, or Republicans (REP), which was founded in 1986 in a split from the center-right Christian Democrats. The first notable regional electoral victories for right-wing parties like REP occurred in the late 1980s and 1990s. Even following reunification, the NPD and DVU had representatives in three out of the five former East German state parliaments. Until 2017, however, no right-wing parties were represented in the Bundestag, the federal parliament.[28]

While these right-wing political parties were unsuccessful on the federal level, they indirect impacted German politics. The governing centrist parties, the

---

[26] Gert Pickel and Alexander Yendell, "Islam als Bedrohung? Beschreibung und Erklärung von Einstellungen zum Islam im Ländervergleich" ["Islam as a Threat? Description and Explanation of Attitudes toward Islam in Comparison"], *Zeitschrift Für Vergleichende Politikwissenschaft* 10 (2016): pp. 273–309.

[27] Michael Minkenberg and Malisa Zobel, "From the Margins, but Not Marginal: Putting the German Radical Right's Influence on Immigration Policy in a Comparative European Context," in *Do They Make a Difference? The Policy Influence of Radical Right Populist Parties in Western Europe*, ed. Benjamin Biard, Laurent Bernhard, and Hans-Georg Betz (London: ECPR Press and Rowman and Littlefield International, 2019): p. 22.

[28] Minkenberg and Zobel, "From the Margins," p. 22.

Christian Democratic Union/Christian Social Union (CDU/CSU) and the Social Democratic Party of Germany (SPD), had significant reactions to the right-wing parties' issues and campaigns. While both of these parties, which shared most of the power in postwar Germany, were able to choose between either demarcation, confrontation, and ignorance or cordon sanitaire, cooptation, and collaboration, the CDU/CSU pursued the strategy of disallowing competitors on its right flank. Consequently, its strategy was to co-opt right-wing positions when it came to their core claims in the areas of asylum, culture, and immigration in the late 1980s and 1990s.[29] When right-wing populist parties like REP campaigned under slogans like "The boat is full"—pledging to stop immigration and promoting a welfare chauvinism, accompanied by murderous violence against asylum seekers and immigrants—the CDU/CSU co-opted this discourse and subsequently implemented a more restrictive approach on asylum.[30]

Subsequently, media and politics began reproducing a discourse that painted immigration as a threat to German society. Laws were amended and tightened in regard to asylum, and a publicly acclaimed project of multiculturalism and integration was delegitimized.[31] Even in 1998, when the SPD governed with the Greens, they did not dare roll back these restrictive laws.[32] Thus, the relevance of right-wing parties was indirect and laid the basis for the advent of an anti-Muslim discourse that was later adopted by the AfD.

When the AfD was founded in 2013, it began as a populist party that favored free-market economic policies and was critical of Europe and the euro. Following party infighting that ended in a victory for the right-wing camp in 2015, the party began primarily campaigning against multiculturalism, Islam, refugees, and asylum seekers.[33] According to some observers, the rise of the AfD is connected to the so-called refugee crisis.[34] By 2018, the AfD held seats in every state of the German Federal Republic. In 2017, it also crossed the voting threshold, enabling it to gain parliamentary seats at the federal level and, indeed, becoming the third-largest political party after the CDU/CSU and the SPD.

Since the outset of the civil war in Syria, more than 1.4 million people have applied for asylum in Germany, many of them young Muslim men; this figure constitutes more than 43 percent of all applications made to the European Union.[35] The AfD leadership successfully exploited these circumstances, drawing

[29] Minkenberg and Zobel, "From the Margins," p. 22.

[30] Minkenberg and Zobel, "From the Margins," pp. 24–25.

[31] Minkenberg and Zobel, "From the Margins," p. 25.

[32] Minkenberg and Zobel, "From the Margins," pp. 23–26.

[33] Frank Decker, "The 'Alternative for Germany': Factors behind Its Emergence and Profile of a New Right-Wing Populist Party," *German Politics and Society* 34, no. 2 (2016): pp. 1–16.

[34] Charles Lees, "The 'Alternative for Germany': The Rise of Right-Wing Populism at the Heart of Europe," *Politics* 38, no. 3 (2018): pp. 295–310.

[35] Jeffrey Gedmin, "Right-Wing Populism in Germany: Muslims and Minorities after the 2015 Refugee Crisis" (working paper, The One Percent Problem: Muslims in the West and the Rise of the

82 FARID HAFEZ

on the mobilization of the anti-Islam social movement Patriotic Europeans against the Islamization of the Occident, or Patriotische Europäer gegen die Islamisierung des Abendlandes (Pegida), which emerged in 2014.[36] Some observers see Pegida and AfD as two sides of the same coin, hinting at the personal connections and the embrace of Pegida street protests by AfD politicians.[37] As a study on the AfD's program, strategies, and actors has revealed, although the AfD is not a single-issue party, it is clearly promoting a nationalist, *völkisch*, and racist discourse that seeks to provoke and scandalize while also presenting itself as a party of the common people.[38] With its pioneering use of social media channels, the AfD creates its own bubble in which it communicates with and educates its followers.[39]

The AfD effectively radicalized public antipathy toward Islam and Muslims. AfD Vice President Beatrix von Storch demanded that German border police be authorized to shoot refugees, including women and children, who tried to cross the German border.[40] In 2016, the party adopted a platform that included several anti-Muslim policies such as banning burkas, minarets, and the call to prayer,[41] all aimed at stopping the so-called Islamization of Germany,[42] and the party adopted a new manifesto that stated, "Islam does not belong to Germany. Its expansion and the ever-increasing number of Muslims in the country are viewed by the AfD as a danger to our state, our society, and our values."[43] The manifesto also described minarets as a "symbol of Islamic supremacy,"[44] called for hijabs to be banned for civil servants and in public education as well as face veils to be banned in public, and stated that "Islamic theology at state universities have to

---

New Populists series, Brookings Institution, Washington, DC, July 24, 2019), https://www.brookings.edu/research/right-wing-populism-in-germany-muslims-and-minorities-after-the-2015-refugee-crisis/.

[36] See Helga Druxes and Patricia Anne Simpson, eds., special issue, *German Politics and Society* 34, no. 4 (2016).

[37] Karsten Grabow, "PEGIDA and the *Alternative für Deutschland*: Two Sides of the Same Coin?," *European View* 15, no. 2 (2016): pp. 173–81.

[38] Benno Hafeneger Hannah Jestädt, Lisa-Marie Klose, and Philine Lewek, *AfD in Parlamenten: Themen, Strategien, Akteure [AfD in Parliaments: Issues, Strategies, Actors]* (Wochenschau Verlag, 2018), pp. 147–50.

[39] Hafeneger, Jestädt, Klose, and Lewek, *AfD in Parlamenten*, pp. 147–50.

[40] Minkenberg and Zobel, "From the Margins," p. 27.

[41] Ruth Bender, "Germany's AfD Adopts Anti-Islam Stance at Party Conference," *The Wall Street Journal*, May 1, 2016, https://www.wsj.com/articles/germanys-afd-adopts-anti-islam-stance-at-party-conference-1462120609.

[42] Kate Connolly, "Frauke Petry: The Acceptable Face of Germany's New Right?," *The Guardian*, June 19, 2016, https://www.theguardian.com/world/2016/jun/19/frauke-petry-acceptable-face-of-germany-new-right-interview.

[43] "Manifesto for Germany, the Political Programme of the Alternative for Germany," AfD, April 12, 2017, https://web.archive.org/web/20191217224623/https://cdn.afd.tools/wp-content/uploads/sites/111/2017/04/2017-04-12_afd-grundsatzprogramm-englisch_web.pdf.

[44] "Manifesto for Germany."

POSTCOLONIALISM, POST-NATIONAL SOCIALISM 83

be abolished."[45] It also said that Germany's Muslims are "a big danger to our state, our society, and our system of values."[46]

During the 2017 federal elections, the AfD ran a staunchly anti-Muslim campaign. The party's election posters presented Islam as a threat to German national identity. One poster included the belly of a pregnant white woman with the slogan, "New Germans? We'll make them ourselves."[47] This poster is reminiscent of Nazi-era propaganda encouraging German women to produce German children for the Fatherland. Another poster showed a piglet with the words "Islam? It doesn't fit in with our cuisine."[48] AfD also released another poster during the elections that included the words "Burkas? We prefer bikinis," with a picture of two women wearing bikinis on a beach,[49] clearly defining Muslims as the target of propaganda around which the white German identity is constructed.

As Ozan Keskinkilic demonstrates in his postcolonial analysis of the German discourse on Islam, the AfD is reproducing many of the discursive strategies that were already dominant during the Colonial Congresses of the German Kaiserreich in 1905 and 1910; these include designating Islam as a cultural threat, defending an imagined Christian-secular order, sexualizing the Muslim other, framing Islam as a security threat, and constructing the "good" and "bad" Muslim."[50] While the AfD's anti-Muslim discourse did not mark the birth of Islamophobia in Germany, it bolstered existing racialization of Muslims as "the other," albeit in a subtler and less offensive form.

Islamophobia as State Praxis, Hegemonic Idea, and Violence

Given German society's problematic relationship with the legacies of colonialism, racism, and the country's Nazi past, Islamophobia became a pillar of German society early on. The strongest driving force of Islamophobia is the state

---

[45] "Manifesto for Germany."

[46] "Manifesto for Germany."

[47] Melanie Amann, "US Ad Agency Boosts Right-Wing Populist AfD," *Der Spiegel*, August 30, 2017, https://www.spiegel.de/international/germany/u-s-ad-agency-boosts-right-wing-populist-afd-a-1164956.html.

[48] Amann, "US Ad Agency."

[49] Wigbert Löer, "Burgunder statt Burka und Bikini-Models—Wahlkampagne entzweit AfD" ["Burgundy Instead of Burqa and Bikini Models—Election Campaign Divides AfD"], *Stern*, June 6, 2017, https://www.stern.de/politik/deutschland/afd-wahlkampagne-entzweit-die-partei-7483 008.html.

[50] Ozan Zakariya Keskinkilic, "Die Islamdebatte gehört zu Deutschland: Rechtspopulismus und antimuslimischer Rassismus im (post-)kolonialen Kontext" ["The Islam Debate Belongs to Germany: Right-Wing Populism and Anti-Muslim Racism in a (Post)Colonial Context"], *AphorismA* (2019): pp. 35–79.

84 FARID HAFEZ

rather than far-right groups.[51] Following the destruction of Manhattan's World Trade Center twin towers on September 11, 2001, German state authorities, especially the interior ministry, implemented a law-and-order policy vis-à-vis the domestic Muslim population. On the security front, the Ministry of the Interior also introduced several programs, including the German Islam Conference, or Deutsche Islamkonferenz (DIK), which was premised on racializing Muslims and framing them as security threats.[52] The underlying idea of the DIK was based on the "exclusionary and racially informed presumption of deficiencies in the immigrants' subjecthood," and thus "the DIK prescribed that they learn German [and] pledge loyalty to the German nation," noting that for immigrants, "integration demands 'a much greater level of adjustment,' which should be attuned to the culture, history, and modern temporality of the German nation."[53]

The security apparatus criminalized many Muslim organizations by labeling them "legalistic Islamists."[54] The secret service of the German Ministry of the Interior defines legalistic Islamism as follows:

> The vast majority of Islamists in Germany are "legalists." This term is used for members of Islamist organisations in Germany who strive to impose ideas of social and individual life based on Islamist ideology whilst abiding by the law. However, their goals are not reconcilable with the free democratic basic order. Officials and supporters of these organisations engage in lobbying to achieve their aims, intensively using the possibilities provided by the German legal system ("march through the courts"). They intend to obtain complete and permanent freedom for their members to live their lives in accordance with sharia. This, however, may lead to the development of parallel societies, which hinder integration. It is also possible that legalist Islamists promote the further radicalisation of (young) Muslims.[55]

As the German secret service explicitly states, this approach included most Islamist (read *Muslim*) organizations in the definition. Observations about large Muslim civil society organizations were included in the annual report

---

[51] Narzanin Massoumi, Tom Mills, and David Miller, "Islamophobia, Social Movements and the State: For a Movement-Centered Approach," in *What Is Islamophobia? Racism, Social Movements, and the State*, ed. Narzanin Massoumi, Tom Mills, and David Miller (London: Pluto Press, 2017), p. 4.

[52] Luis Manuel Hernández Aguilar, *Governing Muslims and Islam in Contemporary Germany: Race, Time, and the German Islam Conference* (Leiden, The Netherlands: Brill, 2018), p. 228. For a theoretical frame on the racialization of Muslims, see Sahar F. Aziz, *The Racial Muslim: When Racism Quashes Religious Freedom* (Berkeley: University of California, 2021).

[53] Aguilar, *Governing Muslims*, p. 228.

[54] Bundesamt für Verfassungsschutz, "Islamist Organisations," https://web.archive.org/web/201 90201044818/https://www.verfassungsschutz.de/en/fields-of-work/islamism-and-islamist-terror ism/figures-and-facts-islamism/islamist-organisations-2015 (n.d.).

[55] Bundesamt für Verfassungsschutz, "Islamist Organisations."

of the secret service, the *Verfassungsschutzbericht* (Report on Constitutional Protection). In 2020, for example, several Muslim organizations like the Millî Görüş movement, which has 207 mosques in Germany,[56] were still included.[57] In the past, other associations like the Muslim Youth in Germany were also included.[58] Some sued the secret service and were no longer mentioned in the report.[59] The repercussions of being mentioned in these reports entailed social marginalization and ineligibility for state funds.[60] As a consequence, Muslims started refraining from participating in Muslim civil society organizations to avoid being surveilled or becoming a state target.[61] In a welfare state like Germany, where the state plays a significant role in fields such as education, health, and public policy, existing class-ethnicity divides[62] have expanded to encompass religious ones. More recently, in April 2021, before losing the September 2021 elections, CDU/CSU had proposed an even harsher platform to tackle so-called political Islamism,[63] drawing explicitly on infamous anti-Muslim policies from Austria, such as the creation of a Documentation Center, to monitor alleged political Islam.[64] Two other proposals claim that state authorities should stop supporting associations that fall under the category of "political Islam" and that there should be stricter financial controls on Muslim groups.[65]

---

[56] Moscheesuche, "IGMG—Islamische Gemeinschaft Milli Görüs e.V." ["IGMG—Islamic Community Milli Görüs"], https://www.moscheesuche.de/frontendMosques/umbrellaOrganizat ion/13959 (n.d.).

[57] Federal Ministry of Interior (BMI), *Verfassungsschutzbericht 2020* [*Intelligence Agency Annual Report 2020*], www.verfassungsschutz.de/SharedDocs/publikationen/DE/2021/verfassungsschutz bericht-2020.pdf;jsessionid=9E5D164DAD49CA9AD9AB267135121EF3.intranet351?__blob= publicationFile&v=6 (2011).

[58] BMI, *Verfassungsschutzbericht 2010* [*Intelligence Agency Annual Report 2010*], https://publik ationen.uni-tuebingen.de/xmlui/bitstream/handle/10900/63273/vsb2010.pdf?sequence=1&isAllo wed=y.

[59] Werner Schiffauer, "Die Logik des Verdachts: Muslime und Sicherheitspolitik" ["The Logic of Suspicion: Muslims and Security Politics"], Mediendienst Integration, February 27, 2019, www. mediendienst-integration.de/artikel/die-logik-des-verdachts-1.html.

[60] Werner Schiffauer, "Suspect Subjects: Muslim Migrants and the Security Agencies in Germany," in *The Social Life of Anti-Terrorist Laws: The War on Terror and the Classification of the "Dangerous Other,"* ed. Julia Eckert (Bielefeld, Germany: Transcript, 2008), pp. 55–78.

[61] Kerem Öktem, *"Signale aus der Mehrheitsgesellschaf:. Auswirkungen der Beschneidungsdebatte und staatlicher Überwachung islamischer Organisation auf Identitätsbildung und Integration in Deutschland* [*Signals from the Majority: Impacts of the Circumcision Debate and State Surveillance of Islamic Organizations on Identity Construction and Integration in Germany*] (Oxford: University of Oxford, 2013), p. 46, http://tezhamburg.files.wordpress.com/2013/09/signale-aus-der-mehrheitsg esellschaft.pdf.

[62] Thomas Faist, "Ethnicization and Racialization of Welfare-State Politics in Germany and the USA," *Ethnic and Racial Studies* 18, no. 2 (1995): pp. 219–50.

[63] Farid Hafez, "Why Is Europe on a Witch Hunt against 'Political Islam'?," *Middle East Eye*, May 25, 2021, https://www.middleeasteye.net/opinion/europe-islamophobia-witch-hunt-against-politi cal-islam.

[64] Hafez, "Why."

[65] Farid Hafez, "Surveilling and Criminalizing Austrian Muslims: The Case of 'Political Islam,'" *Insight Turkey* 23, no. 2 (2021): pp. 11–22.

86 FARID HAFEZ

In addition, the German public has regularly been exposed to biased media coverage of Islam,[66] resulting in approximately half of the population in Germany holding Islamophobic views. According to Bertelsmann Stiftung's Religion Monitor from 2019, 50 percent of the population from the former West Germany and 57 percent of those from the former East Germany believe that Islam poses a threat to them.[67] Also, the Leipzig Authoritarianism Study from 2018 suggests that 42 percent of Germans from the former West Germany and 51 percent from the former East Germany agree with the statement that Muslims should be prohibited from immigrating to Germany.[68]

Apart from the state and media, elite individuals and movements that affect society at large are central to understanding the dissemination of Islamophobic ideas. Prominent, mainstream authors in Germany have publicly espoused Islamophobic views. The Norwegian mass murderer Anders Behring Breivik even quoted one of these authors, Henryk Broder,[69] in his manifesto.[70] In another incident marking the hegemony of Islamophobia, author Thilo Sarrazin, who was an SPD member, published Germany's 2010's bestselling book titled *Deutschland schafft sich ab* (Germany Abolishes Itself).[71] Sarrazin originally applied the term *race* to Muslims from certain regions, but his publishing house advised him to replace it with *ethnicity*. Still, they were clearly aware of the racist reasoning in Sarrazin's book, which argued that Muslims were fundamentally less intelligent but had a higher birth rate and, hence, would jeopardize the evolution of a prosperous Germany.[72] The book's appeal reflects the hegemonic

[66] Carola Richter and Kai Hafez, "The Image of Islam in German Public Service Television Programmes," *Journal of Arab and Muslim Media Research* 2, no. 3 (2009): pp. 169–81.

[67] Gert Pickel, *Weltanschauliche Vielfalt und Demokratie: Wie sich religiöse Pluralität auf die politische Kultur auswirkt* [*Ideological Diversity and Democracy: How Religious Plurality Affects Political Culture*] (Gütersloh, Germany: Bertelsmann Stiftung, 2019), https://www.bertelsmann-stift ung.de/fileadmin/files/BSt/Publikationen/GrauePublikationen/Religionsmonitor_Vielfalt_und_De mokratie_7_2019.pdf.

[68] Oliver Decker and Elmar Brähler, *Flucht ins Autoritäre: Rechtsextreme Dynamiken in der Mitte der Gesellschaft* [*Flight into Authoritarianism: Right-Wing Extremist Dynamics in the Middle of Society*] (Gießen, Germany: Psychosozial-Verlag, 2018).

[69] Thorsten Gerald Schneiders, "Die Schattenseiten der Islamkritik: Darlegung und Analyse der Argumentationsstrategien von Henryk M. Broder, Ralph Giordano, Necla Kelek, Alice Schwarzer und anderen" ["The Dark Sides of Islam Criticism: Presentation and Analysis of the Argumentation Strategies of Henryk M. Broder, Ralph Giordano, Necla Kelek, Alice Schwarzer, and Others"], in *Islamfeindlichkeit: Wenn die Grenzen der Kritik verschwimmen* [*Islamophobia: When the Boundaries of Criticism Become Blurred*] (Wiesbaden, Germany: Verlag für Sozialwissenschaften, 2009), pp. 403–32.

[70] Markus Hesselmann, "Im Terroristen-'Manifest' zitiert Broder über Broder bei Breivik" ["In the Terrorist 'Manifesto,' Broder Quotes about Broder in Breivik"], *Tagesspiegel*, July 24, 2011, https:// www.tagesspiegel.de/gesellschaft/medien/im-terroristen-manifest-zitiert-broder-ueber-broder-bei-breivik/4427010.html.

[71] Sander L. Gilman, "Thilo Sarrazin and the Politics of Race in the Twenty-First Century," *New German Critique* 39, no. 3 (2012): pp. 47–59.

[72] Farid Hafez, *Feindbild Islam: Über die Salonfähigkeit von Rassismus* [*Enemy Image Islam: On the Mainstreaming of Racism*] (Vienna: Vandenhoeck and Ruprecht, 2019), pp. 94–102.

POSTCOLONIALISM, POST–NATIONAL SOCIALISM 87

power of Islamophobia not only within the right-wing extremist political camp but also within the liberal camp.

As Thorsten Gerald Schneiders argues, Islamophobia is a form of racism that is widely shared not only within the right-wing camp[73]—as Muslims are targeted as the "other" not only of tradition and Germanness, an idea held by the Christian-Democratic camp—but also of progress, liberation, Jews, and queer people,[74] serving the Social-Democratic camp. Additionally, in post–World War II West Germany, the SPD did not spearhead challenges against institutional racism but rather reproduced restrictive models for immigration policy, thus adhering to the nativist reproduction of Germanness.[75] Although Sarrazin was finally expelled from the SPD in July 2020—following the third attempt to do so, after more than ten years of conflict[76]—his book is an example of how the widespread acceptance of racist ideas also comes from the political left.

The consequence of Islamophobia is the rise of violence against immigrants and Muslims. The case of the National Socialist Underground (NSU), a right-wing militant underground group that operated for more than thirteen years and killed ten people, raised serious questions about the relationship between right-wing violence and the secret service, which seemed to have protected this network, something questioned only in the aftermath and not fully disclosed yet.[77] In recent years, transnational armed right-wing groups emanating from Germany, such as the Hannibal network, have also made headlines. This network, established in 2015, recruited former security service agents, soldiers, and policemen along with right-wing individuals to prepare them for "Day X": a military coup d'état.[78] According to police investigations, the network had compiled a "kill list" with more than twenty thousand names, including high-ranking politicians who are seen as having "pro-immigration" stances.[79] This

[73] Thorsten Gerald Schneiders, *Islamfeindlichkeit: Wenn die Grenzen der Kritik verschwimmen* [*Islamophobia: When the Boundaries of Criticism Become Blurred*] (Wiesbaden, Germany: Verlag für Sozialwissenschaften, 2009).

[74] Fatima El-Tayeb, "Time Travelers and Queer Heterotopias: Narratives from the Muslim Underground," *German Review* 88, no. 3 (2013): p. 312.

[75] Yasemin Shooman, " . . . *weil ihre Kultur so ist*": *Narrative des antimuslimischen Rassismus* [" . . . *Because Their Culture Is Like That*": *Narratives of Anti-Muslim Racism*] (Bielefeld, Germany: Transcript, 2014), p. 37.

[76] "Parteigericht Sarrazin aus SPD ausgeschlossen" ["Party Court Expels Sarrazin from SPD"], *Tagesschau*, July 31, 2020, https://www.tagesschau.de/inland/spd-sarrazin-ausschluss-105.html.

[77] Dirk Laabs, "Der Verfassungsschutz und der NSU" ["The Secret Service and the NSU"], in *Rechtsextremismus und "Nationalsozialistischer Untergrund": Interdisziplinäre Debatten, Befunde und Bilanzen* [*Right-Wing Extremism and the "National Socialist Underground": Interdisciplinary Debates, Findings, and Assessments*], ed. Wolfgang Frindte, Daniel Geschke, Nicole Haußecker, and Franziska Schmidtke (Wiesbaden: Springer-Verlag, 2016), pp. 225–57.

[78] Enes Bayraklı and Farid Hafez, "The State of Islamophobia in Europe," in *European Islamophobia Report 2018*, ed. Enes Bayraklı and Farid Hafez (Istanbul: SETA, 2018), p. 23; Anna-Esther Younes, "Islamophobia in Germany. National Report 2018," in *European Islamophobia Report 2018*, ed. Enes Bayraklı and Farid Hafez (Istanbul: SETA, 2018), pp. 383–84.

[79] Bayraklı and Hafez, "State of Islamophobia," p. 25.

88 FARID HAFEZ

case demonstrates that right-wing and anti-Muslim attitudes are shared by those in power, bureaucracy, and politics.

For right-wing populist parties and movements like the AfD and Pegida, it was easy to mobilize on preexisting forms of Islamophobia reflected in state policies and public debates. Old-fashioned ideas like those of a German *Leitkultur*, or core culture, were already held in high esteem in elite circles at the end of the 1990s.[80] This idea rejected claims of multiculturalism, while at the same time representing a nativist German identity that designated German language and cultural traditions as part of the essence of Germanness and considered abiding by these a collective prerequisite for social cohesion.[81] In 2006, CDU Interior Minister Wolfgang Schäuble's proclamation at the German Islam Conference that "Islam is part of Germany and part of Europe" sparked a backlash within his own party.[82] CSU politician Hans Peter Friedrich retorted that the notion that "Islam would belong to Germany is a fact without any historical basis,"[83] a more widespread belief in Germany.

When the AfD emerged, it became the natural heir of this hostility toward Islam.[84] Indeed, an analysis of parliamentary debates in the Bundestag between October 2009 and June 2011 reveals that the CDU/CSU discussed Islam widely in negative terms and associated the religion with terrorism, danger, extremism, and human rights violations.[85] The CDU/CSU uses the notion of an imagined Judeo-Christian tradition that excludes the third-largest religion from German society, with Muslims portrayed as unwilling to fit into society (*integrationsun willig*).[86] Islamism was used primarily in connection to extremism as a security threat.[87]

Connecting to the Islamophobic International

Right-wing political parties around the globe have always been in contact with each other, but their respective nationalistic idiosyncrasies have impeded

---

[80] Jana Cattien, "What Is Leitkultur?," *New German Critique* 48, no. 1 (2021): pp. 181–209.

[81] Jeffrey Gedmin, *Right-Wing Populism in Germany* (Washington, DC: Brookings Institution, 2019).

[82] Gedmin, *Right-Wing Populism.*

[83] Gedmin, *Right-Wing Populism.*

[84] Gedmin, *Right-Wing Populism.*

[85] Farid Hafez, "Islamophobie und die deutschen Bundestagsparteien: Eine Analyse vom 27. Oktober 2009 bis 9. Juni 2011" ["Islamophobia and the German Parliamentary Parties: An Analysis from October 27, 2009, to June 9, 2011"], in *Verhärtete Fronten: Der schwere Weg zu einer vernünftigen Islamkritik* [*Hardened Fronts: The Hard Way to a Reasonable Criticism of Islam*], ed. Thorsten Gerald Schneiders (Wiesbaden, Germany: Springer, 2012), pp. 57–75.

[86] Hafez, "Islamophobie."

[87] Hafez, "Islamophobie."

cooperation.[88] One major turn in this dynamic was when former nationalist camps that could not have conceivably worked together became united under the banner of fighting an alleged Islamization.[89] In the past, German nationalism, for instance, had always been at odds with Italian nationalism and vice versa because of various historical questions about borders.[90] But now, European right-wing parties have come together and have even been able to form successful political groups ("Europarties") under joint leadership in the European Parliament.[91] The European Alliance for Freedom (EAF) was formed in 2011; the EAF evolved into the Europe of Nations and Freedom in 2015 and then Identity and Democracy (ID) in 2019.[92] While the original EAF was not able to reach the minimum requirement for representation among the Members of the European Parliament (MEPs) from seven EU member states, today ID is the fourth-largest party in the European Parliament.[93] The AfD has become part of ID at the European level; previously, some of its MEPs had belonged to the European Conservatives and Reformists.[94]

The exchange of ideas and experiences among right-wing parties and camps leads to transnational cooperation both ideologically, in the sense of borrowing discourses, and organizationally, in the sense of building personal networks that can lead to the development of more formal networks and activities. One can clearly see that the AfD models itself after Austria's successful right-wing Freedom Party (Freiheitliche Partei Österreichs), borrowing its anti-Muslim policy platform, communication style, rhetoric, and campaigns from its older Austrian counterpart.[95]

Furthermore, this transnational European cooperation also enabled European right-wing politicians to cooperate with right-wing politicians in Israel and the United States,[96] and it is even expanding to a global level. In one instance, twenty-three MEPs visited Kashmir on October 23, 2019, two months after the Indian government revoked the region's special autonomous status.[97] Most of the visiting MEPs came from far-right political parties, including France's National Rally and Germany's AfD, and they were allowed in at a time when

[88] Farid Hafez, "Shifting Borders: Islamophobia as Common Ground for Building Pan-European Right-Wing Unity," *Patterns of Prejudice*, 48, no. 5 (2014): pp. 479–99.

[89] Hafez, "Shifting Borders."

[90] Hafez, "Shifting Borders."

[91] Hafez, "Shifting Borders."

[92] "Factsheet: Identity and Democracy," Bridge Initiative, December 22, 2020, https://bridge.geo rgetown.edu/research/factsheet-identity-and-democracy/.

[93] "Factsheet: Identity."

[94] "Factsheet: Identity."

[95] "Factsheet: Heinz-Christian Strache," Bridge Initiative, August 15, 2019, www.bridge.georget own.edu/research/3174/.

[96] "Factsheet: Heinz-Christian Strache."

[97] Eviane Leidig, "The Far-Right Is Going Global," *Foreign Policy*, January 21, 2020, https://foreignpol icy.com/2020/01/21/india-kashmir-modi-eu-hindu-nationalists-rss-the-far-right-is-going-global/.

foreign journalists and domestic politicians were barred access to the region.[98] Eviane Leidig points out that, in the 1930s, collaborations existed between Hindu nationalists, fascist Italy, and Nazi Germany.[99] V. D. Savarkar, a leader of Hindu nationalism during that period, once wrote that India should model its approach to its "Muslim problem" on that used by the Nazis to deal with their "Jewish problem."[100] Writing on the MEPs' visit and its historical precedents, Leidig concludes that the visions of these two nationalist movements are not so dissimilar.[101] The AfD succeeded in becoming the third-strongest political party in the German Bundestag and thus managed to normalize right-wing populism in German party politics. As such, it also became an integral part of the far-right international movement that is currently organized as the ID party at the European level.

Responses to Islamophobia in Germany

As the past five editions of the European Islamophobia Report reveal, there have been many recommendations for policy-makers and civil society on how best to combat Islamophobia in Germany. In the 2019 edition, Enes Bayraklı argues that in Germany, "anti-Muslim racism has become socially acceptable in certain milieus and regions. That is why Germany needs a policy which makes it very clear that Islamophobia violates both the anti-discrimination laws and the democratic requirement of freedom of faith."[102] Consequently, he recommends implementing programs to reduce Islamophobia "in all arenas of society such as work, education, state institutions, and civil society."[103] Bayraklı also considers the fight against right-wing extremism to be of the utmost urgency and views the "authoritarian aggression of the far right [as] directed particularly against Muslims."[104]

While many of the recommendations presented in the European Islamophobia Report remain to be implemented, one important step has been taken by the German federal agencies. In 2017, anti-Muslim hate crime was introduced as a separate category in hate crime statistics.[105] This measure was significant in recognizing the problem of Islamophobia. In 2017, seventy-one attacks

[98] Leidig, "Far-Right."
[99] Leidig, "Far-Right."
[100] Leidig, "Far-Right."
[101] Leidig, "Far-Right."
[102] Enes Bayraklı, "Islamophobia in Germany: National Report," in *European Islamophobia Report 2019*, ed. Enes Bayraklı and Farid Hafez (Istanbul: SETA, 2019), p. 354.
[103] Bayraklı, "Islamophobia," p. 354.
[104] Bayraklı, "Islamophobia," p. 354.
[105] Bayraklı and Hafez, "State of Islamophobia," p. 8.

on mosques and 908 crimes against German Muslims, ranging from verbal to physical attacks and murder attempts, were registered.[106] The Turkish-Islamic Union for Religious Affairs, a mosque umbrella organization, listed 101 attacks on mosques in Germany throughout 2017.[107] In 2018, 678 attacks on German Muslims, including forty attacks on mosques, were reported.[108] In 2019, a total of forty-six anti-Muslim hate crimes were reported by the German Federal Police, while the civil society initiative Brandeilig, which covers attacks on mosques, counted 122 attacks on mosques in 2019.[109]

While efforts to tackle Islamophobia are mostly made by various levels of civil society, from academia to nongovernmental organizations (NGOs), German ministries also fund various initiatives that tackle Islamophobia. On June 2, 2019, CDU politician Walter Lübcke was fatally shot in the head at close range by a right-wing perpetrator who targeted Lübcke for his perceived pro-immigration stance. Lübcke's murder raised the alarm that Islamophobia is a problem facing everyone, not just Germany's Muslim minority. In September 2020, the Ministry of the Interior established an Independent Group of Experts on Hostility to Muslims (Unabhängiger Expertenkreis Muslimfeindlichkeit), a group of twelve experts appointed to make recommendations for the fight against *Muslimfeindlichkeit*, or anti-Muslim hostility, within the next two years.[110] As the ministry argues, it was also a "reaction to the racist and anti-Muslim incidents and terrorist acts of recent months."[111] It seems that a growing fear of German elites might also have made them aware that they, too, might become the targets of Islamophobes.

Alongside state initiatives, in civil society the umbrella organization Alliance against IslamoPhobia and Anti-Muslim Hate (CLAIM) was established in October 2017, which currently brings together around forty civil society organizations fighting Islamophobia in Germany.[112] At the same time, the mere term *Islamophobia* remains contested in the German public sphere, and several actors have mobilized to frame it as an Islamist rallying cry.[113] This contention can also

---

[106] Bayraklı and Hafez, "State of Islamophobia," p. 8.

[107] Bayraklı and Hafez, "State of Islamophobia," p. 8.

[108] Younes, "Islamophobia," p. 374.

[109] Bayraklı, "Islamophobia," p. 332.

[110] "Pressemittleilung, Bundesinnenminister Seehofer beruft Mitglieder für Unabhängigen Expertenkreis Muslimfeindlichkeit" ["Press Release, Federal Minister of the Interior Seehofer Appoints Members for Independent Expert Group on Anti-Muslim Hostility"], BMI, September 1, 2020, https://www.bmi.bund.de/SharedDocs/pressemitteilungen/DE/2020/09/expertenkreis-musl imfeindlichkeit.html.

[111] "Pressemittleilung."

[112] "Was wir tun" ["What We Do"], CLAIM, https://www.claim-allianz.de/was-wir-tun/.

[113] Farid Hafez, "Public and Scholarly Debates on the Comparison of Islamophobia and Anti-Semitism in Germany," *Contemporary Church History/Kirchliche Zeitgeschichte* 32, no. 2 (2019): pp. 277–90.

be seen with the selection of the term *anti-Muslim hostility* for the expert group that was established by the German Ministry of the Interior.[114]

One encounters different forces in the struggle against Islamophobia. On one hand, NGOs in particular try to make a difference, and some state authorities are willing to support these initiatives as well as to implement institutions to better fight Islamophobia. On the other hand, the hegemonic force of Islamophobia is not to be underestimated, as institutions are designed in ways that structurally reproduce Islamophobia.

Conclusion

Postcolonialism, post-Nazism, and German reunification are three important factors in the making of Germany's self-imagination that explain the relevance and rise of Islamophobia in Germany today. The belated arrival of AfD, a successful right-wing populist party with an anti-Muslim agenda, does not indicate a belated arrival of Islamophobia. Rather, the AfD was able to mobilize a preexisting narrative about Muslims contained in the centrist parties, first and foremost the CDU/CSU, as well as an existing Islamophobic state praxis in the wake of 9/11.

As a successful right-wing party with a strong Islamophobic component, the AfD became well integrated in the family of Islamophobic right-wing parties in the European Parliament as well as the larger global network of anti-Muslim right-wing movements. With rising violence committed by underground right-wing groups, some state actors have understood the long-term threat of anti-Muslim right-wing organizations. Recent initiatives to combat Islamophobia (though named *Muslimfeindlichkeit*, or anti-Muslim hostility) initiated by the Ministry of the Interior, which is traditionally known for problematizing parts of Muslim civil society, demonstrate the serious threat that Islamophobia and right-wing violence pose to German society.

At the same time, the potential criminalization of Muslim civil society by establishing institutions like the Independent Group of Experts on Political

---

[114] Meanwhile, opposition parties in parliament like The Left (*Die Linke*) push for the recognition of Islamophobia as a social problem by introducing parliamentary requests that critically treat Islamophobia as a structural issue. "Vorgang—Große Anfrage: Antimuslimischer Rassismus und Diskriminierung von Muslimen in Deutschland Initiative" ["Event—Major Interpellation: Anti-Muslim Racism and Discrimination against Muslims in Germany Initiative"], *Deutscher Bundestag*, June 26, 2019, http://dipbt.bundestag.de/extrakt/ba/WP19/2502/250226.html. Relatedly, this author has provided a working definition with CLAIM to be used for monitoring Islamophobia as part of a project funded by the European Commission. See Farid Hafez, "Anti-Muslim Racism: A Working Definition," CLAIM, 2021, https://www.i-report.eu/en/news/downloads/.

Islamism (Unabhängiger Expertenkreis zum politischen Islamismus),[115] which was initiated after the CDU/CSU had proposed an even harsher platform to tackle so-called political Islamism,[116] reveals how various groups and interests contest the future of Islam and Muslims in Germany. This example from within one institution, the Ministry of the Interior, shows the contentious way forward. Within less than one year, two seemingly opposing institutions have been established that can, on the one hand, reinforce Islamophobia as structural violent state praxis and, on the other hand, simultaneously combat Islamophobia.

In the last federal elections in September 2021, the AfD lost eleven seats and overall became "only" the fifth-strongest party. More importantly, the CDU/ CSU, home to normalized anti-Muslim politics, lost its place as the strongest party and its leadership position as the main governing party for the first time since 2005. What does this mean for the future of anti-Muslim politics, especially if the new coalition will be made of SPD, the Greens, and the Liberals? While some politicians could potentially push some of their anti-racist stances in relation to anti-Muslim racism, one should not expect too much, given the level of institutionalization of Islamophobia in the German state.

---

[115] "Neuer Expertenkreis zum politischen Islamismus" ["New Expert Group on Political Islamism"], BMI, June 25, 2021, https://www.bmi.bund.de/SharedDocs/pressemitteilungen/DE/2021/06/expertenkreis-politischer-extremismus.html.

[116] See the discussion within this chapter in the section titled "Islamophobia as State Praxis, Hegemonic Idea, and Violence."

6

Islamophobia

How the Far Right Went Mainstream in Britain

Mobashra Tazamal

In 2011, Baroness Sayeeda Warsi delivered a speech in which she announced that Islamophobia had "passed the dinner-table test," meaning that it was socially acceptable.[1] Eleven years later, Islamophobia remains rampant across British society. From an increase in hate crimes to racist and dehumanizing portrayals in the British media, the types of abuse that target British Muslims remain in all sectors of society.[2] While analysis and commentary have focused on Islamophobia at a societal level, investigations of the widespread discrimination and hate faced by British Muslims must include the prevalence of anti-Muslim racism in British politics and policy.

From the deadly attacks of September 11, 2001, to the global "war on terror" that devastated numerous countries and destabilized entire regions, the past two decades have witnessed a drastic rise in violence, instability, and state-sanctioned Islamophobia. This time period demonstrates the global interconnectedness of these phenomena and, specifically, how an event in one corner of the world affects individuals in others. Moreover, social media has both fostered global relations and exacerbated the division, growth, and spread of conspiracy theories.

The rise of populist politics in Great Britain is inextricably linked to the presence and institutionalization of Islamophobia in society. In the post–9/11 world, rhetoric heightened Islamophobia to new levels and brought forth discriminatory policies that largely remained outside of public criticism in the name of

---

[1] David Batty, "Lady Warsi Claims Islamophobia Is Now Socially Acceptable in Britain," *The Guardian,* January 20, 2011, https://www.theguardian.com/uk/2011/jan/20/lady-warsi-islamopho bia-muslims-prejudice.

[2] Jamie Grierson, "A Third of UK Muslims Report Abuse or Crime While Studying," *The Guardian*, March 19, 2018. https://www.theguardian.com/uk-news/2018/mar/19/a-third-of-uk-muslims-rep ort-abuse-or-while-studying; Aasma Day, "Exclusive: Muslim Medics Taunted about Bacon and Alcohol—by Their Own NHS Colleagues," *Huffington Post*, September 28, 2020, https://www.huffing tonpost.co.uk/entry/islamophobia-nhs-muslim-doctors-institutionalised_uk_5f562e80c5b62b3ad d43cccb; Anushka Asthana, "Islamophobia Holding Back UK Muslims in Workplace, Study Finds," *The Guardian*, September 7, 2017, https://www.theguardian.com/society/2017/sep/07/islamopho bia-holding-back-uk-muslims-in-workplace-study-finds.

Mobashra Tazamal, *Islamophobia* In: *Global Islamophobia and the Rise of Populism.* Edited by: Sahar F. Aziz and John L. Esposito, Oxford University Press. © Oxford University Press 2024. DOI: 10.1093/oso/9780197648995.003.0006

"fighting terrorism."[3] Attacks perpetrated by individuals identifying as Muslims resulted in the collective suspicion and punishment of the wider Muslim community.[4]

Shortly after September 11, 2001, the UK government began treating the British Muslim community as inherently suspect. As a result, the Prevent program introduced under the Labour government in 2003 claimed that there were known "indicators" of "radicalization," which, if observed in time, could derail an individual on the path to terrorism.[5] There were numerous reports demonstrating the pseudoscience underlying the Prevent program, as well as the Islamophobia inherent to the government policy, as these "indicators" often included Islamic religious observance.[6] Despite criticism from legal and human rights organizations,[7] the government continued the program to prevent "violent extremism," further institutionalizing it in 2015 by making it a statutory duty for public bodies.[8] The program has resulted in self-censorship on university campuses, fear among British Muslim communities, and securitization of public sectors.[9]

As government policy de facto singled out the British Muslim community as being prone to "radicalization," "extremism," and "terrorism," the British tabloid media doubled down on this messaging by making sensational and racist claims, warning about "Muslim radicalization," "Islamic terrorism," and eventually a Muslim "invasion."[10] For the British public, the constant messaging only sowed the seeds of anti-Muslim racism deeper and provided far-right populist politicians the avenue to mainstream their views and build support.

[3] Abdullah Al-Arian and Hafsa Kanjwal, "On the Front Lines: American Muslims and the War on Terror," in *The Terror Trap: The Impact of the War on Terror on Muslim Communities since 9/11* (Washington, DC: Coalition for Civil Freedoms, the Bridge Initiative at Georgetown University, the ICNA Council for Social Justice, CAGE, Center for Islam and Global Affairs, Muslim Justice League, and United Voices for America, 2021), pp. 68–74.

[4] Al-Arian and Kanjwal, "On the Front Lines."

[5] Bridge Initiative Team, "Factsheet: Prevent," Bridge Initiative, March 25, 2019, https://bridge.georgetown.edu/research/prevent/.

[6] Karen Armstrong et al., "Anti-Radicalisation Strategy Lacks Evidence Base in Science," *The Guardian*, September 29, 2016, https://www.theguardian.com/politics/2016/sep/29/anti-radicalisation-strategy-lacks-evidence-base-in-science; Sahar F. Aziz, "State Sponsored Radicalization," *Michigan Journal of Race and Law* 27, no. 5 (2021): pp. 125–61.

[7] "End of Mission Statement of the Special Rapporteur on Contemporary Forms of Racism, Racial Discrimination, Xenophobia and Related Intolerance at the Conclusion of Her Mission to the United Kingdom of Great Britain and Northern Ireland," Office of the High Commissioner for Human Rights, May 11, 2018, https://www.ohchr.org/en/statements/2018/05/end-mission-statement-special-rapporteur-contemporary-forms-racism-racial.

[8] Counter-Terrorism and Security Act 2015, p. 5, ch. 1.

[9] Bridge Initiative Team, "Factsheet: Prevent."

[10] Katy Sian et al., "The Media and Muslims in the UK" (working paper, Centre for Ethnicity and Racism Studies, University of Leeds, 2012), https://www.ces.uc.pt/projectos/tolerace/media/Working%20paper%205/The%20Media%20and%20Muslims%20in%20the%20UK.pdf, pp. 229–72.

Over the past two decades, British politics, and more specifically the Conservative Party, has frequently characterized British Muslims as the forever "other," marking the community of three million as a problem point in British society and using this framing to justify prejudicial talk and discriminatory policies. This characterization was particularly visible in the 2016 London mayoral campaign of Conservative Party candidate Zac Goldsmith, who linked the Labour candidate Sadiq Khan, a British Muslim who went on to win the race, to extremism.[11] Little changed in 2020, as the Conservatives chose Shaun Bailey to run against Khan, despite the former's past anti-Muslim rhetoric. In 2005, Bailey complained that immigrants to the United Kingdom who were allowed to "bring their culture, their country" had turned Britain into a "crime-ridden cesspool" and "rob[bed] Britain of its community."[12]

When this level of Islamophobia is observed at the top, it is not surprising that many Britons hold similar anti-Muslim views. In its annual *State of Hate* report, the anti-racism organization Hope Not Hate found that in 2018, more than one-third of people in the United Kingdom believed that Islam was a threat to the British way of life;[13] among those who voted Conservative in the 2017 general election, that figure rose to nearly half.[14] The report also argued that "anti-Muslim prejudice has replaced immigration as the key driver of the growth of the far right."[15] But generally speaking, within the context of British politics in the last decade, immigrants and Muslims were often viewed as interchangeable subjects.

Instances of Islamophobia, along with discriminatory rhetoric and policies, arose year after year with little to no push back from the government. Rather, many of those in power accepted this ideology of oppression and utilized it for their own gains. It was through this existing avenue of Islamophobia that the discriminatory and divisive messaging of right-wing and far-right parties and groups was able to enter the mainstream, most acutely in the Brexit debates.

---

[11] Robert Mackey, "In Race for London Mayor, Trump's Anti-Muslim Playbook Seems to Be Failing Zac Goldsmith," *The Intercept*, May 3, 2016, https://theintercept.com/2016/05/03/least-london-rich-heirs-campaign-instill-fear-muslims-not-going-well/.

[12] Benjamin Kentish, "Conservative London Mayoral Candidate Claimed Celebrating Hindu and Muslim Festivals Turned Britain into 'Cesspool of Crime,'" *Independent*, October 3, 2018, https://www.independent.co.uk/news/uk/politics/conservative-london-candidate-mayor-shaun-bailey-hindu-muslim-festival-crime-a8566341.html.

[13] Nick Lowles et al., "State of Hate 2019: People vs. the Elite?," Hope Not Hate, February 2019, https://www.hopenothate.org.uk/wp-content/uploads/2019/02/state-of-hate-2019-final-1.pdf.

[14] Frances Perraudin, "Third of Britons Believe Islam Threatens British Way of Life, Says Report," *The Guardian*, February 17, 2019, https://www.theguardian.com/world/2019/feb/17/third-of-britons-believe-islam-threatens-british-way-of-life-says-report.

[15] Lowles et al., "State."

The Populist Campaign for Brexit

Thomas Greven defines populism as a political ideology whose central narrative is the idea of the "people" in opposition to a corrupt political class or establishment.[16] I argue that the populism we see today in Britain is best described as ethno-populism because the narrative in use focuses on the us-versus-them dichotomy, whereas the defining characteristics of difference between the *us* and *them* groupings are rooted in race, religion, and culture. The *us* are often white, working-class people who feel that their identity and interests are under attack or threat by the *them*, often framed as immigrants, refugees, and people of color who are all supposedly favored by the elites. Populist politicians thus frame themselves as reining in the power of the corrupt elites and restoring the fortunes of the everyday individual.[17]

Nothing exemplifies this phenomenon better than the campaign for Britain's exit from the European Union (EU), more commonly known as Brexit. The call was led by British politician Nigel Farage, the preeminent figure of the Euroskeptic political party, the United Kingdom Independence Party (UKIP).[18] Farage led Leave.EU, one of the two campaigns calling for Britain's exit from the EU, and deployed populist tactics by playing on perceived grievances among the white working class. The campaign put immigration at the heart of its messaging, claiming that it put a strain on jobs and public services.[19] The argument resonated among the white working class, especially in postindustrial towns in northern England. These communities had been dealing with the consequences of a global financial crash, resulting in limited to no employment opportunities and reduced social services in their areas owing to the government's austerity program.[20] All these factors were in addition to the underlying and persistent racism in British society. A November 2017 study by scientists found that "psychological predictors of xenophobia were strongly linked with voting to leave the

---

[16] Thomas Greven, "The Rise of Right-Wing Populism in Europe and the United States," Friedrich Ebert Stiftung, May 2016, http://dc.fes.de/fileadmin/user_upload/publications/RightwingPopul ism.pdf.

[17] Ali Rattansi, "Racism and the Rise of Populist Movements," Runnymede Trust, March 23, 2020, https://www.runnymedetrust.org/blog/racism-and-the-rise-of-populist-movements.

[18] "Factsheet: UKIP," Bridge Initiative, January 7, 2019, https://bridge.georgetown.edu/research/ factsheet-ukip/.

[19] Adam Lusher, "EU Immigrants Help Create Jobs, Not Take Them, Study Claims," *Independent*, June 20, 2016, https://www.independent.co.uk/news/uk/politics/eu-referendum-immigration-imm igrants-jobs-brexit-remain-what-happens-unemployment-a7091566.html.

[20] Natalie Fenton, "How the British Media Helped Boris Johnson Win," *Al Jazeera*, December 18, 2019, https://www.aljazeera.com/opinions/2019/12/18/how-the-british-media-helped-boris-john son-win; Patrick Butler, "Deprived Northern Regions Worst Hit by UK Austerity, Study Finds," *The Guardian*, January 28, 2019, https://www.theguardian.com/society/2019/jan/28/deprived-north ern-regions-worst-hit-by-uk-austerity-study-finds.

EU and support for the outcome of the referendum."[21] These numerous factors thus served as the perfect mix for politicians to exploit in driving support.

The populist argument was that the political elite had left these white working-class communities behind and favored immigrants and people of color instead. Using populism meant that right-wing politicians would create an in-group and out-group situation; in the case of Britain, given its decades of Islamophobia, the categories already had been constructed and were ripe for exploitation. Islamophobia and fearmongering about immigrants of color threatening the British "way of life" were central to the Brexit campaign. In part because of the Brexit campaign, the mainstream conversation on immigrants and Muslims in particular shifted further to the right, as the Conservative Party generally accepted and adopted many of the right-wing talking points. The 2018 analysis by Hope Not Hate found that almost half of Conservative voters (47 percent) and those who voted to leave the EU (49 percent) believed that Islam was a threat to the British way of life.[22]

UKIP began making positive headway in the second decade of the 21st century under the leadership of Nigel Farage. In 2016, the BBC wrote that Farage brought "UKIP from a fringe force to the third biggest party in UK politics in terms of votes at the 2015 general election."[23] The original founder of the party, professor Alan Sked, observed that UKIP had become "extraordinarily right-wing" and devoted to "creating a fuss, via Islam and immigrants."[24] During this period, the conversations centering on Islam and immigrants were also given greater attention as the media and tabloids went into overdrive with reporting of the refugee crisis.

The Refugee Crisis

Discussion of the refugee crisis in the media and political circles removed the role of Britain, Europe, and the West in creating the conditions that led to the large-scale movement of people. The rhetoric surrounding the humanitarian

---

[21] Agnieszka Golec de Zavala, Rita Guerra, and Claudia Simão, "The Relationship between the Brexit Vote and Individual Predictors of Prejudice: Collective Narcissism, Right Wing Authoritarianism, Social Dominance Orientation," *Frontiers in Psychology*, November 27, 2017, https://doi.org/10.3389/fpsyg.2017.02023. See also Josh Gabbatiss, "Brexit Strongly Linked to Xenophobia, Scientists Conclude," *Independent*, November 27, 2017, https://www.independent.co.uk/news/science/brexit-prejudice-scientists-link-foreigners-immigrants-racism-xenophobia-leave-eu-a8078586.html.

[22] Perraudin, "Third of Britons."

[23] "The Nigel Farage Story," BBC, July 4, 2016, https://www.bbc.co.uk/news/uk-politics-36701855.

[24] Mehdi Hasan, "Ukip Founder Alan Sked Says the Party Is 'Morally Dodgy' and 'Extraordinarily Right-Wing,'" *Huffington Post*, November 26, 2012, https://www.huffingtonpost.co.uk/2012/11/26/ukip-founder-alan-sked-morally-dodgy_n_2190987.html.

crisis was devoid of context, ignoring the root causes—including violence and destabilization caused in part by Western-led wars and historical interference—that resulted in the mass movement of civilians. Instead, refugees were constructed as a physical threat to the stability and existence of Europe. While such coverage was common across Europe, British media was a unique outlier in the ferocity and hardline approach it took when discussing the humanitarian situation.

A study by the Cardiff School of Journalism in 2015, the same year of the peak of the crisis, found that the British "right-wing press consistently endorsed a hardline anti-refugee and migrant, Fortress Europe approach."[25] In the comparative study, researchers found that while "humanitarian themes were more common in Italian coverage than in British, German or Spanish press. Threat themes (such as to the welfare system, or cultural threats) were the most prevalent in Italy, Spain and Britain."[26] Out of the five countries (Italy, Sweden, Germany, United Kingdom, and Spain) the study considered, it found that "coverage in the United Kingdom was the most negative, and the most polarized."[27] When looking at the actual reporting, research found that in the press coverage across European countries, the negative commentary regarding refugees was usually "challenged within the article by a journalist or another source."[28] However, in the British right-wing press, anti-refugee and migrant themes were "continuously reinforced through the angles taken in stories, editorials and comment pieces."[29] The British press routinely used the word *migrant* over *refugee*, a word that Daniel Trilling wrote "appears shorn of context; without even an im- or an em- attached to it to indicate that the people it describes have histories or futures. Instead, it implies an endless present: they are migrants, they move, it's what they do."[30]

One example of this reframing of the humanitarian emergency into a divisive us-versus-them situation comes from Farage's April 2015 comments. In the same week that more than 930 refugees drowned trying to reach Italy, Farage stated that Britain was unable to accept refugees and even questioned whether those

[25] Mike Berry et al., "UK Press Is the Most Aggressive in Reporting on Europe's 'Migrant' Crisis," *The Conversation*, March 14, 2016, https://theconversation.com/uk-press-is-the-most-aggressive-in-reporting-on-europes-migrant-crisis-56083.

[26] Mike Berry et al., "Press Coverage of the Refugee and Migrant Crisis in the EU: A Content Analysis of Five European Countries," United Nations High Commissioner for Refugees, December 2015, https://www.unhcr.org/56bb369c9.html.

[27] Berry et al., "Press Coverage."

[28] Berry et al., "Press Coverage."

[29] Berry et al., "UK Press."

[30] Daniel Trilling, "How the Media Contributed to the Migrant Crisis," *The Guardian*, August 1, 2019, https://www.theguardian.com/news/2019/aug/01/media-framed-migrant-crisis-disaster-reporting.

Fig. 6.1. UKIP, *Breaking Point* poster, 2016.

fleeing were true refugees. He made distinctions stating that it would be "fine" for Britain to offer a "helping hand" specifically to Christian refugees.[31] During this period, the Conservative mayor of London, Boris Johnson, supplemented the narrative of "threat" by suggesting that military involvement might be needed in order to "choke off the problem at source."[32]

Another instance of this fearmongering was the infamous Breaking Point poster (fig. 6.1). Fewer than ten days before Britons would vote on the referendum, Farage unveiled a poster showing a long queue of refugees, primarily people of color, with the slogan "Breaking point: The EU has failed us all" and the subheading "We must break free of the EU and take back control of our borders." *The Guardian* reported that the photograph being used was of refugees crossing the Croatia-Slovenia border in 2015 and that the "only prominent white person in the photograph obscured by a box of text."[33] Along with a number of politicians, including Boris Johnson, responding by distancing themselves from Farage, there were also complaints launched to police stating that the poster was inciting racial hatred and that it breached UK race laws.[34] Social media users were also quick to point out that the poster shared concerning similarities to

---

[31] Tom Mctague, "Send Them Back! Farage Backs Australian PM's Policy of Returning All Migrants to Stop 'Millions' More Trying to Cross the Mediterranean," *DailyMail.com*, April 22, 2015, https://www.dailymail.co.uk/news/article-3050376/Send-Farage-calls-fleeing-migrants-turned-away-stop-millions-trying-cross-Mediterranean.html.

[32] Mctague, "Send Them Back!"

[33] Rowena Mason and Heather Stewart, "Nigel Farage Anti-Migrant Poster Reported to Police," *The Guardian*, June 16, 2016, https://www.theguardian.com/politics/2016/jun/16/nigel-farage-defends-ukip-breaking-point-poster-queue-of-migrants.

[34] Mason and Stewart, "Nigel Farage."

HOW THE FAR RIGHT WENT MAINSTREAM 101

Nazi propaganda footage of migrants that had been shown in a BBC documentary from 2005.[35]

Farage defended the Breaking Point poster by claiming that "most of the people coming are young males," and the "EU has made a fundamental error that risks the security of everybody."[36] In these comments, he played on long-standing racist and orientalist stereotypes that construct black and brown males as violent and sexual predators.[37] Farage went on to claim without evidence that "very few people that came into Europe last year [2015] would actually qualify as genuine refugees."[38] He tied refugees to violent attacks, claiming that individuals behind violence in Europe came to the continent "posing as refugees," and insinuated that those fleeing persecution, bombs, and mass violence were likely to be "jihadi terrorists" rather than refugees.[39] This rhetoric, supplemented by British tabloid media, dehumanized the men, women, and children seeking safety in Europe and painted them as a threat. As such, Farage and the Leave.EU campaign, along with the far-right anti-Muslim voices that had existed in British society for decades, used the humanitarian crisis for political propaganda.

Populism on the International Stage

The reference to Nazi propaganda was also made by the Leave.EU campaign. While Farage was the face of the campaign, it was bankrolled by Aaron Banks, a millionaire insurance magnate, and its communications were managed by Andy Wigmore. Banks, a former Tory Party member, used some of his own fortune—a reported £7.5 million—to fund the Leave.EU campaign.[40] The three styled themselves as the "bad boys of Brexit" and utilized social media to tap into the grievances of the white working class.[41] During an interview with Emma Briant of Essex University, Wigmore reportedly praised Nazi propaganda, stating that

---

[35] @cdbeaton, "Your new poster resembles outright Nazi propaganda, @Nigel_Farage. Thanks to @brendanjharkin for pointing it out," Twitter, June 16, 2016, 11:57 a.m., https://twitter.com/cdbea ton/status/743397112923230212. See also @pmdfoster, "Can you spot the difference? The @Nigel_ Farage Breaking Point poster from 2016, and a Hungarian government 'information' poster during the current parliamentary election campaign. The exact same photo. #hungaryelections," Twitter, April 5, 2018, 8:32 a.m., https://twitter.com/pmdfoster/status/981887263205453824?lang=en.

[36] Mason and Stewart, "Nigel Farage."

[37] Ella Cockbain and Waqas Tufail, "Failing Victims, Fuelling Hate: Challenging the Harms of the 'Muslim Grooming Gangs' Narrative," Race and Class 61, no. 3 (January 6, 2020): pp. 3–32.

[38] Mason and Stewart, "Nigel Farage."

[39] Mason and Stewart, "Nigel Farage."

[40] Martin Fletcher, "Arron Banks: The Man Who Bought Brexit," New Statesman, October 13, 2016, https://www.newstatesman.com/politics/uk/2016/10/arron-banks-man-who-bought-brexit.

[41] "'Brexit Bad Boy' Andy Wigmore and Why Praising the Nazis Is Never a Good Idea," The Guardian, April 17, 2018, https://www.theguardian.com/politics/shortcuts/2018/apr/17/brexit-bad-boy-andy-wigmore-and-why-praising-the-nazis-is-never-a-good-idea.

"[t]he propaganda machine of the Nazis—if you take away all the hideous horror and that kind of stuff—it was very clever, the way they managed to do what they did."[42] While all three men could not be further from the working class, they understood the political currency of tapping into the white working-class resentment.

Leave.EU utilized populist tactics by stoking fears about purportedly uncontrolled immigration and a Muslim invasion—messaging that targeted populations of primarily white working class Britons. A March 2019 *New Yorker* piece reported that a "typical Leave.EU post on Facebook warned voters that 'immigration without assimilation equals invasion.' A post about the dangers of 'free movement' within the EU was accompanied by a photograph of ticking explosives."[43] White Leave-voting Britons told a reporter that "Muslims had changed their community, and that they wanted to 'get [their] country' back."[44] It was hardly an expression of policy but rather emotional responses fueled by resentment and hatred, and they viewed voting for the referendum as an expression of these feelings. Banks understood this and stated that "[t]he remain campaign featured fact, fact, fact, fact, fact. It just doesn't work. You have got to connect with people emotionally. It's the Trump success."[45]

Banks referenced Donald Trump because the Leave campaign looked for inspiration from Trump's presidential campaign, which explicitly relied on and amplified racist, xenophobic, and Islamophobic attitudes. The Leave. EU campaign had connections with Cambridge Analytica (CA), an election-management company employed by the Trump campaign in the United States. A former CA employee testified that the company had analyzed data for the Leave.EU campaign.[46] In yet another reference to Nazi propaganda, the head of the Strategic Communication Laboratories (SCL) Group, the parent company of CA, Nigel Oakes told Briant that Hitler "didn't have a problem with the Jews at all, but the people didn't like the Jews. . . . So he just leveraged an artificial enemy."[47]

---

[42] Emma Briant, "Three Explanatory Essays Giving Context and Analysis to Submitted Evidence" (Digital, Culture, Media and Sport Committee Inquiry into Fake News, UK Parliament, April 2018), https://www.parliament.uk/globalassets/documents/commons-committees/culture-media-and-sport/Dr-Emma-Briant-Explanatory-Essays.pdf.

[43] Ed Caesar, "The Chaotic Triumph of Arron Banks, the 'Bad Boy of Brexit,'" *The New Yorker*, March 18, 2019, https://www.newyorker.com/magazine/2019/03/25/the-chaotic-triumph-of-arron-banks-the-bad-boy-of-brexit.

[44] Caesar, "Chaotic Triumph."

[45] Maya Oppenheim, "Who's in Nigel Farage's Gold Brexit Gang Photo with Donald Trump," *Independent*, November 14, 2016, https://www.independent.co.uk/news/people/donald-trump-nigel-farage-photo-arron-banks-raheem-kassam-andy-wigmore-garry-gunster-a7416836.html.

[46] Alex Hern, "Cambridge Analytica Did Work for Leave.EU, Emails Confirm," *The Guardian*, July 30, 2019, https://www.theguardian.com/uk-news/2019/jul/30/cambridge-analytica-did-work-for-leave-eu-emails-confirm.

[47] Emma Briant, "Transcript" (Digital, Culture, Media and Sport Committee Inquiry into Fake News, UK Parliament, April 2018), p. 4. https://www.parliament.uk/globalassets/documents/commons-committees/culture-media-and-sport/Dr-Emma-Briant-Explanatory-Essays.pdf.

He added, "Well that's exactly what Trump did. He leveraged a Muslim ... I mean, you know, it's ... it was a real enemy. Isis is real, but how big a threat is Isis really to America?"[48] CA was embroiled in a scandal related to revelations that, beginning in 2014, the company had harvested the personal data of millions of Facebook users without their consent. During parliamentary investigation into CA and its role in the Brexit campaign, Damian Collins, a Conservative member of parliament (MP) and the chairman of the Digital, Culture, Media, and Sport Committee, noted that the Leave.EU campaign relied on "extreme messaging around immigration" and used data analytics to target voters worried about the issue.[49] In 2018, following investigations of the company in both the United States and United Kingdom, CA and SCL ceased operations.[50]

Farage leveraged the refugee crisis to stoke fears about a cultural threat, and Leave.EU centered racist and xenophobic attitudes. In a campaign that sought to define and defend the "true" British identity, immigrants of color and Muslims in particular represented the ultimate "other" to British values and culture. It is through this "other" that racism is inserted in the populist message.[51] While Islamophobia has always been present in British society, Brexit—a campaign rooted in populist tactics centering on immigration as its primary issue— brought it to the national stage.

The four components of populism are "a distrust of corrupt or out of touch power elites[,] a fear of the destruction of national cultures and identities[,] relative deprivation[,] and a dealignment between mainstream parties and electorates."[52] Each of these components incorporates or is intertwined with racism and racialization. In the British context, along with the United States and much of Europe, "corrupt leaders" failing to limit or stop immigration in particular Muslim immigration are framed as threatening national culture. Those who are generally supportive of this framework are often white working-class communities who feel the effects of growing economic inequality as a result of the global financial crisis, hyper-capitalism, the end of industrial and blue-collar jobs, and the erosion of social welfare state but who blame immigrants and people of color for the current state. They feel forgotten and let down by mainstream parties and thus support those who claim to be "outsiders" to politics who defend the country's "true" citizens, as Farage and UKIP marketed themselves.

---

[48] Briant, "Transcript."

[49] "Fake News Inquiry Publishes Evidence from Essex Expert," University of Essex, April 17, 2018, https://www.essex.ac.uk/news/2018/04/17/essex-propaganda-expert-gives-evidence-to-fake-news-inquir.

[50] "Cambridge Analytica and British Parent Shut Down after Facebook Scandal," Reuters, May 2, 2018, https://www.reuters.com/article/us-faceboook-privacy/cambridge-analytica-and-parent-scl-elections-shutting-down-idUSKBN1I32L7.

[51] Rattansi, "Racism."

[52] Rattansi, "Racism."

While Islamophobia has always been present in British society, Brexit brought it to the national stage.

Some supporters of the exit from the EU expressed concerns with a loss of sovereignty. However, the Leave.EU campaign harped on populist and racist sentiments. In a deadly and shocking event leading up to the June 2016 referendum, Thomas Mair, a fifty-three-year-old unemployed gardener, shot and stabbed Jo Cox, a Labour Party MP.[53] In the ensuing investigations, law enforcement found that Mair held deeply racist and anti-immigrant views. While he wrote about defending the "white race," his "greatest obsession" was his resentment toward "white people whom he condemned in his writings as 'the collaborators': the liberals, the left and the media."[54] As he stabbed the forty-one-year-old MP, Mair reportedly shouted "This is for Britain," "Keep Britain independent," and "Britain first."[55] While Mair's racist and far-right views had been present long before the deadly murder, an observer concluded that "they germinated during the febrile countdown to the EU referendum."[56]

A week after the brutal and horrific murder, the Brexit referendum occurred on June 23, 2016, with the results causing widespread shock as the majority of Britons voted to leave the EU. In the four days following the vote, the National Police Chiefs' Council reported that reported hate crimes increased by 57 percent in comparison to the corresponding four day period a month before.[57] Media reported that cases of religious and racially motivated hate crimes increased by 23 percent in the eleven months after Brexit.[58] This indicates that the Brexit campaign had set the stage for the right-wing, populist shift in mainstream politics.

In November 2016, the world watched as Donald Trump was declared the 45th president of the United States following a populist campaign that stoked racism, xenophobia, and Islamophobia. The two campaigns converged when the "bad boys of Brexit" met Trump just days after his win, with Farage becoming the first British politician to meet the president-elect. Much has been written about

---

[53] Kester Aspden, "The Making of a Bedsit Nazi: Who Was the Man Who Killed Jo Cox?," *The Guardian*, December 6, 2019, https://www.theguardian.com/news/2019/dec/06/bedsit-nazi-man-killed-jo-cox-thomas-mair.

[54] Ian Cobain et al., "The Slow-Burning Hatred That Led Thomas Mair to Murder Jo Cox," *The Guardian*, November 23, 2016, https://www.theguardian.com/uk-news/2016/nov/23/thomas-mair-slow-burning-hatred-led-to-jo-cox-murder.

[55] Ian Cobain and Matthew Taylor, "Far-Right Terrorist Thomas Mair Jailed for Life for Jo Cox Murder," *The Guardian*, November 23, 2016, https://www.theguardian.com/uk-news/2016/nov/23/thomas-mair-found-guilty-of-jo-cox-murder.

[56] Cobain et al., "Slow-Burning Hatred."

[57] "Post Brexit, Post Trump Islamophobia," Muslim Engagement and Development, October 2017, https://www.mend.org.uk/wp-content/uploads/2017/10/Post-Brexit-Post-Trump-Islamophobia.pdf.

[58] May Bulman, "Brexit Vote Sees Highest Spike in Religious and Racial Hate Crimes Ever Recorded," *Independent*, July 10, 2017, https://www.independent.co.uk/news/uk/home-news/racist-hate-crimes-surge-record-high-after-brexit-vote-new-figures-reveal-a7829551.html.

HOW THE FAR RIGHT WENT MAINSTREAM   105

the similarities between Leave.EU and Trump's campaign in stoking hatred and fear among the white working class in their respective countries in order to mobilize voters.[59] Given that Islamophobia was already present in both countries and, thus, an easy and electorally effective tactic, both populist campaigns had focused on and amplified anti-Muslim and anti-immigrant fearmongering.

Invasion and threats of overtaking the country were consistent themes not just in the mainstream British political scene but also across nativist politicians in Europe and the United States. In a May 2019 BBC interview, Farage recognized how his campaign was changing politics in Europe, stating that "[the Breaking Point poster] has transformed European politicians."[60] These individuals have pandered to the far-right electorate, positioning them as the "real people" who are victimized by the "silent majority." The claim of victimhood is expanded by incorporating conspiracy theories, such as the racist "great replacement" or "white genocide" theory, a far-right claim that the migration of people of color to the west seeks to destroy and replace the "white race."[61] The white-nationalist gunman in the deadly March 2019 attacks in Christchurch, New Zealand, referred to this theory as the rationale for his deadly rampage targeting two mosques in a mass shooting killing fifty-one Muslim worshippers as they prayed.[62] In the last half of the second decade of the 21st century, leading politicians like Hungary's Viktor Orbán and French far-right politician Marine Le Pen have promoted this dangerous and racist belief.[63] Furthermore, the EU incorporated tinges of this theory as it rebranded its head of migration policy as "the commissioner for protecting the European way of life,"[64] accommodating the demands of far-right challengers. The Brexit campaign played on similar tropes by likening immigration to invasion and claiming that British identity was under threat. A 2018 Cambridge University study concluded that approximately 31 percent of Brexit voters subscribed to this conspiracy theory.[65]

[59] Adam Gabbatt, "'Trump and Brexit' Parallel Campaigns Built on Fear, Anger and Charisma," *The Guardian*, June 25, 2016, https://www.theguardian.com/us-news/2016/jun/25/donald-trump-nigel-farage-us-election-brexit.

[60] Andrew Marr Programme, "Nigel Farage: Breaking Point Poster 'Transformed Politics,'" BBC, May 12, 2019, https://www.bbc.co.uk/news/av/uk-politics-48244663.

[61] "Factsheet: White Genocide Conspiracy Theory," Bridge Initiative, February 3, 2020, https://bridge.georgetown.edu/research/factsheet-white-genocide-conspiracy-theory/.

[62] Mobashra Tazamal, "Christchurch, Immigration, and the Fear Mongering That Incites Hate," Bridge Initiative, April 10, 2019, https://bridge.georgetown.edu/research/christchurch-immigration-the-fear-mongering-that-incites-hate/.

[63] See Ivan Kalmar, "Islamophobia without Muslims? Not Only in Eastern Europe," ch. 8 in this volume; Marwan Mohammed, "France's Islamophobic Bloc and the 'Mainstreamization' of the Far Right," ch. 7 in this volume.

[64] Rattansi, "Racism."

[65] "Brexit and Trump Voters More Likely to Believe in Conspiracy Theories, Survey Study Shows," University of Cambridge, November 23, 2018, https://www.cam.ac.uk/research/news/brexit-and-trump-voters-more-likely-to-believe-in-conspiracy-theories-survey-study-shows.

From the Fringe to Ruling-Party Policy

The Brexit campaign also served as a conduit through which far-right voices were amplified and eventually mainstreamed. Anti-Muslim figures such as Tommy Robinson and Katie Hopkins had long been advancing hateful rhetoric. With Brexit and the growing rightward shift in politics, both retained mass followings on social media, as they called for Britain's exit from the EU and were given ample airtime by the press. In Hopkins's case, she was a part of the press, writing columns for *The Sun* and hosting a radio show for Leading Britain's Conversation (*LBC*). She used these outlets to issue gross and shocking anti-Muslim and anti-immigrant views, describing refugees as a "plague of feral humans" and "cockroaches."[66] While Hopkins's and Robinson's views about Muslims, immigrants, and refugees were extreme, they were simply an extension of the anti-Muslim sentiment common in the political right. Fears about immigration, terrorism, and threats to British identity and culture had been consistent themes in British society, and following Brexit, they were wholeheartedly adopted by the Conservative Party.

Widespread Islamophobia in the Conservative Party

Baroness Warsi's observation of the social acceptability of Islamophobia in British society is made even more clear by her party's own actions—or lack thereof. Today, Islamophobia is a normality within the Conservative party, as anti-Muslim rhetoric is present at all levels, from party members to elected representatives.[67] Given that UKIP generally slid from popularity following the approval of Brexit, the Conservatives have adopted much of the Euroskeptic party's anti-immigration platform in an effort to appeal to voters. Despite countless calls for an inquiry into the Conservative party's Islamophobia problem, the Tories continue to evade any responsibility, signaling to the wider public that anti-Muslim racism is acceptable.

Former British prime minister (PM) and current Conservative Party member Boris Johnson has a history of Islamophobia. In 2018, Johnson published a piece in *The Telegraph* in which he stated that Muslim women who wear the burqa

---

[66] "Factsheet: Katie Hopkins," Bridge Initiative, August 7, 2018, https://bridge.georgetown.edu/research/factsheet-katie-hopkins/.

[67] Mobashra Tazamal, "I've Been Researching Islamophobia for Years—Don't Let Anyone Tell You There Isn't an Epidemic within the Tory Party," *Independent*, November 18, 2019, https://www.independent.co.uk/voices/islamophobia-conservative-party-racism-boris-johnson-muslim-inquiry-a9207191.html.

look like "letterboxes" and "bank robbers."[68] In the week following the article, Tell Mama, an organization that monitors Islamophobia, found that anti-Muslim incidents increased by 375 percent, from eight incidents in one week to thirty-eight incidents in the following week.[69] Furthermore, an August 2018 investigation by *The Sunday Times* revealed that Johnson's official Facebook page contained "hundreds of Islamophobic messages," including "calls to ban Islam [and] deport Muslims and 'vile' attacks on London Mayor Sadiq Khan."[70] To illustrate the acceptance and approval of Islamophobia, an independent panel of the Tory Party cleared Johnson of charges that his comments constituted a violation of the party's code of conduct.[71]

Despite Johnson's clear track record of racist statements, the British public voted for him to lead the country in December 2019. The Conservatives also triumphed in the election by winning seats previously held by the Labour Party and gaining an overwhelming majority in Parliament. This victory, as Nesrine Malik observed, served as a "national endorsement for its [the Conservatives'] intolerance of Muslims."[72]

Support for the party is not shocking, given that Islamophobia is persistent among British society and especially among the Tories. A September 2020 report by Hope Not Hate found that nearly 60 percent of Conservative members had a negative attitude toward Muslims.[73] Almost half of the party members (47 percent) believed that Islam is "a threat to the British way of life," and 58 percent believed in the anti-Muslim conspiracy theory about "no-go zones."[74] Hope Not Hate found that this figure "rose to 66% of those who backed Boris Johnson in the 2019 leadership election."[75] When asked about discrimination faced by British Muslims, only 6 percent of party members believed it to be a serious problem, with this figure dropping to just 3 percent among Johnson supporters.[76]

---

[68] Boris Johnson, "Denmark Has Got It Wrong: Yes, the Burka Is Oppressive and Ridiculous—but That's Still no Reason to Ban It," *The Telegraph*, August 5, 2018, https://www.telegraph.co.uk/news/2018/08/05/denmark-has-got-wrong-yes-burka-oppressive-ridiculous-still/.

[69] Nazia Parveen, "Boris Johnson's Burqa Comments 'Led to Surge in Anti-Muslim Attacks,'" *The Guardian*, September 2, 2019, https://www.theguardian.com/politics/2019/sep/02/boris-johnsons-burqa-comments-led-to-surge-in-anti-muslim-attacks.

[70] Joe Watts, "Boris Johnson's Facebook Page Hosts Hundreds of Islamophobic Comments after Burqa Row," *Independent*, August 19, 2018, https://www.independent.co.uk/news/uk/politics/boris-johnson-facebook-page-islamophobic-comments-burqa-row-anti-muslim-a8498021.html.

[71] "Boris Johnson Cleared over Burqa Comments," *The Guardian*, December 20, 2018, https://www.theguardian.com/politics/2018/dec/20/boris-johnson-cleared-over-burqa-comments.

[72] Nesrine Malik, "The Tories Aren't Ashamed of Their Islamophobia: They're Proud of It," *The Guardian*, October 7, 2020, https://www.theguardian.com/commentisfree/2020/oct/07/tories-islamophobia-proud-muslims-scapegoat.

[73] "The Cultural Problem of Islamophobia in the Conservative Party," Hope Not Hate, September 30, 2020, https://www.hopenothate.org.uk/2020/09/30/the-cultural-problem-of-islamophobia-in-the-conservative-party/.

[74] "Cultural Problem."

[75] "Cultural Problem."

[76] "Cultural Problem."

In the past few years, activists and organizations have called attention to the prevalence of Islamophobia within the ruling party, as numerous dossiers have collected hundreds of cases of anti-Muslim and racist sentiment expressed by Tory Party members, representatives, and elected officials.[77] In May 2019, a number of comments advanced the great replacement conspiracy theory, incorporating dehumanizing rhetoric and advancing anti-Muslim racism.[78] Comments made by people alleging to be part of the Conservative Party included "We don't have a politician strong enough in the UK to lead us away from this infestation," "They cause mayhem wherever they decide to invade," and one claiming that "their plan is to turn this country into an Islamic state."[79] In November 2019, old articles from 2002–03 written by Andrew Browne, a Tory candidate and former aide to Boris Johnson, surfaced in which he argued, "It is not through letting in terrorists that the government's policy of mass migration—especially from the third world—will claim the most lives. It is through letting in too many germs."[80] Despite this revelation, Johnson went on to win in the December 2019 general election. Such rhetoric from Browne and others dehumanized Muslims and refugees by describing them as an "infestation" and "aliens," and the reference to "invade" follows the larger conversation that was initiated by Farage's Brexit campaign.[81]

The examples of horrid anti-Muslim sentiments within the party are voluminous. In April 2019, *Buzzfeed* compiled a list of twenty people claiming to be Tory members making anti-Muslim statements, such as posting about a "Muslim invasion" and the white genocide conspiracy theory; this included one individual calling Muslims "muzz rats" and "sub human scum" in a closed Facebook group. He further wrote, "This lot should be rounded up and put on a boat home." One woman wrote that "Britain has an Islamic problem," while another alleged Tory Party member accused the government and the EU of "facilitating Hijrah," which he called "Muslim conquest by emigration." In another comment alluding to an "invasion," a woman who claimed to be a Tory member wrote, "When I look around London, there's no sound of the English language it's completely Asian, what have you done to make me feel like a foreigner in my own country,

---

[77] Rowena Mason, "300 Allegations of Tory Islamophobia Sent to Equality Watchdog," *The Guardian*, March 5, 2020, https://www.theguardian.com/politics/2020/mar/05/300-allegations-of-tory-islamophobia-sent-to-equality-watchdog.

[78] "Dossier Exposes More Than 100 Accusations of Islamophobia and Racism from Conservative Party Members," *ITV News*, May 17, 2019, https://www.itv.com/news/2019-05-17/dossier-expo ses-more-than-100-cases-of-islamophobia-and-racism-from-people-claiming-to-be-conservative-party-members.

[79] "Dossier."

[80] Rowena Mason, "Tory Candidate Faces Calls to Quit over 'Disgusting Racism,'" *The Guardian*, November 11, 2019, https://www.theguardian.com/politics/2019/nov/11/tory-candidate-anthony-browne-faces-calls-quit-over-disgusting-racism.

[81] Caesar, "Chaotic Triumph."

HOW THE FAR RIGHT WENT MAINSTREAM   109

you have gone ahead and decided with Merkel and Junker to flood Britain with Muslims from around the world." Furthermore, a male Tory member shared a post claiming that "Islam wants our entire culture." *Buzzfeed* stated that it had handed over this information to the Conservative Party headquarters, but it was unclear what, if any, action was taken by the party.[82]

The party has failed to be transparent about its oversight process regarding this widespread problem. Importantly, a number of Muslim Conservative Party members have revealed their personal experiences of Islamophobia within the party.[83] Nevertheless, the party has refused to provide information regarding the investigation and suspension process, as it has never revealed how many members have been suspended. Furthermore, a March 2019 investigation by *The Guardian* found that at least fifteen previously suspended members had been "quietly reinstated."[84] It found that "in the majority of cases where a councillor was reprimanded for retweeting or sharing offensive content, they were later readmitted to the party."[85] One such case involved the Councilor David Abbott, who was suspended in April 2019 for anti-Muslim comments, such as writing on Facebook that "[t]he philosophy seems to be 'breed for Islam,' thus the percentage of the population who follow the 'religion of peace' will significantly increase."[86] By May 2019, Abbott appeared to be reinstated as a Conservative councilor.

In 2019, during the run-up to the general election, Tory Party candidates promised to carry out an inquiry into Islamophobia in the party.[87] However, the promise was short-lived, as newly elected PM Johnson retracted his earlier commitment, instead saying that the party would look into broader issues and how it handles discrimination complaints.[88] Much like the "All Lives Matter" response to the Black Lives Matter movement and demand for racial justice, the

---

[82] Alex Wickham, "Anti-Muslim Tory Members on Facebook Are Telling One Another to Stop Sajid Javid from Becoming Prime Minister," *Buzzfeed News*, April 8, 2019, https://www.buzzfeed.com/alexwickham/tory-islamophobia-facebook-stop-sajid-javid?utm_source=dynamic&utm_campaign=bfsharetwitter.

[83] Alex Wickham, "These Leaked Emails Reveal Number 10 Apologised after Conservative HQ Failed to Respond to Islamophobia Complaints," *Buzzfeed News*, March 11, 2019, https://www.buzzfeed.com/alexwickham/number-10-apology-conservative-hq-islamophobia.

[84] Frances Perraudin and Simon Murphy, "Tory Islamophobia Row: 15 Suspended Councillors Quietly Reinstated," *The Guardian*, March 24, 2019, https://www.theguardian.com/politics/2019/mar/24/tory-islamophobia-row-15-suspended-councillors-quietly-reinstated.

[85] Perraudin and Murphy, "Tory Islamophobia Row."

[86] Basit Mahmood, "Conservative Party Slammed for 'Quietly Reinstating' Councillor Who Made Anti-Muslim Comments," *Metro*, November 21, 2019, https://metro.co.uk/2019/11/21/conservative-party-slammed-quietly-reinstating-councillor-made-anti-muslim-comments-11197712/.

[87] "Tory Leadership Rivals Back Islamophobia Inquiry," BBC, June 19, 2019, https://www.bbc.co.uk/news/uk-politics-48688268.

[88] Kevin Rawlinson, "Tories Accused of Ignoring Islamophobia after Dropping Inquiry," *The Guardian*, December 17, 2019, https://www.theguardian.com/politics/2019/dec/17/equalities-professor-to-head-tory-inquiry-into-discrimination-in-party.

party's insistence on focusing on such broad and vague issues only signals to the wider public that Islamophobia is not an issue to be taken seriously. Further demonstrating the party's disinterest in tackling this issue, the promise for any type of inquiry related to this matter has yet to be carried out.

Despite the plethora of evidence confirming the existence of Islamophobia at structural and institutional levels, the party refuses to act, thereby maximizing the harms caused by anti-Muslim racism. The haphazard responses of random suspensions appear to be public relations stunts in response to media scrutiny. Once the focus is off, the party reinstates individuals with little evidence of actual consequences in place. The party does not hold any willingness to root out bigots among its own ranks.

Why has the ruling party not distanced itself from such divisive, hateful, and dangerous rhetoric and theories? Data shows that the majority of Conservative members hold Islamophobic views.[89] In an effort to avoid alienating its membership and losing electoral support, the party has adopted and accepted anti-Muslim racism as part of its platform, causing the Runnymede Trust to conclude that the government is pursuing a white-nationalist agenda.[90] The party believes that it has more to lose if it decides to come out against Islamophobia and instead has chosen to tacitly accept it. Furthermore, the individual behind the Mates Jacob Twitter account that has been documenting Islamophobia within the party and providing information to media organizations has noted that "[t]he scale of the problem—which would become immediately apparent to a genuinely independent inquiry—is so bad that it's preferable to get the bad coverage for ducking the issue than get the worse coverage that would result if the truth came out."[91] The ruling party's failure to explicitly condemn Islamophobia signals to the wider public that anti-Muslim racism is acceptable. The continual normalization of Islamophobia in British society creates a hostile and dangerous environment for Muslims.

Conclusion

Islamophobia has soared in the past two decades, a period in which massive global changes have taken place. The world has experienced increasing economic inequality, devastating wars, mass protests, social movements, multiple financial crises, and changes in the global order. In response, right-wing populism

---

[89] "Cultural Problem."

[90] Haroon Siddique, "UK Government Accused of Pursuing 'White Nationalist' Agenda," *The Guardian*, December 29, 2020, https://www.theguardian.com/politics/2020/dec/29/uk-government-accused-pursuing-white-nationalist-agenda-runnymede-trust.

[91] Interview with @matesjacob, November 15, 2019.

HOW THE FAR RIGHT WENT MAINSTREAM   111

has mushroomed across Europe. Populists claim to be speaking for the "true" citizens and blame mainstream politicians for favoring the "other" (i.e., Muslims) over them. Right-wing and far-right voices pushed anti-Muslim rhetoric to dangerous extremes and were allowed to do so without much opposition, as the media and political establishment generally agreed with these sentiments.

Britain's political shift toward the right is part of a broader trend across Europe. The Brexit campaign by Leave.EU accelerated this change by utilizing populist tactics exploiting anti-Muslim racism and xenophobia to mobilize white working-class voters. For the majority who voted to leave the EU, the data demonstrated that racist beliefs played a role in their decision.[92] The ruling Conservative Party effectively adopted Islamophobia by instrumentalizing these attitudes and willfully ignoring its infestation across every rank. Ultimately, the party decided that it was politically beneficial to ignore the severity of anti-Muslim racism, given that its voting base holds these views. This choice signals to the wider public that Islamophobia is welcomed, as the governing party rubber-stamps discrimination and violence against British Muslims.

[92] Gabbatiss, "Brexit."

7

France's Islamophobic Bloc and the "Mainstreamization" of the Far Right

Marwan Mohammed

Questioning the place and role of the far right in the emergence, development, and current manifestations of Islamophobia requires a detour through social and political history. In the European context, the rise of Islamophobia is regularly associated with the growth of political and electoral forces from the radical right and neofascist movements over the last three decades.[1] One recent development, however, has been the penetration and legitimization—also called the *mainstreamization*—of far-right ideas, theses, and opinions in politics.[2] The idea that the Muslim presence poses a problem as soon as it becomes visible crosses both sides of the political field. This universality is particularly evident in the rhetorical strategies, as well as the political measures proposed, to solve what these different actors call the Muslim problem.[3] France is one of the Western democracies that goes the furthest in developing laws and institutional arrangements for the control, discipline, and legal discrimination of Muslim populations, limiting the legal means to fight against Islamophobia.

Recently, the French government dissolved the two main organizations fighting against Islamophobia on the pretext that their objectives could be seen as incitement to hatred and because of unmoderated hateful comments on their Facebook page,[4] without any prior punitive action or legal sanction.[5] This

[1] Farid Hafez, "Shifting Borders: Islamophobia as the Cornerstone for Building Pan-European Right-Wing Unity," *Patterns of Prejudice* 48, no. 5 (2014): pp. 1–21.

[2] Aristotle Kallis, "Breaking the Taboos and "Mainstreaming" the Extreme: The Debates on Restricting Islamic Symbols in Europe," in *Right-Wing Populism in Europe: Politics and Discourse*, ed. Ruth Wodak, Majid Khosravinik, and Brigitte Mral (London: Bloomsbury Academic, 2013), pp. 55–70.

[3] The "Muslim problem" draws on the theoretical framework of the construction of public problems. Joseph Gusfield, *La Culture des problèmes publics: L'Alcool au volant; la production d'un ordre symbolique* [*The Culture of Public Problems: Drinking and Driving; the Production of a Symbolic Order*] (Paris: Economica, 2009).

[4] Marwan Mohammed, "Défendre un groupe social illégitime: Les Avocats dans la lutte contre l'islamophobie" ["Defending an Illegitimate Social Group: Lawyers in the Fight against Islamophobia"], *Communications* 2, no. 2 (2020): pp. 251–71.

[5] "Dissolution du CCIF: Une bataille juridique se profile contre la décision du gouvernement" ["Dissolution of the CCIF: A Legal Battle Looms against the Government's Decision"], *Le Monde*, December 31, 2020, https://www.lemonde.fr/societe/article/2020/12/31/dissolution-du-ccif-une-batai

FRANCE'S ISLAMOPHOBIC BLOC   113

political measure, denounced by many human rights organizations as an attack on freedom of opinion and association, was called for by Marine Le Pen,[6] leader of the main far-right party, the Republican Right, and then applauded by Manuel Valls, the Socialist former prime minister.[7] This chapter addresses Islamophobia across France's political spectrum, spanning views from the left to the extreme right. I argue that there is an "Islamophobic bloc" whose ideologies and rhetoric converge in the construction of a "Muslim problem." I first describe this process then demonstrate that it is the radical right in France that benefits from this contemporary mainstreaming of Islamophobia.

A Series of Anti-Muslim Events

The series of political events described here is one of the many public controversies concerning the presence of Muslims in French society. Although there are dozens of others, this one deserves attention because it allows us to grasp the multi-partisan and high-level forms of contemporary Islamophobia in France. On September 21, 2019, Laurent Bouvet shared on social media a refashioned poster from the Federation of Student Parents' Councils (FCPE), the largest organization of parents in France.[8] The original poster shows a Muslim woman wearing an Islamic headscarf and her daughter, with the caption: "Yes, I'm going on a school outing, so what? Secularism means welcoming all parents to school without exception" (fig. 7.1a). In reaction to this poster, Bouvet published a version modified by far right-wing militants,[9] replacing the photo

lle-juridique-se-profile-contre-la-decision-du-gouvernement_6064873_3224.html; "Dissolution de la Coordination contre le racisme et l'islamophobie, pour discours haineux" ["Dissolution of the Coordination against Racism and Islamophobia, for Hate Speech"], *Le Monde*, October 20, 2021, https://www.lemonde.fr/societe/article/2021/10/20/dissolution-de-la-coordination-contre-le-racisme-et-l-islamophobie-pour-discours-haineux_6099241_3224.html.

[6] @MLP_officiel, "Il faut dissoudre le CCIF et l'UOIF, structures qui ont en leur sein et développent une pensée islamiste, qui ont refusé d'être auditionnées par la commission d'enquête sénatoriale sur la radicalisation islamiste!" ["We must dissolve the CCIF and the UOIF, structures that have within them and develop Islamist thought, which refused to be heard by the Senate inquiry commission on Islamist radicalization!"], Twitter, October 30, 2020, https://twitter.com/mlp_officiel/status/1322114772951773184?lang=fr.

[7] @manuelvalls, "La dissolution du #CCIF est une bonne nouvelle et le fruit d' une action déterminée" ["The dissolution of the #CCIF is good news and the result of determined action"], Twitter, December 2, 2020, https://twitter.com/manuelvalls/status/1334114282187984897?lang=fr.

[8] "Une fédération de parents d'élèves va porter plainte contre Laurent Bouvet" ["A Parents' Federation Will File a Complaint against Laurent Bouvet"], *Le Monde*, September 25, 2019, https://www.lemonde.fr/societe/article/2019/09/25/une-federation-de-parents-d-eleves-va-porter-plainte-contre-laurent-bouvet_6012979_3224.html.

[9] "Affiche de campagne sur les mères voilées: La FCPE dépose une plainte" ["Campaign Poster on Veiled Mothers: The FCPE Files a Complaint]," *L'Express*, September 25, 2019, https://www.lexpress.fr/actualite/societe/affiche-de-campagne-sur-les-meres-voilees-la-fcpe-depose-une-plainte_2099539.html.

Fig. 7.1a. Laurent Bouvet, photo of FCPE poster, Facebook, n.d.
b. Laurent Bouvet, photo of modified FCPE poster, Facebook, n.d.

Adapted from: @ADM_Action, "L.Bouvet Printemps Républicain propage le racisme antimusulman assimilant les mères voilées, les musulmans aux terroristes. Le PR avec les identitaires font une campagne de haine contre @FCPE_nationale @gouvernementFR @jmblanquer @uvsq n'ont eu aucune reaction" ["L.Bouvet of Printemps Républicain propogates anti-Muslim racism, equating veiled mothers, Muslims with terrorists. The PR with the identities create a hate campaign against @FCPE_nationale @gouvernementFR @jmblanquer @uvsq had no reaction"], Twitter, September 23, 2019, https://twitter.com/ADM_Action/status/1176004416836648961?s=20&t=YvtFxUYScgl u9WH8KTwwSQ.

of the veiled woman and her child with one of two threatening, bearded Islamic State fighters dressed in military garb and armed with Kalashnikovs (fig. 7.1b),[10] thus portraying the woman and child as a terrorist threat and domestic enemy.

Bouvet is a professor of political science at the University of Versailles Saint-Quentin-en-Yvelines who stopped producing and publishing scientific research many years ago. He is also a polemicist, former member of the Socialist Party, and founder of Printemps Républicain, an organization claiming to belong to the left. He embodies a bourgeois, neoliberal, authoritarian, and republicanist center-left in France. Bouvet's ideas resonate as much on the right as on the center-left. In 2018, he was appointed as a member of the National Council of Secularism by the Minister of National Education, Jean-Michel Blanquer. Blanquer called the situation "a regrettable error" and stated on the news channel BFM TV that "the veil in itself is not desirable in our society."[11] On several occasions, the minister also expressed his opposition to veiled mothers going on school trips, even though his government has refused to propose a legislation for the time being.

The media and political uproar resumed shortly after Bouvet made his post. On October 11, 2019, during a plenary session of the Regional Council of Bourgogne-Franche-Comté, Julien Odoul, group leader and member of the national board of the Rassemblement National, which is the main extreme-right-wing party, humiliated a woman wearing a hijab who accompanied her fifth-grade son on a "My Republic and Me" school visit. After spotting her in the room, the far-right elected official took the microphone to ask her to leave the room or remove her hijab. Despite her dignified attitude, the image of this mother consoling her crying son in the media provoked a delayed and ambiguous wave of indignation from some left leaders, reminding observers that even when the aggressor is from the extreme right, solidarity with women wearing the hijab is not self-evident.

Notably, Odoul did not utilize explicitly xenophobic rhetoric but justified his action in the name of "secular principles" of "the law of the Republic" before he and his colleagues published a communiqué denouncing the "Islamist provocation" of women wearing the hijab.[12] In the course of a week, this debate was

---

[10] "Affiche sur les mères voilées en sortie scolaire parodiée: La FCPE porte plainte" ["Poster on Veiled Mothers on School Outings Parodied: The FCPE Files a Complaint]," *Le Parisian*, September 24, 2019, https://www.leparisien.fr/societe/affiche-sur-les-meres-voilees-en-sortie-scolaire-parod iee-la-fcpe-porte-plainte-24-09-2019-8158866.php.

[11] "Sorties scolaires: Blanquer juge le voile islamique 'pas souhaitable' mais rappelle qu'il n'est pas interdit" ["School Outings: Blanquer Deems the Islamic Veil 'Not Desirable' but Recalls That It Is Not Prohibited"], BFM TV, October 13, 2019, https://www.bfmtv.com/politique/sorties-scolaires-blanq uer-juge-le-voile-islamique-pas-souhaitable-mais-rappelle-qu-il-n-est-pas-interdit_AV-201910130 021.html.

[12] Rassemblement National au Conseil regional de Bourgogne Franche-Comte, "Communique de presse de Julien Odoul," Facebook, October 12, 2019, https://m.facebook.com/RassemblementNati onalBFC/photos/a.725052681227884/904960996570384?type=3&sfns=mo.

featured at least eighty-five times on television, with 286 people invited to participate, none of whom were women wearing a hijab.[13]

Meanwhile, viewers also heard the deputy director of the right-wing daily *Le Figaro* assert on the channel LCI that he "hates the Muslim religion" and refuses to stay on a bus when a veiled woman is there.[14] Similarly, LCI presenter Olivier Galzi compared the Islamic headscarf to an SS uniform.[15] Then, on October 22, Éric Ciotti, representative of the right-wing party Les Républicains, reintroduced a bill to prohibit the wearing of religious symbols by parents accompanying school outings.[16]

Throughout this series of events, groups across the political spectrum used similar linguistic elements to criticize Islam and Muslims. Rather than describe the tension between an immutable, white, and Catholic France and an unassimilable, nonwhite, and non-European population, they claimed to defend the "Republic" and "secularism" besieged by "Islamism."[17] In addition to sharing the same elements of language, these mainstream public actors circulated in the same media or ideological spaces, particularly that of the far right.[18] It was therefore unsurprising to see the omnipresent Bouvet on the *Novopress* website, which is known for spreading racist and conspiracy theories.[19] Another example is Patrick Kessel, the honorary president of the Comité Laïcité République (a branch of a fringe group of the Grand Orient of France, one of the French

---

[13] "Une semaine sur les chaînes d'info: 85 débats sur le voile, 286 invitations et 0 femme voilée" ["One Week on the News Channels: 85 Debates on the Veil, 286 Invitations and 0 Veiled Women"], *Liberation*, October 17, 2019, https://www.liberation.fr/checknews/2019/10/17/une-semaine-sur-les-chaines-d-info-85-debats-sur-le-voile-286-invitations-et-0-femme-voilee_1758162.

[14] " 'Je déteste la religion musulmane': Yves Thréard du 'Figaro' en roue libre sur le voile" [" 'I Hate the Muslim Religion': Yves Thréard of 'Figaro' Freewheeling on the Veil"], Les Inrocktuptibles, October 19, 2019, https://www.lesinrocks.com/actu/je-deteste-la-religion-musulmane-yves-threard-du-figaro-en-roue-libre-sur-le-voile-184873-15-10-2019/.

[15] "Le Journaliste Olivier Galzi compare le voile aux 'uniformes SS' sur LCI" ["Journalist Olivier Galzi Compares the Veil to 'SS Uniforms' on LCI"], *L'Obs*, October 17, 2019, https://www.nouvelobs.com/societe/20191017.OBS19931/le-journaliste-olivier-galzi-compare-le-voile-aux-uniformes-ss-sur-lci.html.

[16] "Interdiction du voile lors des sorties scolaires: Ce que contient la proposition de loi des sénateurs LR" ["Banning the Veil on School Outings: What's in the LR Senators' Proposed Law"], BFM TV, October 23, 2019, https://www.bfmtv.com/politique/parlement/interdiction-du-voile-lors-des-sorties-scolaires-ce-que-contient-la-proposition-de-loi-des-senateurs-lr_AN-201910230 056.html.

[17] Abdellali Hajjat and Marwan Mohammed, *Islamophobie: Comment les élites fabriquent le "problème musulman"* [*How the Elites Construct the "Muslim Problem"*] (Paris: La Découverte, 2013), ch. 3.

[18] Concerning the national written press, *Le Figaro, Causeur, Valeurs actuelles, Le Point*, and *Marianne* occupy central positions in the dissemination and popularization of Islamophobic theses, as do the news channels LCI, C'NEWS, and BFM TV.

[19] "La Gauche doit reconquérir les valeurs de la Nation et de la République: Entretien avec Laurent Bouvet, professeur à Sciences-po Paris" ["The Left Must Reconquer the Values of the Nation and the Republic: Interview with Laurent Bouvet, Professor at Sciences-Po Paris"], *Novopress*, December 16, 2011, https://fr.novopress.info/104790/la-gauche-doit-reconquerir-les-valeurs-de-la-nation-et-de-la-republique-entretien-avec-laurent-bouvet-professeur-a-sciences-po-paris-audio/.

Masonic federations), who accepts invitations from the far-right site *Riposte laïque*.[20] Contributors to this website have been condemned several times for inciting racial and religious hatred, as well as being apologists of right-wing terrorism.[21]

At the very highest level, President Emmanuel Macron, along with several of his ministers, agreed to promote the far-right magazine *Valeurs actuelles* by accepting a lengthy interview in which he shared his opinion on the incident at the plenary session of the Regional Council of Bourgogne-Franche-Comté. President Macron stated that "the elected representative of the Rassemblement National Julien Odoul has been caught! Apparently this woman is closer to the circles of political Islam than we thought."[22] President Macron thus validated the thesis of the Rassemblement National, Marine Le Pen's party, which presented the incident as the result of an "Islamist" manipulation rather than as a discriminatory and racist act of a far-right elected official. Besides the fact that the head of state blamed the victim and reversed the roles, he also gave a governmental dimension to the suspicion and presumption of duplicity that surrounds any public manifestation of Muslimness.

One would at least have expected the president to substantiate his accusations, especially in the columns of a press outlet that is at the forefront of the diffusion of racist ideas and opinions in France. Then, an inquiry by the newspaper *Libération* patently contradicted the thesis of "Islamist" manipulation, in that the president of the parent-teacher association noted that "it is precisely because of the small number of chaperones that Fatima E. found herself in this Dijon excursion."[23] Originally, she was not supposed to be able to participate. This mother, Fatima E., was in the middle of a move to a new house and had no childcare for her daughter yet managed to help the teacher who was organizing the visit. The reality was far from the accusations of "Islamism" and duplicity, encouraged

---

[20] "Patrick Kessel, président d'honneur du Comité Laïcité République" ["Patrick Kessel, Honorary President of the Comité Laïcité République"], *Riposte laïque*, January 19, 2009, https://ripostelaique.com/Patrick-Kessel-president-d-honneur.html.

[21] Pierre Cassan, "Riposte laïque condamné pour ses propos Islamophobes" ["*Riposte laïque* Condemned for Its Islamophobic Remarks"], *Riposte laïque*, March 23, 2012, https://www.liberation.fr/societe/2012/03/23/riposte-laique-condamne-pour-ses-propos-islamophobes_805330/; "Ultradroite et apologie du terrorisme" ["Alt-Right and Apology of Terrorism"], *Humanrights.media*, May 6, 2021, https://humanrights.media/ultradroite-apologie-terrorisme/.

[22] Geoffroy Lejeune, Louis de Raguenel, and Tugdual Denis, "Communautarisme: 'C'est un énorme problème pour nous,' reconnaît Emmanuel Macron" ["Communalism: 'It's a huge problem for us,' admits Emmanuel Macron"], Valeurs le club, October 30, 2019, https://www.valeursactuelles.com/clubvaleurs/politique/communautarisme-cest-un-enorme-probleme-pour-nous-reconnait-emmanuel-macron-112307.

[23] "L'élu RN Julien Odoul a-t-il été piégé par Fatima E., comme l'a affirmé Macron dans 'Valeurs actuelles'?" ["Was RN Elected Official Julien Odoul Framed by Fatima E., as Macron Claimed in 'Valeurs actuelles'?"], *Libération*, November 5, 2019, https://www.liberation.fr/checknews/2019/11/05/l-elu-rn-julien-odoul-a-t-il-ete-piege-par-fatima-e-comme-l-a-affirme-macron-dans-valeurs-actuelles_1761427.

118 MARWAN MOHAMMED

by President Macron, proclaimed by politicians from the left to the far right, journalists, and polemicists who criminalized and demonized this mother on television, radio, and social media.

This series of events demonstrates some of the ideological trends regarding the Muslim question that have been shared by political actors and opinion leaders from the republicanist left to the extreme right, particularly the "replacementist" rhetoric that influences all Islamophobic discourse in France. Certainly, the "great replacement" ideology of the supremacists differs from what I identify as an ideology of the "small replacement" among others, but both refer to a dialectic of conquest and conspiracy.

From "Great" to "Small" Replacement

Most of the political actors maintain distance, at least officially, from the great-replacement theory that inspired the white-supremacist terrorists who targeted and killed Latinos in a Walmart store in El Paso, Texas,[24] Jews in a synagogue in Pittsburgh, Pennsylvania,[25] and Muslims in a mosque in Christchurch, New Zealand.[26] The great-replacement theory owes its name to the far-right French writer Renaud Camus. The thesis is that Christian and white Europe is being invaded and threatened with extinction because of "massive" immigration, coupled with uncontrollable fertility and a capacity to numerically surpass and culturally dominate the "original" populations. In particular, Camus and his political and media allies, such as editorialist and presidential candidate Éric Zemmour,[27] focus on the supposedly massive and conquering presence of Muslim populations that are unassimilable.[28] The project thus consists

[24] "Walmart Shooter Allegedly Penned White Supremacist Rant in 'Bible of Evil,'" El Paso Times, August 4, 2019, https://eu.elpasotimes.com/story/news/2019/08/04/el-paso-shooting-patrick-crus ius-white-supremacist-manifesto/1914965001/.

[25] "How Gay Icon Renaud Camus Became the Ideologue of White Supremacy," The Nation, June 17, 2019, https://www.thenation.com/article/archive/renaud-camus-great-replacement-brenton-tarrant/.

[26] "La Théorie du 'grand remplacement,' de l'écrivain Renaud Camus aux attentats en Nouvelle-Zélande" ["The Theory of the 'Great Replacement,' from Writer Renaud Camus to Attacks in New Zealand"], Le Monde, November 22, 2019, https://www.lemonde.fr/les-decodeurs/article/2019/03/ 15/la-theorie-du-grand-remplacement-de-l-ecrivain-renaud-camus-aux-attentats-en-nouvelle-zela nde_5436843_4355770.html.

[27] C'NEWS, "Finkielkraut à l'Académie française: Finkie immortel!—CSD" ["Finkielkraut at the French Academy: Finkie Immortal!—CSD"], YouTube, April 11, 2014, https://www.youtube.com/ watch?v=JKaQ1YcfIxI#t=506.

[28] "Islam, 'grand remplacement,' place des femmes . . . dans son livre, Eric Zemmour Ressasse Ses Obsessions" ["Islam, 'Grand Replacement,' Place of Women . . . in His Book, Eric Zemmour Rehashes His Obsessions"], Le Monde, September 21, 2021, https://www.lemonde.fr/politique/article/2021/ 09/20/islam-grand-remplacement-place-des-femmes-dans-son-livre-eric-zemmour-ressasse-ses-obsessions_6095322_823448.html.

of excluding them from the national territory by various means of "remigration," ranging from compensation to mass deportation and making life impossible.[29] That Muslims are citizens does not matter; their presence is considered harmful and illegitimate.

Even if many public figures refer to the "great replacement" for what it is— a racist thesis and fascist project with an aim to get rid of Muslims and, more broadly, any presence deemed extra-European—far-right ideas, ideologues, and media continue to extend their ideological hold and presence in public debate. Sociologist Abdellali Hajjat demonstrates the growing space for and "mainstreaming" of media like *Valeurs actuelles*,[30] in which the theses of Renaud Camus are regularly defended and the hegemony of far-right ideas actively constructed. Consensus remains that the great-replacement theory is marginal and condemnable, but there are far fewer public voices linking the rise of the great-replacement ideology with the presence of what can be called *small-replacement* ideologues in the public sphere.

What I propose to designate as the ideology of small replacement is close to what Michel Foucault calls a "discursive formation"—that is, a set of ideological statements and schemes found in discourses, traditions, and systems of thought that may be radically different from or opposed to other subjects.[31] The notion of *small replacement* is not a scientific concept but an image and a formula created to show convergence, analogies, and kinship with the promoters of the *great replacement*. Ideologues of these two camps publicly oppose each other most of the time and come from different histories and political traditions. However, this dichotomy does not prevent consideration of their similarities and complementarity as well as of the spaces, notions, and reasoning that they share. In fact, there is an active movement of public figures, academics, and political organizations from both the right and certain branches of the left of people who share the same views on Muslims and participate in ongoing demonization and exclusion.[32] The partisan and philosophical bases of this movement are diverse and often opposed to each other on other issues, but they are united in constructing the Muslim presence as a problem and spreading the idea that "republican values" are urgently threatened.

---

[29] Renaud Camus, *Le Grand remplacement* [*The Great Replacement*], ed. David Reinharc (Neuilly-sur-Seine, France, 2011).

[30] Abdellali Hajjat, "L'Emprise de *Valeurs actuelles*" ["The Grip of *Valeurs actuelles*"], *Carnet de recherche racismes*, November 13, 2020, https://racismes.hypotheses.org/222.

[31] Michel Foucault, *L'Archéologie du savoir* [*The Archaeology of Knowledge*] (Paris: Gallimard, 1969).

[32] For an overview of the main promoters and beneficiaries of the "Islamophobic cause," see Hajjat and Mohammed, *Islamophobie*. In his book on "le grand confusianisme," political scientist Philippe Corcuff analyzes the anti-Muslim convergences that unite sections of the so-called republican left and different sectors of the right. Philippe Corcuff, *Le Grand confusianisme* (Paris: Textuel, 2020).

120   MARWAN MOHAMMED

Discussion of invasion and reconquest is persuasive in the small-replacement movement. If Camus believes that Islam is a threat in itself to the homeland, the nation, Christian civilization, and the values and people of France, then the ideologues of small replacement position themselves as defenders of progress, women's rights, freedom, and, above all, the scarecrows of the "values of the republic." Both defense of the white nation and protection of the secular republic are animated by the same argumentative structure that portrays a caricatured and overgeneralized Islam as an exogenous, threatening, and conquering reality that it is imperative to resist. For ideologues of the great replacement, demographic invasion and cultural conquest are intimately linked, with the latter derived from the former.[33] For agitators of the small replacement, the stake is to resist the substitution of the "way of life," "values," and "laws of the Republic" in the face of Muslim visibility, which is designated as a false nose of "Islamism" and presented as colonizing, underhanded, and hostile to pluralism and all liberties. The ideologues of the great replacement designate immigration and "Islam" as enemies, while the small-replacement voices point to communalism, Islamism, and political Islam, often targeting the same people. The confusion between Islam and Islamism and between defense of the nation and defense of the republic has reached the point that the extreme right has appropriated the language of the ideologues of the small replacement to avoid falling under anti-racism laws.

Great replacement adherents believe that the presence of Muslims and immigrants from former colonies (western and northern Africa) on national territory is illegitimate and advocate for their removal. Thought leaders and media representatives associated with the small-replacement movement, meanwhile, question the legitimacy of Muslim presence in institutions and increasingly in public space, as well as in the workplace and areas of recreation. They do not want to expel them, like Camus and his supporters do, but rather to discipline or to exclude them within borders. The stigmatization of Muslim visibility aims to prevent its routinization.

The method of small-replacement voices is therefore to demonize before turning to legal exclusions or to internal regulations but always in the name of progress and the defense of the Republic and with rare or implicit recourse to nationalist and patriotic rhetoric. With regard to the Muslim presence, the preferred political weapon of this small-replacement movement is the extension of religious neutrality to persons who and spaces that have never been targeted by laws related to separation of state and religion.

The original law, which was passed on December 9, 1905, required religious neutrality only in regard to the state and its representatives. Since the passage of a law in 2004 prohibiting religious symbols in schools, legislators have continued

---

[33] Camus, *Le Grand remplacement.*

to impose religious neutrality on citizens, mainly Muslims, and areas like the private sector, which have never been subject to these requirements. As such, it is an undertaking of "legal discrimination by capillarity,"[34] which is aimed at punishing any resistance to assimilation and invisibility.[35]

Rhetorical Cohesion of the Islamophobic Bloc

While solutions to the so-called Muslim problem differ among groups within the Islamophobic bloc, the convergence of their discursive and political devices is reflected in common discourses, legislative coalitions, and electoral alliances. The bloc shares several common conceptions. They view Muslims as dangerous "Islamists" or "fundamentalists" accused of fueling terrorism by promoting a "victim discourse." Their use of these categories also targets those who question the role of the racial dynamics of French society or organize on the basis of their minority status (in particular blacks, Muslims, and Arabs), who are then treated as "identitarians," "racialists," or "decolonialists." Those among the majority who value the freedom to organize and speak are reduced to the role of "useful idiots," "Islamo-leftists," or "collaborators."

The considerable influence of small-replacement ideologues comes from their ability to criminalize, silence, and exclude their targets. Contrary to the ideologues of the far right, with whom they regularly struggle and from whom it is difficult to distance themselves, these ideologues are "universalists" who protect French society from "communitarization." They do not fight against Muslims but against "Islamism," the "Salafists," the "Muslim Brotherhood," and "political Islam." With solid media and political communications, including those of Socialist former Prime Minister Valls and former Minister of National Education Blanquer,[36] they have managed to spread the idea that behind every woman wearing a headscarf, associate and activist fighting against Islamophobia, and public display of Islam is a male maneuvering to Islamize

---

[34] Hajjat and Mohammed, *Islamophobie*.

[35] Abdellali Hajjat, *Les Frontières de l'identité nationale: L'Injonction à l'assimilation en France métropolitaine et coloniale* [*The boundaries of national identity: The injunction to assimilation in metropolitan and colonial France*] (Paris: La Découverte, 2012).

[36] For instance, according to Valls, the hijab is either "a kerchief worn by elderly women" or "the claim of a political sign that comes to confront the French society." Bernard Gorce, "Ce que révèle la charge de Manuel Valls contre le voile" ["What Manuel Valls's Charge against the Headscarf Reveals"], *LaCroix*, April 5, 2016, https://www.la-croix.com/France/Politique/Ce-revele-charge-Manuel-Valls-contre-voile-2016-04-05-1200751324. The former minister stated that the hijab is "not desirable in society." "Pour Jean-Michel Blanquer, le voile islamique n'est 'pas souhaitable dans la société'" ["For Jean-Michel Blanquer, the Islamic Veil Is 'Not Desirable in Society'"], *Le Monde*, October 14, 2019, https://www.lemonde.fr/politique/article/2019/10/13/sibeth-ndiaye-et-jean-michel-blanquer-con damnent-l-elu-rn-qui-a-agresse-une-mere-voilee_6015346_823448.html.

French society. Any form of Muslim affirmation in public space is equated with an anti-French, antidemocratic, and anti-republican offensive.[37] This powerful machine of suspicion, criminalization, and exclusion is based on Islamophobic conspiracy theories.[38] Targeting Islam and Muslims on the pretext of combating "political Islam," small-replacement ideologues have facilitated an expansion of Islamophobia.

Therefore, it is unsurprising that confusion between visible religiosity and radicalization reaches the highest levels of the state. For instance, after the murder of four intelligence officers by a colleague who had converted to Islam, the debate on how to identify violent radicalization was revived.[39] Since 2015, experts and public authorities have been developing detection and warning systems with criteria that are regularly criticized for their scientific fragility and normative character, which are sometimes discriminatory and prejudicial to individual liberties.[40] After the atrocious massacre of the four intelligence officers, which was also humiliating for the state, the Minister of the Interior Christophe Castaner testified before the law commission of the National Assembly. He adopted a stance aimed at establishing an offensive state.[41] Questioned about the signs of radicalization that should alert citizens and institutions within the framework of the "society of vigilance" called for by President Macron, Castaner pointed out that "a rigorous religious practice, particularly exacerbated in the matter of Ramadan, is a sign that should make it possible to trigger an alert on these subjects."[42] He also stressed that a "change in behavior in the entourage, the wearing of a beard," whether an individual "kisses or no longer kisses," and if he "has a regular or ostentatious practice of ritual prayer" could all be considered signs of "radicalization."[43]

---

[37] Vincent Geisser, *La Nouvelle islamophobie* [*The New Islamophobia*] (Paris: La Découverte, 2003).

[38] Reza Zia-Ebrahimi, *Antisémitisme et islamophobie: Une histoire croisée* [*Antisemitism and Islamophobia: A Crossed History*] (Paris: Éditions Amsterdam, 2021); Alain Bertho, "L'État a-t-il le monopole du complotisme légitime?" ["Does the State Have a Monopoly on Legitimate Conspiracies?"], *Regards.fr*, December 4, 2020, http://www.regards.fr/idees-culture/article/l-etat-a-t-il-le-monopole-du-complotisme-legitime.

[39] "Radicalisation: 7 policiers ont été désarmés depuis l'attaque de la prefecture" ["Radicalization: 7 Police Officers Have Been Disarmed since the Attack on the Local Government Office"], *Europe 1*, October 30, 2019, https://www.europe1.fr/societe/radicalisation-7-policiers-ont-ete-desarmes-dep uis-lattaque-de-la-prefecture-3928405.

[40] Claire Donnet, "Les Signalements pour 'risque de radicalisation' dans les établissements scolaires en France, nouvel outil de régulation de l'islam" ["Reports of 'Risk of Radicalization' in French Schools, a New Tool for Regulating Islam"], *Déviance et société* 3, no. 3 (2020): pp. 420–52.

[41] "Christophe Castaner liste les signes de radicalisation? 'Vous avez une barbe vous-même,' lui répond un depute" ["Christophe Castaner Lists Signs of Radicalization? 'You Have a Beard Yourself,' Replies a Congressman"], *Europe 1*, October 9, 2019, https://www.europe1.fr/politique/christophe-castaner-liste-les-signes-de-radicalisation-religieuse-vous-avez-une-barbe-vous-meme-lui-rep ond-un-depute-3924324.

[42] "Christophe Castaner."

[43] "Christophe Castaner."

This conception of *radicalization* often accompanies the notion of *islamization*, which originated in the repertoire of the far right. However, it is now promoted and theorized by academics like Gilles Kepel[44] and, more recently, Bernard Rougier, who are both active promoters of the ideas of conquest, domination, and a purported Islamist "ecosystem" in the suburbs.[45] They defend the idea of including terrorist Islamism, militancy against Islamophobia, and the presence of Muslim shops or organizations (sandwich shops, halal butcheries, religious bookshops, sports associations, humanitarian or school equality associations, etc.) on a continuum of the same project. As political scientist Laurent Bonnefoy points out about Rougier's book,[46]

> the general approach ignores the interactions between these Islamist movements on the one hand, and global society and its institutions on the other. The situation of Muslim populations in French society, their difficulties inherited from colonial history are never introduced into the analysis: the rejection of society by some would only be the result of Islamist ideologies with maneuvering and initiative. Discrimination and Islamophobia, evident in media representations as well as in state policies, appear in this framework only as epiphenomena, second only to the "conquering" Islamist agit-prop.[47]

These themes of "Islamization," "conquest," and "lost" territories to be regained generally signal the presence of small-replacement discourse. For instance, now former Minister of National Education Blanquer recently stated that "Islamic law" had replaced "republican law" in Roubaix and Maubeuge, working-class cities in northern France.[48] Of course, he provides no proof other than that "it

---

[44] The author uses the term *islamization* without quotes, deconstruction, or contextualization in his essay *Quatre-vingt-treize*. Gilles Kepel, *Quatre-vingt-treize* (Paris: Gallimard, 2012). For a critique, see Vincent Geisser, "Gilles Kepel hanté par l'islamisation de la France" ["Gilles Kepel Haunted by the Islamization of France"], *OrientXXI*, January 15, 2016, https://orientxxi.info/lu-vu-entendu/gilles-kepel-hante-par-l-islamisation-de-la-france,1149.

[45] Hamza Esmili, "Les Nouveaux faussaires: Le Maître, l'Établi et l'Aspirant" ["The New Forgers: The Master, the Established and the Aspirant"], *Contretemps*, June 6, 2020, https://www.contretemps.eu/nouveaux-faussaires-maitre-etabli-aspirant/.

[46] Bernard Rougier contributed arguments and assisted the government in the expansion of a law "consolidating the republican principles" that facilitated the repression of numerous Muslim institutions, in particular the dissolution of the two main organizations fighting against Islamophobia. See Laurent Bonnefoy, "Bernard Rougier, un chercheur conquis par la fièvre identitaire: De la recherche scientifique aux plateaux televises" ["Bernard Rougier, a Researcher Conquered by Identity Fever: From Scientific Research to TV Shows"], *Revue du crieur* 19 (2021): pp. 142–59.

[47] Laurent Bonnefoy, "Idées toutes faites sur 'les territoires conquis de l'islamisme'" ["Ready-Made Ideas on 'the Conquered Territories of Islamism'"], *OrientXXI*, February 10, 2020, https://orientxxi.info/lu-vu-entendu/idees-toutes-faites-sur-les-territoires-conquis-de-l-islamisme,3618.

[48] Bonnefoy, "Idées."

124   MARWAN MOHAMMED

just shows."[49] His conclusion comes merely from the racial profile of the population, as well as their wearing of headscarves and religious dress, the establishment of places of worship, and halal offerings in shops or restaurants. Thus, the minister is pointing to a segment of the population to illustrate replacement by referring to the substitution of "law of the republic" by "Islamic" law.

The existence of a "discursive formation" including the voices of both the small replacement and the great replacement is based on the shared idea that visible Islam is inseparable from an "Islamism" that aims to conquer French society. It remains to be seen how the convergence between nationalist and republican discourse has taken place or, more precisely, how the construction of a "Muslim problem" has allowed the emergence of an Islamophobic consensus.

Contemporary Emergence of the "Muslim Problem"

How did the words of Marine Le Pen end up in the mouth of center-right minister Blanquer and vice versa? During a televised debate, the Minister of the Interior Gérald Darmanin reproached Marine Le Pen for being too "soft" on the issue of Islam, blaming her because she is "not even ready to legislate on cults" and she considers "that Islam is not even a problem?"[50] How was this consensus built? A historical perspective shows how the far right serves as the source and catalyst of the current consensus around the so-called Muslim problem.

The emergence of a "Muslim problem" is associated with the year 1989, which was marked by the fall of the Berlin Wall and the bicentennial of the French Revolution, two events that would give special resonance to the first "affair of the veil," in a public school in Creil, a middle-class city near Paris, and to the book *Satanic Verses*.[51] The fall of the Soviet Union and its socialist system contributed to the emergence of a new "Islamic" peril, first seen in the politicization of the Islamic headscarf in schools and death threats against the writer Salman Rushdie.[52] Other scholars propose inflection points that go back to the Islamic

---

[49] Hélène Tonneillier, "Selon Blanquer, à Roubaix et Maubeuge, la loi islamique a remplacé la loi républicaine et 'ça se voit'" ["According to Blanquer, in Roubaix and Maubeuge, Islamic Law Has Replaced Republican Law and 'It Shows'"], *Franceinfo*, June 11, 2020, https://france3-regions.franc etvinfo.fr/hauts-de-france/nord-0/blanquer-roubaix-maubeuge-loi-islamique-remplace-loi-repub licaine-ca-se-voit-1790651.html?fbclid=IwAR2EQ9vobBm7w2y91omITH5DrZl0qWavFxR1JtPD JHuYJ0AwvWyJDWxDtb4.

[50] "Darmanin accuse Le Pen de 'mollesse' sur l'islam, la majorité se fait discrete" ["Darmanin Accuses Le Pen of 'Softness' on Islam, the Majority Is Discreet"], *Huffington Post France*, February 12, 2021, https://www.huffingtonpost.fr/entry/darmanin-accuse-le-pen-de-mollesse-sur-lislam-la-majorite-se-fait-discrete_fr_60264c01c5b6f88289fad1ee.

[51] See, for example, John Bowen, *Why the French Don't Like Headscarves: Islam, the State and Public Space* (Princeton, NJ: Princeton University Press, 2007), pp. 66–67.

[52] Thomas Deltombe, *L'Islam imaginaire: La Construction médiatique de l'islamophobie en France, 1975–2005* [*Imaginary Islam: The Media Construction of Islamophobia in France, 1975–2005*] (Paris: La Découverte, 2005).

Revolution in Iran in 1979 or that closely associate the rise of Islamophobia with terrorist violence claiming to be Islamic. The 1995 attacks in France and those of September 11, 2001, in the United States marked a turning point in the treatment of Muslims in Western countries by giving vigor to the idea of associations of Muslims being domestic enemies.[53] These moments mark the emergence of discourses explaining the rise of Islamophobia as a legitimate, or at least understandable, reaction to the change in behavior and the radicalization of Muslim minorities. All these contemporary events are part of a longer history that starts from the medieval opposition to the Muslim world to the contemporary Islamophobia through the decisive period of colonization and Western imperialism. An "anti-Muslim archive" has been built up during these centuries and serves today as a breeding ground for perceptions, images, and stereotypes.[54]

In France, however, contemporary Islamophobia appeared at the crossroad of class struggle and the "problem of immigration" during the workers' strikes beginning in 1982 amid massive layoffs in the automobile industry.[55] At that time, the unity government of the left, resulting from the election of François Mitterrand, embarked on a process of neoliberal economic reform, particularly in the automobile industry, a sector that had been one of the engines of France's economic development and whose productivity was running thin at the end of the 1970s. After World War II, this industry was considered both a laboratory of transformation in the workplace and a space of struggle between immigrants and trade unions.[56] Its growth was based on the massive employment of immigrant workers in the most difficult and worst-paying jobs.[57]

The strikes that began in the spring of 1982 at the Citroën-Aulnay and Talbot-Poissy plants in the Paris suburbs were ordinary in that they mainly concerned the preservation of jobs as well as the improvement of working conditions,

[53] Ibrahim Kalin and John Esposito, eds., *Islamophobia: The Challenge of Pluralism in the 21st Century* (Oxford: Oxford University Press, 2011).

[54] Jocelyne Dakhlia and Bernard Vincent, eds., *Les Musulmans dans l'histoire de l'Europe*, vol. 1 [*Muslims in European History*, vol. 1] (Paris: Albin Michel, 2011); Norman Daniel, *L'Islam et l'Occident* (Paris: Éditions du Cerf, 1993); John Tolan, *Les Sarrasins* [*The Saracens*] (Paris: Flammarion, 2003); Edward W. Said, *L'Orientalisme: L'Orient créé par l'Occident* [*Orientalism: The East Created by the West*] (Paris: Seuil, 1980).

[55] Nicolas Hatzfeld and Jean-Louis Loubet, "Les conflits Talbot: Du Printemps syndical au tournant de la rigueur (1982–1984)" ["The Talbot Struggles: From the Union Spring to the Neoliberal Turn"], *Vingtième siècle* 4, no. 84 (2004): pp. 151–60.

[56] Maryse Tripier, *L'Immigration dans la classe ouvrière* [*Immigration in the Working Class*] (Paris: Ciemi and L'Harmattan, 1990).

[57] Laure Pitti, *Ouvriers algériens à Renault-Billancourt de la guerre d'Algérie aux grèves d'OS des années 1970: Contribution à l'histoire sociale et politique des ouvriers étrangers en France* [*Algerian Workers at Renault-Billancourt from the Algerian War to the Strikes of the 1970s: Contribution to the Social and Political History of Foreign Workers in France*] (PhD dissertation, Université Paris VIII, Paris, France, 2002).

126 MARWAN MOHAMMED

wages, and union freedoms.[58] The conflict came at a time when the religiosity of immigrant workers from North and sub-Saharan Africa, who arrived in large numbers during the second half of the 20th century, had not been considered a problem. Trade unions and employers had even responded positively to requests for the religious accommodation of Muslim workers; a mosque was inaugurated in 1976 in the Renault-Billancourt factory.[59] As historian Vincent Gay explains, concerning the strikes at Citroën-Aulnay and Talbot-Poissy plants, "Part of the demands thus concerned the means of practicing the Muslim religion in the workplace, but they occupy a relatively minor place in the list of demands."[60]

Muslim workers mobilized during the strike. They represented an important contingent of the workers but, more importantly, they were the main targets of layoff plans. Following an agreement between the left government and management, 1,905 employees of the Talbot-Poissy factory, consisting mostly of unskilled workers, lost their jobs. As Gay points out, "[A]mong them there are 20% French (a majority of whom come from the overseas departments and territories), 40% Moroccans, 11% Senegalese, 7% Algerians," and "50"[61] union delegates from CGT (General Confederation of Labor) channels and 15 from the CFDT (French Democratic Labor Confederation). The overwhelming majority of those laid off were workers from the Caribbean, especially from the former colonies.

It is in this context that the "Muslim problem" began to appear in public debate at the initiative of company directors, government, and media.[62] In two internal notes dated summer 1982, Peugeot management asserted that the strikers were being manipulated, there was "significant risk of seeing fundamentalist movements, either spontaneous or coming from the Middle East, trying to take advantage of this agitation," and "Moroccan leaders, particularly at Talbot, are known for their links with fundamentalist movements in their countries of origin."[63] In January 1983, Socialist Interior Minister Gaston Defferre denounced

---

[58] Vincent Gay, "Grèves saintes ou grèves ouvrières? Le 'problème musulman' dans les conflits de l'automobile, 1982–1983" ["Holy Strikes or Workers' Strikes? The 'Muslim Problem' in the Conflicts of the Automobile Industry, 1982–1983"], Genèses 98, no. 1 (2015): pp. 110–30.

[59] Catherine Withol de Wenden and René Mouriaux, "Syndicalisme français et islam" ["French Trade Unionism and Islam"], Revue française de science politique 37, no. 6 (1987): p. 804.

[60] Gay, "Grèves saintes," p. 113.

[61] Vincent Gay, "Lutter pour partir ou pour rester?" ["Struggling to Leave or to Stay?"], Travail et emploi no. 137 (2014): p. 42.

[62] Jacques Barou, Moustapha Diop, and Subhi Toma, "Des musulmans dans l'usine" ["Muslims in the Factory"], in Ouvriers spécialisés à Billancourt: Les Derniers témoins [Unskilled Workers in Billancourt: The Last Witnesses], ed. Renaud Sainsaulieu and Ahcène Zehraoui (Paris: L'Harmattan, 1995), pp. 131–61.

[63] "Le Problème musulman dans les événements Citroën et Talbot de mai–juin 1982" ["The Muslim Problem in the Citroën and Talbot Events of May–June 1982"] (Peugeot internal memo), quoted in Vincent Gay, "De la dignité à l'invisibilité: Les OS immigrés dans les grèves de Citroën et Talbot 1982–1984" ["From Dignity to Invisibility: Immigrant Workers in the Citroën and Talbot Strikes 1982–1984"] (master's thesis, School for Advanced Studies in the Social Sciences, Paris, France, 2011), p. 224.

"holy strikes by fundamentalists, Muslims and Shiites."[64] A month later, it was Socialist Prime Minister Pierre Mauroy who affirmed that immigrant workers, mostly Muslims, were being "agitated by religious and political groups that determined themselves according to criteria having little to do with French social realities."[65] Communist Minister of Labor Jean Auroux agreed with his government colleagues that there was "a religious and fundamentalist element in the conflicts we have encountered, which gives them a turn that is not exclusively trade unionist."[66] In February, on the public radio station France Inter, he even declared that "when workers take an oath on the Coran in a union movement, there is data that is extra-union. A certain number of people are interested in the political or social destabilization of our country because we represent too much in terms of freedom and pluralism."[67]

Statements came from various sources, including internal notes from the Talbot plant in Poissy and the Citroën plant in Aulnays-sous-Bois, both part of the PSA Group management who were concerned about the mobilizations, a briefing document prepared by an advisor to the minister of labor that emphasized the "penetration of the theses of Islamic fundamentalism in certain French societies with a Muslim working-class population,"[68] and especially notes and reports from intelligence services. One of these intelligence service notes argues that Moroccan workers were being manipulated by a number of political movements and organizations that were acting jointly with the Association of Moroccans in France. The religious claims of Moroccan workers were explained by "a penetration of the theses of Islamic fundamentalism in certain French societies with a Muslim working-class population."[69]

The media also covered the strikes by making frequent parallels or references to the international situation:[70]

Journalists, press cartoonists, and humorists reproduced the language with recurring references to the Iranian Revolution, notably through the term ayatollah, incarnation of the Islamist threat . . . In *Le Figaro* and *France Soir*, Jacques Faizant and Trez illustrated the penetration of fundamentalist views among immigrant workers and union blindness in the face of this new phenomenon.[71]

---

[64] Radio interview at Europe 1, January 26, 1983, quoted in Gay, "Grèves saintes," p. 123.
[65] Interview at *Nord-Eclair*, January 28, 1983, quoted in Gay, "Grèves saintes," p. 123.
[66] Interview at *L'Alsace*, February 10, 1983, quoted in Gay, "Grèves saintes," p. 124.
[67] Interview at France Inter, February 10, 1983, quoted in Gay, "Grèves saintes," p. 124.
[68] Gay, "Grèves saintes," p. 150.
[69] Thomas Deltombe, *L'Islam imaginaire: La construction médiatique de l'islamophobie en France, 1975–2005* [*Imaginary Islam: The Media Construction of Islamophobia in France, 1975–2005*] (Paris, France: La Découverte, 2007), p. 50.
[70] Deltombe, *L'Islam*, p. 50.
[71] Gay, "Grèves saintes," pp. 124–25.

Indeed, numerous photos showed Muslim workers praying at the mosque, and press cartoons depicted vehicles leaving the production lines covered with an Islamic veil.

These developments were a turning point, and as such, the left inaugurated the current period in which the "immigration problem," "Muslim problem," and class issues continue to be articulated in an unprecedented and perennial manner:

> Knowing that the majority of Muslims are working class, they are in an economic position weakened by the destructuring of industrial capitalism and suffer the full brunt of long-term unemployment and "precariousness." As soon as their economic position is called into question by the transformations of post-industrial capitalism, the legitimacy of their presence has considerably declined in the eyes of the dominant classes for whom the "costs" of their presence are greater than the "benefits."[72]

The occultation of class issues by this left-wing government in favor of the prism of "Islamist" entrism and the "religious problem" manipulated from abroad gives decisive force to the conspiratorial framing of Muslim presence and engagement. But above all, by formalizing the existence of a "Muslim problem," the left relegates the defense of social and workers' rights to the defense of "secularism" and of the Republic against Islam. The most reactionary movements will seize on this new framing of social and immigrant issues to move closer to the center of the political game.

The Opportunistic Repositioning of the Far Right in Europe

The French trajectory of Islamophobia is unique, even if rising hostility toward Muslims can be observed in many Western countries. Despite the plurality and diversity of Muslim populations and their sociopolitical status, the rejection of Islam spread rapidly in the 1990s in European politics as part of a profound recomposition of the partisan landscape. Most nationalist and populist movements of the right and far right integrated a strong anti-Islamic component into their discourse, paralleling the rise of new forms of transnational mobilization based on the threat of "Islamization" and great replacement.

If the radical European right-wing parties always had a political agenda united by opposition to immigration that is perceived as a cultural threat and economic competition, then the refocusing of an anti-Muslim discourse articulated

---

[72] Hajjat and Mohammed, *Islamophobie*, p. 21.

FRANCE'S ISLAMOPHOBIC BLOC   129

in the defense of social progress has broadened the electoral base of many nationalist movements.[73] For example, the Swiss People's Party, which initiated a popular referendum on the construction of minarets in 2009, became the main political movement in the Federal Assembly, taking more than a quarter of the seats.[74] Meanwhile, the Austrian Freedom Party became the third largest political force in that country, as did the Front National (FN) in France, renamed Rassemblement National by its new leader, Marine Le Pen. They followed in the footsteps of political organizations that pioneered the fight against "Islamization" like Pia Kjærsgaard's Danish People's Party and Geert Wilders's Freedom Party in the Netherlands.[75]

The Rassemblement National of Marine Le Pen, which has become one of the main electoral forces in French politics, initially followed the "Nordic way" to develop its own strategy of "de-demonization."[76] According to sociologist and politician Laurent Chambon, to analyze the rise of the Front National of Marine Le Pen,

> it is necessary to know that Pia Kjærsgaard set up the Danish People's Party (the Dansk Folkeparti) on the ruins of a dying xenophobic and nationalist party which suffered greatly from internal divisions. After imposing a new name and structure, Kjærsgaard spent ten years building a well-oiled and obedient electoral machine. She then managed to establish herself for ten years as a key coalition partner of the Danish conservative and liberal right. To do this, she developed several themes that inevitably [recall] the FN of Marine [Le Pen]: no official contact with the racist, homophobic and anti-Semitic far right; a party that obeys the leader without dissent; a discourse centered on Islam as an ideology threatening European civilization; the use ad nauseam of classic nativist nationalist themes; the defense of the welfare state and social achievements against profiteers from elsewhere; the real people against the system confiscated by the multi-culturalist leftists; a strong Zionism.[77]

Other nationalist currents and movements in Europe do not follow this Nordic way in the same way, but the structural character of Islamophobia as well as

[73] Hans-Georg Betz and Carol Johnson, "Against the Current—Stemming the Tide: The Nostalgic Ideology of the Contemporary Radical Populist Right," *Journal of Political Ideologies* 9, no. 3 (2004): pp. 311–27.

[74] Damir Skenderovic, *The Radical Right in Switzerland: Continuity and Change, 1945–2000* (New York: Berghahn Books, 2009).

[75] Annie Benveniste, *The Rise of the Far Right in Europe: Populist Shifts and "Othering,"* ed. Gabriella Campani and Giovanna Lazaridis (London: Palgrave Macmillan, 2016).

[76] Sylvain Crépon, Alexandre Dézé, and Nonna Mayer, *Les Faux-semblants du Front national* [*The False Pretenses of the National Front*] (Paris: Presses de Sciences Po, 2015).

[77] Laurent Chambon, "Le FN ressuscite la droite" ["The FN Resurrects the Right"], *Minorités* no. 129 (2012). www.minorites.org/index.php/2-la-revue/1318-le-fn-ressuscite-la-droite.html.

130 MARWAN MOHAMMED

its political and cultural roots are lasting and supported by the many far-right parties that have scored spectacular electoral victories.

In France, Jean-Marie Le Pen's qualification in the second round of the 2002 presidential election marked a major turning point that allowed the party, which was founded in 1972 by Nazi militants associated with different branches of the nationalist movement, to build a new balance between the quest for respectability and fidelity to the founders ideas.[78] The classic theme of demographic threat was amplified by of the idea of intentional invasion and illustrated primarily by the visibility and institutionalization of Muslim presence in Europe. Jean-Marie Le Pen's daughter Marine Le Pen has extended the defense of the Christian culture of France to that of European civilization. She participated in the hegemony of an Islamophobic discourse in the name of progress by criticizing, at least publicly, certain xenophobic, homophobic, or anti-Semitic positions previously assumed by her father's generation. If this conversion to a seemingly progressive discourse was possible, it was largely because mainstream political parties and movements, from the left under Mitterand to Macron's ultra-liberal right, allowed the anti-Muslim fixation to define issues such as gender equality and the defense of the principle of secularism. And since this progressivism is opposed to Muslims, the most reactionary components of the right have discovered a passion for equality, the fight against homophobia, or the defense of secularism.[79]

The far right has for years capitalized on the efforts, categories, and patient ideological and semantic encoding work of the artisans of the small-replacement ideologies making every visible Muslim (from the striking worker to the high school girl wearing a headscarf) a "fundamentalist" conspiracy, a soldier of "political Islam," a threat to "republican values," or a danger to gender equality or the French secular model. This work of ideological and political encoding allowed the Rassemblement National of Marine Le Pen to appropriate the political grammar of feminism and to present itself as a fervent and intransigent defender of secularism and the Republic. However, this refocusing does not mean that the core of the party abandons its characteristic nationalist, homophobic, and xenophobic thinking. Numerous neo-Nazi cadres and militants surround Marine Le Pen, whose strategy of de-demonization has been supported and endorsed by most of the media.

---

[78] Crépon, Dézé, and Mayer, *Les Faux-semblants*.

[79] Annie Benveniste and Etienne Pingaud, "Far-Right Movements in France: The Principal Role of Front National and the Rise of Islamophobia," in *The Rise of the Far Right in Europe: Populist Shifts and "Othering,"* ed. Gabriella Campani and Giovanna Lazaridis (London: Palgrave Macmillan, 2016), pp. 55–81.

Conclusion

Most contemporary mass atrocities are provoked by multiple causes and justified by conspiratorial beliefs, rhetoric of threat and conquest, and the staging of imminent danger requiring a vigorous response. These tragedies are preceded by a period of construction of an "interior enemy," degradation of the living conditions of the (future) victims, forms of mistreatment, and a powerful culture of suspicion inseparable from practices of discrimination.[80] Currently, global dynamics involving growing uncertainties and insecurities are contributing to the rise of reactionary and supremacist forces that, in many European countries, designate vulnerable minorities, particularly Muslims, as existential threats.

France stands out for the multipartisan and majoritiarian anti-Muslim consensus that is based on the idea that a concerted process of replacement is ongoing and that Muslim claims and visibility are manifestations of this offensive. On this basis, the resistance is organized and relies more on the state, which, ignoring the possibilities of judicial action, increases administrative closures of places of worship and political dissolutions of organizations designated as "Islamist." In addition to the daily campaigns of denigration that target Muslims and their institutions, many human rights organizations consider the practice to be an attack on freedoms and dangerous for the near future. Indeed, Kenneth Roth, executive director of Human Rights Watch, was not mistaken in noting that "France seems to equate Islam in general with the terrorist threat."[81] For that, French Muslims are paying a high price.

---

[80] Yves Ternon, *Génocide: Anatomie d'un crime* [*Genocide: Anatomy of a Crime*] (Paris: Armand Colin, 2016).

[81] "La France semble assimiler islam et menace terroriste, déplore Human Rights Watch" ["France Seems to Equate Islam with Terrorist Threat, Deplores Human Rights Watch"], *20 Minutes*, January 12, 2021, https://www.20minutes.fr/societe/2951115-20210112-france-semble-assimiler-islam-men ace-terroriste-deplore-human-rights-watch.

8

Islamophobia without Muslims?
Not Only in Eastern Europe

Ivan Kalmar

In 2015 and 2016, the "European migration crisis" saw well over one million people arrive in the European Union (EU), most of them Muslim and, for many, after arduous efforts over desert and sea, abuse by "hosts" along the way, and tragic drownings in the Mediterranean. Those lucky to survive had the choice to follow the Balkan route to the wealthy countries of Western Europe like Germany and Sweden. At the Hungarian border, they hoped, at last, to enter the Schengen area of countries that had abolished border formalities; entering one country allows unimpeded travel to the others.

At first, Hungary allowed thousands to cross its territory, but Prime Minister Viktor Orbán soon gave the order to construct a razor-wire fence to block the route of the migrants.[1] The fence made it nearly impossible to cross, even to request asylum, a right granted by international law.[2] The governments of the Czech Republic, Slovakia, and eventually Poland joined Orbán in his stubborn refusal of the migrants.[3] This reaction was clearly racially motivated. Poland had accepted hundreds of thousands of Ukrainian immigrants.[4] The Czech Republic welcomed more immigrants per capita than France or Italy, but the largest group among them was neighboring Slovaks.[5] Clearly, the four countries' objections were not to migrants as such but to *these* migrants.

---

[1] AFP, "Hungary Closes Border with Serbia and Starts Building Fence to Bar Migrants," *The Guardian*, June 17, 2015, https://www.theguardian.com/world/2015/jun/17/hungary-closes-border-serbia-starts-building-fence-bar-migrants.

[2] "Convention and Protocol Relating to the Status of Refugees," United Nations High Commissioner for Refugees, accessed November 12, 2021, https://www.unhcr.org/protection/basic/3b66c2aa10/convention-protocol-relating-status-refugees.html.

[3] Georgi Gotev, "Visegrad Summit Rejects Migrant Quotas," *Euractiv*, September 7, 2015, https://www.euractiv.com/section/justice-home-affairs/news/visegrad-summit-rejects-migrant-quotas/.

[4] See, for example, Olena Fedyuk and Marta Kindler, *Ukrainian Migration to the European Union: Lessons from Migration Studies* (New York: Springer Berlin Heidelberg, 2016); Krystyna Iglicka and Agnieszka Weinar, "Ukrainian Migration in Poland from the Perspective of Polish Policies and Systems' Theory," *Journal of Immigrant and Refugee Studies* 6, no. 3 (2008): pp. 356–65.

[5] "Migration and Migrant Population Statistics, 2019," Eurostat, accessed November 12, 2021, https://ec.europa.eu/eurostat/statistics-explained/index.php?title=Migration_and_migrant_population_statistics.

Ivan Kalmar, *Islamophobia without Muslims? Not Only in Eastern Europe* In: *Global Islamophobia and the Rise of Populism*. Edited by: Sahar F. Aziz and John L. Esposito, Oxford University Press. © Oxford University Press 2024.
DOI: 10.1093/oso/9780197648995.003.0008

Hundreds of thousands of mostly Muslim people of color knocking at the door gave the four countries, united in the previously insignificant Visegrád Group, the opportunity to stand up once and for all to the condescending West. In September 2015, the EU's Justice and Home Affairs Council decided to distribute 120,000 asylum seekers to most member countries.[6] The measure was taken against the opposition of Hungary, the Czech Republic, Slovakia, and Romania; Poland was still ruled by the liberal democratic Civic Platform party.[7] As EU councils normally made decisions unanimously, the Central Europeans felt belittled. Notably, following the 2008 financial crisis, the formerly communist EU countries' economies fared relatively well.[8] The poor cousins were not so poor anymore, and this status may have given them the courage to stand up to preaching from Brussels. Meanwhile, Islamophobia became a political weapon wielded by the Visegrád members in their endeavor to gain more power within the EU, an effort that also played well with domestic audiences. Anti-migrant, Islamophobic rhetoric led to the election of the notoriously nationalist Law and Justice (PiS) party headed by Jarosław Kaczyński in Poland, and it supported an anti-liberal turn in the previously more hesitant Czech Republic.[9]

The resistance of the previously placid East Central Europeans elicited two kinds of emotion in the West. The first was moral shock; many saw the evident Islamophobia of the Visegrád area as a resurgence of authoritarian racism that they rightly or wrongly attributed to this part of Europe. The Islamophobia of today was a modification of an un-mastered predisposition that had previously been expressed mainly in the form of antisemitism. Jan Gross, a leading historian who had already provoked an impassioned reaction in Poland by his discussion of antisemitic crimes by the Polish population during and after the Holocaust, asked, outraged, "Have Eastern Europeans no sense of shame?"[10] Eastern Europe, he protested, "has yet to come to terms with its murderous past. Only

---

[6] The United Kingdom and Denmark were not subject to the council's jurisdiction. "European Commission Statement following the Decision at the Extraordinary Justice and Home Affairs Council to Relocate 120,000 Refugees," European Commission, September 22, 2015, https://ec.eur opa.eu/commission/presscorner/detail/en/STATEMENT_15_5697.

[7] Ian Traynor and Patrick Kingsley, "EU Governments Push through Divisive Deal to Share 120,000 Refugees," *The Guardian*, September 22, 2015, https://www.theguardian.com/world/2015/sep/22/eu-governments-divisive-quotas-deal-share-120000-refugees.

[8] Atanas Kolev, "The Impact of the Recession in 2008–2009 on EU Regional Convergence," ECON Note no. SG/ECON/ES/2012-522/AKo/as (European Investment Bank, Economics Department, December 14, 2012), https://www.eib.org/en/publications/econ-note-2012-regional-converge nce, p. 4.

[9] Bulcsú Hunyadi and Csaba Molnár, "Central Europe's Faceless Strangers: The Rise of Xenophobia," *Nations in Transit*, June 2016, https://freedomhouse.org/sites/default/files/2020-02/July12016_xenophobia_final_brief_FH.pdf.

[10] Jan Gross, "Eastern Europe's Crisis of Shame," *Project Syndicate*, September 13, 2015, https://www.project-syndicate.org/commentary/eastern-europe-refugee-crisis-xenopho bia-by-jan-gross-2015-09.

134 IVAN KALMAR

when it does will its people be able to recognize their obligation to save those fleeing in the face of evil."[11]

The other major emotion was, in contrast to the gravity of such indignation, one akin to amusement. Scholars and journalists alike noted that the upsurge in Islamophobia—and worse, its mainstreaming among much of the political class in Eastern Europe—is taking place in an area where the number of Muslims was negligible. A number of studies describe this situation as "Islamophobia without Muslims" and opine that it needs to be explained as a contradiction or something that is "puzzling."[12]

Analyses that discuss Islamophobia as a specifically Eastern European phenomenon, run into a number of problems. For one, *Eastern Europe* is an area whose parts have little if anything in common with each other, except for their communist past. To assume at the outset that an issue like Islamophobia will show distinctive characteristics over an area extending from mainly Orthodox Russia with its large Muslim minorities[13] to mostly Muslim Albania and predominantly Catholic East Central Europe in between is unfounded. It is a methodological error encouraged among other things by scholarly, but also journalistic, area specialization inherited from the Cold War. Specialists of "Russian and East European studies," to use one of the common monikers in used, produce the area they study, in the same way that academic and popular orientalism, inherited from the height of the imperialist period, created another area called *the Orient*.

But what, in fact, is generally meant when discussing "Islamophobia in Eastern Europe" focuses on the four so-called Visegrád Group countries: Poland, the Czech Republic, Slovakia, and Hungary. These countries have much in common beyond the post-socialist condition that they share with other parts of Eastern Europe: their Latin Christian and Habsburg heritage, their geographic and cultural proximity to Germany, and, above all, their membership in the EU. Collectively, I refer to them here as *East Central Europe*.[14] Another reason to be careful when using the term *Eastern Europe* is that using a single term assumes that countries in the area have more in common with each other than with the West. This contention does not hold true, however, when it comes to the

---

[11] Gross, "Eastern Europe's Crisis of Shame."

[12] See, for example, Gert Pickel and Cemal Öztürk, "Islamophobia without Muslims? The 'Contact Hypothesis' as an Explanation for Anti-Muslim Attitudes—Eastern European Societies in a Comparative Perspective," *Journal of Nationalism, Memory, and Language Politics* 12, no. 2 (December 31, 2018): p. 162.

[13] See Sahar F. Aziz and Sarah Calderone, "Islamophobia in Russia: Ethnicity, Migration, and National Security," ch. 9 in this volume.

[14] Some broad definitions of *central Europe* include Germany and Switzerland; most include Austria. It has been used to include, in the east, the Balkan states, Belarus, Ukraine, Bulgaria, and other countries. My definition is made specifically for the purposes of this chapter.

phenomenon of Islamophobia "without Muslims," as the idea that Islamophobia does not necessarily need Muslims finds support in both the West and east.[15]

In fact, *Islamophobia without Muslims* refers to Islamophobia that thrives *more* where there are *fewer* Muslims, whether that is in Western Europe, eastern Europe, or America. In this chapter, I argue that the reason is not a historical or cultural proclivity to racism found in one specific region or another. Neither is it some automatic dislike for an unfamiliar Other that is dissipated once you get to know them. Rather, *Islamophobia without Muslims* is the consequence of a condition that I identify as *peripherality*, as it manifests itself in the current stage of capitalist society in the EU and elsewhere. The frustrations and insecurities of peripheral areas and groups in the West have found a misdirected outlet in Islamophobia.[16] East Central Europe is one of these peripheral areas, but it is not the only one.

Islamophobia in East Central Europe

Are East (central) Europeans more Islamophobic? Attitude studies seem to say so. One of the most oft-quoted sources on Islamophobic attitudes in Europe is the Pew Research Center, headquartered in Washington, DC. In its 2019 survey, respondents from several countries were asked how they would describe their attitude to Muslims, with the possible answers including "very favorable," "somewhat favorable," "somewhat unfavorable," and "very unfavorable."[17] Table 8.1 divides the combined answers in the two "unfavorable" categories.

The survey demonstrates that East Central Europeans do indeed have higher rates of Islamophobic attitudes.[18] However, note that the sharpest border is not between West and east. The 14 percent difference between Sweden and Spain is great; the 1 percent difference between Greece and Hungary is not.[19] The biggest break comes not between West and East but between the north (unshaded) on one hand, and the south (shaded).[20] The data makes it more meaningful to speak

---

[15] Farid Hafez, "Reading Islamophobia through the Lens of James Baldwin," *Connections*, December 1, 2019, www.connections.clio-online.net/article/id/artikel-4673; Salman Sayyid, "Islamophobia and the Europeanness of the Other Europe," *Patterns of Prejudice* 52, no. 5 (2018): 420–35.

[16] Discourses about Muslims where there are few of them can be more about local non-Muslim identity than about Muslims. In the post-communist space, this discussion is similar to discussions about the Holocaust, which are not only or primarily about Jews. See Jelena Subotic, *Yellow Star, Red Star: Holocaust Remembrance after Communism* (Ithaca, NY: Cornell University Press, 2019).

[17] "Spring 2019 Survey Data," Pew Research Center, October 2, 2019, accessed January 6, 2021, https://www.pewresearch.org/global/datasets/.

[18] Or they are at East more ready to admit these attitudes to researchers.

[19] "Spring 2019 Survey Data."

[20] "Spring 2019 Survey Data."

Table 8.1. Unfavorable Attitudes toward Muslims in Western, Southern, and Central Europe

Country	Non-Muslims who have negative views of Muslims (%)
United Kingdom	18
France	22
Germany	24
Netherlands	28
Sweden	28
Spain	42
Italy	55
Greece	57
Hungary	58
Czech Republic	64
Poland	66
Slovakia	77

Adapted from: Pew Research Center, "Spring 2019 Survey Data," Pew Research Center, October 2, 2019, https://www.pewresearch.org/global/datasets/.

about Western versus eastern *and* southern Europe in the EU, rather than to contrast East and West.

That eastern Europeanness is not the main issue here is further confirmed by the fact that, in the same study, countries bordering the EU to the East had lower rates of disapproval of Muslims, more similar to Western than to Central Europe: 21 percent in Ukraine, comparable to France, and 19 percent in Russia, comparable to the United Kingdom.[21] If we were looking at an "eastern European" phenomenon here, that would not be the case.[22]

Within East Central Europe, the conditions under which Islamophobia has been exploited in party politics vary. The Catholic Islamophobia of the Polish

---

[21] "Spring 2019 Survey Data."

[22] The lower score in these two significant former Soviet countries could be due to a combination of different factors. First, there are more substantial Muslim communities in both. Second, as non-EU members, these countries' experience with the West is very different. They were not affected by the opportunity that EU policies gave to the Visegrád Group to channel its frustration with the West into politicized expressions of Islamophobia. And third—last but not least—particularly for Russia, its undemocratic government arguably has less need to rally the electorate with populist racism. See Aziz and Calderone, "Islamophobia," ch. 9 in this volume.

leadership and the anti-migrant Islamophobia of Viktor Orbán in Hungary are similar in both content and intensity. Czech Islamophobia is fundamental to the program of the far-right Party of Direct Democracy and a consistent feature of President Miloš Zeman's rhetoric, but Zeman's role is mostly ceremonial; although protests against Islamophobia are rare, it is less actively deployed by the government. In Slovakia, former—now discredited—Prime Minister Robert Fico adopted Islamophobic rhetoric, especially in the last, desperate period of his government. Since then, the country has been less known for official Islamophobic statements. President Zuzanna Čaputová is a progressive liberal democrat, although she also serves a largely ceremonial role. Yet rhetoric and practice may differ, as Slovakia is the last EU country not to have recognized Islam as a national religion, meaning that official mosques, as opposed to unofficial prayer halls, are able to receive building permits.[23]

All the above is meant to nuance, but not to reject, the proposition that Islamophobia is ensconced more in East Central than Western Europe. Parties with similar Islamophobic attitudes to those that rule Poland or Hungary exist in the West and have achieved some electoral success. The most obvious examples are Matteo Salvini's Lega in Italy, which had been part of the government in the recent past, and Marine Le Pen's Rassemblement National (RN) in France, which does particularly well in EU parliamentary elections.[24] But in East Central Europe, instead of the difficult and often ephemeral success of such parties, those that express the same Islamophobic rhetoric have been able to run stable governments. Even worse perhaps, their Islamophobia is inadequately, if at all, challenged by the opposition.

"Without Muslims" in East and West

"Without Muslims" is never meant in a literal sense. Estimating the number of Muslims in a country, let alone its regions, is notoriously difficult. In France, for instance, there are an estimated 5.43 million Muslims, but only 66 percent fasted on Ramadan in 2019.[25] There is no evidence that this is any different in central than it is in Western Europe. Even if "religion" is on the census—and it is not in

---

[23] Rebeka Jakubová, "Moslimovia na Slovensku sú stále bez mešity: Islam Slováci vnímajú ako strašiaka a hrozbu, nemajú na to dôvod" ["Muslims in Slovakia Are Still without a Mosque: Slovaks See It as a Scary Threat, but Have No Reason To"], *Startitup.sk*, July 29, 2020, https://www.startitup.sk/moslimovia-na-slovensku-su-stale-bez-mesity-islam-slovaci-vnimaju-ako-strasiaka-a-hrozbu-nie-je-to-pravda/.

[24] Le Pen's movement was formerly known as the National Front. See Marwan Mohammed, "France's Islamophobic Bloc and the 'Mainstreamization' of the Far Right," ch. 7 in this volume.

[25] E. Moyou, "L'Islam en France—faits et chiffres" ["Islam in France—Facts and Figures"], Statista, accessed January 11, 2021, https://fr.statista.com/themes/6482/l-islam-en-france/#dossierSummary__chapter2.

France—then still some individuals who informally identify as Muslim are likely not counted.

That said, according to Pew Research Center statistics, Muslims made up less than 0.1 percent of the population in Poland, 0.1 percent in Slovakia, 0.2 percent in the Czech Republic, and 0.4 percent in Hungary in 2016.[26] In Western EU countries, Muslims accounted for 0.4 percent of Portugal's population, the same as in Hungary, but ranged elsewhere from 1.4 percent in Ireland to 6.1 percent in Germany, 6.3 percent in the United Kingdom, and 8.1 percent in Sweden; the average for the EU was 4.9 percent.[27] So although there were about twenty-two thousand Muslims in the Czech Republic and forty thousand in Hungary,[28] that number is low enough to justify the hyperbole "without Muslims."

The country-by-country method of counting Muslims, however, covers up an all-important difference: that between urban centers and the small towns and villages of the countryside. Najib and Teeple Hopkins argue that "Islamophobia is a spatialized process that occurs at different scales in Muslim-minority countries: globe, nation, urban, neighbourhood, body and emotion."[29] Within large city conglomerations, Muslims are located in different neighborhoods, for example, where they experience different impacts from contact with residents and the built environment. Najib and Temple are correct on the importance of spatialization. One spatialized dimension they do not mention, however, is of the distinction between urban and rural residence.

Although reliable statistics are hard to come by, it is clear to visitors almost anywhere in Europe that country locations that are distant from larger cities have fewer, if any, Muslim inhabitants. In East Central Europe as elsewhere in the EU today, it is unsurprising to find a kebab or a *shisha* shop in a rural town. But the Muslim population there is limited to those operating the business and lacks the numbers to organize any sort of local Muslim community with a mosque, halal meat supplier, or cultural center, institutions that one finds not only in London, Paris, and Berlin but also, if on a smaller scale, in Budapest, Prague, and Warsaw.

Although there are far fewer Muslims on the whole in East Central Europe, the country-city contrast there is similar to that of the West. The smaller the town, the fewer Muslims live there. But there are exceptions both in the East and in the West. Along the major migration routes of southern Italy or Spain, for example, there are small towns with an appreciable transient Muslim migrant population.

---

[26] Conrad Hackett, Phillip Connor, Marcin Stonawski, and Michaela Potančoková, "Europe's Growing Muslim Population," Pew Research Center, November 29, 2017, https://www.pewforum.org/2017/11/29/europes-growing-muslim-population/pf_11-29-17_muslims-update-20/.

[27] Hackett et al., "Europe's Growing Muslim Population."

[28] Hackett et al., "Europe's Growing Muslim Population."

[29] Kawtar Najib and Carmen Teeple Hopkins, "Geographies of Islamophobia," *Social and Cultural Geography* 21, no. 4 (2020): p. 449.

In the town of Teplice, a Czech spa town popular with wealthy Arab visitors,[30] the service industry catering to them employs a number of Muslims. These, however, are exceptions that prove the rule that the Muslim population of Europe is disproportionately urbanized, leaving the geographically peripheral, rural areas comparatively "without Muslims." Yet it is in such areas, both in the East and in the West, that Islamophobia is highest.

Islamophobia in Europe: Quantitative Studies

Although quantitative studies of Islamophobia within regions of a country are rare, we can learn about its prevalence indirectly by studying the statistics for right-wing, nativist parties such as France's RN that are hostile to Muslims. We know, for example, that in France, urban versus rural residence is one of the most common correlates of voter preference for right-wing, nationalist, or populist parties with an Islamophobic tinge. The French *département* that provided for the most votes for RN, outside of the special case of the island of Mayotte, in the European elections of 2019 was Aisne. The province, where the RN received 39.87 percent of the total vote,[31] has no large cities. The largest center, its capital St. Quentin, has a continually decreasing population, numbering 53,856 inhabitants in 2018.[32] The second most pro-RN *département* was Pas-de-Calais, which, although it is densely populated, also lacks large cities. In both provinces, the number of Muslims only constitutes 1 to 3 percent of the population.[33] These figures make these areas more comparable to East Central Europe than to the rest of France, where the average is 5.8 percent,[34] and certainly to the region of Paris, where 10 percent of the population is believed to be Muslim.[35]

---

[30] "5 Důvodů, proč jsou Arabové v pohodě a 'islámské' Teplice jsou dobrým místem pro život" [Five Reasons Why Arabs Are Comfortable and Why 'Islamic' Teplice Is a Good Place to Live"], *G.cz*, accessed November 12, 2021, https://g.cz/5-duvodu-proc-jsou-arabove-v-pohode-a-islamske-teplice-jsou-dobrym-mistem-pro-zivot/.

[31] "Elections européennes 2019: Les Résultats par département rapportés à la population" ["European Elections of 2019: Results by Department and Population"], *Le Monde*, May 27, 2019, https://www.lemonde.fr/les-decodeurs/article/2019/05/27/elections-europeennes-les-resultats-par-departement-rapportes-a-la-population_5468085_4355770.html.

[32] "Comparateur de territoire—commune de Saint-Quentin (02691)," Insee [National Institute of Statistics and Economics], accessed February 28, 2022, https://www.insee.fr/fr/statistiques/1405 599?geo=COM-02691.

[33] "La Repartition territorial des musulmans en France" ["The Distribution of Muslims in France"], *SkyRock*, last modified 2012, https://tpe602.skyrock.com/photo.html?id_article=3066675 967&id_article_media=29046035.

[34] Hackett et al., "Europe's Growing Muslim Population."

[35] "Les Musulmans très présents en Ile-de-France" ["Muslims Are Very Much Present in France"], *Le Parisien*, last modified August 21, 2009, https://www.leparisien.fr/societe/les-musulmans-tres-presents-en-ile-de-france-21-08-2009-612515.php.

140   IVAN KALMAR

In England, according to the 2011 UK census, almost 40 percent of Muslims lived in the Greater London area, where they made up roughly 12 percent of the population.[36] London is also a city where anti-immigrant politics has made relatively little headway. It is traditionally less open to both the mainstream Conservative and more extreme right-wing parties, such as the United Kingdom Independence Party (UKIP), than almost any other part of the country is.[37] Indeed, in 2016, London for the first time elected a Muslim mayor.[38]

The few Muslims in East Central Europe, too, are concentrated in large cities, and rural areas are the ones that have voted for outspoken nationalists with explicit Islamophobic tendencies. The following examples illustrate the overwhelming pattern. In Poland, the ruling party, PiS, bent on protecting the Christian values of the nation, is far more popular outside of the big cities across the nation and also in the east, which is more rural compared to the West. In the 2020 presidential election, the liberal candidate, Rafal Trzaskowski, was the mayor of the country's capital and largest city, Warsaw. Against the victorious PiS candidate and now President Andrzej Duda, Trzaskowski carried Warsaw by 67.65 percent, compared to Duda's 32.35 percent.[39] In the second-largest city, Krakow, the vote went 61.5 percent for Trzaskowski and 38.5 percent for Duda.[40]

The 2018 Czech presidential elections pitted Miloš Zeman, one of the most outspoken Islamophobes in the region, if not the world, against Jiří Drahoš, a chemist who had signed a public letter along with other scientists demanding a humane approach to refugees. Although in the heat of the election campaign he insisted that he was not pro-migration, this earned him the label of *vítač*, or "welcome," among Zeman's supporters.[41] Zeman won with 51.37 percent, as opposed

[36] "Table KS209 EW—Religion, Local Authorities in England and Wales," UK National Archives, 2011, https://webarchive.nationalarchives.gov.uk/ukgwa/20160105160709/http://www.ons.gov.uk/ons/rel/census/201ma.

[37] Jack Glynn, "Mapping Ukip's Vote Share," UK in a Changing Europe, February 16, 2018, https://ukandeu.ac.uk/mapping-ukips-vote-share/.

[38] Stephen Castle, "Sadiq Khan Elected in London, Becoming Its First Muslim Mayor," *The New York Times*, May 6, 2016, https://www.nytimes.com/2016/05/07/world/europe/britain-election-results.html.

[39] "Wybory prezydenckie 2020: Tak głosowała Warszawa" ["Presidential Elections of 2020: This Is How Warsaw Voted"], Radio dla ciebie, accessed January 3, 2021, https://www.rdc.pl/informacje/wybory-prezydenckie-2020-tak-glosowala-warszawa-wyniki/.

[40] Aleksander Gurgul, "Powyborcze lekcje dla opozycji: Jak zdobyć głosy mieszkańców z obrzeży krakowskich dzielnic?" ["Post-Election Lessons for the Opposition: How to Get the Votes of the Residents of Krakow's Outlying Districts"], *Wyborcza.pl*, accessed January 3, 2021, https://krakow.wyborcza.pl/krakow/7,44425,26196610,wyborcze-lekcje-dla-opozycji.html.

[41] Šárka Kabátová, "Je Drahoš 'vítač'? Co kdy přesně řekl o uprchlících a kvótách" ["Is Drahoš a 'Welcomer'? What Exactly He Said about Refugees and Quotas"], *Lidové noviny*, January 18, 2018, https://www.lidovky.cz/domov/prehledne-je-drahos-vitac-co-kdy-presne-rekl-o-uprchlicich-a-kvotach.A180118_105413_ln_domov_sk.

ISLAMOPHOBIA WITHOUT MUSLIMS? 141

to Drahoš's 48.63 percent.[42] But Prague voted decisively, with 68.75 percent for Drahoš, and he received 57.58 percent in the second-largest city of Brno.[43]

Similarly, in Slovakia in 2019, the progressive liberal candidate, Zuzanna Čaputová, received 73.74 percent of the vote in the district (*kraj*) of the capital, Bratislava, far more than in the country as a whole, at 58.4 percent.[44] In this case, that was enough to defeat her opponent, Maroš Šefčovič, who, though he had served as a high EU official, gravitated toward nationalist themes during the election.[45]

In Hungary, by contrast, the president is elected by parliament. In the 2018 parliamentary elections, Viktor Orbán's Fidesz party showed great strength across the country but much less so in the bigger cities. Fidesz won slightly more than the two-thirds majority of seats needed to alter the constitution, but it captured only one third of those representing Budapest.[46] In preparation for the 2022 elections, a major goal of Fidesz's notorious manipulation of the electoral system seemed to be to ensure that the rural vote has more weight than that of the big cities.[47]

In line with the concept of *Islamophobia without Muslims*, both elements of heightened Islamophobia and fewer Muslims are present in East Central Europe. However, their existence does not distinguish East Central Europe from the West, as we have seen that in the West, too, areas with fewer Muslims are more Islamophobic.

Not the Contact Hypothesis

Why should a lower Muslim presence encourage more Islamophobia? A common answer is that it is, rather, the other way around: more Muslims means less Islamophobia. Some scholars see this observation as supporting the so-called intergroup contact hypothesis, or contact hypothesis for short.[48] In our context, the contact hypothesis assumes that where there are fewer Muslims,

[42] "Prezidentské volby 2018: Výsledky v krajích a obcích" ["Presidential Election of 2018: Results by Regions and Communities"], iROZHLAS, accessed January 4, 2021, https://www.irozhlas.cz/volby/prezidentske-volby-2018/vysledky-kraje-obce.

[43] "Prezidentské volby 2018."

[44] "Výsledky prezidentských volieb 2019" ["Results of the Presidential Election of 2019"], *Sme*, accessed January 4, 2021, https://volby.sme.sk/prezidentske-volby/2019/vysledky.

[45] "Výsledky prezidentských volieb 2019."

[46] "Information to Voters Residing beyond the Borders of Hungary," National Election Office of Hungary, accessed January 4, 2021, https://www.valasztas.hu/web/national-election-office.

[47] Gábor Miklósi, "Orbán Brüsszelre Figyelt, a Fideszes Törvénygyár Akadozni Kezdett" ["Orbán Listened Up to Brussels and the Fidesz Law Factory Started to Falter"], *444*, December 15, 2020, https://444.hu/2020/12/15/orban-brusszelre-figyelt-a-fideszes-torvenygyar-akadozni-kezdett.

[48] See, for example, Pickel and Öztürk, "Islamophobia."

142 IVAN KALMAR

people will meet fewer of them,[49] leading to more Islamophobia. Its message is that familiarity breeds acceptance.[50]

The contact hypothesis has the advantage of simplicity. There is no doubt that one of its attractions to quantitative sociologists is that it is based on data that can be counted. But surely an unqualified generalization that intergroup contact lessens prejudice cannot be valid.

Granted, it is easy to see that contact may have a moderating effect on expressions of hostility.[51] In normal circumstances, most people avoid conflict when found in the same space with strangers. Drivers are much more tempted to yell at other drivers from the safe space of their own vehicle. Islamophobia "without Muslims" in East Central Europe may similarly view Muslims as located safely outside their own space. In that case, however, lack of contact does not work directly to increase hostility. Rather, it is the safety afforded by an environment where expressions of hostility are protected. The relative lack of Muslims, and therefore of individuals who are personally affected by Islamophobia, also means that fewer citizens are motivated to protest against manifestations of Islamophobia. Consequently, Islamophobic views may be expressed more safely.

Two of the most brutal and violent prejudices known in the Western Christian world, that against Blacks and that against Jews, belie the contact hypothesis. Slavery and post-slavery violence against Blacks was greatest in the American South, where Blacks were in some places in the majority, as they are in South Africa. That the persecution of Jews was inversely proportional to their presence would likewise be difficult to defend.[52] These hatreds prospered, in spite of the high degree of contact between the haters and the hated, because circumstances (which I do not otherwise compare with East Central Europe today) made hate safe.

---

[49] This may not always be true, however, given the big-city apartness referenced by Najib and Teeple Hopkins. See Najib and Teeple Hopkins, "Geographies."

[50] The originator of the contact hypothesis was Gordon A. Allport, the author of the still influential *Psychology of Prejudice*, first published in 1954. While Allport thought that contact decreased prejudice only in some conditions, in a much-quoted study, Thomas Pettigrew and Linda Tropp analyzed 515 studies of "intercultural contact" and concluded that increased contact "led to less prejudice of the outgroup 94% of the time." Thomas F. Pettigrew and Linda R. Tropp, "How Does Intergroup Contact Reduce Prejudice? Meta-Analytic Tests of Three Mediators," *European Journal of Social Psychology* 38, no. 6 (September 2008): p. 922.

[51] According to a Gallup poll, knowing a Muslim "makes a small difference in reported levels of personal prejudice toward Muslims"; in the United States, for instance, 53 percent of Americans who know a Muslim person said they do not hold prejudice toward Muslims, compared to 44 percent of those who do not know a Muslim person. See "Islamophobia: Understanding Anti-Muslim Sentiment in the West," Gallup, 2011, https://news.gallup.com/poll/157082/islamophobia-understanding-anti-muslim-sentiment-West.aspx.

[52] During the Holocaust, Jews often found refuge in Denmark, where the local Jewish population was small. Poland and parts of Greece, where it was large, have a more controversial record. It is a well-known World War II–era German witticism that the Germans were good Nazis but bad anti-Semites, while the Austrians were good anti-Semites but bad Nazis. (There were many more Jews in Austria, in proportion to the total population.)

Peripherality: Geographic, Class, and Racial

Contact with Muslims does not mitigate Islamophobia directly. Rather, it is itself a consequence of something else: a quality, not of Muslims but of Islamophobes, which I am referring to as *peripherality*. *Peripherality* as a technical term is probably best known from Immanuel Wallerstein's world-systems theory, which is meant to explain the disparity of privilege across the world in spatial ways but not necessarily country by country.[53] The opposite of *peripheral* is *core*. The core is a location of privilege, and the periphery one of disadvantage; the privilege of one, moreover, depends on the disadvantage of the other, within a system of inequality. In the postcolonial world, to use one major example, the former colonial powers like Britain are the core, and the former British colonies—still linked to Britain by economic, political, and social ties—are the periphery.

Peripherality is a relative matter. An area may be more or less peripheral than another. East Central Europe is peripheral compared to the Western European core. But East Central Europe is not as peripheral, within the world system of capitalism, as Central Asia, for example, or most of Africa are. Although the most common use of *periphery* is geographic, this chapter recognizes two other dimensions of peripherality: class peripherality and racial peripherality. As with geographic peripherality, class and race peripheralities function along a scale from the most to the East privileged.

The position from which Islamophobia is most commonly and explicitly articulated is one not quite at the bottom of the core-peripherality hierarchy but rather somewhere in the lower middle. Many of the spiffy rural towns and villages of the Western, but also eastern parts, of the EU today are outwardly charming, cozy places, with their historic centers gleaming under fresh paint bought with funds from Brussels. Insecurity, not desperation, is the major negative emotion most affecting them.[54] It is the insecurity of those not quite at the bottom of the social scale who cling on to what they perceive as disappearing privilege. Writing specifically about Poland, but in a way that applies to East Central Europe as a whole and beyond, Monika Bobako uses the more precise term *semi-periphery*.[55] The Mexican activist Subcommandante Marcos recognized early on the dynamics of

---

[53] See Darrell Arnold, ed., *Traditions of Systems Theory: Major Figures and Contemporary Developments*, Routledge Studies in Library and Information Science, 11th ed. (New York: Routledge and Taylor and Francis Group, 2014).

[54] This is the conclusion of a study, not yet published, that the author and a research team have conducted using semi-structured interviews with urban and rural residents in the four Visegrád countries.

[55] Monika Bobako, "Semi-Peripheral Islamophobias: The Political Diversity of Anti-Muslim Discourses in Poland," *Patterns of Prejudice* 52, no. 5 (2018): pp. 448–60. Bobako is using the term in a slightly different way from its originator's use. See Immanuel Wallerstein, "Semi-Peripheral Countries and the Contemporary World Crisis," *Theory and Society* 3, no. 4 (Winter 1976): pp. 461–83.

144 IVAN KALMAR

anti-migrant sentiment in the neoliberal, globalizing stage of capitalism, which, he wrote,

> brought about the displacement of millions of people. With their nightmares on their backs, their destiny is to wander, and to act as a kind of scarecrow— frightening those who have jobs into forgetting the boss—as well as a pretext for racism.[56]

Marcos concisely describes all three relevant dimensions of peripherality: geography, class, and race. The areas of *Islamophobia without Muslims* in eastern and Western Europe occupy a peripheral, but not the most peripheral, position along each of those dimensions.

The geographic or spatial dimension of peripherality is the most obvious correlate of *Islamophobia without Muslims*. As we have seen, rural regions are more Islamophobic; globally connected urban centers are less so. And although central Europe includes some big cities, such as Warsaw, Prague, and Budapest, that are home to luxury shops and fine restaurants frequented by a clientele that no longer consists only of foreigners, they do not belong to the first ranks of the world's major cities. The Kearney Global Cities Index places no East Central European city among its top 30 cities.[57] The Globalization and World Cities Research Network has none in the top alpha ++, alpha +, and alpha categories, though Prague and Warsaw have made it to the alpha – group, Budapest is beta +, and Bratislava beta –.[58] East Central Europe does not match the rest of Europe or North America in either the size or quality of its urbanization and so remains *as a whole* relatively peripheral in this sense.

Class peripherality also figures into the East Central Europe context. Islamophobic rhetoric and practices belong to a wider set, known as populism, illiberalism, or right-wing nationalism; some simply speak of "fascism."[59] Writers like Wilhelm Reich identified semi-peripheral class insecurity as the social-psychological core of the original, 20th-century fascism.[60] It is hard not to be reminded of such analyses when confronted with the recent history of

---

[56] Subcomandante Marcos, "The Fourth World War Has Begun," *Le Monde diplomatique*, September 1, 1997, http://mondediplo.com/1997/09/marcos.

[57] "Global Cities: New Priorities for a New World," *Kearney Global Cities Index*, last modified January 2021, https://www.kearney.com/global-cities/2020.

[58] "The World According to GaWC 2020," Globalization and World Cities Research Network, last modified August 21, 2020, https://www.lboro.ac.uk/gawc/world2020t.html.

[59] Federico Finchelstein, *A Brief History of Fascist Lies* (Oakland: University of California Press, 2020); Jason Stanley, *How Fascism Works: The Politics of Us and Them* (New York: Penguin Random House, 2018); Ugo Palheta, *La Possibilité du fascisme: France, la trajectoire du désastre* [*The Possibility of Fascism: France—the Trajectory of the Disaster*] (Paris: La Découverte, 2018); Enzo Traverso, *The New Faces of Fascism* (London: Verso, 2019).

[60] Wilhelm Reich, *The Mass Psychology of Fascism* (New York: Farrar, Straus, and Giroux, 1970).

ISLAMOPHOBIA WITHOUT MUSLIMS? 145

support for illiberal leaders like Donald Trump. His supporters have regularly been described as "working class" or given intersectionality with race as "white working class" or with gender as "white working-class men" and, finally, with reference to education, "white working-class men without a college degree."[61]

This categorization has been challenged by Mondon and Winter,[62] among others, but part of their valid criticism is less about the facts and more about the *working-class* label, which is indeed misleading. In the American Rust Belt, Trump supporters in 2016, many of whom switched back to Democrat in 2020, were working class, but more specifically they belonged to what should be called *the white upper working class*, people who have or had solid industrial employment, in which they applied their skills in a disciplined manner, and whose family and friendship networks were predominantly white.[63]

In America, as in Europe, much of the upper working class had long ago become culturally almost indistinguishable in culture and economic interests from some of the lower middle class. Home ownership has made them all indebted, literally, to capital, in an "age of credit."[64] We can therefore understandably debate about whether *working class* is the right way to describe the supporters of Trump or Orbán. At an anti-vaccination rally in Prague, a speaker described the group basically as the ordinary folks one stereotypically imagines at a local neighborhood pub: "We managed to gather together innkeepers, professional boxers, ski lift operators, football fans and hairdressers."[65] It may be hard to find the proper class label for this demographic, but clearly, the urban elite they are not.

The one most typical measurable characteristic of this hard-to-name semi-peripheral group is *without a college degree*. Kaya and Kayaoglu culled data from the World Values Survey and the European Values Study, two large-scale international projects, to find correlates of Islamophobia, and they found the

---

[61] See, for example, Jonathan P. Baird, "How Democrats Lost the White Working Class," *New Hampshire Business Review* 39, no. 14 (2017): p. 15.

[62] Aurelien Mondon and Aaron Winter, "Whiteness, Populism and the Racialisation of the Working Class in the United Kingdom and the United States," *Identities* 26, no. 5 (September 3, 2019): pp. 510–28; Aurelien Mondon and Aaron Winter, *Reactionary Democracy: How Racism and the Populist Far Right Became Mainstream* (Brooklyn, NY: Verso Books, 2020); Christine J. Walley, "Trump's Election and the 'White Working Class': What We Missed," *American Ethnologist* 44, no. 2 (2017): pp. 231–36.

[63] This phenomenon is discussed by Michael McQuarrie, among others. McQuarrie points out that both Black and white workers in the Rust Belt area were disaffected with the Democratic Party for similar reasons. Their common "revolt" against the candidacy of Hillary Clinton "demobilized" Black voters and "mobilized" white ones in support of Trump. Michael McQuarrie, "The Revolt of the Rust Belt: Place and Politics in the Age of Anger," *British Journal of Sociology* 68 (2017): pp. S120–52.

[64] Matthew Day, "The Short Happy Life of the Affluent Working Class: Consumption, Debt and Embourgeoisement in the Age of Credit," *Capital and Class* 44, no. 3 (September 1, 2020): pp. 305–24.

[65] Ludvík Hradilek, "Obrazem: Vakcína neexistuje; dvoutisícový dav na Staroměstském náměstí aplaudoval nesmyslům" ["In Pictures: The Vaccine Does Not Exist; a Crowd of Two Thousand on Old Town Square Applauds Nonsense"], *Deník N*, January 10, 2021, https://denikn.cz/535202/fotogale rie-vakcina-neexistuje-dvoutisicovy-dav-na-staromestskem-namesti-aplaudoval-nesmyslum/.

146   IVAN KALMAR

size of town or city where a person resides to be very influential; as expected, the smaller the city, the greater likelihood that a resident exhibits Islamophobic prejudice (specifically, not wanting to live next to Muslims). However, they also note that even in non-metropolitan locations, the more educated are less likely to show Islamophobia. Their explanation is a standard contact hypothesis, but with a twist. They claim that "having a higher possibility of interaction with Muslim population has a stronger impact on the lower educated than on the higher educated individuals."[66] However, it is not that educated people are more affected by contact with Muslims but that low education is a factor that contributes to an individual's class peripherality. In other words, the degree of contact with Muslims is not what matters here as much as do factors of class peripherality. Class peripherality amplifies geographic peripherality as a correlate of Islamophobia.

Furthermore, racial peripherality intersects with the class dimension. Muslims are often racialized in Europe today together with migrants of color, whether they are themselves phenotypically Brown or Black or not.[67] Migrants of color and their descendants are arguably situated at the most peripheral point of the racial hierarchy in eastern or Western Europe, with the likely exception of the Roma. Islamophobia may therefore be viewed as white supremacist.

But then, eastern Europeans themselves are less privy to racial privilege than are Western Europeans. Recent scholarship enables an understanding of race that, like peripherality, is relative. *Whiteness* becomes in some of recent writing a quality of degree, with some ethnic groups less unambiguously categorized than others as *white* in terms relating to the privilege that whiteness brings. Mary Hickman and Louise Ryan detail, for example, the precarious *whiteness* of Irish immigrants in England and compare it to that of central and eastern Europeans in the country.[68] But unlike the Irish, or Jews in America,[69] eastern Europeans

---

[66] Ayhan Kaya and Ayşegül Kayaoglu, "Individual Determinants of Anti-Muslim Prejudice in the EU-15," *Uluslararası İlişkiler/International Relations* 14, no. 53 (2017): pp. 45–68, 60.

[67] This fact is behind the definition of *Islamophobia* by the Runnymede Trust as "anti-Muslim racism." Farah Elahi and Omar Khan, eds., *Islamophobia: Still a Challenge for Us All* (London: Runnymede Trust, 2017), https://www.runnymedetrust.org/uploads/Islamophobia%20 Report%202018%20FINAL.pdf. See also Nicholas De Genova, "The 'Migrant Crisis' as Racial Crisis: Do *Black Lives Matter* in Europe?," *Ethnic and Racial Studies* 41, no. 10 (August 9, 2018): pp. 1765–82.

[68] Mary J. Hickman and Louise Ryan, "The 'Irish Question': Marginalizations at the Nexus of Sociology of Migration and Ethnic and Racial Studies in Britain," *Ethnic and Racial Studies* 43, no. 16 (2020): pp. 96–114.

[69] Echoing a common expression, see Karen Brodkin, *How Jews Became White Folks and What That Says about Race in America* (New Brunswick, NJ: Rutgers University Press, 1998). See also the sermon by Rabbi Gil Steinlauf on how Jews had to struggle to "become white." Gil Steinlauf, "Jews Struggled for Decades to Become White: Now We Must Give Up White Privilege to Fight Racism," *The Washington Post*, September 22, 2015, https://www.washingtonpost.com/posteverything/wp/2015/09/22/jews-in-america-struggled-for-generations-to-become-white-now-we-must-give-up-that-privilege-to-fight-racism/.

ISLAMOPHOBIA WITHOUT MUSLIMS? 147

seem to be becoming less white, not more. Studies have reported a disturbing increase in violence, physical and verbal, against eastern Europeans in Western Europe.[70] These phenomena are a form of racialization.[71]

The racialization operates with a broader concept of *eastern Europe*, of which East Central Europe is a part, and is happening against a backdrop of both journalistic and scholarly disappointment with the state of democracy, specifically in East Central Europe. For example, Krastev and Holmes state that "the attempt to democratize formerly communist countries was aiming at a kind of cultural conversion to values, habits and attitudes considered 'normal' in the West."[72] This "conversion" suggested that eastern European culture was inherently inhospitable to democracy and needed to be changed. Such a wholesale dismissal of "eastern Europe" as an area where democracy is not "normal" fully complies with Tariq Modood's seminal definition of *cultural racism*.[73]

By a kind of perverted but clear logic, insecurity about being fully Western— that is, "white," and by implication, mobilizing white privilege—requires distancing oneself from the non-Western Other.[74] One needs to differentiate oneself as sharply as possible from those who are not white. In the postcolonial logic marked by migration from the former colonies, that means especially distancing oneself from non-European migrants. During the 2015-16 "migration crisis," migrants of color who were either really or allegedly Muslim supplied the precariously white public of East Central Europe with a ready-made Other to set themselves above within the European racial hierarchy.[75] Although central Europe may be a region that is almost literally "without Muslims" in the flesh, we can see now that, in some Central Europeans' construction of the world and their place in it, Muslims nevertheless play a very large role.

---

[70] Alina Rzepnikowska, "Racism and Xenophobia Experienced by Polish Migrants in the UK before and after Brexit Vote," *Journal of Ethnic and Migration Studies* 45, no. 1 (January 2, 2019): pp. 61–77; József Böröcz and Mahua Sarkar, "The Unbearable Whiteness of the Polish Plumber and the Hungarian Peacock Dance around 'Race,'" *Slavic Review* 76, no. 2 (2017): pp. 307–14.

[71] Ivan Kalmar, "How Eastern Europeans Became Less White," in *White but Not Quite: Central Europe's Illiberal Revolt* (Bristol, UK: Bristol University Press, 2022), Chapter 1, 33–45.

[72] Ivan Krastev and Stephen Holmes, *The Light That Failed: A Reckoning* (London: Allen Lane, 2019), p. 10.

[73] Tariq Modood, "'Difference,' Cultural Racism and Anti-Racism," in *Debating Cultural Hybridity: Multicultural Identities and the Politics of Anti-Racism*, ed. Pnina Werbner and Tariq Modood (London: Zed Books, 1997), pp. 154–72.

[74] Sahar F. Aziz, *The Racial Muslim: When Racism Quashes Religious Freedom* (Berkeley: University of California, 2021).

[75] See Kalmar, *White but Not Quite*, especially "'We Will Not Be a Colony!,'" Chapter 8, 199–226. See also Salman Sayyid, "Islamophobia and the Europeanness of the Other Europe," *Patterns of Prejudice* 52, no. 5 (2018): pp. 420–35; Reza Hasmath and Solomon Kay-Reid, "What Salience Does White Privilege Have in Non-Diverse Societies?" (working paper, American Sociological Association Annual Meeting, virtual, 2021).

Conclusion

My purpose has been to demonstrate that the condition suggested by the somewhat bemused phrase *Islamophobia without Muslims* is not an "eastern European" curiosity but something that reveals crucial aspects of anti-Muslim racism in both Western and eastern Europe, as well as the United States. Islamophobia thrives in what might be called the *white periphery*: regions and social groupings that have been particularly damaged by the ascendancy of neoliberal globalization. And one such region that has been particularly affected is East Central Europe, where communist rule was supplanted quite abruptly by capitalism at the very moment when the neoliberal, globalist form of capitalism appeared to be in its triumphant stage.[76] It is not the lack of contact with Muslims, as the contact hypothesis would suggest, that results in relatively high indices of Islamophobia but rather the peripherality that is the condition of Central Europe as a whole, as well as of parts of the West.

A mistaken form of articulating frustration with peripheralization has, unfortunately, been the effort to set oneself apart from the even more peripheralized— that is, to add to one's precarious social capital of racial and class privilege by attacking an even more peripheralized Other. The Muslim is a particularly suitable target of othering in this context because of the availability of historical discourses like orientalism. The latter's close relationship to antisemitism makes it possible to tap into the affective and rhetorical reservoir also of anti-Judaism, a central part of Christianity's historical baggage.[77] Here, too, there is no principled difference between East and West. It is praiseworthy that several Polish scholars have uncovered the connection between antisemitism and Islamophobia, specifically in Poland,[78] but that connection remains, mutatis mutandis, across the Christian West. As the "migrant crisis" coincided with a major Islamist terrorist attack in Paris and shocking tales of migrant men attacking women in Cologne during the 2015–16 New Year's Eve celebrations, Islamophobia provided politicians across Europe, and in America, with a golden opportunity to take

---

[76] The fall of communism has itself been widely celebrated as the victory of capitalism in this Reaganite-Thatcherite stage. The period of triumph ended with the 2008 financial crisis.

[77] Ivan Kalmar, *Early Orientalism: Imagined Islam and the Notion of Sublime Power* (New York: Routledge, 2014); Ivan Kalmar, "Orientalism," in *Key Concepts in the Study of Antisemitism*, ed. Sol Goldberg, Scott Ury, and Kalman Weiser (Cham, Switzerland: Palgrave, 2020), pp. 187–99.

[78] See, for example, Monika Bobako, "Semi-Peripheral Islamophobias: The Political Diversity of Anti-Muslim Discourses in Poland," *Patterns of Prejudice* 52, no. 5 (2018): pp. 1–13; Elżbieta M. Goździak and Péter Márton, "Where the Wild Things Are: Fear of Islam and the Anti-Refugee Rhetoric in Hungary and in Poland," *Central and Eastern European Migration Review* 17, no. 2 (2018): pp. 125–51; Kasia Narkowicz and Konrad Pędziwiatr, "From Unproblematic to Contentious: Mosques in Poland," *Journal of Ethnic and Migration Studies* 43, no. 3 (February 17, 2017): pp. 441–57.

ISLAMOPHOBIA WITHOUT MUSLIMS? 149

advantage of it as a means to exploit the sense of precariousness and peripherali-zation that illiberal leaders seek.

When the numbers of migrants declined, in part because of the EU's deal to keep them in Turkey,[79] Islamophobic rhetoric subsided somewhat. Early in his four-year presidential term, Donald Trump gave up creating a registry of American Muslims, and his "Muslim ban" was watered down to apply only to Muslim countries that he particularly disliked. Soon enough, he was seen dancing the *al-'ardah,* sword in hand, with his Saudi Arabian hosts.[80] Viktor Orbán, too, initially targeted Islam more explicitly than he would later. In his case, it is the Muslim Turkic states of Asia that he has tried to enlist in his fight against liberal democracy.[81] In the meantime, anti-feminist and anti-LGBTQ rhetoric has become perhaps even more prominent than Islamophobia in East Central Europe has, with the exception of the Czech Republic, although such rhetoric has certainly not replaced Islamophobia.[82]

Islamophobia took the center stage of illiberalism only in 2015–16 and may be losing some of its intensity, perhaps temporarily, as a rhetoric of demagogic pop-ulism. But the origins of the insecurity to which it is a deplorable response have long historical roots. They lie in the worldwide neoliberal revolution, of which the collapse of communism in 1989 can be considered a triumphant apex, but which then began to flounder significantly during the 2008 financial crisis.[83] If Islamophobia has been politically more successful in East Central Europe, then it is not because of any inherent cultural or historical characteristics of the area. Rather, it is because during the disarray of the post-communist transition, ne-oliberal globalization affected the region particularly hard, amplifying all the symptoms and reactions that we see in other peripheral areas of the world, in-cluding the West, as *Islamophobia without Muslims* exists there, too.

There is, however, a practical consideration that may, unfortunately, guar-antee Islamophobia a more lasting place in the political arsenal of illiberalism

[79] Population Council, "The European Commission's Proposal for a Partnership Framework on Migration: Documents," *Population and Development Review* 42, no. 3 (September 2016): pp. 580–83.

[80] Eric Levenson and Noah Gray, "Trump, White House Officials Bounce along to Saudi Sword Dance," CNN Digital, May 20, 2017, https://www.cnn.com/2017/05/20/politics/trump-saudi-ara bia-dance/index.html.

[81] Hamdi Firat Buyuk, "Orban Enlists Turkic States in Fight against Liberal Democracy," *Balkan Insight* (blog), October 22, 2019, https://balkaninsight.com/2019/10/22/orban-enlists-turkic-states-in-fight-against-liberal-democracy/.

[82] Elżbieta Korolczuk, "The Fight against 'Gender' and 'LGBT Ideology': New Developments in Poland," *European Journal of Politics and Gender* 3, no. 1 (2020): pp. 165–67.

[83] A particularly enlightening book on the subject of neoliberalism and its peripheralizing effects on central Europe is Philipp Ther and Charlotte Hughes-Kreutzmüller, *Europe since 1989: A History* (Princeton, NJ: Princeton University Press, 2018). The author of the present chapter has previously discussed the role of neoliberalism in the peripheralization of eastern Europe, specifically in the context of Islamophobia. See Ivan Kalmar, "Islamophobia in the East of the European Union: An Introduction," *Patterns of Prejudice* 52, no. 5 (2018): pp. 389–405.

150 IVAN KALMAR

in central and eastern rather than Western Europe. In Western Europe, political leaders will increasingly have to include in their calculations the voters "of migration background,"[84] who are clustered in urban areas. This trend does not affect politicians in the east, who can still afford to treat their entire country as if it were "without Muslims." One can see why they want to keep it that way.

---

[84] *Mit Migrationshintergund*, translated as "of migration background," has become a common phrase in Germany to identify Germans whose family roots are outside of Germany, especially outside of Europe.

9

Islamophobia in Russia

Ethnicity, Migration, and National Security

Sarah Calderone* and Sahar F. Aziz

"Go back to Kuban, to the Cossacks," Alexander Bastrykin, the head of Russia's Federal Investigative Committee, told a Leningrad region investigator who hails from Anapa.[1] Bastrykin's on-the-record comments referenced a purportedly mishandled investigation on a gas-leak death.[2] Bastrykin continued: "They've just flooded the place. One day, it's the Asians pushing in, then it's the Kyrgyz, then the Tajiks, and now the Krasnodarians are flooding the place. Go back."[3]

---

* Sahar Aziz is professor of law, chancellor's social justice scholar, and the founding director of the Center for Security, Race and Rights at Rutgers Law School. Sarah Calderone is a student at Rutgers Law School, editor-in-chief of *Rutgers University Law Review*, and law fellow at the Center for Security, Race and Rights. She holds a master's degree in international affairs from Columbia University's School of International and Public Affairs, a certificate in Russian, Eurasian, and East European studies from the Harriman Institute, and a bachelor of arts in Russian studies and political science from Drew University. She was awarded a Fulbright grant in 2014–15 to research migration from Central Asia in Ekaterinburg, Russia.

[1] "'Киргизы, таджики, еще и краснодарцы понаехали': Глава СК Бастрыкин велел 'возвращаться обратно' следователю из Анапы" ["Kyrgyz, Tajiks, and Still Krasnodars Have Flooded: Head of IC Bastrykin Told an Investigator from Anapa to 'Return Back'"], *Current Time*, October 19, 2021, https://www.currenttime.tv/a/bastrykin-velel-vozvraschatsya-obratno-sledovatelyu-anapa/31518444.html.

[2] The mother of the deceased claimed that the investigator approached the investigation with a passive attitude and questioned its results on the cause of death. See "'Киргизы, таджики, еще и краснодарцы понаехали': Глава СК Бастрыкин велел 'возвращаться обратно' следователю из Анапы" ["Kyrgyz, Tajiks, and Still Krasnodars Have Flooded: Head of IC Bastrykin Told an Investigator from Anapa to 'Return Back'"], *Current Time*, https://www.currenttime.tv/a/bastrykin-velel-vozvraschatsya-obratno-sledovatelyu-anapa/31518444.html. Cossacks are a non-Muslim minority group in Russia historically portrayed as militaristic and nomadic, and the term *Kazakh* for ethnic Kazakhs from Kazakhstan has the same etymological roots in Turkish as *Cossack*. "Cossack (n.)," Online Etymology Dictionary, accessed November 21, 2021, https://www.etymonline.com/word/Cossack.

[3] "'They're Flooding the City': Russia's Investigative Committee Head Unleashes Racist Tirade While Criticizing Detective in St. Petersburg," *Meduza*, October 19, 2021, https://meduza.io/en/feature/2021/10/19/they-re-flooding-the-city; see also "'Киргизы, таджики, еще и краснодарцы понаехали': Глава СК Бастрыкин велел 'возвращаться обратно' следователю из Анапы" ["'Kyrgyz, Tajiks, and Still Krasnodars Have Flooded': Head of IC Bastrykin Told an investigator from Anapa to 'Return Back'"], *Current Time*.

Sarah Calderone and Sahar F. Aziz, *Islamophobia in Russia* In: *Global Islamophobia and the Rise of Populism*. Edited by: Sahar F. Aziz and John L. Esposito, Oxford University Press. © Oxford University Press 2024. DOI: 10.1093/oso/9780197648995.003.0009

Using the offensive term *ponaekhali*, often used to connote immigrants flooding into, overrunning, or otherwise coming into a location in droves,[4] Bastrykin's statement highlights three social dynamics that contribute to xenophobia and Islamophobia in Russia today. First, Kyrgyz and Tajiks, although hailing from former Soviet republics in Central Asia, are distinguished in public discourse from East Asian migrants from China, Korea, and elsewhere. This differentiation is because Central Asian states have shared Soviet history with Russia. Notwithstanding their diverse ethnic and religious backgrounds, Central Asian nations generally consist of Turkic peoples who practice Islam. Second, migrants from Central Asia are outsiders to Russia's native minorities, which include Cossacks but also Muslim populations from "Tatarstan, Bashkortostan, Dagestan, Adygeya, Chechnya, Ingushetia, Northern Ossetia, Kabardino-Balkaria, and Karachayevo-Cherkessia."[5]

Finally, the demeaning tone of Bastrykin's statement belies the Russian government's stated commitment to multinationalism and tolerance of minority ethnicities, cultures, and denominations. Central Asians, among others, are treated differently (notably worse) than ethnic Russians are, regardless of citizenship status.

Russia has been home to native Muslim minorities since the incorporation of Chechnya, Tatarstan, and Crimea into the Russian Empire starting in the 18th century.[6] Only since the 2000s did migrant populations from Muslim-majority, post-Soviet countries in Central Asia begin arriving in large numbers to current-day Russia.[7] Despite the government's official narrative that Russia is a multinational and multi-denominational country,[8] migrants from Central Asia encounter systematic xenophobia and discrimination,[9] arising in large part from perceived differences in ethnicity, nationality, and religion.

The state treats Muslim migrants from Central Asia as potential security threats, in contrast to Russian Muslims and non-Muslim migrant groups. But the

---

[4] " 'They're Flooding the City.' " The term is понаехали, transliterated as *ponaekhali*. "Понаехали," *Multitran*, accessed November 21, 2021, https://www.multitran.com/m.exe?s=%D0%BF%D0%BE%D0%BD%D0%B0%D0%B5%D1%85%D0%B0%D0%BB%D0%B8+&l1=2&l2=1.

[5] Greg Simons, "Introduction: The Image of Islam in Russia," in *The Image of Islam in Russia* (New York: Routledge, 2021), p. 175.

[6] Shireen Hunter et al., *Islam in Russia: The Politics of Identity and Security* (New York: Routledge, 2004), pp. 7–9.

[7] See Caress Schenk, *Why Control Immigration? Strategic Uses of Migration Management in Russia* (Toronto, Canada: University of Toronto Press, 2018), pp. 1–2.

[8] "Путин: РФ является многонациональной страной, и 'пещерный национализм' может ее развалить" ["Putin: Russian Federation Is a Multinational Country, and 'Caveman Nationalism' Could Break It Up"], *TASS*, October 18, 2018, https://tass.ru/obschestvo/5691434.

[9] Daniil Kislov and Ernest Zhanaev, "Russia: Xenophobia and Vulnerability of Migrants from Central Asia," Foreign Policy Center, December 4, 2017, https://fpc.org.uk/russia-xenophobia-vulnerability-migrants-central-asia/. Note that much academic, advocacy, and media writing on the subject varies widely on the extent of xenophobia and discrimination against migrants; some of this writing will be covered below.

nation's need for cheap labor permits them to migrate to Russia on the condition that they assimilate into Russian society and culture. Moreover, Russia like other European nations is experiencing a rise of xenophobic, right-wing populism that influences the government and public's preference for Slavic, Orthodox migrants from European, post-Soviet countries over Central Asian Muslim migrants.

Thus, Central Asian Muslims also encounter the racialization of Muslim identity experienced by other Muslim diasporas in Western countries.[10] In Russia, however, what determines whether a Muslim Central Asian migrant is "good" or "bad" is shaped by Russia's migration and national security policies.[11] Accordingly, this chapter examines the complicated history of the Russian government's relationship with its Muslim minorities and the effect on migrant populations from post-Soviet states. Muslim migrants from post-Soviet Central Asia experience discrimination in large part because Islamophobia is tied to ethno-religious populism and xenophobia, in contrast to the favored status of Orthodox Christian migrants from post-Soviet countries.

The Complex History of Muslims in Russia

Russia has been home to Muslim populations for centuries. Since imperial times, Chechens, Tatars, Dagestanis, and Bashkirs have experienced periods of hostility, neutrality, and peaceful relations. They are most vulnerable to state repression when they seek political autonomy.[12] During the Soviet period, the central government engaged with Muslim ethnic groups through a nationalities policy centered around republics defined by ethnicity and the state's anti-religion policies.[13] Following the collapse of the Soviet Union, ethnic Russians were

---

[10] See Sahar F. Aziz, *The Racial Muslim: When Racism Quashes Religious Freedom* (Berkeley: University of California Press, 2021).

[11] This Good Muslim/Bad Muslim framework has been applied in the American and global contexts. See, generally, Aziz, *Racial Muslim*; Mahmood Mamdani, *Good Muslim, Bad Muslim: America, the Cold War, and the Roots of Terror* (New York: Doubleday, 2005); Mitra Rastegar, *Tolerance and Risk: How US Liberalism Racializes Muslims* (Minneapolis: University of Minnesota Press, 2021); Saher Selod, "Islamophobia and the Rise of Ethnonationalist Populism in the United States," ch. 4 in this volume; Khaled A. Beydoun, "The Myth of the 'Moderate Muslim': Deconstructing the Mythic 'Good versus Bad' Muslim Paradigm," *Al Jazeera*, May 20, 2016, https://www.aljazeera.com/opinions/2016/5/20/the-myth-of-the-moderate-muslim.

[12] See, generally, Simons, "Introduction"; Iskander Abbasi, "Russian Islamophobia: From Medieval Tsardom to the Post-Soviet Man," Islamophobia Studies Center, 2022, https://iphobiacenter.org/wp-content/uploads/2022/06/Islamophobia-Russia.pdf?fbclid=IwAR26OhzptP9f3jUX9qaKJI9svl-mmdvfry7Doh5yFQ69BpM4bt5P_7l-NzM, p. 11.

[13] See, generally, Elise Giuliano, "Variation of Mass Nationalism across Russia's Republics," in *Constructing Grievance: Ethnic Nationalism in Russia's Republics* (Ithaca, NY: Cornell University Press, 2011), pp. 42–43, 52–53. There are of course accounts that paint Soviet rule as perhaps not as anti-religious as portrayed by others, but scholars also point to this phenomenon as one that explains the relatively secular practice of Islam in post-Soviet Central Asian republics. See Hunter, *Islam in Russia*; Helene Thibault, "The Soviet Secularization Project in Central Asia: Accommodation

154   SARAH CALDERONE AND SAHAR F. AZIZ

prioritized in the repatriation programs of the 1990s.[14] Later, migrants from Central Asia, among others, began arriving in Russia in search of work.[15]

Russia's Native Muslim Populations

In Russia, Muslims—comprising Russian ethnic groups and other ethnicities from former Soviet Union states in Central Asia and the Caucasus—make up approximately 10 to 14 percent of the population.[16] According to a 2009 Pew Research Center report, Russia was home to the largest Muslim population—sixteen million—among European countries, with Germany occupying a far second at four million.[17] Ten years later, Russia is still home to the largest Muslim minority population as compared to Bulgaria's 11.1 million, France's 8.8 million, Sweden's 8.1 million, and Austria's 6.9 million Muslims.[18]

Relations with ethnically diverse Muslim Russian citizens are more complex than the government publicly admits they are. The Russian government's relations with Tatarstan and Chechnya, for example, illustrate how the state offers conditional acceptance to Russian Muslims based on cultural assimilationism and political compliance.[19] These factors serve as a litmus test for differentiating between "Good Muslims" to be tolerated and "Bad Muslims" to be occupied,

---

and Institutional Legacies," *Eurostudia—revue transatlantique de recherche sur l'Europe* 10, no.1 (2015): pp. 11–31; Abbasi, "Russian Islamophobia," p. 15 (detailing relations with Muslim communist groups from abroad).

[14] See Schenk, *Why Control Immigration?*, pp. 1–2.

[15] See Schenk, *Why Control Immigration?*, p. 2. While this chapter will focus on this group in particular, Central Asians were not the only ones migrating to Russia; others were from the Caucasus, including Orthodox Armenians and Georgians as well as Muslim Azerbaijanis.

[16] "Russia Will Be One-Third Muslim in 15 Years, Chief Mufti Predicts," *Moscow Times*, March 5, 2019, https://www.themoscowtimes.com/2019/03/05/russia-will-be-one-third-muslim-in-15-years-chief-mufti-predicts-a64706. The range for this figure is wide depending on which entity is citing it; religious groups emphasize larger percentages, while government and other sources are more conservative in their estimates. However, it is unclear whether these figures include just citizens or Muslim migrants, including those among the estimated three to five million undocumented migrants. See Schenk, *Why Control Immigration?*, p. 2.

[17] "Mapping the Global Muslim Population," Pew Research Center, October 7, 2009, https://www.pewforum.org/2009/10/07/mapping-the-global-muslim-population/.

[18] See "Russia Will Be One-Third Muslim"; "Europe's Growing Muslim Population," Pew Research Center, November 29, 2017, https://www.pewforum.org/2017/11/29/europes-growing-muslim-population/.

[19] Anna Alekseyeva, "The Russian Politics of Multiculturalism," *OpenDemocracy*, March 30, 2015, https://www.opendemocracy.net/en/odr/russian-politics-of-multiculturalism/. Alekseyeva focuses solely on the Russian government's relationship with the north Caucasus in explaining President Vladimir Putin's purported acceptance of Islam, but considering its connection to other Muslim-majority regions helps elaborate the spectrum of treatment of Muslims in Russia, which varies between the examples of Tatarstan and Chechnya. See Aziz, *Racial Muslim*.

deported, or incarcerated, belying the Russian government's official narrative of multinational, multi-denominational harmony.[20]

The Russian government and public opinion define Good Muslims as those who are non-dissident, not overt in their religious practices, and useful to state security and economic goals. The case of Tatarstan exemplifies the government's promotion of Good Muslims. This autonomous republic partially owns one of the major Russian oil companies,[21] and until 2021 maintained an independent presidential office.[22] The Kremlin's apparent trust in Tatar self-governance has been driven in part by a perceived lack of ambition for autonomy that would otherwise threaten centralized rule from Moscow. Moreover, Tatarstan's willingness to separate religion from politics facilitated their semiautonomous governance structure. As a result, the Tatars maintain their region's autonomous status through informal authority, not direct confrontation with the Russian government.[23]

In contrast, Bad Muslims are political dissidents, militaristic, overt in their religious practices, or uncooperative with the Kremlin's national security policies. The case of Chechnya exemplifies the Russian state's violent response to Muslim minorities' demands for political autonomy and, in some cases, outright secession. Following the collapse of the Soviet Union, Russia and Chechnya fought two civil wars, driven partially by a local desire to secede coupled with increased religiosity among Chechens.[24] The wars came along with religiously and ethnically charged language in media, as well as increased security and surveillance.[25]

---

[20] Alekseyeva, "Russian Politics."

[21] OAO Tatneft (Form 20-F), US Securities and Exchange Commission, July 14, 2005, https://www.sec.gov/Archives/edgar/data/1058255/000119312505141948/d20f.htm#rom88804_45; ВЫПИСКА из Единого государственного реестра юридических лиц, ПУБЛИЧНОЕ АКЦИОНЕРНОЕ ОБЩЕСТВО "ТАТНЕФТЬ" ИМЕНИ В.Д. ШАШИНА [Extract from the Unified State Registry of Legal Entities, public joint stock company Tatneft named after V. D. Shashin], July 11, 2022, https://egrul.nalog.ru/index.html; "Fitch Affirms PJSC Tatneft at 'BBB-'; Outlook Stable," Fitch Ratings, February 14, 2022, https://www.fitchratings.com/research/corporate-finance/fitch-affirms-pjsc-tatneft-at-bbb-outlook-stable-14-02-2022.

[22] "Russian Duma Oks Bill That Would Abolish the Title of 'President' in Tatarstan," *Radio Free Europe/Radio Liberty*, October 25, 2021, https://www.rferl.org/a/tatarstan-president-president-title/31528369.html; "Подписан закон о единой системе публичной власти в субъектах России" ["Law Signed on the Unified System of Public Authority in the Federal Subjects of Russia"], President of Russia, December 21, 2021, http://kremlin.ru/acts/news/67399.

[23] Matthew Allen Derrick, "Placing Faith in Tatarstan, Russia: Islam and the Negotiation of Homeland" (dissertation, University of Oregon, 2012), https://scholarsbank.uoregon.edu/xmlui/bitstream/handle/1794/12336/Derrick_oregon_0171A_10305.pdf?sequence=1; András Tóth-Czifra, "How to Be a Successful Region in Russia: The Case of Tatarstan," Institute of Modern Russia, February 1, 2022, https://imrussia.org/en/analysis/3413-how-to-be-a-successful-region-in-russia-the-case-of-tatarstan.o. See, generally, Helen Faller, *Nation, Language, Islam: Tatarstan's Sovereignty Movement* (New York: Central European University Press, 2011).

[24] See Alekseyeva, "Russian Politics"; Marlene Laruelle, "How Islam Will Change Russia," Jamestown Foundation, September 13, 2016, https://jamestown.org/program/marlene-laruelle-how-islam-will-change-russia/.

[25] Abbasi, "Russian Islamophobia," p. 19.

In contrast to the secular and politically compliant Tatarstan, Chechens developed separatist aspirations to establish a state governed by Islamic principles.

The political and cultural borders of the Good Muslim and the Bad Muslim, however, are hierarchical and fluid. Similar to the treatment of Muslims in the United States, the more religious and politically dissident a Muslim, the more harshly they are targeted by state national security and migration exclusion laws.[26] After being subdued by Moscow, Chechnya is now a player in the Russian government's suppression of domestic dissidents. For instance, the murder of opposition politician Boris Nemtsov was ultimately pinned on five Chechens in what appears to be a cover-up.[27] More recently, there were reports that the Chechen government under orders from Moscow sent a special operations team to Ukraine to kill President Volodymyr Zelensky during Russia's war in Ukraine.[28] Meanwhile, Tatarstan—once considered the model of a Muslim-majority region—clashed with Moscow over its refusal to give up its presidential role. In October 2021, Russia's State Duma voted to rescind the presidential title of Tatarstan, whose parliament subsequently denounced the measure.[29] Such changes evince the precarity of Muslims' status as Russian minorities who are subject to double standards and collective punishment.

The Russian government does not readily admit to pursuing Islamophobic policies that differentiate between its Muslim and non-Muslim citizens. When accused of Islamophobia, the Russian government draws upon a history of what it describes as cooperation and coexistence among Russia's many cultures, including Muslim minorities.[30] Former Prime Minister Yevgeniy Primakov, for instance, differentiated between Islamic fundamentalism and extremism in explaining how the government should treat Muslims in Russia, with the former "being an entirely legitimate expression of Islamic faith" and the latter "unacceptable" and one that "needs to be repressed at all cost."[31] President Vladimir Putin expanded on this narrative by "engag[ing] with Islamic states and movements that the West considers as terrorist or as internationally illegitimate, such as Iran, Hamas and Hizbullah."[32] With these approaches, alongside statements on

---

[26] See Aziz, *Racial Muslim*.

[27] "Boris Nemtsov Murder: Five Chechens Jailed for Attack," BBC, July 13, 2017, https://www.bbc.com/news/world-europe-40592248; Marlene Laruelle, "How Islam."

[28] Timothy Bella, "Assassination Plot against Zelensky Foiled and Unit Sent to Kill Him 'Destroyed,' Ukraine Says," *The Washington Post*, March 2, 2022, https://www.washingtonpost.com/world/2022/03/02/zelensky-russia-ukraine-assassination-attempt-foiled/.

[29] "Russian Duma Oks Bill."

[30] See "Путин: РФ является многонациональной страной, и 'пещерный национализм' может ее развалить" ["Putin: Russian Federation Is a Multinational Country, and 'Caveman Nationalism' Could Break It Up"]. Examples include narratives that paint imperial Russia as not colonizing but accommodating, and Soviet conferences that emphasized friendliness toward Islam. See Hunter, *Islam in Russia*.

[31] Ronald Dannreuther, "Understanding Russia's Return to the Middle East," *International Politics* 56 (2019): p. 735.

[32] Dannreuther, "Understanding," p. 735.

Russia's multinationalism and denunciations of some nationalist groups,[33] the Russian government attempts to prove that its policies are not Islamophobic.

However, these claims fall flat when considering that Primakov made the above remarks while visiting Tatarstan amid the beginning of the Second Chechen War because he was seeking buy-in from Russian Muslims.[34] Also, claims that Russia is more accepting of a wider range of Islamist rather than Western Europe groups are belied by the fact that many Islamist groups, such as Hizb ut-Tahrir, the Islamic Party of Turkestan, and the Muslim Brotherhood, are designated as terrorist under Russian law.[35] Thus, the state's multinational, multi-denominational rhetoric glosses over the distinction between Good and Bad Muslims, how the distinction is made, and what happens when extremism is interpreted broadly.[36] Because of this, analysis of Russia's cooperative multinationalism and its differentiated treatment of Muslim populations is complicated.

Russia's experiences with the Chechen wars, alongside legitimation from the post–9/11 Global War on Terror (GWOT), inform how it treats Russian Muslims and Central Asian Muslim migrants. Because Russia faced separatism and terrorist attacks from the Muslim-majority republic of Chechnya, the GWOT provided international political cover for the government's brutal collective punishment of Chechens.[37] And yet Putin engages in the rhetoric of multiculturalism for purposes of quelling instability among the millions of Russian Muslims while simultaneously differentiating Russia as more welcoming of migrants than Western Europe is. A deeper look at the Kremlin's migration and national security policies demonstrates how Islamophobia harms another group of Muslims—Central Asian migrants.

[33] See "Путин: РФ является многонациональной страной, и 'пещерный национализм' может ее развалить" ["Putin: Russian Federation Is a Multinational Country, and 'Caveman Nationalism' Could Break It Up"]; Dannreuther, "Understanding," p. 735.

[34] See "Tatar-Bashkir Report," *Radio Free Europe/Radio Liberty*, October 20, 1999, https://www.rferl.org/a/1346597.html.

[35] "Единый федеральный список организаций, в том числе иностранных и международных организаций, признанных в соответствии с законодательством Российской Федерации террористическими" ["Unified Federal List of Organizations, including Foreign and International Organizations, Recognized in Accordance with the Legislation of the Russian Federation as Terrorist"], Federal Security Service of the Russian Federation, April 22, 2022, http://www.fsb.ru/fsb/npd/terror.htm. See below for discussion on Islamophobia in Russian national security law and the organizations included in this list.

[36] See Dannreuther, "Understanding."

[37] See Dmitri Trenin, "Policy Brief: The Forgotten War: Chechnya and Russia's Future," Carnegie Endowment for International Relations, November 2003, https://carnegieendowment.org/files/Policybrief28.pdf. For information on Russian abuses in the conflict, see "War Crimes in Chechnya and the Response of the West: Testimony before the Senate Committee on Foreign Relations," Human Rights Watch, February 29, 2000, https://www.hrw.org/news/2000/02/29/war-crimes-chechnya-and-response-west#.

Migrants from Former Soviet States

After the collapse of the Soviet Union, various stages of immigration ensued from the early return of ethnically Russian compatriots in newly independent states to a steady stream of labor migration from Muslim-majority, formerly Soviet countries. Stark differences in how the government received these groups is indicative of Russians' attitudes toward Muslim migrants.

Beginning in the 1990s, Russia launched a repatriation program to return ethnic Russians living in other former Soviet republics to Russia.[38] While there are still pockets of ethnic Russians who stayed in those countries, the program was successful in attracting people in search of stability and security through long-term resettlement.[39] Ten years later, migrants from post-Soviet Central Asian republics began arriving in Russia in search of work amid precarious economic conditions at home. This wave of migrants has come primarily from Kyrgyzstan, Tajikistan, and Uzbekistan, and they maintain temporary status, moving across borders seasonally for work in the construction and service sectors.[40] These populations are also ethnically Turkic, with the exception of Tajiks, and practice a secularized form of Islam.[41]

Although migration statistics in Russia are unreliable, official estimates report between one and two million Central Asian labor migrants plus three to five million total undocumented migrants.[42] Their temporary and irregular status, exacerbated by the COVID-19 pandemic,[43] makes them vulnerable to discrimination and violence.[44] Particularly when compared to other migrants from Slavic, Orthodox-majority countries, Central Asian Muslim migrants are among the worst treated noncitizens in Russia, facing harassment, abuse by law enforcement, and mass deportations.[45] Central Asians' Muslim identities intersect with

---

[38] Olga Vykhovanets and Alexander Zhuravsky, "Compatriots: Back to the Homeland," Russian International Affairs Council, May 31, 2013, https://russiancouncil.ru/en/analytics-and-comments/analytics/compatriots-back-to-the-homeland/.

[39] Vykhovanets and Zhuravsky, "Compatriots"; see Schenk, *Why Control Immigration?*, p. 3.

[40] See Schenk, *Why Control Immigration?*, p. 11. Migrants from Kazakhstan play a somewhat different role in the regional migration system, often filling roles that in Russia usually require higher qualifications. While these groups are distinct and have unique challenges, the chapter will often refer to them collectively because of the nature of the Russian government's relationship with them and its broad migration policies.

[41] See, for example, "Central Asia: Islam and the State," International Crisis Group, July 10, 2003, https://www.crisisgroup.org/europe-central-asia/central-asia/uzbekistan/central-asia-islam-and-state.

[42] See Schenk, *Why Control Immigration?*, pp. 2, 11–12.

[43] Aruuke Uran Kyzy, "Coronavirus Exposes Central Asian Migrants' Vulnerability," *The Diplomat*, April 10, 2020, https://thediplomat.com/2020/04/coronavirus-exposes-central-asian-migrants-vulnerability/; "Russia Tells Illegal Migrants from Post-Soviet Countries to Leave by June 15," *Moscow Times*, April 16, 2021, https://www.themoscowtimes.com/2021/04/16/russia-tells-illegal-migrants-from-post-soviet-countries-to-leave-by-june-15-a73623.

[44] See Kislov and Zhanaev, "Russia."

[45] Kislov and Zhanaev, "Russia." See, for example, Victor Agadjanian, Cecilia Menjívar, and Natalya Zotova, "Legality, Racialization, and Immigrants' Experience of Ethnoracial Harassment in

race, ethnicity, geography, and class when the Russian government targets them, nationalist groups attack them, and businesses exploit them.[46]

Since arriving in large numbers to Russia, Central Asian migrants have oscillated between being welcomed workers amid labor shortages, including during the COVID-19 pandemic, and suspicious outsiders prone to radicalization when they practice Islam.[47] Despite alarmist media coverage surrounding a series of terrorist attacks worldwide with connections to Central Asia, there is no evidence of widespread radicalization among Muslims in post-Soviet Central Asian states.[48] The numbers of alleged terrorist attacks committed by Muslim Central Asians are low, at three out of 153 in Russia between 2014 and 2017, yet Central Asian Muslims remain subject to collective suspicion.[49]

Russia," *Social Problems* 21, no. 1 (2017): pp. 558–76 (providing details on the differences in treatment based on interviews). Even the war in Ukraine provided an opportunity to welcome migrants from there, with policies prioritizing their transfer. See the section on migration law below.

[46] See Marlene Laruelle and Natalia Yudina, "Islamophobia in Russia: Trends and Societal Context," in *Religion and Violence in Russia: Context, Manifestations, and Policy*, ed. Olga Oliker (Washington, DC: Center for Strategic and International Studies, 2018) https://csis-website-prod. s3.amazonaws.com/s3fs-public/publication/180530_Oliker_ReligionandViolenceinRussia_Web. pdf?HLUcSpiycSLjwYXjxwk8nM49DfnpOsvT; Umida Hashimova, "Russia's Dependence on Cheap Central Asian Labor Exposed," *The Diplomat*, October 18, 2021, https://thediplomat.com/2021/ 10/russias-dependence-on-cheap-central-asian-labor-exposed/; Catherine Putz, "Central Asia's Migrants Face Suspicion in Russia," *The Diplomat*, April 1, 2016, https://thediplomat.com/2016/04/ central-asias-migrants-face-suspicion-in-russia/.

[47] See "Virus-Driven Migrant Shortage Keeps Russia from 'Ambitious Plans'—Kremlin," *Moscow Times*, April 8, 2021, https://www.themoscowtimes.com/2021/04/08/virus-driven-migrant-short age-keeps-russia-from-ambitious-plans-kremlin-a73524. Again, this welcome is not guaranteed, as foreigners have seen another setback in recommended quarterly tuberculosis tests, which will disproportionately affect Central Asian migrants. See Sergei Guscha, "Foreigners in Russia Outraged by New Medical Checks," *Deutsche Welle*, December 19, 2021, https://www.dw.com/en/foreign ers-in-russia-outraged-by-new-medical-checks/a-60182104; Mohammed Elshimi and Raffaello Pantucci, "Explaining the Radicalization of Central Asian Migrants," *The Diplomat*, January 29, 2018, https://thediplomat.com/2018/01/explaining-the-radicalization-of-central-asian-migrants/; "Syria Calling: Radicalisation in Central Asia," International Crisis Group, January 20, 2015, https://www. crisisgroup.org/europe-central-asia/central-asia/syria-calling-radicalisation-central-asia.

[48] See, for example, Edward Lemon, "Assessing the Terrorist Threat in and from Central Asia," *Voices on Central Asia*, October 18, 2018, https://voicesoncentralasia.org/assessing-the-terror ist-threat-in-and-from-central-asia/; Edward Lemon, Vera Mironova, and William Tobey, "Jihadists from Ex-Soviet Central Asia: Where Are They? Why Did They Radicalize? What Next?," *Russia Matters*, December 7, 2018, https://www.russiamatters.org/analysis/jihadists-ex-sov iet-central-asia-where-are-they-why-did-they-radicalize-what-next; John Heathershaw and David Montgomery, *The Myth of Post-Soviet Muslim Radicalization in the Central Asian Republics* (London: Chatham House, 2014), https://www.chathamhouse.org/sites/default/files/publications/ research/20141111PostSovietRadicalizationHeathershawMontgomeryFinal.pdf.

[49] The number is more likely one because the Global Terrorism Database includes two attacks simply because the perpetrators were from Central Asia. See Lemon, "Assessing." The most recent EU Terrorism Situation and Trend report does not include any such attacks and instead focuses on some of the recent right-wing activities in Russia. Europol, *European Union Terrorism Situation and Trend Report* (Luxembourg: Publications Office of the European Union, 2021), https://www.europol.eur opa.eu/cms/sites/default/files/documents/tesat_2021_0.pdf.

SARAH CALDERONE AND SAHAR F. AZIZ

Another factor influencing Russia's relations with Central Asian migrants is a rise in ethno-religious populism that privileges Russian Orthodox and Slavic identity.

Rise of Ethnonationalist Populism

Islamophobia toward Central Asian Muslim migrants is shaped not only by demographics but also the rise of Russian ethno-nationalist populism.[50] Right-wing groups propagate hyper-nationalism defined by Russian ethnicity and Russian Orthodox Christianity. According to the Center for Eastern Studies, populist groups in Russia fall into two categories: those with ethnocentric views and those with imperialist views. Ethnocentric groups and imperialist groups are diverse in their ideologies but may share a desire for the unification of the former empire, Russian supremacy, and the exclusion of immigrants.[51]

The Russian government, similar to other illiberal states, has co-opted some right-wing populism in order to minimize any threat that these groups pose to the state.[52] But it dissolved groups, such as the "Russians," an ethnocentric group deemed to be a threat to state authority that deviated from the multinational narrative in their attempt to create "an ethnically unified state."[53] The "Russians" sowed discord beyond the government's control.[54]

However, nationalists comprising Eurasian and Orthodox groups—the Night Wolves, the National Liberation Movement, and the Eurasian Youth Association—and xenophobic, government-friendly parties, including the Liberal Democratic and Rodina parties, are permitted to be mainstream.[55] Some groups are more welcoming of Muslims when Muslims are useful to their goals— that is, when they are seen as supportive of imperial ambitions or as traditional, in these groups' views. Some groups, including the Liberal Democratic Party, continue to hold anti-Muslim views as a legacy of its leaders.[56] Again, Good Muslims are, more than anything, those who support the regime.

---

[50] For an account of the rise of and differences among nationalism, populism, and right-wing extremism in Russia, see, generally, Marlene Laruelle, *In the Name of the Nation: Nationalism and Politics in Contemporary Russia* (New York: Palgrave Macmillan, 2009).

[51] Jan Strzelecki, "Russian Nationalism Three Years after the Annexation of Crimea," Centre for Eastern Studies, August 8, 2017, https://www.osw.waw.pl/en/publikacje/osw-commentary/2017-08-08/russian-nationalism-three-years-after-annexation-crimea.

[52] Stratfor, "How Russia Uses Right-Wing Extremism as a Cheap, Deniable Way to Undermine Western Countries," *Business Insider*, January 21, 2021, https://worldview.stratfor.com/article/russia-s-role-stoking-right-wing-extremism-west.

[53] Strzelecki, "Russian Nationalism."

[54] Strzelecki, "Russian Nationalism."

[55] Strzelecki, "Russian Nationalism"; Kira Harris, "Russia's Fifth Column: The Influence of the Night Wolves Motorcycle Club," *Studies in Conflict and Terrorism* 43 (2020): 259–73.

[56] Vladimir Frolov, "Russia Has Its Own Tea Party with Rodina," *Moscow Times*, October 6, 2012, https://www.themoscowtimes.com/2012/10/06/russia-has-its-own-tea-party-with-rodina-a18

The Kremlin enjoys transnational ties with other right-wing populist parties and groups in Europe that draw on President Putin's imperial agenda.[57] For example, the regime has admirers abroad, including in the United States, for its traditional values regarding gender and sexuality and for its hawkish approach toward security.[58] Conservative figures as Pat Buchanan and Tucker Carlson and entities like *Newsmax* positively depict President Putin.[59] A recent pro-Kremlin video encouraging English speakers to move to Russia cited traditional values and Christianity as reasons to do so.[60]

Yet the values that these conservative parties share with others abroad are not necessarily reflected in Putin's speeches when it comes to relations with Muslims. Rather, President Putin's appeals to nationalist sentiments differentiate between Good and Bad Muslims, setting expectations for how Muslims should act in Russian society if they want to avoid becoming ensnared in national security practices or subjected to populist sentiment.[61] Speaking with Muslim leaders, Putin remarked on their role in countering religious extremism, noting that "[t]hese ideas, even destructive ideas, can only be fought with the help of other ideas."[62] Despite an acknowledged attempt to avoid using language that equates Islam and extremism,[63] Putin's distinction between Good and Bad Muslims largely comes down to their religiosity, political ambitions, and usefulness to the government.

The declining ethnic Russian population has triggered fears of a Muslim takeover—in ways that are similar to circumstances in Western European countries—given the higher population growth among native Muslim populations,

---

341; Kira Harris, "A Hybrid Threat: The Night Wolves Motorcycle Club," *Studies in Conflict and Terrorism* 46, no. 9 (2021): 1–29; Anna Nemtsova, "Russia's Trump, Vladimir Zhirinovsky, Wants to Build a Wall, Ban Muslims, and Nuke the White House," *Daily Beast*, April 13, 2017, https://www.thedailybeast.com/russias-trump-vladimir-zhirinovsky-wants-to-build-a-wall-ban-muslims-and-nuke-the-white-house.

[57] See Stratfor, "How Russia."

[58] See Glenn Diesen, "Russia as an International Conservative Power: The Rise of the Right-Wing Populists and Their Affinity Towards Russia," *Journal of Contemporary European Studies* 28, no. 2 (2020): pp. 182–96; Max de Haldevang, "Strongmen Like Putin and Xi Might Seem All Powerful—but They Make Their Countries Weaker," *Quartz*, August 1, 2018, https://qz.com/1231698/strongmen-xi-jinping-and-vladimir-putin-seem-powerful-but-they-make-their-countries-weaker/.

[59] Rich Lowry, "Vladimir Putin Shouldn't Be a Right-Wing Hero," *Politico*, December 9, 2021, https://www.politico.com/news/magazine/2021/12/09/vladimir-putin-shouldnt-be-a-right-wing-hero-524041.

[60] Tim McNulty, "'This for Real?' Moscow Ridiculed as 'Move to Russia' Ad Sparks Hilarious Twitter Slapdown," *Express*, July 29, 2022, https://www.express.co.uk/news/world/1647800/Vladimir-Putin-latest-Moscow-move-to-Russia-ad-twitter-cheap-gas-cancel-culture-vn.

[61] "Putin Calls for a 'Revival' of Islamic Education in Russia," *Moscow Times*, January 25, 2018, https://www.themoscowtimes.com/2018/01/25/putin-calls-for-revival-of-islamic-education-in-russia-a60276.

[62] "Putin Calls for a 'Revival.'"

[63] Dannreuther, "Understanding," p. 735.

coupled with the influx of migrants from Central Asian Muslim-majority countries.[64] Officials' estimates that Muslims will reach 30 percent of the population by 2034 are exploited by right-wing populists to stoke fears among the majority-ethnic and Christian Russians.[65]

Islamophobia in Russia

The Good/Bad Muslim litmus test manifests alongside populist attitudes driven by ethnic and religious considerations. Moreover, counterterrorism law and foreign policy reactively target Muslim populations while restrictive migration law and policy favor Slavic migrants from post-Soviet provinces over Muslim migrants from Central Asia and the Caucasus. Public opinion, migration law, and national security law expose the inconsistency between the government's narrative of multiculturalism, on one hand, and its antagonistic relationship with domestic Muslim populations on the other hand.

Public Opinion and Relations with Muslims

With several right-wing movements and parties promoting populist nationalism, more than half of Russians support the motto "Russia for Russians."[66] Russians' general disdain for foreigners prompts their support for increased immigration controls, especially for Muslims from Central Asia.[67] But xenophobia does not tell the full story of Islamophobia in Russia.

As Marlene Laruelle and Natalia Yudina explain, little is written on the topic of Islamophobia in Russia because of the ways religious identity intersects with nationality and ethnicity.[68] These complicated interactions contribute to discrimination against labor migrants in Russia.[69] Ethnicity appears to play a larger role than religion does in shaping Russian public opinion polls on Muslims. Respondents in one survey expressed more tolerance of Muslims' religious

---

[64] See Violeta Manapova, "Исламофобия в России и мире как отражение миграционных процессов" ["Islamophobia in Russia and the World as an Expression of Migration Processes"], *Gramota* 13 (2020): pp. 112–16; "Russia Will Be One-Third Muslim." As such, Russia likely falls in the camp of illiberal differentialism when it comes to integration structures, in that the regime seeks to keep majorities and minorities separate—providing accommodation but not to the level that is provided to the native population. See Ray Taras, "Norms and Models of Migrant Rights," in *Xenophobia and Islamophobia in Europe* (Edinburgh: Edinburgh University Press, 2012), pp. 26–67.

[65] "Russia Will Be One-Third Muslim."

[66] See Strzelecki, "Russian Nationalism."

[67] See Strzelecki, "Russian Nationalism."

[68] Laruelle and Yudina, "Islamophobia"; Abbasi, "Russian Islamophobia," p. 5.

[69] Laruelle and Yudina, "Islamophobia."

identity than of their ethnicity or immigration status.[70] These findings fail to take into consideration, however, that the relationship between ethnicity and religion make xenophobia and Islamophobia difficult to separate in the Russian context. Hence religion still matters, even if Islamophobia is expressed in terms of ethnicity or immigration status.

Violent attacks on minorities often are aimed at Muslims because of "unprecise motivations."[71] Taking victims' religious background into consideration, however, gives a different picture, one that demonstrates the prevalence of violence against Muslims each year.[72] There are few cases of attacks based explicitly on religion, whereas statistics show that Muslims are targets of approximately 30 to 60 percent of ethnic violence in a given year.[73] What appears to be a relative lack of religious violence or animosity when compared to ethnic violence could be explained by a misinterpretation of the data.

To reconcile what appear to be perceptions and activities motivated more by xenophobia than by Islamophobia in public opinion data, a look at less-direct questions provides a clearer picture. For instance, when asked about attitudes toward Islamic dress, as compared to feelings toward Muslims generally, more than 75 percent of respondents expressed likely or definitive opposition to hijabs in educational spaces.[74] Such aversion to expressions of Muslim identity exists despite waning public support for the populists' ethnonationalist "Russian Marches," which are organized annual gatherings of nationalist groups.[75]

Although Russians responding to polls do not admit that they are Islamophobic, anti-Muslim sentiment exists. At first glance, polls show that Russians find secular Muslims more tolerable than religious Muslims. However, this observation does not align with a self-proclaimed preference for religious Muslims by some populist groups such as the Night Wolves.[76] The group, which only accepts men, purports to stand for patriotism and the defense of Russia, with an imperial bent seen in its motto "Wherever we are, that is Russia."[77] This

---

[70] David Herbert, "A Different Dynamic? Explaining Prejudice against Muslims in the Russian Federation: Islamophobia or Internalised Racial Hierarchy?," *Connections: A Journal for Historians and Area Specialists* (2019), https://www.connections.clio-online.net/article/id/artikel-4692.

[71] Laruelle and Yudina, "Islamophobia."

[72] Laruelle and Yudina, "Islamophobia."

[73] Laruelle and Yudina, "Islamophobia."

[74] Levada Center, "РОССИЯНЕ НЕ ПОДДЕРЖАЛИ НОШЕНИЕ ХИДЖАБОВ В УЧЕБНЫХ ЗАВЕДЕНИЯХ" ["Russians Did Not Support Wearing of Hijabs in Educational Institutions"], June 30, 2015, https://www.levada.ru/2015/06/30/rossiyane-ne-podderzhali-noshenie-hidzhabov-v-uchebnyh-zavedeniyah/. The poll did not distinguish between Russian citizens and migrants.

[75] Levada Center, "РОССИЯНЕ ПОТЕРЯЛИ ИНТЕРЕС К 'РУССКИМ МАРШАМ'" ["Russians Lost Interest in 'Russian Marches'"], November 24, 2015, https://www.levada.ru/2015/11/24/rossiyane-poteryali-interes-k-russkim-marsham/.

[76] Harris, "Hybrid Threat."

[77] Harris, "Hybrid Threat"; Anais Llobet and Maxime Popov, "Leader of Putin's Favorite Biker Gang: 'We Consider Ourselves Part of the Army of Russia,'" *Business Insider*, October 7, 2014, https://www.businessinsider.com/afp-russias-night-wolves-ride-for-the-motherland-2014-10.

translates into less concern with the religiosity of Muslims and more with their political ambitions vis-à-vis the interests of Orthodox Russians. Outside the context of that support, their religiosity is not preferred, especially if it is at odds with political goals. And it does not necessarily equate to support of Central Asian migration into Russia.

Politics of Migration

Islamophobia also interacts with the Russia's labor needs. The government must balance the country's need for migrant labor with nativist xenophobic opposition grounded in perceptions that Muslims are a national security threat. The high demand for foreign labor arises from a decline in the native working population by approximately one million people per year since 2007 because of low birth rates and low life expectancy.[78] Four million labor migrants per year, largely seasonal and from Central Asian states, worked in Russia.[79] During the COVID-19 pandemic, approximately half of them left because of border closures aimed at preventing the spread of the coronavirus. The ensuing labor shortage prompted the government to explore aid to various sectors that relied on migrant labor, such as construction and agriculture.[80] Moreover, entry requirements for labor migrants to return to Russia were relaxed.[81]

This need for foreign labor clashes with domestic politics that prioritize Orthodoxy and Russianness. For instance, during voting on the constitutional referendum in 2020 allowing President Vladimir Putin the ability to "reset" and renew his presidential terms two more times, there were amendments related to belief in God and to the Russian language.[82] While the former was said to apply to all religious groups, according to the Orthodox Patriarch Kirill, the naming of Russian as "the language of the state-forming people" draws on the national

---

[78] Maria Lipman and Yulia Florinskaya, "Labor Migration in Russia," *PONARS Eurasia*, January 9, 2019, https://www.ponarseurasia.org/labor-migration-in-russia/; Benjamin Harvey, "Russia's Population Is Shrinking Even as Putin Seeks Expansion," *Bloomberg*, June 10, 2022, https://www.bloomberg.com/news/articles/2022-06-10/russia-s-population-is-shrinking-even-as-putin-seeks-expansion.

[79] Lipman and Florinskaya, "Labor Migration in Russia."

[80] AFP, "Russia Eyes Measures to Tackle Migrant Labor Shortage," *Moscow Times*, February 10, 2021, https://www.themoscowtimes.com/2021/02/10/russia-eyes-measures-to-tackle-migrant-labor-shortage-a72894.

[81] AFP, "Russia Eyes Measures."

[82] Dmitry Shlapentokh, "New Russian Identity Makes Way into the Constitution," Institute of Modern Russia, June 26, 2022, https://imrussia.org/en/analysis/3126-new-russian-identity-makes-way-into-the-constitution; William E. Pomeranz, "The Putin Constitution," Kennan Institute: The Russia File, March 20, 2020, https://www.wilsoncenter.org/blog-post/putin-constitution.

identity around ethnicity, language, and religion.[83] This situates Central Asian Muslims as permanent outsiders.

Laws on exams, documentation, and other areas involved in the migration process show how Central Asian Muslim migrants are discriminated against, while preference is given to their Slavic Orthodox counterparts. Migration laws and policies require tests about Russian language, history, and culture while also prioritizing visa distribution to Russian-speaking migrants. The tests are increasingly difficult for young Central Asians, given the decline in Russian-language instruction in the region.[84] Furthermore, the history and law sections promote preferred national sentiments, including Christian Orthodox identity.[85]

Three laws govern migration to Russia: (1) the Federal Law on Entry into and Exit from the Russian Federation, (2) the Federal Law on Legal Status of Foreign Citizens in the Russian Federation, and (3) the Federal Law on Migration Registration of Foreign Citizens and Stateless Persons in the Russian Federation. The government also publishes a set of "concepts" that clarify the policy direction of a certain area of law. The Concept of State Migration Policy of the Russian Federation for the Period to 2025 expands on state goals to address socioeconomic, spatial, and demographic development challenges.[86] The process is intended to raise the people's quality of life, preserve national security, protect the national labor market, and support multinational and inter-religious peace and cooperation in Russian society. Each of these goals must align with preserving Russian culture, Russian language, and the historical-cultural legacy of Russia's native people.

Costly documentation to remain and work in Russia, also known as patents, impose a substantial burden on migrants' limited resources that inhibits poorer migrants,[87] including from Central Asia. Quarterly medical exams are also required of all migrants except Belarusians.[88] The so-called passportization

---

[83] Shlapentokh, "New Russian Identity"; Pomeranz, "Putin Constitution"; "God Could Soon Have a Place in Russia's Constitution," *Current Time*, June 24, 2020, https://en.currenttime.tv/a/god-could-soon-have-a-place-in-russia-s-constitution/30688781.html.

[84] Umida Hashimova, "2021: Another Year of the Russian Language in Central Asia," *The Diplomat*, January 3, 2022, https://thediplomat.com/2022/01/2021-another-year-of-the-russian-language-in-central-asia/.

[85] Vanessa Ruget, "'Name the Republic That Was Joined to Russia in 2014': Russia's New Civics and History Test for Migrants," *Journal of Nationalism and* Ethnicity 46, no. 1 (2017): 20–33.

[86] Концепция государственной миграционной политики Российской Федерации на период до 2025 года [Concept of State Migration Policy of the Russian Federation for the Period to 2025], Order of the President of the Russian Federation from October 31, 2018, N 622, https://docs.cntd.ru/document/902352946.

[87] Olga Chudinovskihkh and Mikhail Denisenko, "Russia: A Migration System with Soviet Roots," Migration Policy Institute, May 18, 2017, https://www.migrationpolicy.org/article/russia-migration-system-soviet-roots.

[88] "New Russian Immigration Laws Require Regular Medical Tests, Fingerprinting," Committee to Protect Journalists, February 2, 2022, https://cpj.org/2022/02/new-russian-immigration-laws-require-regular-medical-tests-fingerprinting/.

of residents of Russia-occupied Donbas eases requirements for eastern Ukrainians.[89] Although the Eurasian Economic Union (EEU) and preferential migration policies appear to advantage some Central Asian populations with relaxed requirements,[90] they keep migrants in a nonpermanent status rather than simplifying a path to permanent residency or citizenship. Moreover, the EEU introduced a so-called "blacklist" for migrants who violate laws in other EEU states, with little prospect for removal or other changes of status.[91] Kyrgyz migrants who fall under the EEU and are a majority of labor migrants from Central Asia are especially vulnerable to permanent exclusion without due process rights.[92]

Recent geopolitical conflicts further complicate the Russian government's treatment of Muslim Central Asian migrants as compared to Orthodox Slavic migrants. The Russian war in Ukraine reinforced the Russian government's focus on national security by leveraging migrants' interests in citizenship. In exchange for joining the Russian army and fighting in Ukraine, Central Asian migrants were offered a path to Russian citizenship.[93]

Politics of National Security Law

National security laws and policies affecting Russia's Muslim populations are shaped by Russia's wars with Chechnya and the GWOT. As the United States sought partners in its GWOT, President Vladimir Putin was among the first heads of state to show his support. Putin's motivations, however, had more to do with repressing political opposition at home than with combatting international terrorism.

Putin portrayed the 9/11 attacks against the United States as similar to Russia's experience—a sort of "global Chechnya"—in order to legitimize Russia's violent crackdown on Muslims within its borders.[94] As one analyst put it, "[W]hile the United States wanted Russia to join the [GWOT], the Russians just wanted

[89] Warsaw Institute, "What Is Behind Russia's Passportization of Donbas," May 7, 2021, https://warsawinstitute.org/behind-russias-passportization-donbas/.

[90] Oybek Madiyev, "The Eurasian Economic Union: Repaving Central Asia's Road to Russia?," Migration Policy Institute, February 3, 2021, https://www.migrationpolicy.org/article/eurasian-economic-union-central-asia-russia.

[91] See, for example, Kirill Nourzhanov and Sebastian Peyrouse, *Soft Power in Central Asia: The Politics of Influence and Seduction* (Lanham, MD: Lexington Books, 2021).

[92] Lipman and Florinskaya, "Labor Migration in Russia."

[93] Colleen Wood and Sher Khashimov, "Central Asians in Russia Pressured to Join Moscow's Fight in Ukraine," *Moscow Times*, March 17, 2022, https://www.themoscowtimes.com/2022/03/17/central-asians-in-russia-pressured-to-join-moscows-fight-in-ukraine-a76957.

[94] John O'Loughlin, Gearoid O'Tuathail, and Vladimir Kolossov, "A 'Risky Westward Turn'? Putin's 9-11 Script and Ordinary Russians," *Europe-Asia Studies* 56 (January 2004): pp. 3–34.

ISLAMOPHOBIA IN RUSSIA   167

the United States to join in the GWOC—the Global War on Chechnya."[95] The GWOT thus granted Putin license to maintain a centralized, authoritarian state against the threat of ostensibly religious-driven separatism in the south.

Since the Chechen wars, real and perceived security concerns have been a priority for the Russian government.[96] Even though only 4 percent of attacks in Chechnya "were carried out by actors connected with Islam,"[97] counterterrorism policy still focused on the potential threat stemming from "Russia's large migrant populations (and concurrent trends of marginalization, discrimination, and alienation of migrant workers) . . . turn[ing].the country into a principal target for ISIL recruitment for terrorist violence in Russia's homeland and abroad."[98]

Counterterrorism laws grant the Russian state the political legitimacy and legal authority to single out Muslim political dissidents as national security threats. Following a string of attacks in the north Caucasus, the Russian government adopted the Federal Law on Countering Terrorism, which established the National Anti-Terrorism Committee to be controlled by the Federal Security Bureau (FSB). The Federal Law on Anti–Money Laundering and Terrorism Financing and the Federal Law on Counteracting Extremism, which broadly define extremist activity, selectively target Muslims.[99] The majority of the thirty-eight entities on Russia's list of designated terrorist organizations are alleged to be "Islamist."[100] Moreover, Islamic texts are disproportionately banned, and efforts

[95] Paul Kolbe, "The Global War on Chechnya: What Does 9/11 Teach Us about Counterterrorism Cooperation with Russia?," *Russia Matters*, October 13, 2021, https://russiamatters.org/analysis/global-war-chechnya-what-does-911-teach-us-about-counterterrorism-cooperation-russia.

[96] Lawrence P. Markowitz and Mariya Omelicheva, "The Nature and Sources of Terrorist Threat in Russia: An 'Armed Underground' or ISIL?," PONARS Eurasia, November 26, 2018, https://www.ponarseurasia.org/the-nature-and-sources-of-terrorist-threat-in-russia-an-armed-underground-or-isil/.

[97] Monica Duffy Toft, "Russia's War on Terrorism," in *The Policy World Meets Academia: Designing US Policy toward Russia*, ed. Timothy J. Colton, Timothy Frye, and Robert Legvold (Cambridge: American Academy of Arts and Sciences, January 2010).

[98] Markowitz and Omelicheva, "Nature."

[99] Федеральный закон "О противодействии легализации (отмыванию) доходов, полученных преступным путем, и финансированию терроризма" от 07.08.2001 N 115-ФЗ [Federal Law on Anti–Money Laundering and Terrorism Financing from August 7, 2001, No. 115-FZ], http://www.consultant.ru/document/cons_doc_LAW_32834/; Федеральный закон "О противодействии экстремистской деятельности" от 25.07.2002 г. № 114-ФЗ [Federal Law on Counteracting Extremism from July 25, 2002, No. 114-FZ], http://www.kremlin.ru/acts/bank/18939; Mike Eckel, "'Extremism' as a Blunt Tool: Behind the Russian Law Being Used to Shut Navalny Up," *Radio Free Europe/Radio Liberty*, April 29, 2021, https://www.rferl.org/a/russia-anti-extremism-law-blunt-instrument-navalnu-jehovahs-witnesses/31230149.html.

[100] "Единый федеральный список организаций, в том числе иностранных и международных организаций, признанных в соответствии с законодательством Российской Федерации террористическими" ["Unified Federal List of Organizations, including Foreign and International Organizations, Recognized in Accordance with the Legislation of the Russian Federation as Terrorist"].

to control Islamic education arise from state monitoring and from state control of educational centers under the guise of combatting extremism.[101]

Over time, national security laws targeting designated Islamic terrorist groups have been enforced against other religious groups, including Jehovah's Witnesses, prominent Russian opposition activists and journalists, and most recently, anyone who publicly questions Russia's territorial claims in Ukraine.[102]

Conclusion

Islamophobia in Russia is pervasive against Central Asian Muslim migrants, despite Putin's claims to the contrary. Russia's counterterrorism practices, migration laws, and support for right-wing populist groups do not align with its official narrative of being a multinational, multi-denominational country that respects Muslims. Not only are Muslims the lowest in the hierarchy of migrants, but to avoid expulsion, imprisonment, and exclusion, they must navigate the Good Muslim/Bad Muslim litmus test. The more religious and politically dissident a Muslim, the more harshly they are targeted by state national security and migration exclusion laws. Like their counterparts in other Western nations, Muslims must conform their religious and political beliefs to the government's politics in exchange for mere toleration. Equality, meanwhile, is not an option in countries that begrudgingly allow Muslims entry in order to fill their need for cheap labor. That Muslims offer the government a convenient scapegoat for domestic problems makes them all the more vulnerable to hate crimes as well as government repression. In a context of renewed imperial ambition, these factors intersect in understanding Islamophobia in Russia today.

[101] Victoria Arnold, "Russia: Jehovah's Witness Bible, Jewish, Christian, Muslim Books Banned," *Forum 18*, September 29, 2017, https://www.refworld.org/docid/59d2233e4.html; "Putin Calls for a 'Revival.'"

[102] Eckel, "'Extremism.'"

10
Muslim Life in Belgium
In Search of a *Vivre ensemble*

John Farmer and Ava Majlesi

At a workshop intended to build trust between Brussels and Belgium police forces and the country's Muslim and Jewish communities, Chief Saad Amrani was featured.[1] Chief Armani served as a divisional commander of the Brussels police at the time and later became a senior advisor to the chief of the Belgian National Police.[2] He was an anomaly in the police ranks: a Belgian of Moroccan descent who had grown up in Schaerbeek, a municipality similar in many respects to Molenbeek, the largely Muslim district of Brussels that had become notorious for its large number of foreign fighters[3] and for harboring the terrorists who had attacked Paris and later Brussels's own subway and airport.[4]

Chief Amrani spoke from the heart when addressing his fellow police officers, saying,

> I covet the notion of "vivre ensemble" [living together] and the quality of life of our citizens. In a world that is becoming increasingly complex and diversified, it has become clear to me that it is essential for police officers to build bridges and to work toward a "rapprochement" with the communities that reside within our precincts.[5]

---

[1] Trudy Rubin, "Worldview: Rutgers Team's Antiterror Ideas Travel Far," *The Philadelphia Inquirer*, July 17, 2016, https://www.inquirer.com/philly/columnists/trudy_rubin/20160717_Worldview__Rutgers_team_s_antiterror_ideas_travel_far.html.

[2] "Saad Amrani," Miller Center on Policing and Community Resilience, https://millercenter.rutgers.edu/staff/saad-amrani/.

[3] Robert Jan-Bartunek and Alastair Macdonald, "Guns, God and Grievances—Belgium's Islamist 'Airbase,'" Reuters, November 16, 2015, https://www.reuters.com/article/us-france-shooting-belgium-guns-insight-idUSKCN0T504J20151116.

[4] Matthew Levitt, "The Islamic State, Extremism, and the Spread of Transnational Terrorism" (testimony submitted to the US Senate Committee on Foreign Relations, April 12, 2016), https://www.foreign.senate.gov/imo/media/doc/041216_Levitt_Testimony.pdf.

[5] Miller Center on Policing and Community Resilience archives. The publication of the archives is forthcoming.

John Farmer and Ava Majlesi, *Muslim Life in Belgium* In: *Global Islamophobia and the Rise of Populism*. Edited by: Sahar F. Aziz and John L. Esposito, Oxford University Press. © Oxford University Press 2024.
DOI: 10.1093/oso/9780197648995.003.0010

JOHN FARMER AND AVA MAJLESI

The challenge of discovering a workable life together, or *vivre ensemble*, is one that faces not just Brussels, not just Belgium, but many countries around the world. We have become a world of diasporas, of mixed ethnicities, faiths, and cultures living as never before in close proximity. *The Economist* pointed out after the 2010 census that there are

> [m]ore Chinese people liv[ing] outside mainland China than French people liv[ing] in France, with some to be found in almost every country. Some 22 million ethnic Indians are scattered across every continent. Diasporas have been a part of the world for Millennia. . . . [I]f migrants were a nation, they would be the world's fifth largest.[6]

Between the years 2015 and 2020, the approximate number of international migrants worldwide increased from 248 million to 281 million.[7]

The fact that hundreds of millions of people live in countries where they were not born, coupled with the continued struggles of historic diaspora and minority populations, means that we are also living as never before in a world of vulnerable populations. Sadly, but perhaps not surprisingly, anti-immigrant attitudes have increased worldwide concomitantly with the increase in transnational migration.[8] Anti-immigrant attitudes combined with discriminatory policies aimed at repressing immigrant communities can lead to the alienation of these groups and, in extreme cases, hostilities and even violence by natives of the "host country."[9]

Recent polls indicate that some of the least tolerant countries are found in the European Union (EU).[10] Belgium, for instance, has experienced "some of the largest decreases in tolerant attitudes,"[11] with its score falling by 1.33 index points.[12] This is due in large part to migration being a contentious issue in

---

[6] "Mapping Migration," *The Economist*, November 17, 2011, https://www.economist.com/graphic-detail/2011/11/17/mapping-migration.

[7] An *international migrant* is defined as "any person who changes his or her country of usual residence." See "International Migrant Stocks," Migration Data Portal, February 5, 2021, https://www.economist.com/graphic-detail/2011/11/17/mapping-migration.

[8] Alex Berry, "Anti-Immigrant Attitudes Rise Worldwide: Poll," *Deutsche Welle*, September 23, 2020, https://www.dw.com/en/anti-immigrant-attitudes-rise-worldwide-poll/a-55024481.

[9] Krishnadev Calamur, "Are Immigrants Prone to Crime and Terrorism?," *The Atlantic*, June 15, 2016, https://www.theatlantic.com/news/archive/2016/06/immigrants-and-crime/486884/.

[10] Berry, "Anti-Immigrant Attitudes."

[11] Berry, "Anti-Immigrant Attitudes."

[12] Neli Esipova, Julie Ray, and Anita Pugliese, "World Grows Less Accepting of Migrants," Gallup, September 23, 2020, https://news.gallup.com/poll/320678/world-grows-less-accepting-migrants. aspx. The Gallup index comprises three questions asking "whether people think migrants living in their country, becoming their neighbors and marrying into their families are good things or bad things." The index consists of "the points across the three questions, with a maximum possible score of 9.0 (all three are good things) and a minimum possible score of zero (all three are bad things). The higher the score, the more accepting the population is of migrants."

Belgium. As a result, right-wing political parties directing anti-immigrant rhetoric through a populist lens have made significant gains in recent years.[13] In comparison, the United States placed sixth in the Gallup Migrant Acceptance Index, which assesses the attitude of survey respondents to the idea of "migrants living in their country, moving into their neighborhood and marrying into their family," indicating generally positive attitudes in the United States toward immigrants.[14]

Although the challenge to discover a *vivre ensemble* is a general one that exists internationally, its solutions must be local, taking into account the ethnic and cultural attributes of the host nation as well as the culture and ethnicity of the nations of origin. The tendency to generalize about Muslim migrants in particular, without regard to their countries of origin and how those origins have shaped religious practice, is the very foundation of bigotry; Islamic practice varies from culture to culture, from country to country. On one hand, the specific characteristics of Islam in individual countries must be taken into consideration in assessing the challenges of creating and sustaining a *vivre ensemble*. On the other hand, the ethnic and cultural characteristics of the host communities must also be addressed in any effort to develop strategies for building communities of trust.

This chapter considers Belgium, its growing Muslim populations, and their estrangement amid rising right-wing populism. Drawing upon interviews conducted in Brussels by the authors,[15] it evaluates street-level approaches toward achieving the kind of *vivre ensemble* that Chief Amrani and many of his fellow Belgians so deeply covet.

The Challenge of History: Muslim Migration to Belgium

Many of the issues dividing Belgian communities today can be attributed to policies dating back to the beginning of the 20th century. The first Muslims to migrate to Belgium arrived as economic migrants in the 1910s as a result of French colonization in northwest Africa.[16] North African infantry soldiers played an important role in defeating the Nazi occupying forces during World

---

[13] "Right-wing populism has become very influential in liberal democracies, gaining electoral success in Western and Central Europe and proving to be even stronger in Eastern Europe's younger democracies." Laura Santi Amantini, "Populist Anti-immigrant Sentiments Taken Seriously: A Realistic Approach," *Res Publica*, May 26, 2021, https://link.springer.com/article/10.1007/s11158-021-09516-1#Sec3.

[14] Berry, "Anti-Immigrant Attitudes."

[15] Rubin, "Worldview."

[16] Hassan Bousetta and Laure-Anne Bernes, *Muslims in the EU: Cities Report—Belgium* (Open Society Institute, EU Monitoring and Advocacy Program, 2007), https://www.opensocietyfoundations.org/uploads/3dc37b95-94ca-4c3b-a571-07b9a2451715/museucitiesbel_20080101.pdf, p. 11.

172 JOHN FARMER AND AVA MAJLESI

War II, having joined European Allied powers, including Belgium, in combat.[17] Following World War II, Belgium actively worked to develop its low-skilled labor force through "bilateral agreements with Morocco and Turkey (1964), Tunisia (1969) and Algeria (1970)."[18] Gradually, through legislation, the wives and children of these economic migrants were able to join them and settle in Belgium.[19] Meanwhile, economic migrants were not the only group of Muslims to migrate to Belgium. Some Muslims—in particular, Moroccans—were attracted to the idea of studying in French-speaking Belgium and, in some cases, settled there long-term. Finally, and to a much lesser extent, some Muslims came to Belgium through asylum or as illegal residents.[20]

Recognizing this changing demographic, in 1974, Belgium became the first country in Europe to recognize Islam as an official religion.[21] In "1989, the Belgian Royal Commission for Immigrants Policy released an integration strategy that was seen as a compromise between a purely multicultural approach and the rigid assimilationist views held by right-wing Flemish parties."[22]

The integration strategy left much to be desired. The majority of the North African population living in Belgium has been subjected to discriminatory attitudes and policies, perpetuated through extreme-right political parties, leading to significant disadvantages for multiple generations in the spheres of housing, education, and employment prospects.[23] Not surprisingly, the authors encountered a profound sense of alienation among Muslims from Molenbeek, an alienation felt most keenly in their interaction with police. As the mother of a deceased boy who traveled to Syria to fight for the Islamic State described:

If the police would enter more often into the Muslim community[,] . . . I think an open dialogue between the police and the Muslim community members would be very productive. Additionally, parents would be much more atten-tive to what goes on outside, the relations of their children, and would com-municate much more directly with police and tell them "this one—needs to be watched a little." Without stigmatization, without rushing things. Being able to talk to the police without it becoming necessarily a terrorism file.[24]

---

[17] Institute for Jewish Policy Research, *Mapping Reports of Jewish Muslim Dialogue in 5 European Countries* (CEJI, 2010), https://archive.jpr.org.uk/object-eur1, p. 7.

[18] Bousetta and Bernes, *Muslims*, pp. 11–12.

[19] Institute for Jewish Policy Research, *Mapping Reports*, p. 7.

[20] Bousetta and Bernes, *Muslims*, pp. 11–12.

[21] Vinayak Dalmia "Islamic Radicalization in Belgium," *Air Force Journal of European, Middle Eastern, and African Affairs* (Fall 2020): pp. 78–83, https://media.defense.gov/2020/Aug/31/2002487 580/-1/-1/1/DALMIA.PDF.

[22] Dalmia "Islamic Radicalization," pp. 78–79.

[23] Institute for Jewish Policy Research, *Mapping Reports*, p. 8.

[24] Miller Center.

One Muslim teenager reported that his interaction with police consisted in their "throwing me up against a wall every week or so."[25]

One widely respected crime prevention officer described a society in which isolation had bred mistrust, felt acutely in the relationship between the police and Muslim youth:

> The issue of trust[,] . . . the issue of trust does not only concern the police. The issue of trust must be built every day—across social lines[,] and to build the trust especially of the youngest people. With young people, it is clear that you have to be able to offer something—to them this means that you have to offer them something that you are going to deliver on—because if not, this will result in a total rupture. A difficulty we encounter often with the kids is that you can work with them up until the age of 14 or 15 years old; after 16, 17, 18 it gets extremely difficult because they are more involved in their own activities parallel to what we do—closed, secretive organizations[,] and this means they have broken with all official organizations.[26]

But despite overarching initiatives on the books, there was little to no actual planning related to the meaningful integration of these economic migrants into Belgian society. The impact of this neglect can be felt even today, generations later.[27]

The Challenge of Political Structure: Belgium's Government

In addition to a lack of strategic planning, Belgium's political structure was not built for, nor was it modified to support, a meaningful transition from guest worker to Belgian citizen. Like the United States, Belgium is considered a "federal state," retaining responsibility for foreign affairs, defense, the justice system, and other national issues.[28] The country is divided into three regions, bearing some resemblance to US states: Wallonia (majority French-speaking with a small German-speaking community in the east), Flanders (majority Flemish-speaking), and the Brussels-Capital Region.[29] Each region has its own legislative and executive branches,[30] which undertake a broad range of issues,

---

[25] Miller Center.

[26] Miller Center.

[27] Institute for Jewish Policy Research, *Mapping Reports*, p. 8.

[28] "Belgium, a Federal State," Belgium.be, accessed January 23, 2022, https://www.belgium.be/en/about_belgium/government/federale_staat.

[29] "The Regions," Belgium.be, accessed January 23, 2022, https://www.belgium.be/en/about_belgium/government/regions.

[30] "Regions."

174 JOHN FARMER AND AVA MAJLESI

including power over the economy, employment, housing, and other regional issues.[31] In general, the Flemish areas of Belgium have favored a rigid assimilationist approach to immigrants, while the other areas have been more open to multiculturalism.

According to Belgium's official website, the country has three communities, referring "to persons that make up a community and the bond that unifies them, namely their language and culture."[32] These communities include "the Flemish Community, the French Community and the German-speaking Community."[33] This characterization of Belgian society could have been written prior to the arrival of significant "other" populations; it still makes no mention whatsoever of the other ethnic and religious communities living in the country (e.g., Moroccan, Turkish, Jewish, or Congolese communities).[34] Belgium's official structure, which only recognizes three majority cultures and languages—French, Flemish, and German—is similarly exclusionary.

This structure does not bode well for maintaining a society that is inclusive and that values diversity. Additionally, the nation's haphazard organization complicates any attempt to harmonize efforts to build social cohesion. One Brussels restaurant owner reflected on how the problems in Brussels are a microcosm of a larger, European problem:

> If I could just add something[,] . . . what upsets me the most about Belgium, it's not mainly the police, but the organization, which to me does not seem to work at all. . . . It is unbelievable in Europe, that if there is no communication between countries[,] if there is no communication at high levels, how do you expect there to be communication between the community and the police? That really makes me scared. . . to see all the problems, the discord, especially in a small country like Belgium.[35]

The Challenge of Rhetoric: Rise of Anti-Immigrant and Anti-Muslim Sentiment in Belgium

The more recent growth of far-right movements in Europe, and Belgium specifically, has done little to alleviate tensions between Belgium's majority and minority communities. In 1991, the far-right party, at the time called Vlaams Blok and

---

[31] "The Powers of the Regions," Belgium.be, accessed January 23, 2022, https://www.belgium.be/en/about_belgium/government/regions/competence.
[32] "Belgium, a Federal State."
[33] "Belgium, a Federal State."
[34] "Belgium, a Federal State."
[35] Miller Center.

now known as the Flemish Interest Party, shocked Belgium when it won 6.6 percent of the Flemish vote.[36] The party gained popularity based on various anti-immigrant ideas, "such as abolishing 'multicultural indoctrination' in schools, setting up a 'foreigners' police' charged with tracking down illegal immigrants in Belgium, and a series of limitations on the rights of foreigners in the country."[37] Vlaams Blok prioritized anti-immigration on its agenda. The party considered immigrants a threat to Flemish society and the white, Christian, Dutch-speaking region of Flanders; in this view, Muslim values simply could not be reconciled with the Flemish values of the Flanders region.[38] Vlaams Blok promoted a "law-and-order approach openly focused on immigrant youth, who were vilified and considered the source of urban unrest, waves of petty crime (often drugs-related) and widespread feeling of insecurity in some urban neighborhoods."[39] The party also advocated for restrictions on immigrants' social welfare benefits, civil rights, and political rights—pushing for a "dual system of social policy" and full citizenship rights as a privilege only for "native" Flemish people.[40]

Despite an alliance between the more "mainstream" political parties pledging to avoid collaboration with Vlaams Blok,[41] the party continued to grow and use populist narratives to tailor its appeals to the common man.[42] As the Vlaams Blok party expanded, the more mainstream, traditional political parties were compelled to shed their image as elites.[43] This incremental change led them to also shed policies that the mainstream used to champion, such as reducing unemployment, enhancing education outcomes, and promoting social mobility for immigrants,[44] in favor of rhetoric that increasingly tended to demonize immigrants.[45]

In maintaining its base's favor, Vlaams Blok encountered its share of difficulties. From 2004–14, "a large part of its electorate shifted to the New Flemish Alliance, whose line on migration is tough but more moderate than [Vlaams Blok's] proposals."[46] This shift in support from Vlaams Blok to the New

---

[36] Laurens Cerulus, "Inside the Far Right's Flemish Victory," *Politico*, May 27, 2019, https://www.politico.eu/article/inside-the-far-rights-flemish-victory/.

[37] Cerulus, "Inside."

[38] Jan Blommaert, "25 Years of Right Wing Extremism in Belgium," *Diggit Magazine*, September 25, 2017, https://www.diggitmagazine.com/articles/25-years-right-wing-extremism-belgium.

[39] Blommaert, "25 Years."

[40] Blommaert, "25 Years."

[41] Cerulus, "Inside."

[42] Blommaert, "25 Years."

[43] Blommaert, "25 Years."

[44] Blommaert, "25 Years."

[45] "VB's anti-foreigner rhetoric has always been focused on migrants from Islamic countries, mainly Moroccans and Turks—two major migrant groups in Belgium." Benjamin De Cleen, "Security and the Radical Right in Flanders," *OpenDemocracy*, July 3, 2012, https://www.opendemocracy.net/en/opensecurity/security-and-radical-right-in-flanders/.

[46] Cerulus, "Inside."

Flemish Alliance seems to demonstrate that "center-right parties have the capacity to outperform the populist radical right on key electoral issues such as immigration."[47] Despite the New Flemish Alliance's "more moderate" views on immigration, the softer anti-immigrant message "may serve to further legitimize the rhetoric of the radical right and bring it into the political mainstream."[48] This dynamic should be a concern for anyone advocating for a more inclusive Belgian society. A superficial toning-down of the rhetoric is not a cause for celebration.

The Challenge of Today: Current Attitudes toward Immigrants and Muslims in Belgium

Of great concern is the fact that over time, discriminatory ideas and policies once considered fringe have moved into the mainstream, and with support in the highest levels of Belgian government. The best gauge of Belgian attitudes toward Muslims and immigrants is voting patterns, and political parties on the extreme right continue to win elections.[49] Tensions have certainly flared in recent years, particularly in the aftermath of the May 2014 attack on the Jewish Museum of Belgium in Brussels[50] and the coordinated terror attacks at the Brussels Airport and metro station in March 2016.[51] Additional, likely ISIL-inspired attacks since then, including a 2017 attempted vehicular attack in Antwerp[52] and the 2018 shooting spree in Liege,[53] have brought to the forefront the issue of Islamic radicalization in Belgium and broader Europe.

Molenbeek, a predominantly Muslim neighborhood in Brussels, is "considered a hotbed of extremism" by the state.[54] Many of the perpetrators involved in the November 2015 Paris attacks and the March 2016 Brussels attacks were young Muslims from immigrant families living in the Molenbeek neighborhood.[55] But

[47] James F. Downes, "Why Is the Far Right Losing Voters in Belgium?," *Fair Observer*, January 22, 2019, https://www.fairobserver.com/region/europe/belgium-populism-far-right-politics-flemish-interest-news-18181/; Cerulus, "Inside."

[48] Downes, "Why."

[49] Institute for Jewish Policy Research, *Mapping Reports*, p. 9.

[50] Laura Smith-Spark, Elwyn Lopez, and Pierre Meilhan, "3 Dead in Shooting at Jewish Museum of Belgium," *CNN World*, May 24, 2014, https://www.cnn.com/2014/05/24/world/europe/belgium-jewish-museum-shooting/index.html.

[51] "Brussels Explosions: What We Know about Airport and Metro Attacks," BBC, April 9, 2016, https://www.bbc.com/news/world-europe-35869985.

[52] Milan Schreuer, "Man in Antwerp, Belgium, Tries to Drive into Crowd," *The New York Times*, March 23, 2017, https://www.nytimes.com/2017/03/23/world/europe/antwerp-belgium-car-att ack.html.

[53] "Liege Shootings: Gunman 'Had Killed Day before Attack,'" BBC, May 30, 2018, https://www.bbc.com/news/world-europe-44299952.

[54] Dalmia, "Islamic Radicalization," p. 80.

[55] Andrew Higgins, "A Close Look at Brussels Offers a More Nuanced View of Radicalization," *The New York Times*, April 19, 2016, https://www.nytimes.com/2016/04/20/world/europe/more-than-islam-origin-is-a-marker-for-terror-among-brussels-immigrants.html.

a closer look at the perpetrators' backgrounds shows that most were of Moroccan descent; none was from the Turkish Muslim community.[56] This distinction does not seem to matter to the far- and center-right parties in Belgium, which are more interested in perpetuating the narrative that Islam itself is the enemy. Not only does this narrative benefit these parties, but it benefits *actual* terrorist groups (like ISIS and al-Qaeda), who use the concept of a war between Islam and the West as a recruitment tool.

In the wake of the 2016 terror attacks, far-right groups threatened to attack the Molenbeek neighborhood in retaliation,[57] and Belgium's interior minister proclaimed that Muslims danced, celebrated, and assaulted police and press in response to the attacks—a dubious claim at best.[58] This rhetoric, unsurprisingly, does not help but rather exacerbates the underlying tensions.

Such blanket condemnations gloss over socioeconomic factors that, if addressed, could mitigate attempts to radicalize Muslim youth by ameliorating the grounds for disaffection. Youth unemployment in Belgium overall is 23.2 percent, compared with 45 percent for youth in Belgium born outside of the EU.[59] The overall unemployment rate in Molenbeek is 30 percent, with youth unemployment in Molenbeek at nearly 40 percent.[60] Time and again, studies have shown the relationship between unemployment and crime.[61] Yet the implementation of policies that prevent minority communities from receiving the education and training necessary for gainful employment and that restrict immigrants' access to higher-quality jobs can only increase the isolation and alienation of these communities, leading to worse overall outcomes for Belgian society.

---

[56] Higgins, "Close Look."

[57] "Belgium to Require Immigrants to Sign Up to 'European Values,'" *The Guardian*, April 1, 2016, https://www.theguardian.com/world/2016/apr/01/belgium-to-require-immigrants-to-sign-up-to-european-values.

[58] Adam Taylor, "A Belgian Minister Said Muslims 'Danced' after Terror Attacks: Now He's Facing Questions," *The Washington Post*, April 21, 2016, https://www.washingtonpost.com/news/worldviews/wp/2016/04/21/now-europe-has-its-own-scandal-about-celebrating-muslims/.

[59] Dalmia, "Islamic Radicalization," p. 80.

[60] Dalmia, "Islamic Radicalization," p. 80.

[61] Marc Hooghe, Bram Vanhoutte, Wim Hardyns, and Tuba Bircan, "Unemployment, Inequality, Poverty and Crime: Spatial Distribution Patterns of Criminal Acts in Belgium, 2001–06," *British Journal of Criminology* 51, no. 1 (January 2011): p. 14 (indicating that "unemployment is positively associated not just with property, but also with violent crime" in Belgium); Fredj Jawadi, Sushanta K. Mallick, Abdoulkarim Idi Cheffou, and Anish Augustine, "Does Higher Unemployment Lead to Greater Criminality? Revisiting the Debate over the Business Cycle," *Journal of Economic Behavior and Organization* 182 (February 2021): p. 467 (concluding that "maintaining stable economic activity is critical to stabilize the incidence of crime" and arguing that "unemployment persistence or long-term unemployment might drive criminality more than the short-term fluctuations in the labour market").

The Challenge of Policies: Affecting (and Alienating) Muslims in Belgium

With its core communities and their well-defined, common bonds of language and culture, Belgium never seems to have made it a priority to welcome and to integrate immigrants into Belgian society. An obvious contrast is the United States, which, because it is not defined by an ethnicity, a religion, or increasingly even a common language, is arguably better suited for integration. Indeed, "[a]t the core of the American experience is a conviction that immigrants who come to America can and should become Americans. Patriotic assimilation turns profoundly dissimilar foreigners into proud and happy Americans."[62] In comparison with Europe, American Muslims "have either similar or greater socio-economic status and levels of education than the average American," and they are "active in civil and political society."[63] In contrast, Muslim immigrants in Europe "tend to have worse labor market outcomes, are less well educated, and less socially integrated."[64]

While there are multiple factors to consider, the "isolation of Muslims in neighborhoods like Molenbeek played a role in radicalizing some Belgian youth of foreign descent."[65] And though the Brussels attacks in 2016 were not committed by asylum-seekers but by those born and raised within Europe, leaders curiously called for "tighter restrictions on refugees."[66] This rhetoric is yet another example that serves to mobilize the far right and is likely to alienate minority communities.

Indeed, Belgian policies affecting Muslims in the last decade have been informed by political rhetoric and too often have served to exacerbate divisions rather than to seek common ground. One law proposed in the aftermath of the 2016 coordinated attacks would require non-EU migrants to sign a European values statement, including a "pledge to prevent and report any attempts to commit 'acts of terrorism.'"[67] This approach misguidedly presumes Belgian Muslims' tendency to commit terrorism.

---

[62] Jeff Jacoby, "Why There Are Muslim Ghettos in Belgium, but Not in the US," *The Boston Globe*, March 24, 2016, https://www.bostonglobe.com/opinion/columns/2016/03/27/why-there-are-muslim-ghettoes-belgium-but-not-united-states/zek1CSRR0epWhLmSCiPWKK/story.html.

[63] Alex Nowrasteh, "Muslim Immigration and Integration in the United States and Western Europe," CATO Institute, October 31, 2016, https://www.cato.org/blog/muslim-immigration-integration-united-states-western-europe.

[64] Nowrasteh, "Muslim Immigration."

[65] Heather Murdock, "Refugees in Brussels Cope with Anti-Immigrant Sentiment," VOA News, March 28, 2016, https://www.voanews.com/a/refugees-brussels-cope-anti-immigrant-sentiment/3258349.html.

[66] Murdock, "Refugees."

[67] "Belgium to Require Immigrants."

Other efforts serve only to further isolate the Muslim population. A July 2011 ban on wearing full-face veils in public was subsequently extended to hijabs.[68] The extension of this prohibition to headscarves has had a harmful impact on Muslim women, in some cases preventing them from integrating into Belgian society and pursuing various educational and employment opportunities.[69] Furthermore, in June 2020, the Constitutional Court of Belgium ruled that banning religious clothing in universities does not violate religious freedom.[70] Meanwhile, local officials in Wallonia recently announced that "[r]eligious symbols, including the hijab[,] will be permitted in universities in the French-speaking Wallonia region of Belgium starting in September 2021."[71] The announcement provided a glimmer of hope for advocates who have pushed for lifting similar bans across other regions of Belgium.[72] Despite this welcome change in the Wallonia region, however, the court's opinion does not affect the bans in place in the majority Flemish Flanders region and the Brussels region. There is currently no legislation in place at the federal level to protect the right to wear a hijab in universities across Belgium.[73]

The recently enacted ban on ritual animal slaughter affects not only the Muslim community but the Jewish community as well. A January 2019 law in the Flemish-speaking Flanders region of Belgium prohibited ritual animal slaughter—potentially affecting the 500,000 Muslims and thirty thousand Jews in Belgium.[74] Under the auspices of animal rights protection, the law removed the religious exemption that had allowed the Islamic and Jewish practices of animal slaughter without stunning.[75] Belgian laws had a long-standing requirement that animals must be "stunned before slaughter to prevent unnecessary pain."[76] Even with the animal welfare rationale behind the legislation, the affected communities fear that Islamophobia and anti-Semitism are the actual impetus for the legislation.[77] In December 2020, the European Court of Justice,

---

[68] Marco Müller, "Where Are 'Burqa Bans' in Europe?," *Deutsche Welle*, January 8, 2019, https://www.dw.com/en/where-are-burqa-bans-in-europe/a-49843292.

[69] "Lifting of Hijab Ban in Southern Belgium Offers Hope for Muslim Women," TRT World, January 18, 2021, https://www.trtworld.com/magazine/lifting-of-hijab-ban-in-southern-belgium-offers-hope-for-muslim-women-43365.

[70] Othman El Hammouchi, "Belgium's Other Racism Problem," *Politico*, June 23, 2020, https://www.politico.eu/article/belgiums-islamophobia-denial-discrimination-muslim-population/.

[71] "Lifting of Hijab Ban."

[72] "Lifting of Hijab Ban."

[73] "Lifting of Hijab Ban."

[74] Molly Quell, "Ban on Ritual Animal Slaughter Upheld by EU High Court," Courthouse News Service, December 17, 2020, https://www.courthousenews.com/ban-on-ritual-animal-slaughter-upheld-by-eu-high-court/.

[75] Rachel Elbaum, "Ritual Animal Slaughter Law Leaves Belgium's Muslims and Jews Facing Shortages, Price Hikes," NBC News, March 10, 2019, https://www.nbcnews.com/news/world/ritual-animal-slaughter-law-leaves-belgium-s-muslims-jews-facing-n975566.

[76] Elbaum, "Ritual."

[77] Elbaum, "Ritual."

the EU's highest court, ruled that "member states can require that animals be stunned before being killed" and that the law does not violate the rights of the Islamic and Jewish communities.[78] It is yet another example of a policy that, regardless of its other public policy merits, is likely to cause resentment in these communities, as they will need to import halal and kosher meats at higher cost. Furthermore, the measures have not been counterbalanced by others designed to bring communities together.

For many Muslims, these laws have common underlying themes: You do not belong here. Your values are inconsistent with Belgian values. Your way of dress, which is an expression of your faith, has no place here. Even the food you eat is unacceptable. The message is one of not belonging, and it will continue to unnecessarily alienate Muslim communities in Belgium.

Conclusion: Toward a *Vivre ensemble*

Like so many other nations, Belgium is undergoing a crisis of identity and a challenge to the meaning of citizenship. What does it mean to be Belgian? According to Belgium's own official website, "[t]he concept of 'community' refers to persons that make up a community and the bond that unifies them, namely their language and culture."[79] And Belgium's official website limits the options to communities that are Flemish-speaking, French-speaking, or German-speaking.[80] It leaves no room for immigrants and descendants of immigrants, including those in the Muslim community. The Europe of the past could be "defined by near-homogeneous ethnically-demarcated nation-states."[81] This notion no longer holds true, and certainly not in Belgium. But there is a real need to rethink what it means to be a member of a nation—of Belgium—before tackling the increasingly complex and more difficult issues the country faces.

Any attempts at potential solutions to create a more inclusive and welcoming environment for minority communities in Belgium will need to address the structural barriers inherent in Belgian government, anti-immigration and anti-Muslim rhetoric propagated from the far- and center-right parties, and discriminatory policies and ideas that prevent existing and future generations of Belgian Muslims from enjoying all that full Belgian citizenship can offer. Without specific policies that encourage inclusion and discourage exclusion, the same cycle of Islamophobia will perpetuate to the benefit of no one, and realizing the dream of *a vivre ensemble* will remain elusive.

78 Quell, "Ban."
79 "Belgium, a Federal State."
80 "Ethnic Groups and Languages."
81 Nowrasteh, "Muslim Immigration."

PART III
ISLAMOPHOBIA IN ASIA
Genocide, Pogroms, and Detention

11

Displacing and Disciplining Muslims in India's Burgeoning Hindu *Rashtra*

Audrey Truschke

India was founded in 1947 as a constitutionally secular state with a vision of equal rights accorded to all religious groups. But that foundation has come under severe strain in recent years as another, quite distinct vision for India as articulated by Hindu nationalists has gained popularity. Hindu nationalists seek to remake democratic India into an ethnonationalist homeland for and by Hindus. Their political vision of Hindu supremacy is sometimes referred to as Hindutva and has proved attractive on social and political levels, as evidenced by the rise of the Bharatiya Janata Party (BJP). The BJP—a Hindu nationalist party—took control of India's central government in 2014, and they won general elections again in 2019.[1] Given the demographics of modern India—where nearly 80 percent of the population is Hindu and just over 14 percent is Muslim[2]—the BJP's push for Hindu supremacy is a form of populism that aims to enforce majoritarian norms at the expense of non-Hindu Indian communities.

In the past several years, Hindu nationalists have accelerated their agenda to transform the constitutionally secular nation of India into an ethnonationalist state intolerant of religious minorities. This chapter surveys three major developments in this ongoing transition: the 2019 state policy changes regarding Kashmir, the late 2019 Citizenship Amendment Act, and the February 2020 Delhi riots. These three case studies vary significantly in terms of their locations and the specific communities involved, while occurring within a short timeframe. Common across all three cases is Hindu nationalists' penchant for using force and coercion to achieve their aims at the expense of Muslim communities. This chapter situates each case study against the overlapping backdrops of Hindu

---

[1] TNN, "Modi 2019 Beats Modi 2014: What This Lok Sabha Verdict Means," *The Times of India*, May 24, 2019, https://timesofindia.indiatimes.com/india/modi-2019-beats-modi-2014/articleshow/69473897.cms.

[2] These percentages are based on the 2011 Indian census. Anuja Gyan Varma and Pretika Khanna, "Census 2011 Shows Islam Is the Fastest Growing Religion in India," *Mint*, August 26, 2015, https://www.livemint.com/Politics/XkVYBX2IaBk5Sqf8yr2XMM/Hindu-population-declined-Muslims-increased-2011-census.html. The Indian census has included questions about religious identity dating back to British colonialism.

Audrey Truschke, *Displacing and Disciplining Muslims in India's Burgeoning Hindu* Rashtra In: *Global Islamophobia and the Rise of Populism*. Edited by: Sahar F. Aziz and John L. Esposito, Oxford University Press. © Oxford University Press 2024. DOI: 10.1093/oso/9780197648995.003.0011

184 AUDREY TRUSCHKE

supremacy and Islamophobia, arguing that Hindu nationalists deploy these intertwined frameworks in contemporary India with dangerous results for the nation's largest religious minority.

Overlapping Frameworks: Hindutva and Islamophobia

Hindu nationalism, also known as Hindutva, is a political ideology that dates back roughly a century. It was codified into a defined set of ideas in the 1920s with two events: the publication of V. D. Savarkar's *Hindutva: Who Is a Hindu?* and the formation of the paramilitary Rashtriya Swayamsevak Sangh (RSS).[3] Savarkar was a Maharashtrian Brahmin known for his personal cowardice and encouragement of others to commit acts of violence.[4] Savarkar and the RSS both endeavored to reorganize Indian society and the state to promote Hindu identity—defined in terms of culture or even ethnicity rather than religion—above all others.[5] Early RSS leaders took inspiration for their ideology and organization from European fascist movements of the early to mid-20th century.[6] Hindutva's early articulators did not see their ideology as religious in nature; in fact, Savarkar, an atheist, "was personally contemptuous of religious Hinduism."[7] Today, those who advance the ideology of Hindutva make claims on and attempt to narrow Hinduism, but this political project is resisted by many Hindus.[8] Consistent in Hindutva ideology from Savarkar's time until now is the promotion of Hindu cultural and political supremacy.

---

[3] Christophe Jaffrelot, "Introduction," in *Hindu Nationalism: A Reader*, ed. Christophe Jaffrelot (Princeton, NJ: Princeton University Press, 2007).

[4] Vinay Lal, "Veer Savarkar: Ideologue of Hindutva," *Manas*, accessed July 27, 2021, https://southasia.ucla.edu/history-politics/hindu-rashtra/veer-savarkar-ideologue-hindutva/.

[5] Bridge Initiative Team, "Factsheet: Rashtriya Swayamsevak Sangh (RSS)," Bridge Initiative, May 18, 2021, https://bridge.georgetown.edu/research/factsheet-rashtriya-swayamsevak-sangh-rss/.

[6] The ties between early Hindutva ideologues and European fascism are well documented, especially through Golwalkar. See, for example, Bridge Initiative Team, "Factsheet: Rashtriya Swayamsevak Sangh (RSS)." Many scholars describe Hindutva as fascist today. See, for example, numerous articles in Ram Puniyani, ed., *Religion, Power and Violence: Expression of Politics in Contemporary Times* (New Delhi: Sage, 2005). For an argument for *national populism* as a more precise descriptor, see Sidharth Bhatia, "Interview: 'Concentration of Power in Just a Few Hands Has Always Met with Resistance,'" *The Wire*, February 24, 2021, https://thewire.in/politics/christophe-jaffrelot-interview-bjp-hindutva-populism-caa.

[7] Walter Andersen and Shridhar D. Damle, *Messengers of Hindu Nationalism: How the RSS Reshaped India* (London: Hurst, 2019), p. 80.

[8] See, for example, "Hindutva 101: A Primer," *Sadhana*, December 2019, https://www.sadhana.org/hindutva-101; Sunita Viswanath, "Modi's Religious Nationalism Hurts India's Hindus, Too," *Foreign Policy*, May 26, 2021, https://foreignpolicy.com/2021/05/26/modi-hindu-nationalism-hindutva-hurts-hindus-too/; Anand Patwardhan, "If Hindutva Is Hinduism Then the Ku Klux Klan Is Christianity," *Scroll.in*, September 12, 2021, https://scroll.in/article/1005159/anand-patwardhan-if-hindutva-is-hinduism-then-the-ku-klux-klan-is-christianity.

DISPLACING AND DISCIPLINING MUSLIMS   185

In their pursuit of an ethnonational state that enforces Hindu majoritarian ideas, Hindutva ideologues have shown a century-long proclivity for intolerance, enforced through violence. Vinayak Chaturvedi has argued that the use of force was baked into Savarkar's vision of Hindu identity:

> Savarkar argued that violence was central to any understanding of Hindu civility—and by extension Hindu civilization. The idea of violence as civility was a provocative intervention in the conceptual history of "civility" in the twentieth century. For Savarkar, to marginalize the centrality of violence was not only to overlook the basic foundation of civility, but it was to ignore the foundation of what it meant to be a Hindu.[9]

Early Hindutva proponents often envisioned such violence on a grand scale, to be wielded against entire groups. For instance, M. S. Golwalkar wrote in 1939 endorsing Nazi Germany's recognition of unbridgeable differences between "[r]aces and cultures," and specifically its "purging the country of the Semitic races—the Jews," as "a good lesson for us in Hindusthan to learn and profit by."[10] Golwalkar became the second head of the RSS in 1940, shortly after penning this chilling endorsement of Nazi Germany's anti-Semitic violence.[11] The RSS took other inspirations, both big and small, from European fascist and colonial movements. An example of such fascist influences is the RSS's organization as a paramilitary group with arms training, which persists to this day, and an example of colonial influences is a sartorial taste for men's khaki shorts.[12]

While it remained a fringe ideology for many decades following its initial articulation, Hindutva inspired the killer of India's most famous leader. In 1948, Nathuram Godse, an RSS man and devotee of Hindutva, assassinated Mahatma Gandhi, India's historic independence leader and inspiration for Martin Luther King Jr.[13] Godse felt compelled, in his own words, to "disregard non-violence

---

[9] Vinayak Chaturvedi, "Violence as Civility: V. D. Savarkar and the Mahatma's Assassination," *South Asian History and Culture* 11, no. 3 (2020): pp. 240–41.

[10] M. S. Golwalkar, *We or Our Nationhood Defined* (Nagpur, India: Bharat, 1939), pp. 87–88.

[11] Christophe Jaffrelot, ed., *Hindu Nationalism: A Reader* (Princeton, NJ: Princeton University Press, 2007), p. 97.

[12] On khaki shorts, see Christophe Jaffrelot, "The Hindu Nationalist Strategy of Stigmatisation and Emulation of 'Threatening Others': An Indian Style Fascism?," in *Politics of the "Other" in India and China: Western Concepts in Non-Western Contexts*, ed. Lion Konig and Bidisha Chaudhuri (New York: Routledge, 2016), p. 17.

[13] On the evidence that Godse was an RSS member, see Dhirendra K. Jha, "The Apostle of Hate: Historical Records Expose the Lie That Nathuram Godse Left the RSS," *Caravan Magazine*, January 1, 2020, https://caravanmagazine.in/reportage/historical-record-expose-lie-godse-left-rss; A. G. Noorani, *Savarkar and Hindutva: The Godse Connection* (New Delhi: Leftword Books, 2002), p. 29. For a view that it is not especially critical for determining the state of Godse's RSS membership at the moment he assassinated Gandhi, see Vinay Lal, "Nathuram Godse, the RSS, and the Murder of Gandhi," *Manas*, accessed July 23, 2021, https://southasia.ucla.edu/history-politics/hindu-rashtra/nathuram-godse-rss-murder-gandhi/.

186   AUDREY TRUSCHKE

and to use force" because of "Gandhi's persistent policy of appeasement towards the Muslims."[14] Invoking Savarkar's view of inevitable Hindu-Muslim conflict, Godse pleaded in 1949 to the judge who would sentence him to death, "[A]ll of [Mahatma Gandhi's] experiments were at the expense of the Hindus."[15]

Whereas India's independence leaders across a broad political spectrum identified European colonialists as the primary obstacle to their goal of self-rule, Hindutva ideologues saw Muslims as the main roadblock to their goal of a Hindu state (*rashtra*).[16] Initially, few Indians found such a fierce, anti-Muslim perspective appealing. Indeed, after Gandhi's brutal murder, the RSS was temporarily banned, and Hindutva failed to break into mainstream Indian politics for decades. The RSS was banned a second time during Indira Gandhi's Emergency (1975–77), when democratic rule was suspended in India for twenty-one months.[17]

Hindutva's political fortunes began to change in the 1980s, and the ideology increasingly defines the Indian mainstream today. The year 1980 witnessed the birth of the BJP, a political party that openly champions Hindutva and has close ties with the RSS.[18] Continuing the Hindu nationalist reliance on violence, two events helped further raise the profile of Hindutva ideology: the 1992 extrajudicial destruction of the Babri Mosque in Ayodhya, along with subsequent anti-Muslim violence, and the 2002 Gujarat Pogrom targeting Muslims.[19] The destruction of the Babri Masjid came after years of agitation, especially by L. K. Advani, a BJP leader.[20] Narendra Modi—a lifelong RSS member and a BJP politician—oversaw the 2002 Gujarat Pogrom as an early signature act of his tenure as chief minister of Gujarat.[21] In contrast to Gandhi's assassination, these violent acts increased Hindutva's popularity and helped propel the BJP to further political victories.[22] Today, the BJP, whose official platform endorses

---

[14] Nathuram Godse, "Why I Killed Gandhi (Simla, May 1949)," in *The Great Speeches of Modern India*, ed. Rudrangshu Mukherjee (Noida, India: Random House India, 2011), pp. 327, 337.

[15] Godse, "Why," p. 333.

[16] See Gyan Prakash, "Secular Nationalism, Hindutva, and the Minority," in *The Crisis of Secularism in India*, ed. Anuradha Dingwaney Needham and Rajeswari Sunder Rajan (Durham, NC: Duke University Press, 2007) pp. 177–88.

[17] Andersen and Damle, *Messengers*, pp. xii, 3.

[18] Jaffrelot, *Hindu Nationalism*, pp. 178–79.

[19] For a broader contextualization of the Ayodhya movement, see Christophe Jaffrelot, *Modi's India: Hindu Nationalism and the Rise of Ethnic Democracy*, trans. Cynthia Schoch (Princeton, NJ: Princeton University Press, 2021), pp. 14–23.

[20] Anand Patwardhan's 1992 documentary film, *Ram ke Naam* (In the Name of God), traces Advani's role in these agitations, including his use of religious rhetoric and imagery.

[21] Jaffrelot, *Modi's India*, pp. 39–44; Parvis Ghassem-Fachandi, *Pogrom in Gujarat: Hindu Nationalism and Anti-Muslim Violence in India* (Princeton, NJ: Princeton University Press, 2012).

[22] Raheel Dhattiwala and Michael Biggs, "The Political Logic of Ethnic Violence: The Anti-Muslim Pogrom in Gujarat, 2002," *Politics and Society* 40, no. 4 (2012): pp. 483–516; Howard Spodek, "In the Hindutva Laboratory: Pogroms and Politics in Gujarat, 2002," *Modern Asian Studies* 44, no. 2 (2010): pp. 349–99.

Hindutva, controls India's central government; Narendra Modi serves as India's prime minister.[23]

A consistent feature of Hindutva ideologues is the treatment of Muslims as their primary enemy. Savarkar devoted a great deal of energy to retelling Indian history from a perspective that relentlessly demonized Muslims. He imagined a nine-hundred-year "epic Hindu-Muslim war" in which Muslims sought, in Savarkar's words, "to destroy the Hindu religion which was the life-blood of the Nation."[24] This view is ahistorical and factually incorrect, but it was and remains a core animating grievance within Hindutva thought. Many Hindutva discussions and writings cast Muslims as "internal threats" and bloodthirsty conquerors, from Savarkar to Indian propaganda regarding the spread of COVID-19.[25] As a result of such virulent rhetoric, Muslims have long been targets of Hindutva violence, which has accelerated since the BJP took control of India's central government in 2014.[26] Christophe Jaffrelot, one of the leading experts on Hindutva, has put it bluntly: Hindu nationalism was, in the 20th century, "structured in opposition to Islam."[27] Jaffrelot has also argued in his wide-ranging writings and interviews that Hindu nationalism has not "fundamentally changed" over the last century regarding its chief enemies and its primary objective.[28] Such continuity in Hindutva's anti-Muslim agenda pursuant to creating a Hindu *rashtra* features in each of this chapter's case studies, beginning with major policy changes regarding the disputed territory of Kashmir.

---

[23] Jaffrelot, *Modi's India*, pp. 34–38 (Modi-RSS relationship), ch. 3 (BJP under Modi's leadership).

[24] V. D. Savarkar, *Six Glorious Epochs of Indian History*, trans. and ed. S. T. Godbole (Bombay: Bal Savarkar, 1971), pp. 129–30. See also Chaturvedi, "Violence," p. 246.

[25] On "internal threats," see M. S. Golwalkar's *Bunch of Thoughts*, quoted in Jaffrelot, ed., *Hindu Nationalism*, p. 117. On disinformation concerning Muslims and COVID-19 in India, see Shakuntala Banaji and Ram Bhat, "How Anti-Muslim Disinformation Campaigns in India Have Surged during COVID-19," *LSE COVID-19 Blog*, September 30, 2020, https://blogs.lse.ac.uk/covid19/2020/09/30/how-anti-muslim-disinformation-campaigns-in-india-have-surged-during-covid-19/; Harsh Mander, "The Coronavirus Has Morphed into an Anti-Muslim Virus," *The Wire*, April 13, 2020, https://thewire.in/communalism/coronavirus-anti-muslim-propaganda-india; Billy Perrigo, "It Was Already Dangerous to Be Muslim in India: Then Came the Coronavirus," *Time*, April 3, 2020, https://time.com/5815264/coronavirus-india-islamophobia-coronajihad/.

[26] Amnesty International, "India 2020," 2020, https://www.amnesty.org/en/countries/asia-and-the-pacific/india/report-india/; Human Rights Watch, "India: Events of 2020," 2021, https://www.hrw.org/world-report/2021/country-chapters/india#; US Commission on International Religious Freedom, "Annual Report 2021," 2021, https://www.uscirf.gov/, pp. 22–24.

[27] Jaffrelot, *Modi's India*, p. 12.

[28] Ajoy Ashirwad Mahaprashasta and Christophe Jaffrelot, "'Not Hindu Nationalism, but Society That Has Changed': Christophe Jaffrelot," *The Wire*, January 25, 2020, https://thewire.in/religion/christophe-jaffrelot-rss-narendra-modi. See also Jaffrelot's comments in Edward Anderson and Christophe Jaffrelot, "Hindu Nationalism and the 'Saffronisation of the Public Sphere': An Interview with Christophe Jaffrelot," *Contemporary South Asia* 26, no. 4 (2018): p. 473; Jaffrelot, *Modi's India*, p. 14.

Kashmir: Accelerating a Settler-Colonial Agenda

In August 2019, the Indian government, led by the Hindu nationalist Narendra Modi, revoked Articles 370 and 35a of the Indian Constitution, thereby stripping the territory of Jammu and Kashmir of its semiautonomous status, while simultaneously imposing a harsh lockdown of the entire region. Kashmir is situated, geographically, between India, Pakistan, and China. The three bordering nations, as well as residents of Kashmir who claim their right to self-determination, have disputed political control of the region for more than seven decades. Consequently, Kshmir's India-Pakistan border, known as the Line of Control, is the world's most heavily militarized area.[29] In the early 1950s, the Indian government extended certain protections to residents of the part of the region under its administration by Articles 370 and 35a, reserving for Kashmiris alone the rights to work, own land, and vote in the region.[30] But the Indian government has long eroded even the limited autonomy of Indian-administered Jammu and Kashmir—the only Muslim-majority state in contemporary India—through military actions as well as judicial and extrajudicial measures.[31] Accordingly, many scholars and human rights advocates find the language of occupation and colonialism apt for describing the Indian approach to Kashmir as well as Kashmir's importance in the imagination of Indian nationalisms.[32] Since the BJP took control of the central Indian government in 2014, it has both built upon and accelerated these earlier Indian trends vis-à-vis Kashmir, positioning the region as critical in the realization of larger Hindu nationalist objectives.

When India's BJP government revoked Articles 370 and 35a in 2019, they effectively canceled any measure of Kashmiri territorial sovereignty. The decision eliminated protections that Kashmiris had enjoyed for years that restricted employment, property rights, and electoral participation to the region's population.[33] In eliminating these protections, the BJP opened the door to

[29] As Suchitra Vijayan notes, the entire Indian-Pakistan border is militarized, complete with fencing and floodlights so bright they can be seen from space at night. Suchitra Vijayan, *Midnight's Borders: A People's History of Modern India* (Brooklyn, NY: Melville House, 2021), p. 183.

[30] Goldie Osuri, "Kashmiris Are Living a Long Nightmare of Indian Colonialism," *The Conversation*, August 21, 2019, http://theconversation.com/kashmiris-are-living-a-long-nightmare-of-indian-colonialism-121925.

[31] Vijayan, *Midnight's Borders*, pp. 187–226; Ather Zia, "Straw Man Arguments and the Removal of Article 370," *Asia Dialogue*, September 27, 2019, https://theasiadialogue.com/2019/09/27/the-long-read-straw-man-arguments-and-the-removal-of-article-370/. On the penning of Article 370, see A. G. Noorani, *Article 370: A Constitutional History of Jammu and Kashmir* (Delhi: Oxford University Press, 2011).

[32] Nosheen Ali, Mona Bhan, Sahana Ghosh, Hafsa Kanjwal, Zunaira Komal, Deepti Misri, Shruti Mukherjee, Nishant Upadhyay, Saiba Varma, and Ather Zia, "Geographies of Occupation in South Asia," *Feminist Studies* 45, nos. 2–3 (2019): p. 576.

[33] Aditi Saraf, "The Lie of the Land: Why Losing Territorial Sovereignty Poses an Existential Threat to Kashmiris," *Caravan Magazine*, October 1, 2019, https://caravanmagazine.in/commentary/los ing-territorial-sovereignty-poses-existential-threat-to-kashmiris; Zia, "Straw Man Arguments."

DISPLACING AND DISCIPLINING MUSLIMS   189

non-Kashmiris settling in the region and thereby fundamentally altering Kashmiri demographics, religions, and cultures. Indeed, while the BJP government seems intent on controlling the land of Kashmir, they are hostile to the people—predominantly Muslims—who currently live on that land. For instance, the Kashmiri legislature was dissolved by Indian-appointed state representatives in late 2018.[34] Disappearances and other human rights violations are heartbreakingly common in Indian-controlled Jammu and Kashmir, spurring a large body of literature that attempts to capture and communicate these horrors.[35] It is still too early to know to what extent, and within what timeframe, internal displacement of Kashmiri Muslims will be actualized in the aftermath of abrogating Articles 370 and 35a. But, as discussed below, this change in Indian state policy was accompanied by severe restrictions on Kashmir's population that promote a view of Muslim Kashmiris as enemies of the Indian state.

The 2019 changes to the status of the territory of Jammu and Kashmir were accompanied by a series of other measures designed to control information, both within and beyond Kashmir, chiefly a seven-month communications blackout. That phrase—*communications blackout*—risks minimizing as merely administrative what was a brutal assault on human rights and everyday life.[36] For seven months, Kashmiris had no access to internet or cell phone service. Their schools and shops were shuttered. Many Kashmiri civilians, including politicians, were detained. No independent journalists were allowed to enter Kashmir, lest they document the actions of the Indian military and the hardships foisted upon Kashmiris.

The loss of contact and the uncertainties created were devastating for residents of the region, prompting humanitarian calls for India to end the blackout from corners far and wide. In October 2019, two months into the blackout, the US House Foreign Affairs Committee urged India to lift the communications blockade because of its "devastating impact on the lives and welfare of everyday

---

[34] Umer Maqbool, "Under Central Rule since June 2018, Soon J&K Won't Have Representatives in Rajya Sabha," *The Wire*, January 14, 2021, https://thewire.in/rights/jammu-kashmir-rajya-sabha-mps-vacant-central-rule.

[35] In this regard, the amount of literature and poetry on Stand with Kashmir's syllabus is instructive. Stand with Kashmir, "The Kashmir Syllabus," 2019, https://standwithkashmir.org/the-kashmir-syllabus/. It reminds me, in some ways, of literature on Partition and how many have felt that personal stories, objects, and even fiction that is rooted in reality can best convey the traumas of that experience.

[36] For sources written at different points during and after the blackout, see, for example, "US Congress Committee Urges India to Lift Kashmir Communication Blackout," *Wire*, October 8, 2019, https://thewire.in/diplomacy/us-congress-committee-urges-india-to-lift-kashmir-communication-blackout; Majid Maqbool, "I'm a Journalist Who Lived through Kashmir's Traumatic Internet Blackout, Which Started One Year Ago: Here's What It's Like to Have Your Freedoms Ripped Away for 213 Days," *Business Insider*, August 5, 2020, https://www.businessinsider.com/india-kashmir-internet-blackout-anniversary-i-lived-through-it-2020-8; Anuradha Bhasin Jamwal, "4G Is Back in J&K after 18 Months, but It Can't Compensate for What We Lost," *The Wire*, February 7, 2021, https://thewire.in/rights/jammu-and-kashmir-4g-internet-costs.

190　AUDREY TRUSCHKE

Kashmiris" who struggled to find medical care without phones and with their streets full of roadblocks and hostile soldiers.[37] In December 2019, four months into the blackout, Kashmiris began disappearing from the WhatsApp groups of their families and friends, triggered by WhatsApp's policy that accounts expire after 120 days without activity.[38] Many did not know if their loved ones in Kashmir were even still alive, much less anything about their welfare. In January 2020, five months into the blackout, a doctor who had been involved in a WhatsApp-based initiative to address cardiac emergencies in Kashmir said, "I don't know how many patients we have lost."[39]

Finally, in March 2020, India began to roll back its lockdown restrictions. Kashmiris slowly reestablished communication with the outside world and with each other, sharing who had died, who had been born, and what those harrowing 213 days had been like for them.[40] Still, the Indian government retained tight control of information flows for months to come. Authorities did not restore 4G internet until February 2021, eighteen months after it was suspended, and even then only with a stated agenda of increased state surveillance of Kashmiris.[41]

Understanding the place of Kashmiris in the Indian nationalist imaginary helps make sense of why India's BJP government devotes immense national resources to restricting the mundane, everyday actions of people across this region. Kashmiris serve as a foil for India's Hindu nationalist government, with Kashmiri oppression being projected as a key activity through which the Indian state defines itself and exhibits its power. As Mridu Rai has put it, "Kashmiri Muslims are made to serve as contrapuntal symbols—of terrorist violence, illegitimate religious impulses, sedition—for contriving a mythical Hindu nation."[42] Kashmiris are useful enemies in BJP rhetoric precisely because they are deemed a threat, through being both Kashmiri and Muslim.[43] The BJP deploys these paired identities to attempt to justify state oppression of Kashmiris as well

---

[37] "US Congress Committee."

[38] "Internet Curbs: Kashmiris Lose WhatsApp Accounts on 120th Day of Inactivity, Thrown Out of Groups," *Scroll.in*, December 5, 2019, https://scroll.in/latest/945860/internet-curbs-kashmiris-lose-whatsapp-accounts-on-120th-day-of-inactivity-thrown-out-of-groups.

[39] Hannah Ellis-Petersen, "'Many Lives Have Been Lost': Five-Month Internet Blackout Plunges Kashmir into Crisis," *The Guardian*, January 5, 2020, http://www.theguardian.com/world/2020/jan/05/the-personal-and-economic-cost-of-kashmirs-internet-ban. See also Sameer Yasir and Jeffrey Gettleman, "In Kashmir, a Race against Death, with No Way to Call a Doctor," *The New York Times*, October 7, 2019, https://www.nytimes.com/2019/10/07/world/asia/kashmir-doctors-phone.html.

[40] Maqbool, "'I'm a Journalist.'"

[41] Jamwal, "4G Is Back."

[42] Mridu Rai, "Kashmiris in the Hindu Rashtra," in *Majoritarian State: How Hindu Nationalism Is Changing India*, ed. Angana P. Chatterji, Thomas Blom Hansen, and Christophe Jaffrelot (New York: Oxford University Press, 2019), p. 259.

[43] Ather Zia, "The Killable Kashmiri Body: The Life and Execution of Afzal Guru," in *Resisting Occupation in Kashmir*, ed. Haley Duschinski, Mona Bhan, Ather Zia, and Cynthia Mahmood (Philadelphia: University of Pennsylvania Press, 2018), pp. 103–28.

as to advance a broader mission of fundamentally altering the nature of Kashmiri society and life.

While the BJP has an aggressive agenda concerning Kashmir, they bristle at frank discussion of it both within and beyond the region. In an Orwellian move, the Indian government unveiled new textbooks in mid-2020 in the territory of Jammu and Kashmir that taught about the revocation of Article 370 less than a year earlier without any mention of its associated key events of mass detentions and the communications blockade.[44] In such a brazen rewriting of events—which openly contradicts the memories and traumas of Kashmiris— the Indian administration builds upon a history of silences when it comes to writing Kashmiri history that has long erased, among other things, the everyday experiences of Kashmiris and the excesses of the Indian state.[45] Breaking that silence is a powerful weapon against such propaganda and the oppressive structures that it supports. The disruptive power of learning and speaking about the Hindu nationalist agenda holds true as well for another case that exemplifies the anti-Muslim sentiments that undergird Hindutva ideology: a legislative combination that threatens to strip many Indian Muslims of citizenship.

CAA-NRC: Endangering the Citizenship of Indian Muslims

In December 2019, India's BJP-led government unveiled plans to fundamentally alter the makeup of the Indian citizenry through two related mechanisms. They sought to rapidly enact the Citizenship Amendment Act (CAA), which provides a fast track to Indian citizenship for refugees who identify with all major religious groups, except Muslims. The bill more than halves the amount of time required for non-Muslims to reside to India prior to gaining citizenship and lifts a bar on illegal migrants attaining citizenship.[46] At the same time, BJP leaders announced that they would conduct an India-wide National Register of Citizens (NRC), which forces all those living within Indian borders to prove their citizenship using specific documents or else risk being declared noncitizens, thus becoming stateless.[47] Each action is independently problematic. The CAA targets Muslims

---

[44] Majid Maqbool, "New Chapter on Article 370 in J&K Textbooks: No Mention of Clampdown, Internet Shutdown, Detentions," *The Wire*, March 4, 2020, https://thewire.in/education/article-370-new-textbooks-kashmir.

[45] Amit Kumar and Fayaz A. Dar, "Marginality and Historiography: The Case of Kashmir's History," *Economic and Political Weekly* 50, no. 39 (2015): pp. 37–44.

[46] Jhalak M. Kakkar, "India's New Citizenship Law and Its Anti-Secular Implications," *Lawfare Blog*, January 16, 2020, https://www.lawfareblog.com/indias-new-citizenship-law-and-its-anti-secular-implications.

[47] "Citizenship Amendment Bill: India's New 'Anti-Muslim' Law Explained," BBC, December 11, 2019, https://www.bbc.com/news/world-asia-india-50670393. Initially, the CAA was called the Citizenship Amendment Bill.

192 AUDREY TRUSCHKE

alone for exclusion among refugees who seek a fast track to Indian citizenship. Notably, many Rohingya Muslims have sought refuge in India in recent years, and the nation is also home to many Bangladeshi Muslims.[48] The NRC requires individuals to produce formal documents to retain their citizenship within a nation where a minority of people have received birth certificates.[49] When working together, the CAA and NRC may prove to be catastrophic. The NRC is likely to strip many Indians of their citizenship, leaving Muslims alone without a quick path back to citizenship through the CAA.[50] In short, the combined implementation of the CAA and the NRC will disenfranchise many Indian Muslims, leaving them stateless persons within a burgeoning Hindu nation.

Scholars and human rights activists rely upon several pieces of evidence as the basis for their projections of the negative impact of the combination of the CAA and the NRC on Indian Muslims. For starters, the BJP was relatively forthcoming about its agenda. BJP politicians openly stated in debates over the CAA legislation that they will not deprive Hindus or anybody of citizenship, except Muslims or "infiltrators," in the words of Amit Shah, one of the most powerful men in the BJP.[51] Mohan Bhagwat, the current RSS chief, too, assured "no Hindu will have to leave over NRC."[52] Given the ideology and history of both the BJP and the RSS, it is reasonable to interpret these statements as they appear to have been intended: as a proclamation that Indian citizenship is, first and foremost, for Hindus.

In addition to BJP and RSS pronouncements, the state of Assam in northeastern India offers a regional test case. Indian officials conducted the NRC in Assam in the 2010s, and the gathering of the list of confirmed Indian citizens had some notably callous moments. For instance, the Indian state ordered thousands of Assamese to travel up to four hundred kilometers away to attend hearings, with little notice. At the time, the events were reported in the news periodically, especially when they resulted in the deaths of some travelers.[53]

---

[48] "India: Citizenship Bill Discriminates against Muslims," Human Rights Watch, December 11, 2019, https://www.hrw.org/news/2019/12/11/india-citizenship-bill-discriminates-against-muslims.

[49] Swagata Yadavar and Disha Shetty, "Almost 38% of Indian Children under the Age of Five Don't Have a Birth Certificate," Scroll.in, January 4, 2020, https://scroll.in/article/948667/almost-38-of-ind ian-children-under-the-age-of-five-dont-have-a-birth-certificate.

[50] This also works in reverse, such that the CAA offers a fast track to Indian citizenship for all except Muslims, leaving them uniquely exposed to the NRC. Jaffrelot, Modi's India, p. 375. Rahul Rao points out that that Adivasi communities may also find themselves at risk because of the combined effects of the CAA and NRC, which could incentivize conversion to Hinduism, a longstanding Hindutva project. Rahul Rao, "Nationalisms by, against and beyond the Indian State," Radical Philosophy 2, no. 7 (Spring 2020): p. 23.

[51] Rohan Venkataramakrishnan, "Who Is Linking Citizenship Act to NRC? Here Are Five Times Amit Shah Did So," Scroll.in, December 20, 2019, https://scroll.in/article/947436/who-is-linking-citi zenship-act-to-nrc-here-are-five-times-amit-shah-did-so.

[52] Jaffrelot, Modi's India, pp. 375–76.

[53] See, for example, Abhishek Saha, "Four Dead as Thousands Rush across Assam for Fresh NRC Hearings," The Indian Express, August 8, 2019, https://indianexpress.com/article/north-east-india/ assam/four-dead-as-thousands-rush-across-assam-for-fresh-nrc-hearings-5887082/.

In late August 2019, the Indian government released its final list that declared stateless nearly two million of the thirty-two million residents of Assam.[54] After the list was released, Indian officials made assurances that those who had been stripped of their Indian citizenship by the NRC would be able to challenge their exclusion, but one year later, no such appeals had been heard.[55] The most concrete action that India has taken to address this situation is to build mass detention camps to house those women, men, and children—largely Bengali Muslims—divested of citizenship.[56] Building camps for newly dubbed internal enemies has been a terrifying move in the eyes of many. Based on this model and precedent in Assam, a BJP government might gather into camps tens of millions of Muslims once they are deemed no longer Indian by a nationwide NRC. Giving voice to this alarming possibility, Secretary-General of the United Nations António Guterres warned in February 2020 that, with the CAA, "there is a risk of statelessness" for Indian Muslims.[57]

In December 2019, the BJP-proposed CAA and NRC met with fierce resistance from substantial parts of the Indian population. The protests began in Assam, which had already witnessed the carnage of its own NRC; demonstrations and other forms of peaceful resistance soon spread to districts across the nation, drawing the participation of hundreds of thousands of Indian citizens.[58] Commentators have described the agitations against the CAA and the NRC as "the most significant upheaval since the Emergency of 1975–77."[59] Students and women were among the key organizers and participants in these acts of

[54] "Assam NRC: What Next for 1.9 Million 'Stateless' Indians?," BBC, August 31, 2019, https://www.bbc.com/news/world-asia-india-49520593.

[55] Priyali Sur, "A Year after Rendering Millions Stateless, India Has Yet to Hear a Single Appeal," *Foreign Policy*, September 10, 2020, https://foreignpolicy.com/2020/09/10/2-million-people-india-assam-stateless-year-nrc/.

[56] Sigal Samuel, "India's Massive, Scary New Detention Camps, Explained," *Vox*, September 17, 2019, https://www.vox.com/future-perfect/2019/9/17/20861427/india-assam-citizenship-muslim-detention-camps. As of September 2021, fewer than one thousand Assamese remain in detention, owing partly to mercy releases granted because of the COVID–19 pandemic; the construction of camps in Assam is ongoing. Siddhartha Deb, "'They Are Manufacturing Foreigners': How India Disenfranchises Muslims," *The New York Times Magazine*, September 15, 2021, https://www.nytimes.com/2021/09/15/magazine/india-assam-muslims.html.

[57] "Citizenship Amendment Act May Leave Muslims Stateless, Says UN Secretary-General António Guterres," *The Hindu*, February 19, 2020, https://www.thehindu.com/news/national/citizenship-amendment-act-may-leave-muslims-stateless-says-un-secretary-general-antnio-guterres/article30863390.ece.

[58] Kaushik Deka, "Citizenship Amendment Bill Protests: Here's Why Assam Is Burning," *India Today*, December 12, 2019, https://www.indiatoday.in/mail-today/story/citizenship-bill-protests-here-why-assam-is-burning-1627538-2019-12-12; Soumya Shankar, "India's Citizenship Law, in Tandem with National Registry, Could Make BJP's Discriminatory Targeting of Muslims Easier," *The Intercept*, January 30, 2020, https://theintercept.com/2020/01/30/india-citizenship-act-caa-nrc-assam/.

[59] Rao, "Nationalisms," p. 17.

194 AUDREY TRUSCHKE

anti-CAA civic engagement.[60] One area that caught much media attention was Shaheen Bagh, a Muslim-majority neighborhood of Delhi, where a multi-month sit-in protest took place between December 2020 and March 2021, inspiring many other similar events.[61]

Across India, protestors turned to the Indian Constitution and other symbols of national pride as their rallying cry. Many held up copies and read the Constitution's preamble as a way to protest against what they perceived as a significant step toward mutilating constitutionally secular India until it was a Hindu *rashtra*.[62] Images of Bhimrao Ambedkar, a key author of India's Constitution, were recurrent at protests, as were Indian flags.[63] Across India and, indeed, across the world, protestors against the CAA and NRC heard, read, recited, and sang one of the Indian writer Varun Grover's Hindi poems:

> *Hum samvidhan ko bachaenge,*
> *Hum kagaz nahin dikhaenge,*
> *Hum jan gan man bhi gaenge,*
> *Hum kagaz nahin dikhaenge.*

> We will save the Constitution,
> We will not show [NRC] papers,
> We will sing Jan Gan Man [the national anthem]
> We will not show papers.[64]

These lines capture what so many protestors said using different symbols and language—namely, that they perceived the CAA and NRC to be against the higher values of the Indian state and that their protests were an act of patriotism.

The BJP and supporting Hindu nationalist groups reacted to the anti-CAA protests with force. Repressive state action against the protestors began almost immediately, especially targeting Muslim students at universities in Delhi and

---

[60] Sangbida Lahiri, "We Are Seeing, for the First Time, a Sustained Countrywide Movement Led by Women," *The Wire*, January 13, 2020, March 8, 2020, https://thewire.in/women/caa-nrc-prote sts-women.

[61] Rao, "Nationalisms," pp. 17–18. See Stuti Govil and D. Asher Ghertner, "Contesting the Spatialization of Islamophobia in Urban India," ch. 12 in this volume.

[62] Rohit De and Surabhi Ranganathan, "We Are Witnessing a Rediscovery of India's Republic," *The New York Times*, December 27, 2019, https://www.nytimes.com/2019/12/27/opinion/india-constitution-protests.html. As Jaffrelot points out, the CAA contravenes Article 14 of the Indian Constitution. Jaffrelot, *Modi's India*, p. 374. On engagements with the Indian Constitution beyond elite communities, see Rohit De, *A People's Constitution: The Everyday Life of Law in the Indian Republic* (Princeton, NJ: Princeton University Press, 2018).

[63] Sujatha Subramanian, "Icons and Archive of the Protests against the Citizenship (Amendment) Act and the National Register of Citizens," *Journal of Feminist Studies in Religion* 37, no. 2 (2021): pp. 128–32.

[64] Rao, "Nationalisms," pp. 20–21.

Aligarh.[65] Many Hindu nationalist leaders dubbed all protestors as anti-national and even issued calls to "shoot the traitors."[66] In repeated instances, the police unleashed violence against peaceful protestors, resulting in a double-digit death toll and hundreds of political prisoners.[67] More than two-thirds of the dead were in the northern state of Uttar Pradesh, whose Hindu supremacist leader, Yogi Adityanath, justified the police brutality.[68] The Indian state even resorted to Section 124a of the Indian Penal Code, which criminalizes sedition, to imprison anti-CAA protesters.[69] Notwithstanding such repression, the anti-CAA protests raged across India for months, coming to an end only with the dawn of the COVID-19 pandemic in March 2020 and associated requirements of social distancing.[70] The COVID-19 pandemic ravaged the globe for more than 3 years, including an estimated death toll of four million in India as of June 2021.[71] This health crisis delayed the BJP's plans for implementing both the CAA and the NRC across India, and they have not yet pursued the matter after the pandemic's formal end in May 2023. At present, it is unclear when these will take place; the Modi government has received seven extensions for issuing guidelines to frame the CAA, with the most recent being in January 2023.[72]

Even without implementation, the CAA and NRC have already had negative effects for numerous Indian communities. The terms of the CAA and NRC debate homogenize both Hindus and Muslims. D. Parthasarathy explains this relationship as follows: "[T]he idea of a homogenous Muslim citizen and identity can be opposed through constructed notion of a homogenised Hindu collective. In the process, the dangers of ignoring the hierarchies and discriminations

[65] Audrey Truschke, "Exclusion, Affect, and Violence in the Many Sites of Indian History," *Indian Cultural Forum*, June 9, 2020, https://indianculturalforum.in/2020/06/09/exclusion-violence-ind ian-history-constitution-truschke/.

[66] Jayshree Bajoria, "'Shoot the Traitors': Discrimination against Muslims under India's New Citizenship Policy," Human Rights Watch, April 9, 2020, https://www.hrw.org/report/2020/04/09/ shoot-traitors/discrimination-against-muslims-under-indias-new-citizenship-policy.

[67] See, for example, "CAA Protests: 22 People Killed, 322 Still in Jail for Violence in December, Uttar Pradesh Tells HC," *Scroll.in*, February 18, 2020, https://scroll.in/latest/953529/caa-protests-22-people-killed-322-still-in-jail-for-violence-in-december-uttar-pradesh-tells-hc.

[68] Jaffrelot, *Modi's India*, p. 384.

[69] Mahek Shivnani and Aashna Mansata, "Wounded Government Pride: 'Sedition' Discrediting the Voice of Dissent," *Criminal Law Research and Review Blog*, April 7, 2021, https://crlreview.in/ wounded-government-pride-sedition-discrediting-the-voice-of-dissent/.

[70] Raghu Karnad, "Farewell to Shaheen Bagh, as Political Togetherness Yields to Social Distance," *The Wire*, March 24, 2020, https://thewire.in/politics/farewell-to-shaheen-bagh-as-political-toget herness-yields-to-social-distance.

[71] Sushmita Pathak, Lauren Frayer, and Marc Silver, "India's Pandemic Death Toll Estimated at about 4 Million: 10 Times the Official Count," NPR, July 20, 2021, https://www.npr.org/sections/ goatsandsoda/2021/07/20/1018438334/indias-pandemic-death-toll-estimated-at-about-4-million-10-times-the-official-co.

[72] "Centre Gets 6th Extension to Frame Rule for Citizenship Act," *The Times of India*, January 11, 2022, https://www.thehindu.com/news/national/home-ministry-seeks-another-extension-of-six-months-to-frame-caa-rules/article66350317.ece .

within and among Hindus are temporarily disregarded politically."[73] More generally, the BJP and its allies seek to tamp down on lower-class discontent by promising a Hindu supremacist future. Although, as Sunita Viswanath has reflected, Hindutva harms Hindus also, especially the poor and marginalized.[74] In the case of Muslims, homogeneity renders any individual as representative of the larger class of potential state enemies. Additionally, the fallout from the protests, especially police brutality and arrests, continues to reverberate in Muslim communities.[75] The BJP persists in wielding violence against Muslims and exerts significant pressure on the journalists who might report on such human rights violations.[76]

February 2020 Pogrom in Delhi

In late February 2020, Hindu mobs and the police unleashed violence against Muslim communities and individuals in northeast Delhi. The bulk of the riots occurred on three days, February 23–25, with some violence spilling into February 26–27. The violence centered on an area of Delhi where Muslims constitute nearly 30 percent of the population and Hindus are close to 70 percent.[77] BJP leaders had been deploying inflammatory language about parts of Delhi for weeks before the violence.[78] The immediate catalyst was that BJP leader Kapil Mishra gave a speech on February 23, 2020, calling for the clearing—either legally or using extrajudicial violence—of anti-CAA protestors from the streets of northeast Delhi, where protests had been inspired by the resistance in Shaheen Bagh.[79] Within hours, Hindu mobs violently attacked protesters. Over the next

[73] "Citizenship (Amendment) Act: The Pitfalls of Homogenising Identities in Resistance Narratives," *Economic and Political Weekly* 55, no. 25 (June 20, 2020): p. 4.

[74] Viswanath, "Modi's Religious Nationalism."

[75] Betwa Sharma, "One Year after Mass Protests, India's Muslims Still Live in Fear," *Foreign Policy*, December 18, 2020, https://foreignpolicy.com/2020/12/18/one-year-mass-caa-protests-india-muslims-citizenship-amendment-act-modi/.

[76] See, for example, Rana Ayyub, "A Timeline of Hate, Intimidation and Injustice in Modi's India," *The Washington Post*, August 16, 2021, https://www.washingtonpost.com/opinions/2021/08/16/india-modi-muslims-journalists-dissent-democracy-rana-ayyub/; Rana Ayyub, "The Indian Government Continues to Harass Journalists: I'm Facing Prison over a Tweet," *The Washington Post*, June 29, 2021, https://www.washingtonpost.com/opinions/2021/06/29/rana-ayyub-india-journalism-modi-harassment/. As Reporters without Borders put it bluntly in explaining India's tumble in the World Press Freedom Index in recent years, "India is one of the world's most dangerous countries for journalists." "India," Reporters without Borders, accessed January 9, 2022, https://rsf.org/en/india.

[77] These percentages are as of the 2011 census. Jaffrelot, *Modi's India*, p. 384.

[78] Jaffrelot, *Modi's India*, pp. 384–86.

[79] Delhi Minorities Commission, *Report of the DMC Fact-Finding Committee on North-East Delhi Riots of February 2020* (Government of NCT of Delhi, 2020), https://sanhati-india.in/2020/07/28/report-of-the-dmc-fact-finding-committee-on-north-east-delhi-riots-of-february-2020/, pp. 30–31, 99.

three days, at least fifty-three people died, 250 were hospitalized, and an unknown number went missing.[80] The majority of casualties were Muslim.[81] There was also widespread arson and other damage to Muslim-owned shops, mosques, and homes in the area. These events appear to have been designed to instill fear in Muslim communities and their allies to deter further resistance to the ongoing project to remake India as a homeland for Hindus.

The February 2020 Delhi riots were organized and traded on anti-Muslim sentiments. A fact-finding report by the Delhi Minorities Commission notes that Hindu mobs of one hundred to one thousand people roamed around, enacting violence in a systematic manner.[82] Locals in northeast Delhi identified the attackers as a mix of outsiders and residents, many of whom were visibly armed.[83] The mobs discriminated on the basis of religion during their attacks, including by asking for identification cards in order to ensure that they targeted Muslims.[84] The attackers also shouted slogans that advanced extreme Islamophobic sentiments and, relatedly, allegiance to the BJP, such as "Modiji, kaat do in mullon ko" ("Mr. Modi, cut these Muslims into pieces").[85] The Indian government tried to prevent groups from disseminating information about the mob violence. Some regional news channels who tried to accurately report on the Delhi riots found themselves banned by India's Ministry of Information and Broadcasting.[86] Still, major news organizations and human rights groups documented police brutality and complicity during the riots, both in real time and subsequently.[87]

Viewing this mob violence on both micro and macro levels, one can see the harsh imprint of Islamophobia. On the ground during these riots, Hindu mobs targeted numerous mosques. For instance, during the height of the violence, members of the Hindu mobs climbed atop the minarets of two mosques in different neighborhoods in northeast Delhi and raised saffron flags (one to Hanuman and the other accompanied by placing a statue of Hanuman at the mosque's entrance).[88] In doing so, they marked Muslim religious spaces as

---

[80] Bajoria, "'Shoot'"; Delhi Minorities Commission, *Report*, p. 33.

[81] Bajoria, "'Shoot.'"

[82] Delhi Minorities Commission, *Report*, p. 99.

[83] Delhi Minorities Commission, *Report*, pp. 99–100.

[84] Delhi Minorities Commission, *Report*, p. 39.

[85] Delhi Minorities Commission, *Report*, p. 50.

[86] Jaffrelot, *Modi's India*, p. 393.

[87] See, for example, "Delhi 2020 Religious Riots: Amnesty International Accuses Police of Rights Abuses," BBC, August 28, 2020, https://www.bbc.com/news/world-asia-india-53891354.

[88] Naomi Barton, "Delhi Riots: Mosque Set on Fire in Ashok Nagar, Hanuman Flag Placed on Minaret," *The Wire*, February 25, 2020, https://thewire.in/communalism/delhi-violence-mosque-set-on-fire-in-ashok-vihar-hanuman-flag-placed-on-top; Betwa Sharma, "Delhi Hero: Meet the Hindu Man Who Removed the Saffron Flag from a Burnt Mosque," *Huffington Post*, March 5, 2020, https://www.huffingtonpost.in/entry/delhi-riots-hero_in_5e60cf49c5b6bd126b7643e8.

subservient to Hindu majoritarian norms and, specifically, to a Hindu deity.[89] The mob later set one of the mosques on fire and damaged it. These acts were among the numerous cases of desecration and destruction of mosques in recent decades in India, perhaps most powerfully in the 2002 Gujarat pogrom that was overseen by then Chief Minister of Gujarat Narendra Modi. During that horrific violence, more than five hundred places of Muslim religious significance, including many mosques, were damaged or destroyed, and Hindus sometimes placed saffron-colored flags and icons of Hanuman on the rubble.[90] Like with Gujarat in 2002, acts of mosque desecration in Delhi in February 2020 were accompanied by violence, including of a lethal nature, against Muslims.

A further chapter in the story of one of these mosques offers hope while also pointing to the severe Islamophobia that constrains the possibilities for Muslim political action and daily life for Muslims in Delhi at present. A few days after a saffron flag was placed atop the minaret, another Hindu man climbed the same minaret and removed it; this second man was hailed as a hero.[91] The incident was an example of Indian Hindus rejecting the hateful agenda of Hindu nationalism that is seeking, among other things, to hijack their religious tradition and reduce it to a violent political ideology.[92] But it is noteworthy that only a Hindu could have committed this action in the current Indian environment and reasonably expected to live to tell the tale. A Muslim would have put himself or herself in far greater danger in seeking to remove a mark of Hindu supremacy from an Islamic religious space. In fact, the Hindu man who removed the saffron flag was asked to do so by an elderly Muslim cleric who knew that an Indian Muslim could not safely accomplish this feat.[93] Indian Muslims are already living, to a great degree, within a Hindu *rashtra* in which they are being increasingly denied religious freedom.

On a worldwide scale, the political events of Delhi during the February 2020 riots and the aftermath displayed a harsh indifference to Muslim lives. Then President Donald Trump was visiting India on February 24 and 25, 2020, when Hindu mobs were enacting violence against Muslim communities in northeast Delhi. President Trump made no public comments on the horrific attacks.

---

[89] Ziya Us Salam, "Plot to Turn a Mosque in North East Delhi into a Temple Foiled," *Frontline*, December 4, 2020, https://frontline.thehindu.com/social-issues/delhi-riots-february-2020-plot-to-turn-mosque-allahwali-masjid-under-jamiat-ulema-e-hind-in-karawal-nagar-north-east-delhi-into-a-temple-foiled/article33099659.ece.

[90] Christophe Jaffrelot, "The 2002 Pogrom in Gujarat: The Post–9/11 Face of Hindu Nationalist Anti-Muslim Violence," in *Religion and Violence in South Asia: Theory and Practice*, ed. John R. Hinnells and Richard King (New York: Routledge, 2007), p. 176.

[91] Sharma, "Delhi Hero."

[92] This point was made powerfully by Hindu community leaders and scholars who identify as Hindu during the virtual conference Dismantling Global Hindutva: Multidisciplinary Perspectives, held September 10–12, 2021.

[93] Sharma, "Delhi Hero."

Nearly immediately, many interpreted this silence as a sign of the United States' permission, if not outright approval, for the bloodletting.[94] For his part, Prime Minister Narendra Modi acted with similar, and predictable, callousness. Modi had overseen the 2002 Gujarat Pogrom, for which he was banned from visiting the United States for over a decade.[95] Modi has never shown remorse for the 2002 Gujarat pogrom, only continuing to dehumanize the Muslims who died under his watch.[96] Similarly, Modi had few words of comfort for those who were displaced or lost property or worse during the 2020 Delhi riots.

More broadly, the BJP refused to take responsibility for the 2020 riots in Delhi and, instead, promoted a disinformation campaign that blamed Muslims for the attacks. Hindu nationalist groups and mouthpieces went so far as to say that the greatest victim of the February 2020 Delhi riots was Kapil Mishra, whose inflammatory language had sparked the lethal anti-Muslim violence.[97] The Indian state allowed the perpetrators of the riots to go free and, instead, arrested prominent Indian Muslims as retribution, including the well-known activist Umar Khalid. As of August 2023, Umar Khalid remains incarcerated, a reminder of the potential costs of being an outspoken Muslim in Modi's India.[98] The Islamophobia is truly staggering that undergirds the Modi administration's logic of imprisoning Muslims for exercising their democratic right to protest and for being targeted in violent assaults. The message, quite clearly, is that within the burgeoning Hindu *rashtra*, Muslims must endure a loss of rights, up to and including the right to liberty and life.

Conclusion: Saffron Nation

India's government continues down an alarming path of advancing authoritarianism, enforcing majoritarian norms, and encouraging Islamophobia. In the

---

[94] See, for example, Priyanka Bansal, "Trump's India Trip Ignored the New Delhi Riots: But His Silence Isn't the Most Damning," NBC News, February 28, 2020, https://www.nbcnews.com/ think/opinion/trump-s-india-trip-ignored-new-delhi-riots-his-silence-ncna1144986. On Trump's comments supporting Modi during that visit, see Joanna Slater, "Violence in Delhi and Support for Modi on 'Religious Freedom,'" *The Washington Post*, February 25, 2020, https://www.washingtonp ost.com/world/2020/02/24/trump-india-live-updates-2/.

[95] Modi was denied one visa to the United States and had another US visa revoked. Jaffrelot, *Modi's India*, pp. 451–52.

[96] In 2013, Modi compared Muslim victims of the 2002 Gujarat pogrom to dogs. See, for example, Sruthi Gottipati and Annie Banerji, "Modi's 'Puppy' Remark Triggers New Controversy over 2002 Riots," *Reuters*, July 12, 2013, https://www.reuters.com/article/narendra-modi-puppy-reuters-interv iew-idINDEE96B08S20130712.

[97] Jaffrelot, *Modi's India*, p. 393.

[98] Richa Banka, "Umar Khalid Gets Bail in a Riots Case, to Stay in Jail," *Hindustan Times*, April 16, 2021, https://www.hindustantimes.com/cities/delhi-news/umar-khalid-gets-bail-in-a-riots-case-to-stay-in-jail-101618527542670.html.

aftermath of the events discussed in this chapter—the 2019 changes in Indian policies on Kashmir, the Citizenship Amendment Act and protests against it between December 2019 and March 2020, and the February 2020 Delhi riots—there have been no resignations, no suspensions, and no formal apologies. Many of the protestors and others unjustly imprisoned remain incarcerated as of 2023. In contrast, many of the violent actors who were supported by the state, whether formally or informally, walk free.

India is turning into a saffron nation—an ethnonationalist Hindu state—before our eyes. This rebirth has extensive ramifications for Indians, especially non-Hindu religious communities and those who would participate in civil society or criticize the state. For those outside of India, India's turn to the hard right makes it increasingly dangerous to talk and write about anti-Muslim events and the broader contours of Hindutva within India and as a global phenomenon. Academics, journalists, and human rights advocates are often unable to travel to the subcontinent and, in different ways, face threats from an aggressive, pro-Hindutva wing of the Indian diaspora.[99] Like other kinds of populism, Hindutva proponents rely on the silence of both the oppressed and their allies. Combating Hindutva and Islamophobia, thus, requires painstaking documentation of anti-Muslim aggressions in India.

---

[99] See, for example, Hannah Ellis-Petersen, "Death Threats Sent to Participants of US Conference on Hindu Nationalism," *The Guardian*, September 9, 2021, https://www.theguardian.com/world/2021/sep/09/death-threats-sent-to-participants-of-us-conference-on-hindu-nationalism.

12

Contesting the Spatialization
of Islamophobia in Urban India

Stuti Govil and D. Asher Ghertner

The Preamble to the Constitution of India begins with the resolution to establish "India as a sovereign, socialist, secular and democratic republic."[1] In the Indian context, secularism has never meant the withering away of religious identity or even the separation of religion and state. Rather, the secularization process in India was intended to recognize all religions as equal under law.[2] As a result, India constitutionally and politically opposed the adoption of a national religion, but the centrality of political identification and the codification of religion in law created a persistent tension in how secular policy and law were to be adjudicated within a polity that comprises multiple religious communities. This tension is playing out in the current moment through an ascendant Hindu nationalism that seeks to bring to fruition what, in the eyes of its proponents, is a long overdue Hindu *rashtra*, or the political project of defining India as a Hindu nation. This project is premised on practices aimed at establishing Muslim cultural, religious, and political forms in a relation of exteriority vis-à-vis this Hindu nation, most prominently via the discursive framing of Islam as a religion alien to the subcontinent.[3]

Multiple studies trace the intensifying forms of Islamophobic political discourse in India in recent decades.[4] Most of these accounts rightly register December 6, 1992, as a crucial inflection point when Hindu fundamentalism,

---

[1] The Constitution of India, https://cdnbbsr.s3waas.gov.in/s380537a945c7aaa788ccfcdf1b99b5 d8f/uploads/2023/05/2023050195.pdf.

[2] Rajeev Bhargava, "The Distinctiveness of Indian Secularism," in *The Future of Secularism*, ed. T. N. Srivastava (New York: Oxford University Press, 2007), ch. 3; Christophe Jaffrelot, "India's Democracy at 70: Toward a Hindu State?," *Journal of Democracy* 28, no. 3 (2017): 52–63.

[3] Angana P. Chatterji, Thomas Blom Hansen, and Christophe Jaffrelot, eds., *Majoritarian State: How Hindu Nationalism Is Changing India* (New Delhi: Oxford University Press, 2019).

[4] Edward Anderson and Christophe Jaffrelot, "Hindu Nationalism and the 'Saffronisation of the Public Sphere,'" *Contemporary South Asia* 26, no. 4 (2018): 468–82; Nitasha Kaul, "Islamophobia in India," *Society and Space*, December 7, 2020, https://www.societyandspace.org/articles/islamopho bia-in-india; Niranjan Sahoo, "Mounting Majoritarianism and Political Polarization in India," in *Political Polarization in South and Southeast Asia*, ed. Thomas Carothers and Andrew O'Donohue (Washington, DC: Carnegie Endowment for International Peace), pp. 9–24.

Stuti Govil and D. Asher Ghertner, *Contesting the Spatialization of Islamophobia in Urban India* In: *Global Islamophobia and the Rise of Populism*. Edited by: Sahar F. Aziz and John L. Esposito, Oxford University Press.
© Oxford University Press 2024. DOI: 10.1093/oso/9780197648995.003.0012

represented by the political ideology known as Hindutva, asserted itself on a national stage.[5] That day, there was a rally in Ayodhya, Uttar Pradesh, revered as the birthplace of the Hindu deity Lord Ram, led by the Vishwa Hindu Parishad and the Bharatiya Janata Party (BJP), the main religious organization and political party within the wider family of Hindu-nationalist organizations referred to as the Sangh Parivar.[6] Protesters-turned-rioters attacked the Babri Masjid, a 16th-century mosque built during the rule of the Mughal emperor Babur. The ideological resurgence of Hindutva, which fell to the political fringes in the heyday of Nehruvian secularism (1947–90), following the Ayodhya riots and subsequent mobilization to build a Ram Janmabhoomi (birthplace) temple in its place contributed to the BJP's national electoral triumph, first from 1998 to 2004 and again from 2014 until present.[7]

Hindutva and its political weapon of Islamophobia are conventionally understood to operate primarily at the level of realpolitik, electoral equations, and contestations over national belonging. This chapter flips this analytical perspective by contending that alongside the rise of Islamophobia as a national political discourse that differentially excludes, stigmatizes, and punishes Muslim citizens, there has also been a more entrenched rise of Islamophobia as a spatial project of material denial, infrastructural disconnect, municipal exclusion, and spatial relegation.[8] Understanding Islamophobia in the context of an ascendant Hindu *rashtra* requires not only attention to the grand political denials and spectacular anti-Muslim violence that are most commonly portrayed in international media and human rights conversations but also the everyday lived experience of Muslims struggling to access clean water and safe neighborhoods and to enjoy residential tenure security, economic facilities, and other basic needs. Infrastructural neglect and Muslim ghettoization, on the one hand, and threatened national citizenship, on the other, are two faces of Islamophobia in contemporary India. While national citizenship debates in India have rightfully garnered major scholarly and humanitarian attention, the question of urban belonging is less well understood and yet is as significant to understanding and challenging the politics of fear confronting Muslim Indians across multiple arenas of everyday life. The broad question we explore in this chapter, then, is

[5] See Audrey Truschke, "Displacing and Disciplining Muslims in India's Burgeoning Hindu *Rashtra*," ch. 11 in this volume; David Ludden, ed., *Making India Hindu: Religion, Community, and the Politics of Democracy in India* (Oxford: Oxford University Press, 2006); Chatterji, Hansen, and Jaffrelot, *Majoritarian State*.

[6] Tapan Basu, Pradip Datta, Sumit Sarkar, Tanika Sarkar, and Sambuddha Sen, eds., *Khaki Shorts and Saffron Flags: A Critique of the Hindu Right* (Delhi: Orient Longman, 1993).

[7] BJP, "BJP Election Manifesto 2014: Ek Bharat—Shreshtha Bharat," http://library.bjp.org/jspui/handle/123456789/260; Deepak Mehta, "The Ayodhya Dispute: The Absent Mosque, State of Emergency and the Jural Deity," *Journal of Material Culture* 20, no. 4 (2015): pp. 397–414.

[8] Nikhil Anand, "Municipal Disconnect: On Abject Water and Its Urban Infrastructures," *Ethnography* 13, no. 4 (2012): pp. 487–509.

how the mechanics of Islamophobia can be understood—and subverted—when we attend to their operation on the terrain of urban citizenship.

Urban Citizenship and Islamophobia

Over the past thirty years, urban citizenship has (re-)emerged as a key analytical and political category for recognizing the variegated mechanisms by which citizenship entitlements are granted or denied in everyday life.[9] While much of the framing of citizenship rights historically emphasized formal citizenship entitlements, such as the right to vote or access national healthcare, urban citizenship focuses on how substantive citizenship entitlements pertaining to material needs—including clean water and sanitation, residential tenure security, freedom of movement, and access to public space and resources—are inflected by municipal belonging as much as by national belonging. This position was vociferously articulated by urban social movements across the world in the first decade of the 21st century, specifically in response to neoliberal economic policies that led to splintered infrastructural access and unequal resource distribution within and across neighborhoods.[10] These movements collectively showed that the city had become the primary social and political community within which individuals and groups exercise and make claims for this set of rights.[11] Indeed, the United Nations has more recently codified urban citizenship, via its adoption of the language of "The right to the city," as a key pillar for recognizing the substantive citizenship rights necessary to ensure material and bodily security.[12] Without reviewing this wider policy orientation, this chapter builds on the observation that the contested terrain of urban citizenship, which concerns who has the right to contribute to the collective organization of urban space and the urbanizing national (metro)polis, is increasingly not only shaped by but in turn shapes debates over the parameters of national citizenship.

To understand this dynamic, we examine the critical events that rocked Delhi in 2019–20, when contestations around the meaning of national citizenship played out literally within the fabric of urban space. The passage of the controversial Citizenship Amendment Act (CAA), which reframed national citizenship on the basis of religion in late 2019, led to spontaneous protests in the heart

---

[9] James Holston and Arjun Appadurai, eds., *Cities and Citizenship* (Durham, NC: Duke University Press, 1999); James Holston, *Insurgent Citizenship: Disjunctions of Democracy and Modernity in Brazil* (Princeton, NJ: Princeton University Press, 2008).

[10] Stephen Graham and Simon Marvin, *Splintering Urbanism* (New York: Routledge, 2001).

[11] Renu Desai and Romola Sanyal, eds., *Urbanizing Citizenship: Contested Spaces in Indian Cities* (New Delhi: Sage, 2012).

[12] United Nations, "Policy Paper 1: 'The Right to the City and Cities for All'" (Conference on Housing and Sustainable Urban Development, Habitat III, United Nations, New York, NY, 2017).

of Muslim neighborhoods across the nation, bringing hundreds of thousands of people to the streets.[13] As we show through a focus on the iconic protest in New Delhi that catalyzed this nationwide mobilization, protestors joined an explicitly anti-CAA message with spatial articulations of Muslim neighborhoods as central places of urban social life. Claims to national belonging, in other words, emerged as simultaneous expressions of the right to the city, what the French sociologist Henri Lefebvre famously termed, in the aftermath of the global protests of 1968, "the right to centrality."[14]

Examining how national citizenship struggles took place upon and responded to a terrain of hollowed-out urban citizenship rights in India guides us to attend to the more infrastructural logics of Muslim exclusion that have materially disadvantaged Muslim communities from well before the more muscular forms of Islamophobia articulated via ascendant Hindutva politics. This attention to Islamophobia as spatial practice as much as political discourse helps make evident the spatial predicates of Islamophobia within a longer history of Muslim ghettoization that predates the national rise of the BJP and the Babri Masjid demolition as well as the global, post-War-on-Terror discourse of "Muslim terror" that often frames how Islamophobia is understood in South Asia and beyond.[15] The violence of Hindu fundamentalists burning mosques and terrorizing families during the so-called Delhi Riots of February 2020, which occurred as retribution against the neighborhoods staging anti-CAA protests, thus must be understood as building upon a spatial politics in which Muslim peripherality is the default organizational form of the Hindu *rashtra*. Rendering Muslims as symbolically and politically exterior is possible because of their geographical marginalization.

Hindu Majoritarianism and Islamophobia: Creating a New Spatial Order

The year 2014 ushered in a key shift in how religion is entrenched in Indian politics. After ten years in the political opposition, the BJP secured a landmark victory in the Lok Sabha, the lower house of the Indian Parliament, under the leadership of Narendra Modi, who had been accused but subsequently acquitted in 2020 of leading a state-sponsored pogrom against Muslims in the state of

---

[13] Jayshree Bajoria, "'Shoot the Traitors': Discrimination against Muslims under India's New Citizenship Policy," Human Rights Watch, April 9, 2020, https://www.hrw.org/report/2020/04/09/shoot-traitors/discrimination-against-muslims-under-indias-new-citizenship-policy.

[14] Henri Lefebvre, *The Urban Revolution*, trans. Roberto Bononno (Minneapolis: University of Minnesota Press, 2003 [1970]).

[15] Andrew Shryock, ed. *Islamophobia/Islamophilia: Beyond the Politics of Enemy and Friend* (Bloomington: Indian University Press, 2010).

Gujarat in 2002.[16] As part of its campaign, the BJP promised to bring back *acche din*, or "the good days," and reinforced its commitment to the Hindu *rashtra* through its evocations of a national need to recover past Hindu glories.[17]

Since then, India has witnessed a slow erosion of secular public life. A spectacular example came in the form of a petition filed before the Supreme Court seeking to remove the words *socialist* and *secular* from the Preamble to the Constitution, which claimed that they were "antithetical to the constitutional tenets as well as historical and cultural themes of India."[18] Even when not overtly challenging the constitutional basis of secularism, well-organized Hindu nationalists have mounted a massive ethno-religious mobilization to "Hinduize" the public sphere.[19] This mobilization has operated, in part, through an affective politics of *bahumat*, a communalist sense of "the majority" as a particular kind of scorned yet righteous moral force. This form of majoritarianism, as Thomas Blom Hansen puts it, "increasingly adopted a style of forceful anger that foregrounded hurt sentiments."[20] It did so by mobilizing a revisionist historical account of Hindu cultural degeneration understood to be an effect of a long history of foreign subjugation first by Mughals, then by the British, and, since Independence in 1947, by a false secularism that, in Hindutva political thought, is understood to have denied the cultural hegemony that Hindus rightly deserve. The 1992 demolition of the Babri Masjid by an angry mob radiated across the nation as a performative display of Hindutva masculine rage, driving this sense of historical wrong to the core of national politics.[21] The Supreme Court of India's 2020 judgment allowing the final construction of the Ram Janmabhoomi temple in the place of the demolished Babri Masjid provided judicial validation of this form of *bahumat*, concretizing both material and symbolic replacement of Muslim spaces as a project of Hindu nation-building.[22]

Guided by the Ram Janmabhoomi movement in the early 1990s, smaller and more routine political displays of Hindu *bahumat* have become increasingly

[16] Christophe Jaffrelot, *Modi's India: Hindu Nationalism and the Rise of Ethnic Democracy* (Princeton, NJ: Princeton University Press, 2021). See also Parvis Ghassem-Fachandi, *Pogrom in Gujarat: Hindu Nationalism and Anti-Muslim Violence in India* (Princeton, NJ: Princeton University Press, 2012).

[17] BJP, "BJP Election Manifesto 2014."

[18] "Plea in SC to Remove 'Socialist' and 'Secular' from Constitution's Preamble," *The Wire*, July 29, 2020, https://thewire.in/law/supreme-court-plea-socialist-secular-constitution-preamble.

[19] Christophe Jaffrelot, "India's Democracy"; Rizwan Ahmad, "Renaming India: Saffronisation of Public Spaces," *Al Jazeera*, October 12, 2018, https://www.aljazeera.com/opinions/2018/10/12/renaming-india-saffronisation-of-public-spaces.

[20] Thomas Blom Hansen, "Democracy against Law: Reflections on India's Illiberal Democracy," in *Majoritarian State: How Hindu Nationalism is Changing India*, ed. Angana P. Chatterji, Thomas Blom Hansen, and Christophe Jaffrelot (New Delhi: Oxford University Press, 2019), p. 33.

[21] Veena Das, *Life and Words: Violence and the Descent into the Ordinary* (Berkeley: University of California Press, 2007).

[22] M Siddiq (D) Thr Lrs vs. Mahant Suresh Das and Others, Civil Appeal Nos. 10866–67 of 2010 in the Supreme Court of India, November 9, 2019.

common in Indian cities. For instance, a "beef ban" was enacted in the early tenure of the BJP's first term, leading to a spate of lynchings and killings of Muslims and Dalits (former "untouchable" outcastes) by Hindu vigilantes in small cities, villages, and on the peripheries of metro areas in the name of *gau rashka*, or "defense of the cow"—a specific elevation of Brahmin hegemony.[23] In these tragic events, Muslims suspected of consuming or selling beef were lynched by their neighbors, village compatriots, and others who shared community space with them, often with conspicuous abdication of police responsibility for quelling communal violence. Shocking to India's secular public sphere was the occurrence of such violence within major metropolitan regions, actions that confirm Nair's observation that lynching in India has always operated as "a ritual that explicitly enforces the outcaste status of its victims," often via displays meant to shock and boldly bring to the surface communalist social relations.[24]

Hindutva, as a right-wing ideology, holds that Hindus are "a people descending from ancestral sons of the soil, the 'Vedic fathers.'"[25] In this sense, Hindutva meets the criteria of ethnic nationalism, with its motto "Hindu, Hindi, Hindustan" tying faith to language to land.[26] Within this paradigm, Indian Muslims are discursively othered and rendered alien to their own country, despite the more syncretic religious traditions of the subcontinent and the strong evidence that "Hinduism" as a religious singularity is a colonial construction.[27] Muslims under this political dispensation are subjected to discriminatory rhetoric that casts them as an inherent threat to the spatial form of the "Hindu" nation, city, and neighborhood.[28] This spatial imaginary works via different registers, including through a rhetoric of demographic competition that frames Hindus as being in danger of becoming outnumbered (*Hindu khatre mei hain*, or Hindus are in danger, is the common Hindi line evoking the sense of demographic risk). This claim circulates through routine media portrayals and social commentary intimating that Indian Muslims, as agents aligned to Pakistan or as having questionable allegiance to the Indian nation, are deliberating taking over pure ethno-religious spaces in India.[29]

---

[23] Kaul, "Islamophobia."

[24] Supriya Nair, "The Meaning of India's 'Beef Lynchings,'" *The Atlantic*, July 17, 2017, https://www.theatlantic.com/international/archive/2017/07/india-modi-beef-lynching-muslim-partition/533739/.

[25] Chatterji, Hansen, and Jaffrelot, *Majoritarian State*, p. 3.

[26] Christophe Jaffrelot, ed., *Hindu Nationalism: A Reader* (Princeton, NJ: Princeton University Press, 2007), p. 5.

[27] Esther Bloch, Marianne Keppens, and Rajaram Hegde, eds., *Rethinking Religion in India: The Colonial Construction of Hinduism* (New York: Routledge, 2010).

[28] Kaul, "Islamophobia."

[29] Eviane Leidig, "Hindutva as a Variant of Right-Wing Extremism," *Patterns of Prejudice* 54, no. 3 (2020): p. 230.

This discursive construction of the spatial idea of a pure Hindu land leads Indian Muslims to be increasingly alienated by a political rhetoric that uses state machinery to strengthen its ideological project and to normalize prejudice among its populace, keeping immense support for the ruling BJP party intact.[30] This othering takes concrete, material form in Indian cities, where bourgeois and plebian concerns with neighborhood character build on a longer history of Muslim segregation that frames the Muslim threat to the Hindu "inside" as a geographical struggle over habitat. Here, the Muslim can only figure as an alien encroacher threatening to deprive Hindu environments of resources and security.[31]

The legacy of urban segregation forms a crucial spatial backdrop for ongoing neighborhood and citywide spatializations of Muslim exteriority. That is, Muslim ghettoization and exclusion serve as the foundation upon which fear of Muslims encroaching on the ordinary public spaces of the city becomes possible. Such patterns of segregation have a longer, colonial history but took a more dramatic form in the aftermath of India's violent Partition with Pakistan, which occurred at the dawn of Independence from British rule in 1947.[32] New Delhi, at the time, witnessed an exodus of approximately two-thirds of its Muslim population, a majority of whom were "elite Muslims."[33] Delhi was especially devastated by the Partition and its communal logic of dividing land on the basis of religion, becoming what Gyan Pandey called the quintessential "partition city."[34] Immediate post-Partition riots were fueled by stories of rape, pillage, murder, and abductions from both sides of the border. The riots in north India during this period included attacks on Muslim neighborhoods and homes, the desecration and occupation of Muslim monuments and places of worship, and numerous incidents of abduction and rape of women. An estimated 25,000 Muslims were killed while others sought refuge in "evacuee camps," zones that emerged in established Muslim-majority neighborhoods or prominent religious sites like the Jama Masjid.[35]

---

[30] Jaffrelot, *Modi's India*; Dibyesh Anand, "The Violence of Security: Hindu Nationalism and the Politics of Representing 'the Muslim' as a Danger," *The Round Table* 94 (2005): pp. 203–15; D. Asher Ghertner, "Hindu Extrastatecraft? Coding the Future Hindu, or the Infrastructural Inertia of Indian Urbanism," in *Global Asias: Essays on Futurity Past and Present*, ed. Tim Bunnell and Daniel Goh (Berlin: Jovis, 2018), pp. 97–107.

[31] Madeeha Mujawar, "Muslims Not Allowed: The Stereotypes of Mumbai's Rental Property Market," CNBC, September 18, 2020, https://www.cnbctv18.com/views/muslims-not-allowed-the-stereotypes-of-mumbais-rental-property-market-6970051.htm.

[32] Joya Chatterji, "Of Graveyards and Ghettos: Muslims in Partitioned West Bengal," in *Living Together Separately: Cultural India in History and Politics*, ed. Mushirul Hasan and Asim Roy (Oxford: Oxford University Press), pp. 222–49.

[33] Laurent Gayer, "Safe and Sound: Searching for a 'Good Environment' in Abul Fazl Enclave, Delhi,'" in *Muslims in Indian Cities: Trajectories of Marginalisation* (New York: Columbia University Press, 2012), pp. 213–36.

[34] Gyan Pandey, *Remembering Partition: Violence, Nationalism and History in India* (Cambridge: Cambridge University Press, 2001).

[35] Pandey, *Remembering Partition*.

Newly arrived Hindu and Sikh refugees who had fled Pakistan as well as resident locals soon started occupying empty houses and spaces left behind by Muslims, often driving out Muslims from non-Muslim majority neighborhoods.[36] The illegal occupations prompted the establishment of the Office of the Custodian of Evacuee Property, intended to guard abandoned properties until the return of their original owners.[37] In many instances, however, the custodian acquired abandoned properties of Muslims who were still in the city, part of what Geva aptly calls "the scramble for houses."[38] This painful history of Muslim erasure and ghettoization in Delhi set the stage for the post–Babri Masjid entrenchment of exclusionary regimes of urban citizenship, whereby more muscular forms of Islamophobia could be both publicly announced and practically enforced in the lived spaces of the city.

Contesting Exclusionary Citizenship

In its 2014 election manifesto, the BJP declared that "India shall remain a natural first home for persecuted Hindus and they shall be welcome to seek refuge here."[39] The BJP won its second consecutive term in power after the 2019 General Elections, when it garnered a resounding majority in both houses of the Indian Parliament.

Despite a tumultuous first term, the party secured public support through divisive populist politics that led to bolder articulations of a Hindu *rashtra*. Toward that end, the BJP-controlled Parliament repealed Article 370 of the Indian Constitution, which had accorded special status to the state of Jammu and Kashmir, India's only Muslim-majority provinces.[40] The party also reiterated its commitment to the "enactment of the Citizenship Amendment Bill for the protection of individuals of religious minority communities from neighboring countries escaping persecution."[41] This served as a default citizenship guarantee for Hindus, regardless of national origin. The BJP manifesto further stated that the party would "combat infiltration" of foreign aliens by expeditiously completing the National Register of Citizens (NRC), a comprehensive legal list of all citizens that would include personal data markers, including religious identification.[42] In

---

[36] Pandey, *Remembering Partition*, p. 122.

[37] Vazira Zamindar, *The Long Partition and the Making of Modern South Asia: Refugees, Boundaries, Histories* (New York: Columbia University Press, 2007).

[38] Rotem Geva, "The Scramble for Houses: Violence, a Factionalized State, and Informal Economy in Post-Partition Delhi," *Modern Asian Studies* 51, no. 3 (2017): pp. 769–824.

[39] BJP, "BJP Election Manifesto 2014," p. 40.

[40] Geeta Pandey, "Article 370: What Happened with Kashmir and Why It Matters," BBC, August 6, 2019, https://www.bbc.com/news/world-asia-india-49234708.

[41] BJP, "BJP Election Manifesto 2019: Sankalpit Bharat, Sashakt Bharat," http://library.bjp.org/jspui/handle/123456789/2988, p. 12.

[42] BJP, "BJP Election Manifesto 2019."

CONTESTING THE SPATIALIZATION OF ISLAMOPHOBIA   209

a country where paper-based documentation of legal standing is nowhere near universal, adult illiteracy is high, and forced migration is common, critics understood the NRC to be a bureaucratic technology to be used for denying the citizenship status of Muslim and other minoritized religious communities.[43] In contrast to the Citizenship Act of 1955, the first national law defining the parameters of citizenship for the Indian republic, the 2019 CAA, passed by the BJP-led Parliament in December 2019, introduced religion as a metric for citizenship for the first time.

The passage of the CAA led to several months of public protest by those enraged by the government's apparent abandonment of secular principals.[44] These protests targeted the CAA as a legislative act; they also targeted the associated removal of recognized elements of the social infrastructure of Muslim belonging, including the abrogation of Article 370 and the statewide curfew and internet blockade in Jammu and Kashmir.[45] Protests across India in late 2019 and early 2020, first in universities and in New Delhi's public arenas, spread to areas of persistent Muslim ghettoization as a new generation of Muslim women tied these exclusions to the lived experiences of material denial and spatial dis-privilege they lived on a daily basis.[46]

The most resilient protest emerged spontaneously in Shaheen Bagh, a neighborhood in the south of Delhi. On December 15, 2019, the Delhi police, a force that operates under the authority of the central government led by the BJP, broke into Jamia Milia Islamia University, one of India's largest public universities known for having mostly Muslim students.[47] Police attacked students on the grounds that they were antinational protesters, and closed-circuit video footage from inside Jamia's Zakir Hussain Library showed police forcibly entering and randomly beating students immersed in study. An estimated twenty-six million rupees (approximately $356,000) worth of damage occurred, and the library remained closed for three months because of the physical devastation.[48] The shattered windows and battered bookcases represented an infrastructural assault on the model of secular Muslim education for which Jamia stands.

---

[43] Bajoria, "'Shoot the Traitors.'"

[44] Nayanika Mathur, "'NRC se Azadi': Process, Chronology, and a Paper Monster," *South Asia Multidisciplinary Academic Journal* 24/25 (2020), https://doi.org/10.4000/samaj.6917.

[45] Maitrayee Basu, "When 'Muslimness Could Bring Trouble into Secular Spaces': Anti-CAA Protests and Religious Slogans," *Journal of Feminist Studies in Religion* 37, no. 2 (2021): pp. 151–55.

[46] Betwa Sharma, "One Year after Mass Protests, India's Muslims Still Live in Fear," *Foreign Policy*, December 18, 2020, https://foreignpolicy.com/2020/12/18/one-year-mass-caa-protests-india-muslims-citizenship-amendment-act-modi/.

[47] Ali Khan Mahmudabad, "Indian Muslims and the Anti-CAA Protests: From Marginalization Towards Exclusion," *South Asia Multidisciplinary Academic Journal* 24/25 (2020), https://doi.org/10.4000/samaj.6701.

[48] "One Jamia Library Reopens 3 Month Damage during Anti-CAA Stir," *Hindustan Times*, March 12, 2020, https://www.hindustantimes.com/cities/three-months-after-damage-during-anti-caa-stir-one-jamia-library-reopens/story-9zWxh55AmKi7z1yXNbWrdJ.html.

Muslim Ghettoization: The Case of Shaheen Bagh

Soon after the attack on Jamia, a small group of women in Shaheen Bagh, located near the Jamia campus, launched an indefinite sit-in. The round-the-clock protest grew as first neighbors then thousands more from across Delhi and the nation joined them on the street in an encampment that grew into a blockade of the main thoroughfare to the satellite city of Noida, across the Yamuna River.[49] Motivated by the desire to secure a better future for their children, Saima Khan, a thirty-three-year-old woman who helped organize communications for this leaderless movement, told journalist Rajvi Desai, "After Jamia, there's no more fear in our hearts. There's no future for our children now; our lives are meaningless, except for Shaheen Bagh."[50]

Shaheen Bagh emerged as a profound moment of national political reckoning for Muslim women's voices, which had been hitherto ignored or essentialized in Indian political discourse. A neighborhood on the fringes of posh South Delhi, Shaheen Bagh is a Muslim middle-class space suffering from persistent infrastructural neglect and violence.[51] Its narrow, cramped lanes are bereft of drainage systems and an adequate potable water supply, and it suffers from faulty electrical wiring, leading to frequent local power outages. Pleas to the local government for service upgrades have long gone unheeded, marking it off starkly from nearby middle-class Hindu neighborhoods that benefit from more routine maintenance and repair.[52] As an extension of the larger Muslim-majority neighborhood of Jamia Nagar, auto-rickshaw and taxi drivers are hesitant to go inside Shaheen Bagh for fear of violence: "*Mahaul kharab hai*" ("The situation is very tense") is the common refrain that one hears.

The emergence of the sharpest critique of and opposition to the CAA from this particular neighborhood draws attention to the interdependency between rising national Islamophobia and Muslim ghettoization. Shaheen Bagh was conspicuously absent from public and popular discourse until late 2019. Until the mid-1980s, Jamia Nagar was a barely populated grassland with only a few Jamia professors' houses scattered about.[53] After the 1984 anti-Sikh riots that ravaged

---

[49] Jean-Thomas Martelli and Kristina Garalytė, "How Campuses Mediate a Nationwide Upsurge against India's Communalization: An Account from Jamia Millia Islamia and Shaheen Bagh in New Delhi," *South Asia Multidisciplinary Academic Journal* 22 (2019), http://journals.openedition.org/samaj/6516.

[50] Ravji Desai, "In Shaheen Bagh, Muslim Women Redefine Carework as Resistance," *The Swaddle*, January 6, 2020, https://theswaddle.com/in-shaheen-bagh-muslim-women-redefine-carework-as-resistance/.

[51] Farah Farooqi, "To Better Understand the Shaheen Bagh Protest, We Must Understand the Locality Itself," *The Caravan*, January 20, 2020, https://caravanmagazine.in/politics/shaheen-bagh-locality-caa-protest.

[52] Farooqi, "Better Understand."

[53] Farooqi, "Better Understand."

CONTESTING THE SPATIALIZATION OF ISLAMOPHOBIA   211

Delhi, precipitated by the assassination of Prime Minister Indira Gandhi by her Sikh bodyguards, Jamia Nagar grew rapidly as Muslims moved there out of fear of falling victim to similar Hindu mob violence that had befallen their better-off Sikh neighbors. Following increased communal violence in the aftermath of the demolition of the Babri Masjid in 1992, the neighborhood, like Muslim neighborhoods nationally, saw the relocation of wealthier Indian Muslims seeking refuge.[54] Nationally circulating images of communal riots in Mumbai and growing neighborhood-level discourses of religious tension at the time led non-Muslim residents of the area to leave, further consolidating Jamia Nagar's and Shaheen Bagh's Muslim-majority status. The area's population continued to grow as Muslim ghettoization deepened through the systematic exclusion of Muslim families from mixed neighborhoods over ensuing years.[55]

The socioeconomic backgrounds of Shaheen Bagh residents is deeply heterogeneous today. Even though it is more densely populated than similar middle-class Hindu neighborhoods are, it went through phases of gentrification following the arrival of residents from wealthier areas of the city.[56] Despite the considerable presence of a Muslim middle class in the neighborhood, it is overcrowded and bustling, located very close to a busy intersection leading to Noida. The neighborhood lacks a proper drainage system and a government school. Every year, the shoddy drainage infrastructure means that monsoon rains flood ground-floor homes with sewage. Neighborhoods in Jamia Nagar and adjacent Zakir Nagar do not have a reliable water supply, forcing residents to rely on informal networks of water sources and private vendors for everyday use.[57] Residents must also hire manual laborers to clean out pipes frequently because of shallow municipal drainage, a material reminder of the systemic disinvestment and municipal neglect they face. Daily logistical challenges associated with neighborhood maintenance and social reproduction there came to require a complex choreography of collective care, including hiring sewage and trash workers, ensuring water delivery, coordinating parking, negotiating school commutes, and caring for children in the absence of government daycare centers. This collective care work falls disproportionately on women. Anger over the CAA and the assault on national citizenship that it represented were therefore combined with a fragile grasp on urban citizenship to propel the "brave

---

[54] Thomas Blom Hansen, "Babri Masjid and Its Aftermath Changed India Forever," *Scroll.in*, December 7, 2017, https://thewire.in/communalism/babri-masjid-aftermath-changed-india-forever.

[55] Laurent Gayer and Christophe Jaffrelot, *Muslims in Indian Cities: Trajectories of Marginalisation* (New York: Columbia University Press, 2012).

[56] Farooqi, "Better Understand."

[57] Shivam Patel, "In Southeast Delhi, Most Rely on Bottled Water over Taps," *Indian Express*, February 9, 2021, https://indianexpress.com/article/cities/delhi/in-southeast-delhi-most-rely-on-bottled-water-over-taps-residents-cite-quality-issues-7180340/.

women of Shaheen Bagh" into a powerful protest that was implicitly organized around claims for citizenship repair.[58]

Reparative Urban Citizenship

Although it is tempting to read Shaheen Bagh as a self-styled segregated space, external forces have led to the immigration of hundreds of Muslim families to Shaheen Bagh from elsewhere in Delhi. The ethos of fear and imminent danger drives this in part, but so does the lack of affordable and accessible housing for Muslim families, a normalized outcome of anti-Muslim housing discrimination now widespread in urban India.[59] Islamophobia, the xenophobic fear *of* Muslims, operates in this context as the majoritarian demand for spaces visually and sensorily free of the always-dangerous Muslim other. Ghettoization is further enforced through Muslims' own fear of majoritarian violence. Muslim peripherality is maintained by subtle codes of neighborhood order, often supported by the state through patterns of infrastructural neglect and the strategic un-policing of Muslim spaces during moments when rupturing violence emerges to reassert majoritarian dominance.[60]

Against these spatializing logics of segregation and Muslim peripheralization, the Shaheen Bagh protest emerged as a platform for reparative urban citizenship, even while it gained political visibility primarily for challenging the CAA. Its first public form was a spontaneous sit-in that grew into an extensive encampment, a localized social network, that soon exploded into something bigger. Ringed by a wall of men, thousands of Muslim women filled a billowing tent, delivering cries for justice and songs of peace. They sat in protest, sending echoes of their call for freedom around the country.[61] Out of the bare existence of a community living on the street, a platform emerged for transforming women's everyday care work into a new secular infrastructure, a reparative commons taking citizenship as such as its material terrain. The tasks of caring for children, preparing meals, and tidying the home that were normally carried out as private affairs were turned into extroverted webs of mutual aid: blanket sharing, preparing collective meals, street sweeping, providing communal childcare, and establishing police lookouts characterized the area. These webs came to extend across the country,

[58] Syed Hameed, "The Brave Women of Shaheen Bagh," *The Wire*, December 23, 2019, https://thewire.in/women/caa-nrc-protests-shaheen-bagh.

[59] Gayer and Jaffrelot, *Muslims*.

[60] Bajoria, " 'Shoot the Traitors.' "

[61] Sarang Narasimhaiah, "Azaadi with a Circle A? Nurturing the Seeds of Anti-Authoritarian Abolitionism in Modi's Current Mass Mobilization," *Society and Space*, April 6, 2020, https://www.societyandspace.org/articles/azaadi-with-a-circle-a-nurturing-the-seeds-of-anti-authoritarian-abolitionism-in-indias-current-mass-mobilizations.

CONTESTING THE SPATIALIZATION OF ISLAMOPHOBIA   213

with dozens of "Shaheen Baghs" popping up across the country to care for those living through the ruins of secular citizenship and to confront the violence of Hindu majoritarianism enshrined in the CAA.[62]

Shaheen Bagh, as both a network of urban occupations and a political imaginary, modeled what Sharik Laliwala calls a new, vernacularized secularism that is ascendant in Muslim political fora.[63] This development is represented in such "post-Islamist" rituals as the reading of the Preamble of the Indian Constitution, the display of the Indian flag, and the use of portraits of prominent non-Muslim democratic leaders such as B. R. Ambedkar and M. K. Gandhi alongside religious iconography. One Shaheen Bagh banner played on a song from Guru Dutt's classic film *Pyaasa* (1957): "Jinhe naaz hain Hind par, woh kahaan hain? Yahaan hain, yahaan hain, yahaan hai" ("Those proud of India, where are they? They are here, they are here, they are here"). Shaheen Bagh shows this trend to be as much a material as a representational innovation, though with the social-reproductive labor and political power of Muslim women placed front and center under the Indian flag. Alongside holding interfaith prayers, Shaheen Bagh built a community kitchen, a blanket depot to manage Delhi's frigid winter nights, a street library for children to maintain their studies, and an open-air art gallery.[64] A designated space for offering *namaz* (daily prayers) was set up; *iftar* (the fast-breaking evening meal) was served for fasting women.

When a caravan of buses carrying hundreds of Sikh farmers traveling from Punjab to join the protest was blocked by the police, Shaheen Bagh women fired up their stoves, escorted the weary travelers to the protest site, laid out bedrolls, served them a hot meal, and opened the mosque for bathing.[65] One day, the owners of a restaurant sent biryani for the protestors; another day, a meat trader delivered provisions. The police on duty were also offered biryani and kebabs, even when they tried to block the deliveries that supplied ingredients for these meals.

This makeshift infrastructure sustained thousands of people for months. They also produced a makeshift community—not in the sense of a temporary or insecure network but in Abdoumaliq Simone's sense of being rooted in an improvisational mode of becoming, a prefigurative citizenship not defined by identity

---

[62] Furquan Ameen, "Shaheen Bagh Inspires More Protests across Country," *The Telegraph*, January 15, 2020, https://www.telegraphindia.com/india/shaheen-bagh-inspires-many-protests-across-the-country/cid/1736089.

[63] Sharik Laliwala, "How Muslims Are Creating a New Vocabulary of Secularism for Indian Democracy," *Scroll.in*, February 16, 2020, https://scroll.in/article/952470/how-muslims-are-creating-a-new-vocabulary-of-secularism-for-indian-democracy.

[64] Paroma Mukherjee, "Shaheen Bagh's Revolutionary Highway," *Mint*, January 30, 2020, https://www.livemint.com/mint-lounge/features/shaheen-bagh-s-revolution-highway-11580373131891.html.

[65] These observations are based on Stuti Govil's attendance of the protest.

214 STUTI GOVIL AND D. ASHER GHERTNER

papers or religion.[66] Shaheen Bagh performed an ethos of care that circulated within an infrastructure that both made evident the democratic deficit in existing infrastructural arrangements and operated as a demand to institutionalize the democratizing impulse that it advanced. It functioned as what Ashraful Alam and Donna Houston call a "care collective," or a social form in which care operates as an infrastructure holding together diverse coalitions of "haves" and "have-nots," affirming the commonality implicit in the model of citizenship[67]— the "camaraderie of citizens" addressed in the Indian Constitution.[68] As an intervention into the material conditions of livability, Shaheen Bagh was a platform for reparative urban citizenship posited as a means of challenging damaged national citizenship.

The remedial forms of material provisioning—carrying water, running backup generators, stringing lights, pooling kitchen resources, and shuffling chairs and beds—at the occupation site were not incidental to a place like Shaheen Bagh. They should be seen as part of a learned "make-shift" practice of confronting constantly mutating forms of Muslim marginalization, or as the relegation of Muslim life to a zone of nonbeing.[69] They were a spatial claim that we are here, we belong; they were a physical materialization of a life made to matter through political protest offering reparative care as both the demand and the model of national redress.

Urbicide and Islamophobia

Confronted with this infrastructure of care, the Delhi police weaponized infrastructural disconnect, targeting the vital systems sustaining Shaheen Bagh by setting up blockades that cut off road access, the supply of water brought in by tanker, and sometimes electricity. These measures were justified by characterizing the encampment, a force pushing back against violence, as itself a violent affront to public order. The chain of justifications grew weekly. The police first asserted that the protest must move to a park—although there is none in the area—to preserve the public's right of way and urban normalcy. Shaheen Bagh is nothing but a "mini Pakistan" aimed at keeping the Indian law out, declared

---

[66] Abdoumaliq Simone, "Living as Logistics: Tenuous Struggles in the Remaking of Collective Urban Life," in *The Routledge Companion to Planning in the Global South*, ed. Gautam Bhan, Smita Srinivas, and Vanessa Watson (London: Routledge, 2017), ch. 21.

[67] Ashraful Alam and Donna Houston, "Rethinking Care as Alternative Infrastructure," *Cities* 100 (May 2020): pp. 264–75.

[68] Hannah Ellis-Petersen and Shaikh Azizur Rahman, "'Modi Is Afraid': Women Take Lead in India's Citizenship Protests," *The Guardian*, January 21, 2020, https://www.theguardian.com/world/2020/jan/21/modi-is-afraid-women-take-lead-in-indias-citizenship-protests.

[69] Simone, "Living."

CONTESTING THE SPATIALIZATION OF ISLAMOPHOBIA   215

BJP leader Kapil Mishra.[70] Such a cohesive mobilization could not possibly be the work of Muslim women, who must be mindlessly following the command of more nefarious men or foreign agents, the mainstream media openly speculated. Finally, Shaheen Bagh in the time of COVID-19 came to be seen itself as a viral outbreak, "terrorists on a suicide mission," a health scourge to be eradicated.[71] And so the power of law, institutional or vigilante, had to reclaim the mantle of "the people" for the *bahumat*—the majority.

The denigration of, false propaganda against, and infrastructural assault on Shaheen Bagh show just how clearly effective the hegemonic powers of denied care—Hindutva—understood the Shaheen Bagh protest to be. To shut it down, deny the relationality it invoked, and reinscribe citizenship as a masculinist play of demographic numbers and neighborhood representation—to reassert *bahumat* as political currency—was the logic of majoritarian power; this is where the February 2019 Delhi riots come in.

On February 23, Kapil Mishra, the BJP leader who had earlier characterized Shaheen Bagh as a mini-Pakistan, stood with a band of supporters in Maujpur, where an anti-CAA protest modeled on Shaheen Bagh was taking place, and issued an ultimatum to the police: either clear out the demonstrators or his followers would do it themselves.[72] Over the following week, Hindu-supremacist mobs stormed Muslim-majority neighborhoods in North East Delhi, areas not incidentally where the BJP had just won some of its few state assembly seats (in contrast to Shaheen Bagh, which like most of Delhi was won by the less-communal Aam Aadmi Party).[73] Fifty-three people died, the majority of whom were Muslim; four hundred more were injured, 226 houses were severely damaged, 487 shops were gutted, and fourteen mosques were left desecrated. "The common object" of this raid, the Delhi high court later declared, "was to assault the persons belonging to Muslim community, damage their vehicles, loot and set ablaze the houses."[74] In riot-affected Gokulpuri, a group of two hundred people

---

[70] "BJP Candidate Kapil Mishra Terms Delhi Polls Contest between India, Pakistan," *The Economic Times*, January 23, 2020, https://economictimes.indiatimes.com/news/elections/assembly-elections/delhi/bjp-candidate-kapil-mishra-terms-delhi-polls-contest-between-india-pakistan/articleshow/73549302.cms?from=mdr.

[71] Ria Kapoor, "'Terrorists on Suic*de [*sic*] Mission': Amid COVID-19 Scare, Kapil Mishra Says Shaheen Bagh Now Direct Threat to Life," *Times Now News*, March 17, 2020, https://www.timesnownews.com/delhi/article/terrorists-on-suicde-mission-amid-covid-19-scare-kapil-mishra-says-shaheen-bagh-now-direct-threat-to-life/565516.

[72] Jeffrey Gentleman, Suhasini Raj, and Sameer Yasir, "The Roots of the Delhi Riots: A Fiery Speech and an Ultimatum," *The New York Times*, February 26, 2020, https://www.nytimes.com/2020/02/26/world/asia/delhi-riots-kapil-mishra.html.

[73] Bharti Jain, "Northeast Delhi Riots: Population Density, Narrow Lanes Restricted Movement of Forces, Says MoS Home in Rajya Sabha," *The Times of India*, March 18, 2020, https://timesofindia.indiatimes.com/city/delhi/northeast-delhi-riots-population-density-narrow-lanes-restricted-movement-of-forces-says-mos-home-in-rajya-sabha/articleshow/74698604.cms.

[74] Karn Pratap Singh, "700 Victims of Delhi Riots File Claims for Damages," *Hindustan Times*, January 25, 2021, https://www.hindustantimes.com/cities/delhi-news/700-vict

gathered around a Muslim cemetery armed with hammers, sickles, and axes; "[o]n one call, all of them raised their tools and struck the building's boundary wall. '*Jai Shri Ram* [Glory to Lord Ram],' they said, and struck again."[75] No police emerged, despite the fact that the action was taking place adjacent to the area police station, so the group's assault continued on the gravestones inside, after which they set fire to two shops that had the Muslim surname Khan written on them.[76]

In the face of evidence of police collusion with the rioters, the Ministry of Home Affairs (under the BJP-led central government), which oversees the Delhi police, stated that the police were unable to prevent the attacks because the neighborhoods were unnavigable.[77] The narrow lanes, dense settlement structure, and lack of signage and street lighting in Muslim-majority neighborhoods—the very product of infrastructural disconnect—was here offered as the basis for the withdrawal of state protection. "Little Pakistan" was left outside the sphere of Indian law. By reaffirming the Muslim political subject as a body perpetually subject to gratuitous violence, the riots also showed that subject to be beyond the need for care, beyond a place within the national body, unworthy of citizenship. Shaheen Bagh and all places of visible Muslim urbanity—where the right to centrality as both public visibility and national belonging—must be denied relationality, it is asserted; this is the Hindutva stance on urban citizenship. This is its position of urbicide.[78]

In the wake of the Delhi riots, residents in affected areas erected metal sheets, bamboo poles, and wooden boards as barricades to cordon off Hindu spaces from Muslim ones.[79] A divided city was quickly reproduced. If Islamophobia gets spatialized through the masculinist performance of neighborhood *bahumat*—boys and men in streets asserting Hindu strength, testing for echoes of their chants of "Jai Shri Ram!"—then women-led infrastructure of care must be understood as a spatial claim to citizenship offered against the majoritarian assertion

---

ims-of-delhi-riots-file-claims-for-damages-101611527062593.html; Apoorva Mandhani, "Rioters Had 'Common Object' to Assault Muslims: What Court Said in 1st Delhi Riots Conviction," *The Print*, December 7, 2021, https://theprint.in/judiciary/rioters-had-common-object-to-assault-musl ims-what-court-said-in-1st-delhi-riots-conviction/777876/.

[75] Ananya Bhardwaj, "Muslim Cemetery Desecrated and Shops Set on Fire, but Police Missing in Action in Delhi," *The Print*, February 25, 2020, https://theprint.in/india/muslim-cemetery-desecra ted-and-shops-set-on-fire-but-police-missing-in-action-in-delhi/371014/.

[76] Bhardwaj, "Muslim Cemetery."

[77] Jain, "Northeast Delhi Riots."

[78] On urbicide as infrastructural violence against communal systems of care, see Stephen Graham, "Lessons in Urbicide," *New Left Review* 19 (2003): p. 63.

[79] Vijayta Lalwani and Karnika Kohli, "Divided City: How Barricades Came Up Overnight between Hindu and Muslim Neighbourhoods in Delhi," *Scroll.in*, February 28, 2020, https://scroll.in/ article/954574/divided-city-how-barricades-came-up-overnight-between-hindu-and-muslim-nei ghbourhoods-in-delhi.

CONTESTING THE SPATIALIZATION OF ISLAMOPHOBIA   217

of us versus them, nationalists versus antinationals, Hindus versus Muslims. In exposing themselves to police power, Shaheen Bagh women put into play a style of persistence that holds the potential to defeat violence's aim of pushing the marginalized into a permanent zone of nonbeing. Against Islamophobia's urbicidal tendencies, Shaheen Bagh emerged as an infrastructure of care that showed struggles over the terrain of urban citizenship and material belonging to be central to struggles over the definition of national citizenship.

Resisting the national citizenship laws and the gradual imposition of bureaucratic tests for Muslim identification and qualification for national benefits, the protests at Shaheen Bagh stretched for 101 days, until India's national coronavirus lockdown was initiated on March 24, 2020.[80] As an insurgent political imaginary that some have called the most powerful citizenship movement since Indian Independence, Shaheen Bagh posited a counter-reality to violence's realism.[81] Women from the neighborhood joined the sit-in as a response to the violence against innocent students and, in their calls for *azaadi* ("freedom") from police brutality and inhumane laws, they sought a different future for Muslim children in an increasingly Hindu-nationalist India.

[80] Jeffrey Gentleman and Kai Schultz, "Modi Orders 3-Week Total Lockdown for All 1.3 Billion Indians," *The New York Times*, March 24, 2020, https://www.nytimes.com/2020/03/24/world/asia/india-coronavirus-lockdown.html/.

[81] "The Greatest Movement since Independence but What's Shaheen Bagh's Future?," *Outlook India*, March 8, 2020, https://www.outlookindia.com/newsscroll/the-greatest-movement-since-independence-but-whats-shaheen-baghs-future-comment/1755426. See also Suddhabrata Deb Roy, "Locating Gramsci in Delhi's Shaheen Bagh: Perspectives on the Iconic Women's Protest in India," *Capital and Class* 45 (2021): p. 183.

13

(Un)Made in China

Uyghur Muslims at the Intersection of Islamophobia and Ethnic Cleansing

Khaled A. Beydoun[*]

> *"My brother passed away in East Turkistan [Xinjiang]. It's been hard for us being so far away; we are completely helpless. We can't even send money because we might put the rest of the family in danger."*
> [Four days later]
> *"We just got news that they were forced to give him a Chinese funeral. . . . There is no tombstone allowed. Just a number at the grave. No identity, just a number. He was #770."*[1]

Beijing's objective is to bury every marker of Uyghur life under soil that it seeks to remake in the form of Han Communism. To enforce an unyielding, cultural genocide against a minority population that calls Xinjiang—the disputed territory in northwest China—home. This aim is illustrated by the burial of the brother of Rima R., a Uyghur refugee, and the culture he struggled to keep alive until his last breath, which he was finally stripped of when assigned a lifeless number on his headstone, #770, a lasting symbol of submission that marks the final resting place of the dead who lay among Uyghur struggling to live.

This chapter examines the architecture of Islamophobia within the province of Xinjiang, the disputed territory in northwest China that the Uyghur rebelliously call East Turkistan. It highlights the political and legal pillars of the architecture of Islamophobia that imperil the Uyghur today, and how the state enforces Islamophobia as structural campaign to submit the Uyghur to its Communist

---

[*] Khaled A. Beydoun is a scholar-in-residence at Harvard University's Berkman Klein Center for Internet and Society and the Initiative for a Representative First Amendment. Beydoun is an associate professor of law at Arizona State University College of Law. He is also the co-director of the Damon J. Keith Center for Civil Rights.

[1] Direct messages to author from Rima R., now living in Melbourne, Australia, via Instagram, on November 27 and December 1, 2020. Rima R.'s name has been changed to protect anonymity.

Khaled A. Beydoun, *(Un)Made in China* In: *Global Islamophobia and the Rise of Populism*. Edited by: Sahar F. Aziz and John L. Esposito, Oxford University Press. © Oxford University Press 2024. DOI: 10.1093/oso/9780197648995.003.0013

Han vision. Islamophobia is the strategic framing of Muslim identities and behavior as presumptive evidence of terrorism.[2] The War on Terror mainstreamed this profile in the United States and beyond and equipped the Communist Party–controlled Chinese government in Beijing with a tool to further crack down on and persecute the Indigenous Uyghur Muslim population in Xinjiang. In short, Beijing strategically deployed Islamophobia to demonize, then subjugate, a Muslim minority population that refused to bend to its Communist grip and Han-supremacist will.

Beginning in 2014, Islamophobia in China devolved into ethnic cleansing, climaxing with strident crackdowns on Uyghur life in Xinjiang and criminalization of the Muslim practices that serve as the lifeline of Uyghur society. As Kait Strittmeyer writes in *We Have Been Harmonized: Life in China's Surveillance State*, "The Communist Party is not just Big Brother. It's Big Mother, too."[3]

Uyghur Identity and Society

Before it bore the name *Xinjiang*, the territory home to fourteen million Uyghur in northwest China was known as East Turkistan. The land, bordering Turkic nations like Kazakhstan and Kyrgyzstan to the west and Mongolia to the east, sits along the ancient Silk Road, a gateway historically linking China to vital regional and global markets.[4] Xinjiang's economic importance, geographic proximity, abundant resources, and size figure heavily into Beijing's stake in the disputed territory and, with that, its commitment to stamp out opposition within it,[5] however subtle or remote.

For the Uyghur, a Turkic and Muslim people, their very culture is perceived as subversive by the Han Communist regime in Beijing.[6] In 1944, during the Chinese Civil War between the Nationalists and Communists, the Uyghur established the East Turkestan Republic.[7] This independent Uyghur nation-state, however, would only last for four years; in 1949, the victorious People's

---

[2] Khaled A. Beydoun, *American Islamophobia: Understanding the Roots and Rise of Fear* (Berkeley: University of California Press, 2018).

[3] Kait Strittmeyer, *We Have Been Harmonized: Life in China's Surveillance State* (New York, NY: Custom House, 2020), p. 48.

[4] *Turkic nations* refers to a group of states in Central and West Asia where the populations speak Turkic languages.

[5] Xinjiang is roughly one-sixth of China's landmass. Xinjiang also "contains huge coal and oil reserves, believed to be three times those of the United States." Matthew Moneyhon, "Controlling Xinjiang: Autonomy on China's 'New Frontier,'" *Asian-Pacific Law and Policy Journal* 3 (2002): pp. 120, 121.

[6] For a popular book examining the PRC's crackdown on the Uyghur, see Sean Roberts, *The War on Uyghurs: China's Internal Campaign against a Muslim Minority* (Princeton, NJ: Princeton University Press, 2020).

[7] Roberts, *War*, pp.126–27.

Liberation Army of China annexed the coveted land and renamed it *Xinjiang*, meaning "new frontier" in Mandarin.[8]

Since then, the Uyghur have lived under the thumb of Beijing. And today, they remain vulnerable to the Chinese government's integrated campaign of ethnic, political, and religious persecution. Early Communist regimes, given their aversion to organized religion at large and Islam in particular, have targeted Islam to suppress the Uyghur.

Islam remains intrinsic to Uyghur identity.[9] The population in Xinjiang overwhelmingly adheres to the faith, and Uyghur script adopts the Arabic rooted in the Qur'an, Islam's holy book. The fundamental rituals and symbols of Muslim life thus permeate Uyghur culture and society.[10] The mosque is a center of religious, social, and civic gathering, the imam is a leading community figure, and the notion of a transnational Muslim community, or ummah, figures heavily into the Uyghur worldview.[11] Beijing views these cornerstones of Islamic life as obstacles to controlling the Uyghur.[12]

Turkic ethnicity and nationhood are another cornerstone of Uyghur identity: "In addition to religious affinity Uyghur ethnicity resembles and overlaps with that of its Central Asian neighbors, such as Kyrgyzstan, Kazakhstan, and other countries populated with predominantly Turkic peoples."[13] Shared ethnicity and history breed greater affinity among the Uyghur with neighboring Turkic societies, while linguistic ties allow for greater political solidarity and cultural exchange.

The Han-controlled Chinese government looks upon these ties with great suspicion. Beyond Uyghur aspirations for self-determination, Beijing also fears transnational unity among the Turkic Central Asian states that orbit Xinjiang. After all, Bishkek and Tashkent, the capitals of the Turkic nations of Kyrgyzstan and Uzbekistan, respectively, are far closer to Xinjiang than to the large Chinese cities along the eastern coastline.

Physical appearance is another unifier between the Uyghur and their Turkic neighbors. Domestically, phenotype is a central differentiator between Uyghur and Han identity. It marks another divide that the state seizes upon to root its campaign of submission and push the program of Han supremacy. Ultimately,

---

[8] Roberts, *War*, pp. 126–27.

[9] Colin Mackerras, "Ethnicity in China: The Case of Xinjiang," *Harvard Asia Quarterly* 8 (2004): p. 10.

[10] Mackerras, *Ethnicity*, pp. 10–15.

[11] The imam is the spiritual head of the mosque.

[12] For a survey of Uyghur religious life and the salience of Islam to Uyghur culture and society in Xinjiang, see Gardner Bovingdon, *The Uyghurs: Strangers In Their Own Land* (New York: Columbia University Press, 2010).

[13] Khaled A. Beydoun, "China Holds One Million Uyghur Muslims in Concentration Camps," *Al Jazeera English*, September 13, 2018, https://www.aljazeera.com/opinions/2018/9/13/china-holds-one-million-uighur-muslims-in-concentration-camps.

(UN)MADE IN CHINA   221

Beijing's Sinicization efforts of the Uyghur converge along cultural, religious, and racial divides.

Han Supremacy

The racial dimension of Beijing's repression of the Uyghur is central to understanding the cultural genocide unfolding in Xinjiang. The Han, the majority ethnic group in China that presides over the Communist Party and the state, view the Uyghur as the greatest obstacle to Sinicizing the entire polity. While China remains "an incredibly diverse nation with fifty-six recognized" ethnicities, the Han are keen on supplanting them with a monolithic Chinese identity made exclusively in their image.[14]

The claim of Uyghur indigeneity to Xinjiang stands as a threat to this racial project. A leading Chinese official declared at a United Nations Permanent Forum on Indigenous Issues hearing that "China has no indigenous peoples," echoing the state's dismissal of Uyghur's indigeneity.[15] Furthermore, the statement manifests the Communist regime's disavowal of any piece of history that conflicts with the party's carefully crafted political narrative and the Han-supremacist aim to erase deeply rooted histories and identities that cannot be squared with authoritarian groupthink.[16] For Beijing, Chinese equals Han, and ethnic "blood" is the central marker of belonging.[17]

The perseverance of Uyghur nationhood in Xinjiang, both cultural and political, conflicts with Beijing's assimilatory project. Its Sinicization campaign is an "inherently imperial project" seeking to suppress every manifestation of Uyghur identity and, most forcefully, to punish overtly political activity.[18] There are elements among the Uyghur who remain committed to political self-determination, with the ultimate hope of restoring an independent East Turkistan.[19] However, that vision is fleeting in light of China's rising global

---

[14] Brennan Davis, "Being Uyghur . . . with 'Chinese Characteristics': Analyzing China's Legal Crusade against Uyghur Identity," *American Indian Law Review* 44 (2019): pp. 81, 83.

[15] "Statement by Counsellor Yao Shaojun of the Chinese Delegation at the 15th Session of the Permanent Forum on Indigenous Issues," Permanent Mission of the People's Republic of China to the United Nations, May 10, 2016, https://www.mfa.gov.cn/ce/ceun/eng/chinaandun/socialhr/3rdco mmittee/t1308351.htm.

[16] For a critical examination of China's strategic disavowal of past events and incidents to further the regime's political aims, see Margaret Hillenbrand, *Negative Exposures: Knowing What Not to Know in Contemporary China* (Durham, NC: Duke University Press, 2020).

[17] Michael Ignatieff, *Blood and Belonging: Journeys into the New Nationalism* (New York: Farrar, Straus, and Giroux, 1993), p. 5.

[18] Michael Clarke, "China and the Uyghurs: The 'Palestinianization' of Xinjiang?," *Middle East Policy* 22 (2015): pp. 127, 128.

[19] Lindsay Maizland, "China's Repression of Uyghurs in China," Council on Foreign Relations, June 30, 2020, https://www.cfr.org/backgrounder/chinas-repression-uyghurs-xinjiang.

222 KHALED A. BEYDOUN

hegemony and Xiangiang's centrality to Beijing's international ambitions.[20] The vast majority of Uyghur living in Xinjiang have capitulated to China's authoritarianism, while the teetering push for an independent state rises from disparate Uyghur diaspora groups.[21] Beyond survival, the domestic Uyghur appeal is for mere tolerance of their distinct traditions and customs, which is one that, particularly under the administration of President Xi Jinping, runs afoul of the People Republic of China's (PRC) accelerated Han-supremacy project.[22]

In this political landscape, the very notion of Uyghur distinctiveness is often interpreted as an affront to Chinese authority. This peculiarity is displayed through religious expression, and namely, the exercise of Islam, through dress, grooming, outward expression, and the daunting daily ritual of "acting Muslim" within a surveillance state where even the most benign indication of religious fidelity triggers suspicion.[23]

Faith, therefore, is where Beijing fixates its submission strategy on the Uyghur.[24] Because Islam stands as the lifeline of Uyghur society, China has turned its surveillance campaign against the faith and its cornerstone practices to submit the Uyghur.[25] While this racial project was already in process before 9/11, Beijing's aim was elevated intensely by the Global War on Terror that followed.

War-on-Terror Interest Convergence

"September 11, 2001 was a world event but it was also a globalized event," surveillance scholar David Lyon writes.[26] The ensuing War on Terror evolved into,

[20] For a history of the origins of the East Turkistan independence movement by a prominent Chinese history scholar, see Wang Ke, *The East Turkistan Independence Movement* (New York: Columbia University Press, 2019).

[21] See Shafik Mandhai, "Uyghurs Marking 'Independence Day' Call for International Help," *Al Jazeera English*, November 13, 2018, https://www.aljazeera.com/news/2018/11/13/uighurs-marking-independence-day-call-for-international-help.

[22] See Sheena Chestnut Greitens, Myunghee Lee, and Emir Yazici, "Counterterrorism and Preventive Repression: China's Changing Strategy in Xinjiang," *International Security* 44 (2019): pp. 9, 10.

[23] See Khaled A. Beydoun, "Acting Muslim," *Harvard Civil Rights–Civil Liberties Law Review* 53 (2018): p. 1. The author defines *acting Muslim* as the process whereby Muslim Americans strategically negotiate and publicly perform a religious identity stigmatized by counterterrorism policy.

[24] "Where the Soviets broke you, made you confess to invented charges, and then killed you, the Chinese wanted to remake its citizens." Phil Tinline, "How Orwell Foretold the Remaking of Xinjiang," *The New Statesman*, July 29, 2020, https://www.newstatesman.com/world/asia/2020/07/how-orwell-foretold-remaking-xinjiang.

[25] Mackerras, *Ethnicity*, p. 10.

[26] David Lyon, *Surveillance after September* (Cambridge, MA: Polity, 2003), p. 109. For a leading treatise examining how the 9/11 terror attacks spawned the wholesale formulation and enforcement of surveillance on a global scale, see Lyon, *Surveillance*, pp. 28–37.

to echo Lyon, a war of global proportions.[27] This new crusade revolutionized the security state in the United States and swung open the door for China to intensify its subjugation of the Uyghur.

Under the banner of "fighting terrorism," Beijing seized the opportunity to tie the predominantly Muslim minority group to transnational terrorism.[28] This category included al-Qaeda, the group that carried out the terror plots in New York City and Washington, DC, then local Uyghur groups that pushed for self-determination.[29] Beijing welcomed the global demonization of Muslims, which was mainstreamed by the War on Terror because it created the opportunity to intensify Beijing's crackdown on Xinjiang. In a reversal of critical race theorist Derrick Bell's interest-convergence theory, 9/11 and the ensuing War on Terror aligned with Beijing's project of subjugating the Uyghur, and Beijing then used the War on Terror to persecute the Muslim minority with full-fledged American support.[30]

Five weeks after 9/11, President George W. Bush landed in Beijing to woo China as an ally in the upstart global war. For the neoconservative Bush administration, the War on Terror was an imperial project devised to broader American influence.[31] For the war's prospective enlistees, including China, the broadening mandate of counterterrorism provided renewed opportunity to crack down on the oppositional Uyghur.

Standing alongside (then) President Jiang Zemin, Bush stated, "We have a common understanding of the magnitude of the threat posed by international terrorism," following meetings in which Zemin briefed Bush about the "security" concerns posed by the Uyghur.[32] With Beijing's interest in persecuting the Uyghur converging with the Bush administration's Global War on Terror, the stage was set in Xinjiang for an accelerated crackdown on Islam as the lifeline

[27] See Sahar F. Aziz, "The Authoritarianization of US Counterterrorism," *Washington and Lee Law Review* 75 (2018): p. 1573 (demonstrating how authoritarianism became increasingly transnational under the banner of the global war on terror).

[28] Greitens, Lee, and Yazici, "Counterterrorism," pp. 9, 10.

[29] On September 3, 2002, the US Treasury Department listed the East Turkistan Islamic Movement on the departmental list of terrorist organizations. Beijing used this designation to claim that the Uyghur population in Xinjiang was linked to the group, which was a ploy to galvanize American support for its crackdown on the Uyghur. Akbar Shahid Ahmed, "China Is Using US 'War on Terror' Rhetoric to Justify Detaining 1 Million People," *Huffington Post*, December, 2, 2018, https://www.huffpost.com/entry/china-is-justifying-its-biggest-human-rights-crisis-in-decades-with-made-in-the-usa-war-on-terror-rhetoric_n_5bae375be4b0b4d308d2639c.

[30] See Derrick A. Bell Jr., "Brown v. Board of Education and the Interest Convergence Dilemma," *Harvard Law Review* 93 (1980): pp. 518, 524. Bell theorizes how geopolitics currently shapes domestic policy. For an examination of the convergence of the War on Terror and Beijing's Sinicization interests after 9/11, see also Khaled A. Beydoun, "Exporting Islamophobia in the Global 'War on Terror,'" *New York University Law Review* 95 (2020): pp. 81, 92–96.

[31] Deepa Kumar, *Islamophobia and the Politics of Empire: 20 Years after 9/11* (Brooklyn: Verso, 2021), p. 9.

[32] Robin Wright and Edwin Chin, "Bush Says China Backs War on Terror," *Los Angeles Times*, October 18, 2001, https://www.latimes.com/la-101901bush-story.html.

of Uyghur identity and society.[33] As a result, the "war on the Uyghur people" commenced roughly a month after 9/11.[34] This campaign echoed the language of Washington's "See something, say something," campaign, enlisting private citizens alongside the state to track and keep tabs on Muslim communities.[35]

In line with the American War on Terror strategy, Beijing instantly conflated Uyghur identity with terrorism after 9/11.[36] State police began to openly associate benign expressions of Islam with terrorism.[37] Islamic institutions and leaders were linked to foreign terror groups. Beijing's strategy behind this structural "Islamophobia" was *not* counterterrorism; rather, it peddled these activities as a Trojan Horse for its preexisting Sinicization and Han-supremacy objectives.[38]

The traditional appearances and customs of the Uyghur, combined with the culture of piety that pervades their society in Xinjiang, corroborated the stereotypical Islamic images of terrorism found in Western and, later, Chinese media.[39] Uyghur Muslims, like their co-religionists in the United States and beyond, were "racialized as terrorists."[40] Uyghur men donning beards and women wearing headscarves were branded "extremists," which Beijing matched with the very anti-Muslim caricatures that saturated Western media.[41] This "redeployment of Orientalist tropes" that drove damaging anti-Muslim caricatures in the United States rose to the fore in China.[42] And it also provided the ideal geopolitical impasse for Beijing to elevate its Sinicization and Han-supremacy campaigns to full scale.[43]

---

[33] Ahmed, "China."

[34] See Roberts, *War*.

[35] For a brief analysis of the "See something, say something" campaign that was spawned on September 12, 2001, see Hanson O'Haver, "How 'If You See Something, Say Something' Became Our National Motto," *The Washington Post*, September 23, 2016, https://www.washingtonpost.com/posteverything/wp/2016/09/23/how-if-you-see-something-say-something-became-our-national-motto/.

[36] "China tapped into the prevailing anger at Islamic extremists Thursday by calling for international backing for its effort to quell Muslim [Uyghur] separatists in the western region of Xinjiang," Chinese officials stated during President Bush's meeting with President Zemin on October 18, 2001. Wright and Chin, "Bush."

[37] Michael Clarke, "China's 'War on Terror' in Xinjiang: Human Security and the Cases of Violent Uyghur Separatism," *Terrorism and Political Violence* 20 (2008): p. 271.

[38] *Islamophobia* is "the presumption that Islam is inherently violent, alien, and inassimilable[,] . . . [c]ombined with the belief that expressions of Muslim identity are correlative with a propensity for terrorism." Khaled A. Beydoun, "Islamophobia: Toward a Legal Definition and Framework," *Columbia Law Review Online* 116 (2016): pp. 108, 111.

[39] Ahmed, "China."

[40] Natsu Taylor Saito, "Symbolism under Siege, Japanese American Redress and the 'Racing' of Arab Americans as 'Terrorists,'" *Asian American Law Journal* 8 (2001): pp. 1, 12; Sahar F. Aziz, *The Racial Muslim: When Racism Quashes Religious Freedom* (Berkeley: University of California 2021).

[41] For a critical examination of the most prominent stereotypes of Muslim men and women after the 9/11 terror attacks, see Evelyn Alsultany, *Arabs and Muslims in the Media: Race and Representation after 9/11* (New York: NYU Press, 2012).

[42] Leti Volpp, "The Citizen and the Terrorist," *UCLA Law Review* 49 (2002): p. 1586.

[43] Beydoun, "Exporting Islamophobia," pp. 92–96.

Virtually overnight, 9/11 flipped the state's formal framing of its Sinicization efforts in Xinjiang. It transitioned from suppressing "Turkic separatism in Xinjiang" to dubbing it "the 'main battlefield' in China's fight against terrorism."[44] This shift marshalled the United States, and many other nations, to support China's crackdown in Xinjiang or to remain silent as the violence mounted. Two decades into the War on Terror began, Beijing has deepened its counterterrorism rhetoric as a ploy to assimilate the Uyghur into Han culture. Wang Li, China's foreign minister, justified the government's actions in Xinjiang as part of the Global War on Terror witch-hunt:

> It's the necessary way to deal with Islamic or religious extremism. [China's] efforts are completely in line with the direction of the international community has taken to combat terrorism, and are an important part of the global fight against terrorism.[45]

With Uyghur life purportedly linked to terrorism, the War on Terror equipped Beijing with the "moral blank check for [the] human rights abuses" against the Uyghur that it had long coveted.[46] The War on Terror became a potent political justification for systematically destroying any and every semblance of Uyghur identity and society in its very cradle.

In June 2012, the National People's Congress of China enacted legislation that echoed the rhetoric of the War on Terror and foreshadowed the coming of the Strike Hard on Terror campaign.[47] The new counterterrorism law was based on the "preventative" and "preemptive-strike" logic of the War on Terror.[48] More nefariously, the law enabled the state through its policing and surveillance agents to arbitrarily assess the "subjective intent" of a Uyghur subject who had yet to commit an "act of terror."[49] In turn, this assessment enabled the state to fabricate both the mens rea and actus reus components of a terror act and to manufacture terror charges entirely based on Uyghur identity.

This state of Uyghur existence in Xinjiang was made real by law and unmade by the War on Terror license that Washington, DC, granted Beijing. Darren Byler, a scholar of the Uyghur crisis, observed how the modern state of subjugation in China is "[a] system premised on a rhetoric of a war on Muslim 'terrorism'

---

[44] Greitens, Lee, and Yazici, "Counterterrorism," p. 11.

[45] Ahmed, "China."

[46] Greitens, Lee, and Yazici, "Counterterrorism," p. 12.

[47] The Chinese law is titled Opinions on Several Issues on the Application of Law in Cases of Terrorist Activities and Extremism Crimes, *China Law Translate*, June 6, 2018, https://www.chinal awtranslate.com/en/opinions-on-several-issues-on-the-application-of-law-in-cases-of-terrorist-act ivities-and-extremism-crimes/.

[48] "[Terrorism] also includes individuals preparing to carry out, or currently carrying out, terrorist activities." Opinions on Several Issues, p. 4.

[49] Opinions on Several Issues, p. 4.

that the Chinese state has imported form its US and its allies post–September 11, 2001."[50] It is a war that is extending into its third decade and expanding into distinct fronts of anti-Muslim populism and scapegoating. The COVID-19 pandemic has caused many to declare that the 9/11 era has ended.[51] However, this conclusion is contradicted by the draconian Chinese Counterterror Law enacted in 2012, accompanied by surveillance campaigns that strike at Uyghur life alongside an unrelenting pandemic.[52]

The Terror of Chinese Counterterrorism

Beijing initiated its Strike Hard against Violent Terrorism campaign in 2014 to escalate its submission of the Uyghur. President Xi focused his administration's attention on "three evil forces," separatism, extremism, and, most forcefully, terrorism, in line with Washington's War on Terror mandate.[53] The campaign aimed to crush separatist elements and to crack down on "illegal religious activities" under the banner of fighting terror, branding the Uyghur collectively as putative terrorists.[54]

The campaign took a drastic turn in 2016. On August 29, President Xi appointed hardliner Chen Quanguo to serve as Communist Party secretary of Xinjiang. Shortly after assuming that role, Quanguo authorized ongoing mass arrests and the detention of Uyghur in major cities, enforcing the preemptive mandate of the 2012 counterterrorism laws.[55] Most notably, he ushered in the rapid expansion of the concentration camps that currently detain as many as two million Uyghur and ethnic Muslims.[56]

The network of concentration camps became Quanguo's signature surveillance program.[57] The high-tech camps are postmodern panopticons where the punitive and disciplinary aims of the state, conducted behind walls of concrete

---

[50] See Darren Byler, *In the Camps: China's High Tech Penal Colony* (New York: Columbia Global Reports, 2021), p. 22.

[51] Ben Rhodes, "The 9/11 Era Is Over," *The Atlantic*, April 6, 2020, https://www.theatlantic.com/ideas/archive/2020/04/its-not-september-12-anymore/609502/.

[52] For an examination of the distinct threats faced by the Uyghur during the pandemic, see Vaishnavi Chaudry, "The Impact of COVID-19 on Uyghur Muslims: An Ignored Crisis," LSE Human Rights, April 23, 2020, https://blogs.lse.ac.uk/humanrights/2020/04/23/the-impact-of-covid-19-on-uighur-muslims-an-ignored-crisis/.

[53] Sarah A. Topol, "Her Uyghur Parents Were Model Citizens: It Didn't Matter," *The New York Times*, January 29, 2020, https://www.nytimes.com/2020/01/29/magazine/uyghur-muslims-china.html.

[54] Clarke, "China's 'War on Terror,'" p. 280.

[55] Opinions on Several Issues.

[56] Greitens, Lee, and Yazici, "Counterterrorism," pp. 16–17.

[57] See Byler, *In the Camps.*

and secrecy, have no bounds.[58] Under Quanguo's authority, the camps tripled in size between April 2017 and August 2018.[59] This expansion was heavily subsidized by the state, such that "construction spending on security-related facilities in Xinjiang increased by twenty billion yuan (around $2.96 billion) in 2017."[60] The Uyghur did not cease expressing their cultural and religious way of life were arrested and forced to endure the violence within the camps. The camps are where the state program of mass punishment and discipline is most aggressively enforced, as manifested by penetrative brainwashing programs and, for those who resist, physical punishment.

Within a year's time, Quanguo had lived up to his "reputation as an ethnic policy innovator" and a "pioneer of aggressive policing techniques."[61] He earned that status by presiding over another domestic site of mass surveillance, Tibet, where Quanguo mutated the federal surveillance program to one of full-scale punishment, an approach that he later intensified in Xinjiang. In addition to mass arrests and detention, Quanguo deployed "200,000 [Communist] cadres from government agencies, state-owned enterprises, and public institutions" to Xinjiang.[62] He thus coupled the technological might of digital surveillance with the Strike Hard campaign's wide assignment of on-the-ground spies and informants.[63]

The Chinese Counterterror Law of 2012 was intended to stifle the routine and benign expression of faith by Uyghur residents.[64] With the Strike Hard on Terror campaign, Xi adapted China's Sinicization to the Islamophobic rhetoric that strongmen across the world, including Donald Trump and Narendra Modi, peddled to stoke populist angst.[65] However, unlike the American or Indian heads of state, Xi is not stifled by constitutional restraint or term limits. Chinese anti-terror laws enabled him to unleash whatever disciplinary or punitive horror he chose upon the Uyghur.[66]

---

[58] China restricts foreign journalists from entering the camps. "Why It's So Difficult for Journalists to Report from Xinjiang," *Asia Society*, May 23, 2019, https://asiasociety.org/blog/asia/why-its-so-difficult-journalists-report-xinjiang.

[59] The number of camps tripled from thirty-nine to 141. Maizland, "China's Repression."

[60] Maizland, "China's Repression."

[61] Greitens, Lee, and Yazici, "Counterterrorism," p. 27.

[62] Human Rights Watch, *"Eradicating Ideological Viruses": China's Campaign of Repression against Xinjiang's Muslim* (September 2018), https://www.hrw.org/sites/default/files/report_pdf/china0918_web.pdf, p. 11.

[63] Human Rights Watch, *"Eradicating,"* p. 11.

[64] See Opinions on Several Issues.

[65] For an analysis of the Indian Prime Minister's use of anti-Muslim imagery to further his Hindu-nationalist vision, see Catarina Kinnvall, "Populism, Ontological Insecurity and Hindutva: Modi and the Masculinization of Indian Politics," *Cambridge Review of International Affairs* 32 (2019): p. 283. For an examination of Donald Trump's use of Islamophobia as a political strategy, see Khaled A. Beydoun, "'Muslim Bans' and the (Re)Making of Political Islamophobia," *University of Illinois Law Review* (2017): p. 1756.

[66] See Opinions on Several Issues.

228　KHALED A. BEYDOUN

The persecution that followed was immediate and violent. Arbitrary arrests proliferated, the Islamic holy month of Ramadan was banned in the province in 2015, Uyghur were force-fed pork and alcohol, and the presence of Communist Party informants increased within religious spaces and private homes.[67] Another "anti-extremism" law was enacted in 2017, this time explicitly prohibiting Uyghur men from growing long beards and women from wearing hijabs in public.[68] The new law also prohibited Uyghur from using Islamic emblems like crescents and stars to decorate their homes or showcasing them atop their mosques or cultural centers.[69] "In the eyes of Beijing, all Uyghur could potentially be terrorists or terrorist sympathizers,"[70] a view that makes every conceivable form of Islamic expression punishable by the state.

The Strike Hard campaign mutated China's Sinicization campaign of the Uyghur into one of full-scale subjugation against the Uyghur. The myriad forms of punitive violence revealed Beijing's genuine intent: to force the Uyghurs to assimilate into Han Chinese culture by erasing their cultural and religious identity for good.[71] Scholars and human rights advocates have dubbed China's designs as a "genocide" and "cultural genocide," while others have labeled it "ethnic cleansing."[72] On the eve of Joe Biden's inauguration as the 46th president of the United States, Trump's Secretary of State Mike Pompeo formally accused China of "committing genocide and crimes against humanity in Xinjiang."[73]

The Strike Hard campaign opened the door for the expansion of the concentration camps. As the cornerstone of Beijing's subjugation strategy in Xinjiang, the scale of the spread of the network of camps throughout the massive province shows no sign of slowing.[74] Every strata of Uyghur society, from rank-and-file workers to "singers, musicians, novelists, scholars, and academics," have been

---

[67] Jon Sharman, "China 'Forcing Muslims to Eat Pork and Drink Alcohol' for Lunar New Year Festival," *Independent*, February 7, 2019, https://www.independent.co.uk/news/world/asia/china-muslims-xinjiang-pork-alcohol-lunar-new-year-spring-festival-uighur-islam-a8767561.html.

[68] Sharman, "China."

[69] Clarke, *China and the Uyghurs*, p. 130.

[70] Maizland, "China's Repression."

[71] Yasmeen Serhan, "Saving Uyghur Culture from Genocide," *The Atlantic*, October 4, 2020, https://www.theatlantic.com/international/archive/2020/10/chinas-war-on-uighur-culture/616513/.

[72] Erkin Alptekin, the (former) president of the World Uyghur Congress, framed the crisis in terms of cultural genocide, stating, "The Chinese want to replace us with their own people as colonists, and assimilate those of us who remain, wiping out our culture." Clarke, *China and the Uyghurs*, pp. 127–128.

[73] Bill Chappell, "Pompeo Accuses China of Genocide against Uyghur Muslims," NPR, January 19, 2021, https://www.npr.org/2021/01/19/958468971/pompeo-accuses-china-of-genocide-against-muslim-uighurs-in-xinjiang.

[74] For a Uyghur expert's analysis of the state intent behind the rapid expansion of the concentration camps, see Rian Thum, "China's Mass Internment Camps Have No Clear End in Sight," *Foreign Policy*, August 22, 2018, https://foreignpolicy.com/2018/08/22/chinas-mass-internment-camps-have-no-clear-end-in-sight/.

detained in the camps.[75] The camps are sites of mass discipline and control, where captives are forced to sing Communist songs and slogans and undergo ideological brainwashing and, in some instances, physical torture. Roughly 12 percent of the Muslim population between the ages of twenty and seventy-nine have been imprisoned.[76] There is no due process, and "most people in the camps have never been charged with crimes and have no legal avenues to challenge their detentions."[77]

The camps sit at the center of a broader system of physical Hanization. For decades, Beijing has incentivized Han Chinese to move into Xinjiang to build a majority in the Uyghur homeland, shifting the demographics sharply.[78] Since 2014, President Xi quartered Communist Party members inside Uyghur homes to monitor and report "extremist" behavior.[79] This aspect of the Strike Hard Campaign, dubbed the Becoming Family program, diverted one million Communist Party members, overwhelmingly Han, into Uyghur homes for as long as five months.[80] The compulsory homestay program converted private homes into perpetual surveillance stations, where activities such as praying, fasting during Ramadan, speaking Uyghur, and eating halal (Islamically blessed) meat would routinely be branded as violations of the counterterrorism laws.[81]

Breaking up the Uyghur family is another strategy of the Strike Hard campaign. Uyghur adults are arrested for the slightest "anti-extremism" infractions[82] or no infraction at all. These circumstances lead to the detention and the funneling of Uyghur children into Xinjiang's swelling network of "brainwashing" orphanages and kindergartens.[83] These centers are where children are separated from their parents and subjected to Communist disciplinary drills tailored for

[75] Serhan, "Saving Uyghur Culture."
[76] Editorial Board, "China Is Creating Concentration Camps in Xinjiang: Here's How We Hold It Accountable," *The Washington Post*, November 24, 2018, https://www.washingtonpost.com/opini ons/china-is-creating-concentration-camps-in-xinjiang-heres-how-we-hold-it-accountable/2018/ 11/23/93dd8c34-e9d6-11e8-bbdb-72fdbf9d4fed_story.html.
[77] Maizland, "China's Repression."
[78] As of 2019, the Han make up approximately 40 percent of the population in Xinjiang. The province is also segregated along urban-rural lines. The "Uyghurs have been effectively pushed out of now-Han dominated metropolitan areas, with 98% of Han in Xinjiang living in urban centers and 90% of Uyghurs living in rural areas." Davis, "Being Uyghur," p. 97.
[79] Dominic J. Nardi, *Religious Freedom in China's High-Tech Surveillance State*, US Commission on International Religious Freedom, September 2019, https://www.uscirf.gov/sites/default/files/ 2019%20China%20Surveillance%20State%20Update.pdf, p. 2.
[80] Human Rights Watch, *"Eradicating,"* p. 11.
[81] The halal food prohibition was "heralded by government officials as fighting a fictional pan-halal trend under which Muslim influence was supposedly spreading into secular life." "For Uighur Muslims in China, Life Keeps Getting Harder," *Foreign Policy*, October 26, 2019, https://foreignpol icy.com/2019/10/26/uighur-concentration-camps-surveillance-spies-china-control/.
[82] Opinions on Several Issues.
[83] Sigal Samuel, "China's Jaw-Dropping Family Separation Policy," *The Atlantic*, September 4, 2019, https://www.theatlantic.com/international/archive/2018/09/china-internment-camps-uig hur-muslim-children/569062/.

youth.[84] The number of these so-called kindergartens doubled in 2017, in line with Quanguo's expansion of concentration camps.[85]

The alienation of children from their parents continues after they are physically reunited. In cases in which parents return from the camps and children are reassigned to their homes, the state deputizes youth to serve as in-home informants. These youth are authorized to monitor their parents, siblings, and whoever else may enter their home.[86] This nefarious tentacle of the surveillance state in Xinjiang simultaneously disintegrates families and co-opts future Uyghur generations into a Han-supremacist society.[87]

The mosque, the institutional symbol of Muslim life, has been violently targeted by Xi's Strike Hard campaign. To further subjugate the Uyghur, Xi razed more than thirty mosques in Xinjiang.[88] Many of these mosques were longstanding shrines, destroyed to sever the Uyghur from vital spaces of spiritual and civic congregation and to erode the practice of Islam among the Uyghur.[89]

The mosques that still stand have not been spared. Upon the direction of Beijing, Quanguo has, "installed video cameras over mosque doorways to monitor worshippers" who frequent individual mosques.[90] He also directed that additional video recorders be placed inside mosques to monitor individuals who choose to maintain their spiritual observance despite Beijing's criminalization of Islam.[91] The Chinese Counterterror Law of 2012 restricts "exploiting religious teaching, sermons, exegesis, [and] study" so as not "to advocate terrorism or extremism," which in turn equips state police with the unilateral authority to shutter, or destroy, Islamic houses of worship in Xinjiang.[92]

The Strike Hard campaign has obscured the line between punishment, discipline, and control. Reports of women being sterilized to prevent Uyghur births are widespread.[93] Han men are incentivized by the state to sleep with and marry

---

[84] See also Nicole Bozorgmir, "Uyghur Parents Say China Is Ripping Their Children Away and Brainwashing Them," *Vice*, July 1, 2019, https://www.vice.com/en/article/7xgj5y/these-uighur-parents-say-china-is-ripping-their-children-away-and-brainwashing-them.

[85] Isobel Yeung, "They Came for Us at Night: Inside China's Hidden Wars on Uighurs," *Vice*, June 29, 2019, https://www.vice.com/en/article/8xz3qg/they-come-for-us-at-night-inside-chinas-hidden-war-on-muslim-uighurs.

[86] Samuel, "China's Jaw-Dropping Family Separation Policy."

[87] Samuel, "China's Jaw-Dropping Family Separation Policy."

[88] Thirty-one mosques and two major Islamic shrines were destroyed, in whole or in part, between 2016 and 2018 in Xinjiang. Of the thirty-one, fifteen were "completely or almost completely razed." Amy Gunia, "China Destroyed Mosques and Other Muslim Sites in Xinjiang, Report Says," *Time*, May 7, 2019, https://time.com/5584619/china-xinjiang-destroyed-mosques/.

[89] Gunia, "China."

[90] "Authorities have installed surveillance cameras both inside and outside houses of worship to monitor and identify attendees." Nardi, *Religious Freedom*, p. 1.

[91] Topol, "Her Uyghur Parents."

[92] Opinions on Several Issues.

[93] "China Forcing Birth Control on Uyghurs to Suppress Population, Report Says," BBC, June 29, 2020, https://www.bbc.com/news/world-asia-china-53220713. See also Adrian Zenz, "China's Own

Uyghur women.[94] The harvesting of Uyghur organs sold on global black markets further illustrates the macabre physical and psychological violence inflicted on the Uyghur.[95] It is a violence that usually follows, and sometimes precedes, efforts to control and discipline the Uyghur. The state may not be directly linked with these morbid practices, but its campaign against the Uyghur has enabled, if not incentivized, black-market actors to seize upon the vulnerable population.

Through the Global War on Terror and the domestic Strike Hard campaign, Beijing has wielded the guise of counterterrorism policy to mine every ounce of Uyghur Muslim life out of Xinjiang and, in its place, impose Han culture and Communist groupthink.[96] Chinese studies scholar Joanne Smith Finley deftly connects counterterrorism motives with the state aim of the Uyghur's submission to China's agenda, arguing that "state counterterrorism becomes terrorism when it fails to distinguish between the innocent and the guilty, it is highly disproportionate, and it aims to terrify or intimidate the wider population or a particular community into submission."[97]

Conclusion

Islamophobia is a global phenomenon that is emerging and intensifying on many fronts. Home to the largest population in the world and a Communist government keen on eliminating dissidents domestically and expanding its hegemony globally, China has the Uyghur trapped in the middle. They are stuck in the belly of an authoritarian beast that brands Uyghur and Muslim identity as inassimilable and suspicious, and it does so within a geopolitical landscape where humanitarian appeals to slow Beijing's crackdown on the Uyghur have been silenced by China's economic and political might, not to mention Western-led Islamophobic geopolitics.

China remains a horrific theater of unrestrained and unimaginable Islamophobia. It is one in which fathers are kidnapped in the night and thrown

---

Documents Shown Potentially Genocidal Sterilization Plans in Xinjiang," *Foreign Policy*, July 1, 2020, https://foreignpolicy.com/2020/07/01/china-documents-uighur-genocidal-sterilization-xinjiang/.

[94] "Xinjiang Authorities Push Uyghurs to Marry Chinese," *Radio Free Asia*, September 2017, https://www.rfa.org/english/news/special/uyghur-oppression/ChenPolicy2.html.

[95] Will Martin, "China Is Harvesting Thousands of Human Organs From Its Uyghur Muslim Minority, UN-Human Rights Body Hears," *Business Insider*, September 25, 2019, https://www.businessinsider.com/china-harvesting-organs-of-uighur-muslims-china-tribunal-tells-un-2019-9.

[96] "Those outside the camps are required to attend weekly, or even daily, Chinese flag-raising ceremonies, political indoctrination meetings, and at times Mandarin [Chinese] classes." Human Rights Watch, *"Eradicating,"* p. 4.

[97] Joanne Smith Finley, "Securitization, Insecurity, and Conflict in Contemporary Xinjiang: Has PRC Counterterrorism Evolved into State Terror," *Central Asian Survey* 38 (2019): pp. 1, 15.

into concentration camps for praying, mothers are arrested and detained in prisons for donning the hijab, and children are separated from their parents and placed into brainwashing orphanages designed to "cleanse" their minds of the ancient culture and Islamic customs passed down to them from their elders. The world may never know the full scale of the horror unfolding behind the thick walls of secrecy and iron curtains of authoritarianism in Xinjiang. Short of humanitarian intervention or a global movement exposing China for the crimes against humanity inflicted upon the Uyghur, the Communist regime in Beijing will remain committed to its brutal designs of cultural genocide.

14

Islamophobia and Genocide

Myanmar's Rohingya Genocide

Ronan Lee

Barbed wire, sandbags, and soldiers delimit the boundaries of the Aung Mingalar quarter of Sittwe, the capital of Myanmar's[1] Rakhine state. In this ghetto live around four thousand Rohingya, a mostly Muslim minority, confined since 2012 to a space no larger than a couple of square kilometers (see fig. 14.1).[2] Income opportunities are severely limited, and residents rely on remittances from outside the ghetto to survive. Aung Mingalar's residents cannot freely travel even the few hundred yards to the city's hospital or to visit the market.[3] If they did, they would see shuttered Rohingya businesses defaced with anti-Rohingya graffiti reminiscent of Nazi defacement of Jewish homes and businesses.[4] Further disturbing similarities with Nazi atrocity crimes can be witnessed on the outskirts of Sittwe where concentration camps housing around 140,000 Rohingya were also established in 2012.[5] As with the city center's Aung Mingalar ghetto, camp residents are not free to leave, work opportunities are scarce, and education and health access are extremely limited.

In 2015, ghetto and camp residents who had already been confined for three years told me they lived with the daily fear that Myanmar's authorities might cut off their access to food or water at any time.[6] They were right to be worried about the threat to Rohingya lives posed by Myanmar's authorities. Just

---

[1] Where names are concerned, the aim is to maintain meaning and avoid confusion. While the military junta officially changed the country's name from Burma to Myanmar in 1989, throughout this chapter the name *Myanmar* is generally used. In Myanmar, names are commonly personal names, so Aung San Suu Kyi and others' Myanmar names are used in full, rather than being arbitrarily changed to comply with Western naming expectations.

[2] Human Rights Watch, *"An Open Prison without End": Myanmar's Mass Detention of Rohingya in Rakhine State* (October 8, 2022), https://www.hrw.org/report/2020/10/08/open-prison-without-end/myanmars-mass-detention-rohingya-rakhine-state.

[3] Human Rights Watch, *"Open Prison."*

[4] Ronan Lee, *Myanmar's Rohingya Genocide: Identity History and Hate Speech* (London: Bloomsbury, 2021).

[5] "Remarks by Special Envoy Noeleen Heyzer at the Informal Meeting of the General Assembly on Myanmar," UN Department of Political and Peacebuilding Affairs, June 13, 2022, https://dppa.un.org/en/remarks-special-envoy-noeleen-heyzer-informal-meeting-of-general-assembly-myanmar.

[6] Lee, *Myanmar's Rohingya Genocide.*

Ronan Lee, *Islamophobia and Genocide* In: *Global Islamophobia and the Rise of Populism.* Edited by: Sahar F. Aziz and John L. Esposito, Oxford University Press. © Oxford University Press 2024.
DOI: 10.1093/oso/9780197648995.003.0014

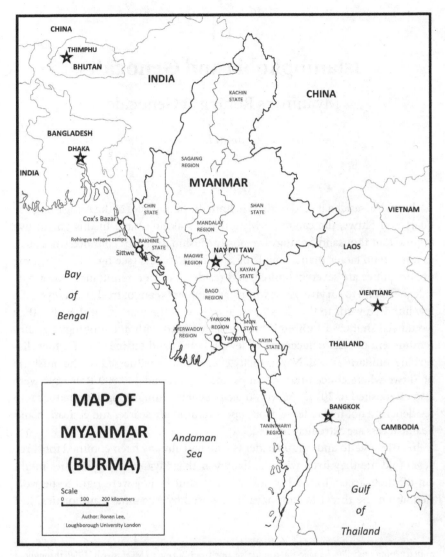

Fig. 14.1. Ronan Lee, *Map of Myanmar (Burma)*, 2023.

two years later, the Rohingya community endured the largest forced migration in the region since World War II, when Myanmar's military, known as the Tatmadaw, unleashed a months-long scorched-earth campaign that laid waste to more than three hundred Rohingya villages.[7] The Tatmadaw claimed to be

---

[7] Human Rights Watch, "Burma: New Satellite Images Confirm Mass Destruction," October 17, 2017, https://www.hrw.org/news/2017/10/17/burma-new-satellite-images-confirm-mass-destruction.

ISLAMOPHOBIA AND GENOCIDE 235

seeking out members of a recently emerged militant group. But their "clearance operation" was characterized by extrajudicial killings on a massive scale with the targeting of educated Rohingya and community leaders, the widespread use of sexual violence against women and girls as a military tactic, and the razing of the Rohingya's largely bamboo villages with fire launched from military helicopters. United Nations (UN) High Commissioner for Human Rights Zeid Ra'ad Al Hussein called it "a textbook example of ethnic cleansing,"[8] and damning reports published by human rights groups described Tatmadaw violence as "crimes against humanity"[9] and "a human rights and humanitarian catastrophe."[10]

Within the space of just a few months, more than 700,000 Rohingya refugees arrived in Bangladesh by foot, carrying whatever possessions they could.[11] Many now live in Kutupalong, the world's largest refugee camp that is part of a complex of camps adjacent to the Myanmar frontier that house, beneath flimsy tarpaulin and bamboo, most of the world's Rohingya population. The 2017 forced migration prompted the International Criminal Court to investigate war crimes, crimes against humanity, and genocide.[12] A UN Human Rights Council (UNHCR) fact-finding mission described rampant human rights violations, recommending the "investigation and prosecution of Myanmar's Commander-in-Chief, Senior General Min Aung Hlaing, and his top military leaders for genocide, crimes against humanity and war crimes."[13] There is also a high-profile case underway at the International Court of Justice (ICJ) accusing Myanmar of committing genocide and of failing to live up to its responsibilities as a signatory of the Genocide Convention to prevent genocide taking place.[14] Scholars, too,

---

[8] "UN Human Rights Chief Points to 'Textbook Example of Ethnic Cleansing' in Myanmar," UN News, September 11, 2017, https://news.un.org/en/story/2017/09/564622-un-human-rights-chief-points-textbook-exampleethnic-cleansing-myanmar.

[9] Human Rights Watch, "Burma: Military Commits Crimes against Humanity," September 25, 2017, https://www.hrw.org/news/2017/09/25/burma-military-commits-crimes-against-humanity.

[10] Amnesty International, "Myanmar: Crimes against Humanity Terrorize and Drive Rohingya Out," October 18, 2017, https://www.amnesty.org/en/latest/news/2017/10/myanmar-new-evidence-of-systematic-campaign-to-terrorize-and-drive-rohingya-out/.

[11] "Myanmar: UN Fact-Finding Mission Releases Its Full Account of Massive Violations by Military in Rakhine, Kachin and Shan States," UN Human Rights Council, September 18, 2018, https://www.ohchr.org/EN/HRBodies/HRC/Pages/NewsDetail.aspx?NewsID=23575&LangID=E.

[12] "ICC Prosecutor, Fatou Bensouda, Requests Judicial Authorisation to Commence an Investigation into the Situation in Bangladesh/Myanmar," International Criminal Court, July 4, 2019, https://www.icc-cpi.int/news/icc-prosecutor-fatou-bensouda-requests-judicial-authorisation-commence-investigation-situation.

[13] "Myanmar: UN Fact-Finding Mission Releases Its Full Account of Massive Violations by Military in Rakhine, Kachin and Shan States," UN Human Rights Council, September 18, 2018, https://www.ohchr.org/EN/NewsEvents/Pages/DisplayNews.aspx?NewsID=23575.

[14] Application of the Convention on the Prevention and Punishment of the Crime of Genocide (The Gambia v. Myanmar), ICJ, https://www.icj-cij.org/en/case/178.

categorized crimes against the Rohingya as genocide,[15] and in 2022, the United States made a formal genocide declaration.[16]

Myanmar's egregious mistreatment of the Rohingya was not new. During the preceding four decades, the Tatmadaw undertook semi-regular anti-Rohingya pogroms that forcibly deported as many as hundreds of thousands of Rohingya each time, and the apartheid conditions that Rohingya continue to endure within Rakhine state have frequently been highlighted by human rights groups.[17] The vast majority of Rohingya camp residents arrived in Bangladesh as victims of two major forced deportations from Myanmar. In 1991–92, more than 200,000 fled Myanmar for the relative safety of Bangladesh, and while some subsequently returned to Myanmar, at least 200,000 remained, joined in 2017 by a further population of more than 700,000 refugees. Those Rohingya who remain in Myanmar are locked down in their villages, trapped in Sittwe's ghetto, or in concentration camps. Travel and other rights restrictions are severe, as they have been for decades, and according to UN investigators, Rohingya in Myanmar continue to live with the looming threat of genocide.[18]

In light of the Rohingya's long-term mistreatment by Myanmar's authorities, for many international observers the greatest shock was not the brutality of Tatmadaw violence against the Rohingya but, instead, the seeming endorsement of the Tatmadaw's anti-Rohingya violence by the leader of Myanmar's quasi-civilian administration, the State Counselor Aung San Suu Kyi, the country's de facto prime minister. While UN Secretary-General António Guterres described the 2017 crisis as "a humanitarian and human rights nightmare" and explained that the "situation has spiraled into the world's fastest developing refugee emergency,"[19] Aung San Suu Kyi described international media reports of military atrocities as "a huge iceberg of misinformation,"[20] resisted international

[15] Alicia de la Cour Venning, Thomas MacManus, and Penny Green, *Countdown to Annihilation: Genocide in Myanmar* (London: International State Crime Initiative, 2015); Penny Green, Thomas McManus, and Alicia de la Cour Venning, *Genocide Achieved, Genocide Continues: Myanmar's Annihilation of the Rohingya* (London: International State Crime Initiative, 2018); Azeem Ibrahim, *The Rohingyas: Inside Myanmar's Genocide* (London: Hurst, 2018); Lee, *Myanmar's Rohingya Genocide*; Maung Zarni and Alice Cowley, "The Slow-Burning Genocide of Myanmar's Rohingya," *Pacific Rim Law and Policy Journal Association* 23, no. 3 (2014): pp. 683–754.

[16] "Secretary Antony J. Blinken on the Genocide and Crimes against Humanity in Burma," US Department of State, March 21, 2022, https://www.state.gov/secretary-antony-j-blinken-at-the-united-states-holocaust-memorial-museum/.

[17] Amnesty International, *"Caged without a Roof": Apartheid in Myanmar's Rakhine State*, 2017, https://www.amnesty.org.uk/files/CagedwithoutaRoof-ApartheidMyanmar-AIreport.pdf.

[18] "Genocide Threat for Myanmar's Rohingya Greater Than Ever, Investigators Warn Human Rights Council," UN News, September 16, 2019, https://news.un.org/en/story/2019/09/1046442.

[19] "Rohingya Refugee Crisis a 'Human Rights Nightmare,' UN Chief Tells Security Council," UN News, September 28, 2017, https://news.un.org/en/story/2017/09/567402-rohingya-refugee-crisis-human-rights-nightmare-unchief-tells-security-council.

[20] "Rohingya Crisis: Suu Kyi Says 'Fake News Helping Terrorists,'" BBC, September 6, 2017, https://www.bbc.co.uk/news/world-asia-41170570.

ISLAMOPHOBIA AND GENOCIDE   237

intervention, and later led Myanmar's defense against genocide accusations at the ICJ in the Hague.[21] Many questioned how a Nobel Peace Prize laureate, regarded internationally as an icon of democracy and human rights, could seemingly be so inconsistent in her politics and prepared to enable and defend appalling human rights abuses against a Muslim minority.[22] This chapter outlines how this occurred, mapping the Rohingya's progressive exclusion from Myanmar's political mainstream.

The genocide against the Rohingya provides a disturbing example of how a well-integrated Muslim minority over time can be progressively excluded from political and social life and mistreated by the authorities to the point of genocide without any significant domestic political outcry. This chapter considers Myanmar's history in order to outline the Rohingya's indigeneity, noting important aspects of the country's demographics, and common attitudes toward religion, ethnicity, and race. An examination of the progressive mistreatment of the Rohingya follows and is divided into two parts. The first traces the diminution of the Rohingya's social and political standing during the period of military dictatorship from 1962 to 2011, while the second considers the period of quasi-civilian rule from 2011 to 2021.

Rohingya History in Myanmar, National Demographics, and Attitudes toward Religion, Ethnicity, and Race

Today, the Rohingya are most visible internationally through a crisis lens, seen as refugees in Bangladesh and genocide victims at home in Myanmar. It is certainly true that most Rohingya, around one million,[23] live in a state of protracted displacement in Bangladesh, where they are unable to build permanent structures, have limited access to education and work opportunities, and little expectation of when, if ever, it might be safe for them to return to Myanmar. Denied citizenship rights by Myanmar's authorities, Rohingya living in Bangladesh are

[21] Application of the Convention on the Prevention and Punishment of the Crime of Genocide (The Gambia v. Myanmar), verbatim record, ICJ, 2019, https://www.icj-cij.org/public/files/case-related/178/178-20191211-ORA-01-00-BI.pdf.

[22] "Critics Circle Aung San Suu Kyi over Rohingya Crisis," *Al Jazeera*, September 11, 2017, https://www.aljazeera.com/news/2017/9/11/critics-circle-aung-san-suu-kyi-over-rohingya-crisis; James Doubek, "Malala Yousafzai Criticizes Aung San Suu Kyi over Violence on Myanmar's Rohingya," NPR, September 4, 2017, https://www.npr.org/sections/thetwo-way/2017/09/04/548436637/malala-yousafzai-criticizes-aung-san-suu-kyi-over-violence-on-myanmars-rohingya?t=1657813728762; Rebecca Wright, Katie Hunt, and Joshua Berlinger, "Aung San Suu Kyi Breaks Silence on Rohingya, Sparks Storm of Criticism," CNN, September 19, 2017, https://edition.cnn.com/2017/09/18/asia/aung-san-suu-kyi-speech-rohingya/index.html.

[23] "Joint Government of Bangladesh—Rohingya Population by Location as of 30 June 2022," UNHCR, July 12, 2022, https://data.unhcr.org/en/documents/details/94163.

238 RONAN LEE

effectively stateless.[24] However, for Myanmar's Rohingya, things were not always so bleak. How this Muslim minority came to be victims of a genocide within Myanmar, with the seeming support of the country's democratically elected civilian authorities and without any meaningful public outcry, provides a salutary warning about how easily this could happen to minorities elsewhere.

Myanmar's history, demographics, and how people in the country routinely understand religion, ethnicity, and race provide important context to explain the motivations of key political actors. In Myanmar, religious identity is routinely understood as an indicator of ethnic identity, which is commonly conflated with racial identity, which many regard as essential and unchanging.[25] Belonging to a particular ethnic or racial group is commonly accompanied by an assumption about religious adherence. While a group like the Rohingya could be understood as an ethnic group with mostly Muslim adherents, most people in Myanmar, and certainly the military leadership, regard the Rohingya as essentially Muslim. As a result, policies and practices designed to harm the group should be understood as representations of Islamophobia rather than simply attacks upon a minority ethnic group.

Myanmar's majority religion is overwhelmingly Theravada Buddhism, with 87.9 percent of the country's approximately 51 million people claiming it as their religion.[26] There is a substantial Christian minority accounting for 6.2 percent of the population, while Muslims make up just 4.3 percent of the nationwide population. Myanmar's ethnic composition complicates identity matters, and this is particularly the case in Rakhine state, the Rohingya's ancestral home. Nationwide, the majority ethnicity, the Bamar (also identified as Burman), a mostly Buddhist group, is by far the largest, comprising an estimated 68 percent of the population.[27] Since independence, Bamar Buddhists have dominated Myanmar's government institutions, military, and businesses. In Rakhine state, another mostly Buddhist group, the Rakhine, is dominant, accounting for around two thirds of the state's 3.1 million people. Many Rakhine regard themselves, and the land they historically shared with the Rohingya, to have been illegally annexed by the Burma Empire in 1784, just decades before the start of the British colonial era, and they retain strong separatist tendencies. The Rohingya, an overwhelmingly

[24] "Stateless Rohingya Refugee Children Living in 'Untenable Situation,' UNICEF Chief," UN News, February 27, 2019, https://news.un.org/en/story/2019/02/1033722; "Statelessness and the Rohingya Crisis," UNHCR, November 2017, https://data.unhcr.org/en/documents/details/60575.

[25] Robert H. Taylor, "Refighting Old Battles, Compounding Misconceptions: The Politics of Ethnicity in Myanmar Today," ISEAS Perspective, March 2, 2015, https://www.iseas.edu.sg/images/pdf/ISEAS_Perspective_2015_12.pdf.

[26] "The 2014 Myanmar Population and Housing Census," Myanmar Information Management Unit, https://themimu.info/census-data.

[27] Lex Rieffel, "Peace in Myanmar Depends on Settling Centuries-Old Ethnic Conflicts," Brookings Institution, March 20, 2017, https://www.brookings.edu/blog/up-front/2017/03/20/peace-in-myanmar-depends-on-settling-centuries-old-ethnic-conflicts/.

Muslim group (and routinely regarded as Muslim by most in Myanmar) comprise most of the remaining Rakhine state population. Enumerators of the most recent census in 2014 were prevented from recording any individual's identity as "Rohingya," so various estimates have been made about the size of the Rohingya population at that time. In Rakhine state, approximately 1.09 million people were unrecorded by census enumerators, which suggests a Rohingya population of at least that size.[28] The UN High Commissioner for Refugees estimated that 1.3 million Rohingya lived in Rakhine state before the 2017 crisis,[29] meaning that Rohingya accounted for less than 2.5 percent of the national population.

During the centuries before Myanmar's colonial era, the Rohingya's ancestors were a well-integrated part of Arakan, an independent trading kingdom at the north of the Bay of Bengal that included the lands of modern Rakhine state and that at its peak controlled territory as far north as Chattogram (previously Chittagong).[30] Arakan was multiethnic and multi-religious, and its rulers, at times, minted coins displaying the *Kalima*, the Islamic declaration of faith, and adopted Muslim titles.[31] When Arakan was invaded by the Burma Empire in 1784, Persian was still the kingdom's court language.[32] During that short-lived period of Burmese imperial rule, an East India Company delegation documented the presence of a specific Rohingya identity, noting them as Indigenous to Arakan.[33] Within four decades, war between the British and Burma Empire saw Arakan ceded to British control, and from 1885, the whole of the country (closely approximating the territory that is today Myanmar) fell to British colonial rule. Throughout the colonial period, Rohingya continued to be well integrated in society.

However, for many Bamar and Buddhists, the colonial era represented a period of national humiliation. The colonial British often privileged foreigners

---

[28] "2014 Myanmar Population."

[29] "Global Trends Forced Displacement in 2017," UNHCR, 2018, https://www.unhcr.org/5b27be547.pdf.

[30] Michael Charney, *Where Jambudipa and Islamdom Converged: Religious Change and the Emergence of Buddhist Communalism in Early Modern Arakan, 15th–19th Centuries* (PhD dissertation, University of Michigan, 1999), https://www.academia.edu/320060/Where_Jambudipa_and_Islamdom_Converged_Religious_Change_and_the_Emergence_of_Buddhist_Communalism_in_Early_Modern_Arakan_15th_19th_Centuries.

[31] Tahir Ba Tha, "A Short History of Rohingya and Kamans of Burma," *Kaladan Press Network*, September 13, 2007, https://archive.org/details/a-short-history-of-the-rohingyas-and-kamans; Nurul Islam, "Muslim Influence in the Kingdom of Arakan," *ARNO*, January 13, 2012, https://www.rohingya.org/muslim-influence-in-the-kingdom-of-arakan/; Htay Lwin Oo, "Mr Htay Lwin Oo Speech in ANU on Rohingya History," YouTube, March 17, 2013, https://www.youtube.com/watch?v=jE-JV4d1cx8.

[32] East India Company, company letter to king of Raccan, 1686, India Office Records and Private Papers IOR/E/3/91 f. 42.

[33] Francis Buchanan, journal of progress and observations during the continuance of the deputation from Bengal to Ava in 1795 in the dominions of the Barma monarch, 1795, India Office Records and Private Papers, Mss. Eur C12, 172; Francis Buchanan, "A Comparative Vocabulary of Some of the Languages Spoken in the Burma Empire," *Asiatic Researches* 5 (1799): pp. 219–40.

within their administration and imported from the subcontinent considerable numbers of administrators and low-income laborers who frequently undercut local wages.[34] Through loan defaults, Indian moneylenders became major landholders, adding to feelings of economic alienation among the Indigenous population.[35] Anti-colonial narratives continue to be powerful within Myanmar today. There is considerable resentment of British colonial rule as well as of those perceived to have benefited from it, such as colonial-era migrants. When weaponized, these narratives can be powerful political tools in Myanmar. The contemporary Tatmadaw traces its organizational and ideological roots to the Bamar Buddhist-dominated anti-colonial movement led by Aung San (father of Aung San Suu Kyi), which allied with the Imperial Japanese to force a British retreat during World War II.[36] Many among the country's non-Buddhist minorities (including the Rohingya) are believed by the military to have been insufficiently supportive of the independence movement, to have been too closely aligned with the colonial British, and to have retained separatist ambitions.[37] These circumstances provide some explanation for the xenophobia and aggressive anti-Rohingya attitudes of Tatmadaw leaders, and they point to Aung San Suu Kyi's personal attitude toward the Rohingya and other minority groups.

When Myanmar gained independence in 1948, Rohingya had full civil and political rights, serving in senior government roles and as MPs in the national parliament.[38] Rangoon University was home to high-profile Rohingya student groups, and Rohingya language was broadcast on the Burma Broadcasting Service's radio station. Throughout the early years of independence, senior national political and military figures openly recognized the Rohingya as legitimate members of the country's national political fabric and were prepared to grant majority Rohingya communities a degree of self-government. U Nu, Myanmar's longest serving civilian-era prime minister, made clear the Rohingya's legitimate integration into the newly independent country, asserting, "The people living in Maungdaw and Buthidaung regions are our nationals, our brethren. They are called Rohingyas. They are one of the same par in status of nationality with

[34] David Steinberg, *Burma/Myanmar: What Everyone Needs to Know* (Oxford: Oxford University Press, 2010).

[35] Sean Turnell, *Fiery Dragons: Banks, Moneylenders and Microfinance in Burma* (Copenhagen: NIAS Press, 2009).

[36] Michael Charney, *A History of Modern Burma* (Cambridge: Cambridge University Press, 2009).

[37] Charney, *History*; Lindsay Maizland, "Myanmar's Troubled History: Coups, Military Rule, and Ethnic Conflict," Council on Foreign Relations, January, 31, 2022, https://www.cfr.org/backgroun der/myanmar-history-coup-military-rule-ethnic-conflict-rohingya; "Identity Crisis: Ethnicity and Conflict in Myanmar," International Crisis Group, August 28, 2020, https://www.crisisgroup.org/ asia/south-east-asia/myanmar/312-identity-crisis-ethnicity-and-conflict-myanmar.

[38] "Burma's Path to Genocide: Leading A New Nation," US Holocaust Memorial Museum, Washington, DC, 2023. https://exhibitions.ushmm.org/burmas-path-to-genocide/chapter-1/lead ing-a-new-nation.

ISLAMOPHOBIA AND GENOCIDE   241

Kachin, Kayah, Karen, Mon, Rakhine and Shan. They are one of the ethnic races of Burma."[39] This situation changed after a military dictatorship came to power in 1962.

From Indigenous to Foreigners: Rohingya Rights Restrictions from 1962

The Rohingya's exclusion from Myanmar's political mainstream was not instantaneous but involved a steady process of rights erosions taking place over decades. From the time of the military coup in 1962 until 2011, when a quasi-civilian administration headed by an ex-general came to power, soldiers dominated Myanmar's politics. The military leadership were overwhelmingly Bamar Buddhists and notoriously xenophobic. The Rohingya's situation deteriorated steadily under military rule. Aiming to make Bamar Buddhist identity the national norm, the junta undertook widespread processes of Burmanization, forced cultural assimilation that involved discrimination against religious and ethnic minorities on matters of culture, language, and education, and aggressively silenced alternative historical narratives.[40] During the 1960s, the military regime expelled hundreds of thousands of Chinese and Indian residents living in the country's largest urban centers, Rangoon (Yangon) and Mandalay.[41] However, at that time the junta lacked the capacity to forcibly deport the Rohingya, a well-established community, from the country's periphery. Large-scale expulsions of Rohingya from Myanmar were not undertaken by the military authorities until other Rohingya rights had been restricted for some years and the group had been actively portrayed as a foreign population.

Weaponizing history to dominate a divided nation that resisted military rule, the junta linked collective citizenship rights with recognition as a *taingyintha*, which they defined as groups who traced ancestry within the country to 1823, before the start of the colonial era. In 1982, these criteria were included in a redrafted citizenship law, which remains in force today.[42] Over time, the recognition as a *taingyintha* came to represent the peak of the country's rights hierarchy.[43] Those groups the junta believed to be *taingyintha* were clarified with the

[39] Md. Mahbubul Haque, "Rohingya Ethnic Muslim Minority and the 1982 Citizenship Law in Burma," *Journal of Muslim Minority Affairs* 37, no. 4 (2017): pp. 454–69.

[40] Jean A. Berlie, *Burma: The Burmanization of Myanmar's Muslims* (Bangkok: White Lotus Press, 2008); Benedict Rogers, *Burma: A Nation at the Crossroads* (London: Rider Books, 2012); Steinberg, *Burma/Myanmar*.

[41] Robert A. Holmes, "Burmese Domestic Policy: The Politics of Burmanization," *Asian Survey* 7, no. 3 (1967): pp. 188–97.

[42] Burma Citizenship Law, 1982, https://www.refworld.org/docid/3ae6b4f71b.html.

[43] Nick Cheesman, "How in Myanmar 'National Races' Came to Surpass Citizenship and Exclude Rohingya," *Journal of Contemporary Asia* 47, no. 3 (2017): pp. 461–83.

242   RONAN LEE

1990 publication of a list of 135 "national" groups.[44] The Rohingya were excluded from this list and increasingly portrayed by the junta as being Bengali migrants who were brought by the British during the colonial era or who had arrived after independence and so by no means Indigenous to Myanmar.

Genocide perpetrators have commonly used identity documents as a tool to discriminate against, dehumanize, and exclude victims. The junta used a range of methods to diminish the ability of Rohingya to evidence their legitimate presence in Myanmar.[45] Processes of citizenship scrutiny were used to enable the active downgrading of Rohingya identity documents, and the authorities also frequently refused to acknowledge the legitimacy of Rohingya identity documents, including passports. The junta then further limited Rohingya rights on the basis that Rohingya could not prove their legitimate residency within Myanmar. Throughout military rule, the Rohingya not only experienced rights restrictions but were steadily excluded from mainstream society. Limits on Rohingya travel rights, given a facade of legality by the junta's refusal to recognize Rohingya identity documents, prevented Rohingya from leaving Rakhine state. Soon, Rohingya were confined to their village areas and many eventually to ghettos such as Aung Mingalar or to concentration camps. The physical separation and limits on contact between Myanmar's Buddhist population and the Muslim Rohingya helped the junta, over time, portray the Rohingya as outsiders and genuinely foreign.

Rohingya collectively faced strategies of oppression common to other genocidal contexts, including increasingly severe restrictions on access to education, healthcare, travel (even to adjacent villages), and their ability to work, marry, and have children.[46] Rohingya found themselves trapped in an apartheid state, and despite centuries of ancestry and uncontroversial post-independence recognition as part of the country's political fabric, they were excluded from the government's list of Indigenous groups, were well along on a path to collective statelessness, and increasingly regarded by the majority of Myanmar's population as foreigners.

A shockingly violent indication of the diminution of Rohingya standing came in 1978. The junta linked a citizenship verification process, *Nagamin* ("King Dragon"), billed as the registration of foreigners prior to the 1983 census, with a military campaign to seek out militants within Rohingya

---

[44] Cheesman, "How."
[45] "Genocide by Attrition: The Role of Identity Documents in the Holocaust and the Genocides of Rwanda and Myanmar," Fortify Rights, June 8, 2022, https://www.fortifyrights.org/mya-inv-rep-2022-06-08/.
[46] Amnesty International, *"Caged"*; "Report of the Independent International Fact-Finding Mission on Myanmar," UN Human Rights Council, 2018, https://documents-dds-ny.un.org/doc/UNDOC/GEN/G18/274/54/PDF/G1827454.pdf.

communities close to the Bangladesh border. The Tatmadaw used its "Four Cuts" method—denying opponents access to food, funds, fresh recruits, and information—which by design targets civilian communities with scorched-earth tactics; the 2017 "clearance operation" methods were an updated version of this approach.[47] This military violence understandably provoked panic among Rohingya civilians, and hundreds of thousands fled to Bangladesh. Another violent forced deportation was undertaken by the military in 1991–92, when, again, hundreds of thousands of Rohingya fled across the international frontier. Rohingya who returned to Myanmar after those waves of forced deportation were subsequently portrayed by the military authorities as illegal Bangladeshi incursions.

By the late 2000s, when Myanmar's military regime announced a new constitution that would provide for a degree of civilian rule and competitive elections, the Rohingya had been made effectively stateless, subjected to apartheid conditions, and physically separated from mainstream Myanmar life for decades. From having been uncontroversially recognized as full members of society until the early 1960s, the Rohingya's domestic standing was incrementally diminished so that by 2011, the group was widely regarded, with little domestic opposition, as foreign and subjected to egregious human rights abuses. While opportunities for public expression of discontent during military rule were limited, when chances did arise such as during the 8888 Uprising that first brought Aung San Suu Kyi to political prominence, the overwhelming focus of opposition activists was on removing the military from power rather than highlighting concerns about human rights abuses against groups like the Rohingya.[48] Prioritizing the removal of the military from power above the human rights concerns of minorities has been the long-preferred approach of Aung San Suu Kyi's National League for Democracy (NLD).[49] Since the 2021 coup, there are indications that the country's alternative leadership, the National Unity Government, which is strongly influenced by the NLD and regards Aung San Suu Kyi as Myanmar's legitimate head of government,[50] has adopted a similar approach, prioritizing removing the Tatmadaw from power above all other national concerns.[51]

---

[47] Martin Smith, *Burma: Insurgency and Politics of Ethnicity* (London: Zed Books, 1991).

[48] Charney, *History*.

[49] Prashanth Parameswaran, "What's Behind the New Constitution Change Push in Myanmar?," The Diplomat, January 30, 2019, https://thediplomat.com/2019/01/whats-in-the-new-constitution-change-push-in-myanmar/.

[50] "Heads of Government," National Unity Government of the Republic of the Union of Myanmar, 2022, https://www.nugmyanmar.org/en/.

[51] "About NUG," National Unity Government of the Republic of the Union of Myanmar, 2022, https://gov.nugmyanmar.org/about-nug/.

Democracy, Hate Speech, and Buddhist Nationalism

When the military junta delivered long-promised constitutional change in 2008, it instituted a quasi-civilian system of government that enshrined Tatmadaw power within a procedural democracy. The military would avoid civilian oversight and retain significant direct political influence. The Constitution of the Republic of Myanmar 2008 designated government ministries (border affairs, defense, home affairs) and one quarter of parliamentary seats reserved for serving military representatives provided an effective veto on future constitutional change. State-managed nationwide elections in 2010 guaranteed that the Tatmadaw's choice of president, ex-General Thein Sein, could take up office in 2011.[52] However, a rapprochement between the military and opposition leader Aung San Suu Kyi that freed her from house arrest and enabled her election to parliament at a 2012 by-election meant the 2015 national election would be a competition between the military-backed Union Solidarity and Development Party (USDP) and Aung San Suu Kyi's NLD.[53] Despite Aung San Suu Kyi's huge domestic popularity, in this competitive electoral environment in which the USDP was widely believed to have the advantage of guaranteed support from the military's appointed 25 percent of parliamentary representatives,[54] the NLD was always likely to fear they might not win the 2015 election, and consequently they pivoted toward policy approaches that they believed were supported by a majority of voters.[55] This political environment, coupled with two significant policy reforms by Thein Sein's administration—the liberalization of the telecommunications industry and increased opportunities for free expression—enabled and encouraged an increase in and normalization of anti-Muslim and anti-Rohingya discourse. Consequently, anti-Muslim and specifically anti-Rohingya policy positions were taken by both the USDP and the NLD.

Throughout the decades of direct military rule, Myanmar had one of the world's most restricted media environments, with severe limits on freedom of expression, extensive domestic censorship, and access to foreign news sources

---

[52] Sean Turnell, "Myanmar in 2010: Doors Open, Doors Close," *Asian Survey* 51, no. 1 (2011): pp. 148–54.

[53] Turnell, "Myanmar."

[54] "The Myanmar Elections: Results and Implications," International Crisis Group, October 29, 2015, https://www.crisisgroup.org/asia/south-east-asia/myanmar/myanmar-elections-results-and-implications.

[55] Hanna Hindstrom, "NLD Blocked Muslim Candidates to Appease Ma Ba Tha: Party Member," *Irrawaddy*, August 31, 2015, https://www.irrawaddy.com/election/news/nld-blocked-muslim-candidates-to-appease-ma-ba-tha-party-member; Martin Woollacott, "Anti-Muslim Paranoia Could Still Derail Myanmar's Journey to True Democracy," *The Guardian*, October 29, 2015, https://www.theguardian.com/commentisfree/2015/oct/29/anti-muslim-military-myanmar-democracy; Poppy McPherson, "No Vote, No Candidates: Myanmar's Muslims Barred from Their Own Election," *The Guardian*, November 3, 2015, https://www.theguardian.com/world/2015/nov/03/no-vote-no-candidates-myanmars-muslims-barred-from-their-own-election.

ISLAMOPHOBIA AND GENOCIDE 245

and social media applications blocked. This situation began to change early in the Thein Sein administration with increased opportunities for public expression and reforms to censorship requirements. In 2011, access to foreign news media, including to Myanmar's exiled news media outlets, was unblocked, and prepublication press censorship ended in 2012.[56] This change gave Myanmar's residents access to foreign news sources and previously inaccessible social media applications. This new access coincided with economic liberalizations, including the opening of the previously notoriously restricted telecommunications industry. Before 2012, Myanmar's mobile phone ownership levels were among the world's lowest, bettering only North Korea.[57] In a country where per capita gross domestic product barely exceeded one thousand dollars,[58] SIM cards were previously prohibitively expensive luxury items, often costing thousands of dollars each and well beyond the reach of most in Myanmar. However, liberalization of the telecommunications industry changed that, reducing SIM card prices to as little as one dollar and opening the domestic market to international carriers. Myanmar's residents quickly embraced the opportunity of mobile phone ownership. Mobile phone penetration rates reached 80 percent by the 2015–16 fiscal year and were estimated to have exceeded 90 percent by 2016.[59]

Facebook's "Free Basics" program turbocharged internet use.[60] Pitched as providing a service to developing countries by giving them unmetered access to Facebook and a curated web experience, "Free Basics" also became a vehicle that delivered Facebook dominance of the domestic internet.[61] For most of Myanmar's residents, their first experience of the internet involved accessing Facebook on a mobile phone rather than accessing an established search engine on a desktop or laptop computer.[62]

[56] Helen Pidd, "Burma Ends Advance Press Censorship," *The Guardian*, August 20, 2012, http://www.theguardian.com/world/2012/aug/20/burma-ends-advance-press-censorship.

[57] Jason Motlagh, "When a SIM Card Goes from $2,000 to $1.50," *Bloomberg*, September 29, 2014, https://www.bloomberg.com/bw/articles/2014-09-29/myanmar-opens-its-mobile-phone-market-cuing-carrier-frenzy.

[58] "GDP Per Capita (Current US$)—Myanmar," World Bank, https://data.worldbank.org/indicator/NY.GDP.PCAP.CD?locations=MM.

[59] Motokazu Matsui, "Foreign Providers, Price Competition Spur Growth," *Nikkei Asian Review*, April 7, 2015, http://asia.nikkei.com/Business/Trends/Foreign-providers-price-competition-spur-growth.

[60] Manish Singh, "After Harsh Criticism, Facebook Quietly Pulls Services from Developing Countries," *The Outline*, May 1, 2018, https://theoutline.com/post/4383/facebook-quietly-ended-free-basics-in-myanmar-and-other-countries

[61] Olivia Solon, "'It's Digital Colonialism': How Facebook's Free Internet Service Has Failed Its Users," *The Guardian*, July 27, 2017, https://www.theguardian.com/technology/2017/jul/27/facebook-free-basics-developing-markets.

[62] Annie Gowan, "Cellphone Use Transforms Burmese Life after Government Opens Mobile Market," *The Washington Post*, November 22, 2014, https://www.washingtonpost.com/world/asia_pacific/new-private-companies-spark-mobile-phone-revolutionin-once-isolatedburma/2014/11/21/eb4479c2-6c41-11e4-bafd-6598192a448d_story.html; Casey Hynes, "Internet Use Is on the Rise in Myanmar, but Better Options Are Needed," *Forbes*, September 22, 2017, https://www.forbes.

246 RONAN LEE

These developments revolutionized the way Myanmar's residents consumed information and communicated with each other, providing new opportunities for political expression. The outcomes were not always positive. For generations under military rule, there had been strong restrictions on freedom of expression, and a free press had been unknown in Myanmar. Low rates of media and news literacy contributed to frequent moral panics spurred by social media posts that were often treated as though they represented reliably sourced news. New media freedoms, while giving a platform to long-suppressed voices advocating for human rights and democracy, also provided ready platforms to ultranationalists to provoke religious and ethnic conflict. Uncritical consumption of so-called news posted to Facebook and its users' widespread sharing came to global attention in 2012, when prominent Buddhist nationalists were noted to be actively using social media to encourage religious and ethnic discord.

The negative influence of social media on discourse was highlighted by the chairman of the UN Independent International Fact-Finding Mission on Myanmar, Marzuki Darusman, who namechecked Facebook when describing how social media played a "determining role" and "substantively contributed to the level of acrimony and dissension and conflict, if you will, within the public. Hate speech is certainly of course a part of that. As far as the Myanmar situation is concerned, social media is Facebook, and Facebook is social media."[63] There was widespread international criticism, too, of Facebook's poor record at removing inciting anti-Rohingya and anti-Muslim posts from its platform, an issue raised by US politicians when Facebook CEO Mark Zuckerberg was grilled by the US Senate's Commerce and Judiciary Committee in 2018. This action strongly suggests that, rather than being specific to Myanmar, these problems are widespread where Facebook operates, and the negative outcomes experienced in Myanmar should be expected in other contexts, too.[64]

Buddhist nationalists like the extremist monk Wirathu, the aggressively anti-Muslim 969 Movement (named to symbolize the virtues of the Buddha, aping Muslims' use of 786 as a numerological representation of the *Basmala*, the opening phrase of the Koran) and the Association for the Protection of Race and Religion, commonly known by its Burmese-language acronym, Ma Ba Tha, used new media freedoms to foment a moral panic about the supposed threat

com/sites/chynes/2017/09/22/internet-use-is-on-the-rise-in-myanmar-but-better-options-are-needed/.

[63] Tom Miles, "UN Investigators Cite Facebook Role in Myanmar Crisis," *Reuters*, March 13, 2018, https://www.reuters.com/article/us-myanmar-rohingya-facebook/u-n-investigators-cite-facebookr ole-in-myanmar-crisis-idUSKCN1GO2PN.

[64] "In Senate Hearing, Zuckerberg Faces Blame over Violence in Myanmar," *The Washington Post*, April 10, 2018, https://www.washingtonpost.com/news/the-switch/wp/2018/04/10/transcript-of-mark-zuckerbergs-senate-hearing/.

to Myanmar's Buddhist character posed by Islam.[65] Despite a nearly 90 percent Buddhist population, and just 4.3 percent of Myanmar's residents being Muslim, nationalists insisted that the country's national interest was served by protecting Buddhism from an alleged looming Muslim threat, and they called for limits on the civil and political freedoms of Muslims.

Using similar language to that of advocates for Great Replacement theory in the United States, Buddhist nationalists pointed to the demographic changes that had taken place historically in other Asian countries, including Afghanistan, Malaysia, and Indonesia, which they portrayed as Buddhist countries taken over by Islam as evidence of a contemporary Muslim threat to Myanmar's Buddhist character.[66] Myanmar's Buddhist nationalists frequently tapped into global anti-Muslim narratives and War on Terror language, making ready reference to the 9/11 attacks, Al Qaeda, the Taliban's destruction of the Baniyan statues, and ISIS to portray Islam as an inherently violent religion.[67] Nationalists routinely presented anti-Muslim perspectives and direct actions as Buddhist religious duties, and they extensively used social media to mobilize supporters in opposition to any government action they believed might grant improved rights to Muslims.[68] The Rohingya were a particular target of nationalist ire. At best, Myanmar's Buddhist-nationalist movement was racist, xenophobic, sexist, and Islamophobic, but at worst, it incited violence against Muslims and encouraged genocide against the Rohingya.[69]

Myanmar's Buddhist nationalists took full advantage of new media freedoms. Wirathu, the most prominent Buddhist-nationalist monk, who described himself as the "Buddhist Bin Laden" and was labeled "the Face of Buddhist Terror" by a *Time* cover story,[70] was a prodigious user of social media, quickly amassing a large online following and producing a substantial volume of online content.

---

[65] Andrew R. C. Marshall, "Special Report: Myanmar Gives Official Blessing to Anti-Muslim Monks," *Reuters*, June 27, 2013, https://www.reuters.com/article/us-myanmar-969-specialreport-idUSBRE95Q04720130627.

[66] Niklas Foxeus, "The Buddha Was a Devoted Nationalist: Buddhist Nationalism, Ressentiment, and Defending Buddhism in Myanmar," *Religion* 49, no. 4 (2019): pp. 661–90.

[67] Marshall, "Special Report"; "Buddhism and State Power in Myanmar," International Crisis Group, September 5, 2017, https://www.crisisgroup.org/asia/south-east-asia/myanmar/290-buddh ism-and-state-power-myanmar; Peter Coclanis, "Terror in Burma: Buddhists vs. Muslims," *World Affairs* 176, no. 4 (2013): pp. 25–33.

[68] Laignee Barron, "Nationalist Monk Known as the 'Burmese bin Laden' Has Been Stopped from Spreading Hate on Facebook," *Time*, February 28, 2018, https://time.com/5178790/facebook-remo ves-wirathu; Nadica Pavlovska, "Myanmar's Wirathu: The Social Influencer in Sectarian Violence," *RSIS Commentary*, September 18, 2013, https://www.rsis.edu.sg/wp-content/uploads/2014/07/ CO13169.pdf; "The Mad Monks of Myanmar," *The Diplomat*, July 9, 2013, https://thediplomat.com/ 2013/07/the-mad-monks-of-myanmar.

[69] Joe Freeman, "Can Anyone Stop Burma's Hardline Buddhist Monks?," *The Atlantic*, September 6, 2017, https://www.theatlantic.com/international/archive/2017/09/can-anyone-stop-burmas-hardline-buddhist-monks/538992/.

[70] Hannah Beech, "When Buddhists Go Bad," *Time*, June 20, 2013, https://time.com/3800431/ when-buddhists-go-bad-photographs-by-adam-dean/.

248 RONAN LEE

As Myanmar's preeminent Buddhist-nationalist figure, Wirathu provides an exemplar for the kind of language and message commonly adopted by Buddhist-nationalist leaders. Wirathu's statements frequently engaged violent language, and he has been regularly associated with inciting anti-Muslim violence. Wirathu called mosques "enemy bases,"[71] opposed interfaith marriages, and said, "In every town, there is a crude and savage Muslim majority," warning that Muslims "target innocent young Burmese girls and rape them."[72]

Highlighting a claimed demographic threat, Wirathu declared, "Muslims are like the African carp. They breed quickly, and they are very violent and they eat their own kind. Even though they are minorities here, we are suffering under the burden they bring us."[73] Right-wing politicians like Thein Sein echoed nationalist sentiments about a demographic threat from Islam, targeting the Rohingya, whom they portrayed as colonial-era migrants. He also commonly misnamed the Rohingya, calling them Bengali (a name with pejorative connotations in Myanmar) and rejecting Rohingya claims to long-term residency, declaring for instance, "There are no Rohingya among the races. We only have Bengalis who were brought for farming [during the colonial era]."[74] Statements like this helped make the Rohingya a potent symbol of the purported demographic threat posed by Islam. These sentiments were echoed by military boss and 2021 coup instigator Min Aung Hlaing, who said, "The Bengalis were not taken into the country by Myanmar, but by the colonialists. . . . They are not the natives," and "[t]he native place of the Bengalis is really Bengal."[75] Even Aung San Suu Kyi avoided the Rohingya name, suggesting "people who believe in Islam in Rakhine state" in its place.[76]

The use of victimization narratives is common to far-right actors worldwide. Wirathu often framed Myanmar's dominant Buddhist population as victims threatened by Islam, using this victimization framing to justify rights restrictions and ultimately violence, saying for example, "We were blamed by the world,

---

[71] Marshall, "Special Report."

[72] Kate Hodal, "Buddhist Monk Uses Racism and Rumours to Spread Hatred in Burma," *The Guardian*, April 18, 2013, http://www.theguardian.com/world/2013/apr/18/buddhist-monk-spre ads-hatred-burma.

[73] Tin Aung Kyaw, "Buddhist Monk Wirathu Leads Violent National Campaign against Myanmar's Muslims," *GlobalPost*, June 21, 2013, https://theworld.org/stories/2013-06-21/buddhist-monk-wira thu-leads-violent-national-campaign-against-myanmars-muslims.

[74] Anne Gearan, "Burma's Thein Sein Says Military 'Will Always Have a Special Place' in Government," *The Washington Post*, May 20, 2013, https://www.washingtonpost.com/world/natio nal-security/burmas-thein-sein-says-military-will-always-have-a-special-place-in-government/ 2013/05/19/253c300e-c0d4-11e2-8bd8-2788030e6b44_story.html.

[75] Robert Birsel and Wa Lone, "Myanmar Army Chief Says Rohingya Muslims 'Not Natives,' Numbers Fleeing Exaggerated," *Reuters*, October 12, 2017, https://www.reuters.com/article/us-myan mar-rohingya-idUSKBN1CH0I6.

[76] "Myanmar Bans Officials from Saying 'Rohingya,'" *Al Jazeera*, June 22, 2016, https://www.aljaze era.com/news/2016/6/22/myanmar-bans-officials-from-saying-rohingya.

ISLAMOPHOBIA AND GENOCIDE   249

but we are just protecting our people and country."[77] Further illustrating how Myanmar's nationalists have been influenced by right-wing nationalism internationally, Wirathu commonly pointed to Donald Trump as a source of inspiration and to justify his extreme anti-Muslim positions: "The World singled us out as narrow-minded. But as people from the country that is the grandfather of democracy and human rights elected Donald Trump, who is similar to me in prioritizing nationalism, there will be less finger-pointing from the international community."[78] Ultimately, nationalist activism was not only carried out online. It regularly involved meetings, rallies, anti-Muslim and business boycotts, and all too often it led to violence targeting Muslims.

Buddhist nationalists created the strong perception among Myanmar's political class that nationalist values were widely supported among the country's substantial Buddhist population and that standing against them risked electoral backlash. Facing a competitive election in 2015, the country's major political parties, the USDP and NLD, raced to adopt policies and positions that would appeal to Buddhist nationalists or that at least would avoid drawing nationalist criticism. Three significant episodes prior to the 2015 national election highlight this point and are worth particular attention: nationalists' successful advocacy for Protection of Race and Religion laws, the NLD's failure to nominate a single Muslim candidate nationwide, and the ongoing mistreatment of Rohingya in Rakhine state, including the removal of legacy voting rights from Rohingya holders of "White Card" identity documents.

Strongly advocated by Buddhist nationalists, the Protection of Race and Religion legislative package was made up of four parts: the Population Control Health Care Law, the Religious Conversion Bill, the Myanmar Buddhist Women's Special Marriage Bill, and the Monogamy Bill.[79] Together, these laws represented serious limits on religion and personal freedom and were strongly opposed by civil society groups outside the nationalist space. A joint statement by 180 civil society groups declared that the laws would "destroy the stability" of Myanmar society by "inciting hatred, discrimination, conflict and tension."[80] Thein Sein's administration pushed ahead with these laws. Despite initial opposition from the NLD, then a parliamentary minority, after coming to power Aung San Suu Kyi's government did not revoke them. That these racist and sexist laws could

[77] Associated Press, "Anti-Muslim Buddhist Monk in Myanmar: Trump 'Similar to Me,'" *Voice of America*, November 17, 2016, https://www.voanews.com/a/ap-anti-muslim-buddhist-monk-in-myanmar-trump-similar-to-me/3602121.html.

[78] Associated Press, "Anti-Muslim Buddhist Monk."

[79] "Myanmar: UN Rights Experts Express Alarm at Adoption of First of Four 'Protection of Race and Religion' Bills," UNHCR, May 27, 2015, https://www.ohchr.org/en/press-releases/2015/05/myanmar-un-rights-experts-express-alarm-adoption-first-four-protection-race.

[80] "Civil Society Groups Urge Myanmar to Drop Bills to 'Protect' Religion, Race," *Radio Free Asia*, January 29, 2015, https://www.rfa.org/english/news/myanmar/bills-01292015150834.html.

remain in place for the duration of Aung San Suu Kyi's administration (2016–21) demonstrates the significant rightward movement of Myanmar's politics, with Buddhist-nationalist positions increasingly normalized.

Another indication of the power that Buddhist nationalists exercised within Myanmar's democratic system was the NLD's choice of candidates to face national and sub-national elections in 2015. In an environment in which Myanmar's online discourse was dominated by nationalist voices, the Aung San Suu Kyi–led NLD demonstrated its willingness to acquiesce to a nationalist agenda and did not field a single Muslim among the 1,151 candidates they put forward.[81] While the military-aligned USDP was expected to alienate Muslim candidates, the NLD at that time was home to many Muslim activists, and dozens applied to represent the party. All were rejected, a decision that ensured that from 2016, no Muslim would sit in parliament for the first time since independence. There would be fewer Muslim voters, too, with those Rohingya holders of White Card identity documents who retained legacy voting rights being disenfranchised just months before the 2015 election. This development broke the Rohingya's last, tenuous institutional connection with mainstream Myanmar political life. The decision to revoke White Cards and disenfranchise the Rohingya was taken by Thein Sein, but there was no meaningful opposition to the decision by Aung San Suu Kyi's NLD. This approach by Aung San Suu Kyi and the NLD was reflected, too, in the party's lack of interest in the Rohingya's ongoing repression. That Rohingya endured apartheid conditions in Rakhine state was well known to political elites, and there had been international pressure for Aung San Suu Kyi to speak up in defense of Rohingya human rights. She stayed silent.

Violence in 2012 involving ethnic Rakhine Buddhist communities and the Muslim Rohingya had resulted in around two hundred deaths and displaced around 140,000.[82] This episode was characterized by Thein Sein's government as communal conflict between Buddhists and Muslims. However, Buddhist nationalists and the authorities were accused of instigating the violence, with police and soldiers disarming Rohingya before then standing aside while Buddhist mobs stormed defenseless Muslim communities. The government's response was to physically separate Buddhists and Muslims by confining Rohingya to concentration camps and places like the Aung Mingalar ghetto, where they remain today. Displaced Buddhists were quickly returned to their home communities.

---

[81] Oliver Holmes, "Myanmar's Muslims win no seats in new parliament," *The Guardian*, November 15, 2015, https://www.theguardian.com/world/2015/nov/15/myanmars-muslims-win-no-seats-in-new-parliament.

[82] "Burma Violence: UN Calls for Rohingya Deaths Inquiry," BBC, January 24, 2014, https://www.bbc.co.uk/news/world-asia-25866350; "Situation Remains Bleak One Year on for 140,000 People Displaced in Rakhine State by Inter-Communal Violence," UN Office of the Resident and Humanitarian Coordinator, June 17, 2013, https://reliefweb.int/report/myanmar/situation-remains-bleak-one-year-140000-people-displaced-rakhine-state-inter-communal.

Presaging her response to the 2017 genocidal forced deportation of Rohingya, Aung San Suu Kyi generally followed the government's line that there was violence on both sides, a position not wholly different from Donald Trump's "blame on both sides" comment about far-right violence in Charlottesville, Virginia.[83] Even before the 2015 national election, Aung San Suu Kyi and her party were much more closely aligned with the politics of Buddhist nationalism than with any human rights agenda. Anti-Rohingya political positions had become the norm within Myanmar, routinely adopted by both the pro-military USDP and Aung San Suu Kyi's NLD.

When Aung San Suu Kyi took up the reins of political office in 2016—becoming the country's state counselor, the de facto prime minister—the NLD, while not using the deliberate, public-facing racist language of Wirathu or the Ma Ba Tha, had nonetheless committed to a range of policy approaches that undermined the standing of Muslims, leaving minorities like the Rohingya vulnerable to further serious human rights abuses. While anti-Rohingya policies had previously been instituted by an ideological military dictatorship that wished to exclude the Rohingya from Myanmar, now these same policies and practices persisted within a democratic framework and with seemingly little public opposition. A majority of Myanmar's voters were not prepared to support the USDP (the Tatmadaw's preferred party), and the NLD won the 2015 election by a landslide. But neither were there any widespread public calls to support the aspirations of (or to advocate for action to the end rights abuses against) the Rohingya, a Muslim minority whom many in Myanmar had come to regard as foreigners.[84] Despite the removal of the pro-military USDP from office, the Rohingya's collective circumstances would only deteriorate further during Aung Sang Suu Kyi's NLD administration.

Once in office, the NLD administration prioritized constitutional change, aiming to remove clauses preventing Aung San Suu Kyi (because of her marriage to a foreigner) from becoming president. Aung San Suu Kyi's public position on important matters affecting Muslims generally and the Rohingya specifically only became more closely aligned with those of Buddhist nationalists.[85] It is possible to read aspects of Aung San Suu Kyi's politics as motivated by her

---

[83] Kathryn Watson, "Trump on Charlottesville: 'I Think There's Blame on Both Sides,'" CBS News, August 15, 2017, https://www.cbsnews.com/news/trump-on-charlottesville-i-think-theres-blame-on-both-sides/.

[84] "Observing Myanmar's 2015 General Elections: Final Report," Carter Center, August 1, 2016, https://reliefweb.int/report/myanmar/observing-myanmars-2015-general-elections-final-report; "Burma Elections 2015," Human Rights Watch, November 16, 2015, https://www.hrw.org/blog-feed/burma-elections-2015; Michael Martin, *Burma's 2015 Parliamentary Elections: Issues for Congress* (Congressional Research Service, March 2016), https://sgp.fas.org/crs/row/R44436.pdf.

[85] Aung San Suu Kyi, *Aung San* (Brisbane: University of Queensland Press, 1984); Ronan Lee, "A Politician, Not an Icon: Aung San Suu Kyi's Silence on Myanmar's Muslim Rohingya," *Islam and Christian–Muslim Relations* 25, no. 3 (2014): pp. 321–33.

own personal commitment to Buddhist nationalism, and there is certainly evidence to support this, including her favorable writing about her family's nationalist credentials and her statements and policy approaches toward the Rohingya. However, whatever the views of the party leader, there is strong evidence that by the time the NLD came to power, mainstream political attitudes within Myanmar had come to accept Buddhist-nationalist positions as the norm.

Policies of Rohingya oppression like Rakhine state's apartheid system, once instituted, continued throughout Aung San Suu Kyi's time as state counselor. Aung San Suu Kyi did engage former UN Secretary-General Kofi Annan to undertake a study and make recommendations to improve the situation in Rakhine state, but the Annan Commission's report presentation was quickly followed by the Tatmadaw's 2017 "clearance operation" changing the domestic and international policy focus from seeking a long-term solution to managing the refugee crisis. Annan's pivotal proposal of delinking ethnicity from Myanmar citizenship has been ignored.[86] Foreshadowing Aung San Suu Kyi's later high-profile disregard for Rohingya human rights, in 2016, she questioned the accounts of Rohingya women who detailed Tatmadaw atrocities, including widespread sexual violence, by making a Trump-esque capitalized two-word post, "FAKE RAPE," to the official state counselor's website and Facebook page.[87] Human rights groups have frequently documented Tatmadaw use of sexual violence as a military tactic, and Aung San Suu Kyi's seeming indifference to the accounts of Rohingya women reflected a wider indifference by her and her administration toward human rights violations against the Rohingya. This sent a strong message to the Tatmadaw that future violence against the Rohingya was unlikely to be met by any strong opposition from Aung San Suu Kyi or her government, an effective green light to the 2017 genocidal forced deportation of Rohingya to Bangladesh. That Tatmadaw troops then violently deported most Rohingya from Myanmar in 2017 should have come as no surprise, and neither should Aung San Suu Kyi's defense of the military's genocidal campaign.

If It Can Happen There, It Can Happen Here

The Rohingya's exclusion from Myanmar's political mainstream, the genocide against them that this enabled, and their high-profile 2017 forced deportation provide a disturbing illustration of how quickly Islamophobia can be weaponized

[86] "Towards a Peaceful, Fair and Prosperous Future for the People of Rakhine: Final Report of the Advisory Commission on Rakhine State," Kofi Annan Foundation, 2016, https://www.rakhinecommission.org/the-final-report.

[87] Jonah Fisher, "Hounded and Ridiculed for Complaining of Rape," BBC, March 17, 2017, https://www.bbc.co.uk/news/magazine-39204086.

to diminish the social and political standing of a previously well-integrated minority. Using language about demographic threat that mirrors Great Replacement narratives, Myanmar's Buddhist nationalists successfully advocated for policies that severely limited Muslim rights and had devastating real-world consequences for the Rohingya. While Islamophobic policies might have been expected from Myanmar's military rulers, these practices—continued and aided by improved access to modern media technologies—seemingly achieved widespread community support in a democratic context. Despite Myanmar's moves toward democracy, Buddhist nationalists were able to normalize anti-Muslim speech and to capture the state apparatus. Once this happened, the path to genocide was a short one and occurred with little meaningful public outcry. This should provide a serious warning that in democratic contexts, normalized hate rhetoric can lead to atrocity crimes against even previously well-integrated groups.

PART IV
CONCLUSION
Lessons from South Africa

15

Confronting Islamophobia

Defeating Colonial Bigotries, Learning From South Africa

Ebrahim Rasool

The Gathering Clouds

The phenomenon of Islamophobia is no longer confined to antagonism toward Muslims by those whose origins are predominantly in the West. That antagonism—in attitude, speech, and action—is shifting from its Western axis, where relatively emergent and smaller Muslim minorities assert citizenship. It is now a phenomenon pervading longer-standing and sizeable Asian Muslim communities. These include the Uyghur Muslims in China, the significant minority in India, the Rohingya in Burma, and other settings[1]—antagonism against whom is worthy of confrontation—alongside Islamophobia in the West.

Shifts in demographics may well illustrate Islamophobia as a phenomenon of discrimination based on racial, ethnic, religious, and other cultural and physical distinctions. But increasingly it is mobilized and purposed by the political shifts in society, including the growth and emergence of populism and the attainment of power by certain right-wing or malignant political forces. Such power is either formal and affects the legislative and institutional framework of government or informal through the power to shape the discourse and narrative in society, both of which shaped apartheid South Africa.

As a Muslim who grew up in apartheid South Africa, I experienced discrimination and dispossession as both Black and Muslim. Apartheid was an instrument of oppression applied by a white minority colonial regime with laser precision: an ability to detect difference from or, rather, inferiority to, the white, European, civilized template, followed by the application of differentiated, even hierarchical, measures against each such different community. Such differentiated attention to detail was the outcome of the needs of the white rulers to impose division among those oppressed by unevenly applying both benefits and punishment. In this context, just like women started with a double bind

---

[1] See the respective chapters on these groups in this volume.

Ebrahim Rasool, *Confronting Islamophobia* In: *Global Islamophobia and the Rise of Populism*. Edited by: Sahar F. Aziz and John L. Esposito, Oxford University Press. © Oxford University Press 2024.
DOI: 10.1093/oso/9780197648995.003.0015

(race and gender), Muslims, who were overwhelmingly of 'non-white' African and Malay slave and Indian merchant heritage, started with one, too (race and religion). South African colonialism had a complex mission of dispossessing, discriminating, civilizing, and Christianizing in sophisticated and complex ways with tailor-made instruments of oppression against groups within the Black majority, while discriminating against all who were Black.

This phenomenon, however, is not a 21st-century one but an inherited narrative as old as colonialism itself that has been rendered normal and integrated into the dominant discourses, reaching as far back as the works of William Shakespeare.

The Tempest: The Template of Colonialism

The colonial precepts rendering themselves as a normality that masks heinous crimes has persisted for centuries as racism, xenophobia, anti-Semitism, and misogyny. If Shakespeare were a yardstick of colonialism's booming era, then these themes were not simply the unthought but were actively digested in the process of normalization. Similarly, Shakespeare's *The Tempest* allows for new ways of understanding Islamophobia as yet another step in the evolution of colonial discourse, the unfolding of discrimination and dispossession. Indeed, it is an illustration of how attitude and thought transitions to speech and action when the power differential increases significantly in favor of the supposed superior and against the supposed inferior. Shakespeare's renaissance colonial discourse in *The Tempest* must be read not in the light of its colonial prospects with its stated noble intents but rather in the light of the colonial aftermath—of conquest, dispossession, slavery, genocide, and a range of bigotries.

Shakespeare's *The Tempest* is a tale of a scholarly man of letters, Prospero, who is so devoted to participating in the civilizational proclivities of literature, science, and art that he is deposed and exiled from his governorship of Naples to a land purportedly uninhabited, except by those unlettered and masterless who, in their unsupervised masterless-ness, remain wild and savage and potentially rebellious, as epitomized by Caliban. Hence is born the enlightened colonizer bringing the gifts of education and civilization to the savage, who would do well to learn how to subject libido to discipline, body to soul, and passion to reason.

However, because of Caliban's persistence in his barbarism, his resistance to being civilized, and his rebellion to colonialism, Prospero's daughter, Miranda, retaliates as follows:

> Abhorred slave, which any print of goodness will not take . . . when thou did not, savage, know thine own meaning . . . I endowed thy purposes with words that

CONFRONTING ISLAMOPHOBIA   259

made them known. But thy vile race . . . had that in't which good natures could not abide to be with; therefore wast thou deservedly confined within this rock.[2]

Is the Muslim identity and adherence to Islam, signifying unevolved barbarism and savagery, not equivalent to the obduracy of Caliban, the abhorred slave? Fanon's interpretation of Caliban's choice is that he, the colonized, is forced to live out Prospero's dream of being civilized—the imperative of the Black man to "turn white, or disappear."[3]

In Shakespeare's *The Tempest*, all these themes are brought to a head. The masterless, savage, wild man is essentially antisocial and therefore a threat to civilized society. Lest he foment a counterculture within society, he requires the restraining influences of discipline and subjection to a civilizing project, further necessitating constant surveillance, regular punishment, and even expulsion from society. This context is the sum total of the historical colonial experience transposed today into an almost perfected Islamophobia.

The threat from the so-called wild man is the most important glue that holds the colonizers together and gives them internal coherence amid ruling-class squabbles. Prospero, Caliban's colonizer, reconciles with his brother, who usurped his throne in the face of such a threat from the colonized. Is Islamophobia not a glue that creates coherence across left and right, liberal and conservative, religious and secularist, and nationalist and communist today? More significantly, the threat may not actually exist but may often need to be exaggerated, even manufactured, to paper over the many fissures in such discriminatory and oppressive societies.

The conclusion is that the savage (the Muslim) is deemed completely irredeemable, irreformable, and impervious to any influence, education, civilizing, or progress: "A born devil, on whose Nature, Nurture can never stick."[4]

Edward Said, in his epic work *Orientalism*, gives a clue that nurturing is not the objective: "Orientalism is not simply a discourse that produces a certain knowledge of the Orient, but a Western style for dominating, restructuring and having authority over the Orient."[5]

Reform of the savage is not the answer, but neither is coexistence or the harmony of difference; it is domination with authority. Such domination results in what John Nichols describes as the "metamorphised wild man," who submits to Queen Elizabeth as follows:

[2] William Shakespeare, *The Tempest*, Act I: Scene ii.
[3] Frantz Fanon, "The So-Called Dependency Complex of Colonised People," in *Black Skin, White Masks* (London: Pluto Press, 1986), p. 107.
[4] Shakespeare, *Tempest*, Act IV: Scene i.
[5] Edward Said, *Orientalism* (London: Routledge 1978), pp. 2–3.

260 EBRAHIM RASOOL

O Queen, I must confesse, it is not without cause these civile people so rejoice
that you should give them lawes. Since I which live at large, a wild and savage
man, and have ronne a wilful race since first my life began, do here submit my-
self, beseeching you to serve.[6]

The Tempest is thus an ambiguous reaction to a growing colonial enterprise.
It is ambiguous because Shakespeare, like others of his class, was a beneficiary
of such colonialism: the very idea of exploration beyond known borders, the
encounters with the strange and the exotic, the inflow of resources like riches
and spices that made life infinitely better and more convenient, and the opportunity both to fuel civilization at home and to export it abroad. But the emergence
from the Dark Ages and the onset of the Enlightenment did not easily compass
inhumanity. Yet civilized sensibility, while not allowing rampant discrimination,
dispossession, and dehumanization at home, not just tolerated such abroad but
actively justified them.

It was in this justification that the production of stereotypes was critical and
in which the threat of imminent civilizational danger was amplified. The two,
in tandem, created the platform for double standards. The stereotypes of the
wild man, the savage, and the barbarian created the idea that the colonials or
the Indigenous or the Other were subhuman and, therefore, not to be treated as,
or deemed to be, human. This conception, in turn, strengthened the idea that
their natures, or natural state, needed disciplining and restraining, surveillance
and patrolling, and repression and punishment. The means needed to subject
the Other may not be acceptable *in* a civilization but were necessary *for* a civilization. Left unchecked, the instinctive, libidinous, and undisciplined nature of
the savage poses danger: danger to women—hence the punishment by Prospero
of Caliban after the latter's attempted "rape" of Miranda—and to society. Society
cannot countenance a subculture that ultimately leads to resistance and rebellion
on the margins of society.

How different is this to the world today in which Islamophobia flourishes?
Muslims are experienced as a subculture when they enter the colonial or Western
heartlands and are, therefore, subjected to measures of containment. Yet in the
Muslim homelands, a different standard is allowed, effectively a triple bypass of
democracy, human rights, and freedom (especially for women) in which Western
values are not the precondition for politics and commerce. Islam is infantilized
because, ostensibly, the religion and its sharia has not evolved to a civilizational
level because its primordial nature is so deep that nurture cannot undo it. Yet
Muslim deviance from the democratic and rights norm can be tolerated, and

[6] John Nichols, *The Progress and Public Processions of Queen Elizabeth in 1823* (New York: Burt
Franklin, 1966), p. 436.

geopolitical accommodations can be made, *if* confined geographically to the periphery—the Muslim homelands! But should the Other—the wild, the savage, and the barbarian—transgress these geographical boundaries and come into proximity with the civilized worlds, then the "Other" poses an existential danger to the very foundations of civilization, a danger posed by sharia to the values of civilization, a danger posed by the hijab to the iconography of civilization, a danger posed by the righteously angry to the supply lines of resources that feed the civilization. Then immigration, diversity, and integration are a curse and no longer the blessing they used to be when, for example, America was originally peopled by the refugees and the downtrodden from Europe.

Historically, the surveillance and punishment of the savage were a responsibility shared between the geopolitical gendarme with the capacity to intervene militarily and the local "metamorphised wild man" (e.g., the array of local authoritarians imposed on, and kept in power over, the former colonies, ready to serve the civilized master).[7] For both the gendarme and the local Muslim authoritarian, extremism must be constructed and maintained as the stereotype for the whole of the Muslim community, notwithstanding the fact that extremists are more of a danger to other Muslims who differ with them religiously, politically, and in gender. The extremist becomes more necessary for the Islamophobe when the Other seeks citizenship in the colonial centers, which leads to a ramping up of surveillance that comes ready with a self-fulfilling narrative and is always on the alert to avert an existential threat.

Right-wing populism has certainly given momentum to Islamophobia. The right-wing populists may not have invented it, but they have learned from even liberal administrations about how to purpose Islamophobia. Islamophobia is a useful domestic distraction from real crises in society, a source of national coherence by otherwise fractious ruling elites in the face of threat, and the fig leaf behind which to cement an alliance with their "metamorphised wild men"[8] in the Middle East, to bind them to the colonial master in the West, and to subject them to the regional power in the Muslim heartlands—Israel.

The Cape of Storms: Muslims as Slaves and Outlaws

The Tempest was written by William Shakespeare as a reflection of colonialism around the 17th century and was performed for the first time in 1611. By this time, the Portuguese colonial explorers had already—in the 15th century—set foot in the Cape. *The Tempest* coincides with the occupation by the Dutch of

---

[7] Nichols, *Progress*, p. 436.
[8] Nichols, *Progress*, p. 436.

both Indonesia and what was then called the Cape of Storms: Cape Town, South Africa. By 1658, the Dutch brought the first Muslims to Cape Town as slaves and exiles from Indonesia, supplemented later with others from India, Africa, and elsewhere. These groups would become the so-called Malay community of Muslims who evolved into the Muslims of South Africa today.[9]

Today's Post-Apartheid Muslims

The experience of post-apartheid South African Muslims today seems substantially at odds with the earlier situation in South Africa, as well as with the minority condition that Muslims find themselves in across the world. In some countries, Muslims have been around for about as many centuries as they were in South Africa—Indians in Asia and African Americans in the United States come to mind. In others, however, including most of Europe as well as the recent immigration of Arab and Asian Muslims to the United States, Muslims are relative newcomers. Very few of these Muslim communities would describe their situation positively, pointing to examples of unfriendliness, suspicion, and hostility toward them. Indeed, South Africa may well be a beacon of hope for enjoying the right to live in ways that are consistent with their identity as Muslims.

When visiting South Africa today, many people, both Muslim and non-Muslim, are quite confused about the size of the Muslim population in the country. They cannot believe that Muslims make up at most one million in a population of fifty-nine million—a mere 1.7 percent.[10] This statistic is confounded by the visibility of Muslims in the broader nation, the presence of Islamic symbols, the spectrum and variety of practices that are observed by Muslims, and the generally constructive role played by Muslims in the broader society.

The presence and acceptability of Muslims in South Africa is confirmed by an abundance of halal-friendly food outlets, the amplified echo of the adhan and the minarets on the South African skyline. The freedom of Muslims is evidenced by the variety in the observance of dress codes from the simple headscarves to the full veil, from the Arab *thoub* to the Indian kurta, and from traditional African to modern Western. The contribution of Muslims to the nation is in how they occupy their positions in the boardroom, classroom, courtroom, caucus room, and game room. Such active engagement of Muslims with their fellow citizens—harmoniously and, sometimes, robustly—all speak to a community that is at home in its country. This situation is not that of most Muslim minorities.

---

[9] Jackie Loos, *Echoes of Slavery—Voices from South Africa's Past* (Cape Town: David Philip, 2004), pp. 47–48.

[10] "Official Guide to South Africa, 2019," Statistics SA, accessed February 16, 2022, https://www.gov.za/about-sa/south-africas-people.

CONFRONTING ISLAMOPHOBIA   263

But this position in South Africa, where Muslims are more integral to the nation as a whole, has not been easily or instantly achieved. In the evolution of this coexistence lies the lesson and example of constructing an abode of peace, security, integration, engagement, and equality for Muslims and all fellow citizens. In learning these lessons, we must also be aware that there are fundamental differences in the evolution of the South African Muslim community compared to that of others in the West—an important one being that this community has evolved over three centuries. In order to engage critically with the phenomenon of Islamophobia, it is important to reflect on South Africa's path from being hostile to Muslims to integrating them as part of the South African mosaic.

Roots in Slavery and Exile

The establishment and persistence of Islam in South Africa—at the Cape of Storms—more than three hundred years ago is a tribute to the resilience of exiles and slaves from other Dutch colonies who were brought to the Cape to blunt the anti-colonial struggles they led, and as a pool of labor to service Dutch needs as they developed transport routes between the colonies and Europe.[11] As time went on, other slaves were brought from the rest of Africa to join their Malay counterparts and found in this community both solidarity and spiritual sustenance. This Malay community had spiritual and political luminaries among the political exiles, who facilitated the integration of slaves—Malays, Indians, Africans, and the Indigenous—into one ethnic identity, the Cape Malays, and an overarching religious identity, Islam, with the formation of a pidgin language, Afrikaans.[12] This environment made for a durable Muslim presence in South Africa.

Almost two centuries later, in 1860, on the east coast at Port Natal, the British colonizers started the transfer of Indian indentured laborers from places like Madras and Calcutta to South Africa to work on the sugar plantations; traders soon followed.[13] This development started the second major wave of Muslims, as merchants, to South Africa. This wave, unlike in the Cape, had a different process of identity formation, as common conditions of hardship forced them to seek ways, difficult as they were, to transcend their fault lines of religion, class, and

[11] Yusuf Da Costa and Achmat Davids, *Pages from Cape Muslim History* (Cape Town: Naqshabandi-Muhammadi SA, 1994), p. 13.

[12] Alan Mountain, *An Unsung Heritage—Perspectives on Slavery* (Cape Town: Davis Philip, 2004), p. 98.

[13] Hermann Giliomee and Bernard Mbenga, *New History of South Africa* (Cape Town: Tafelberg, 2007), p. 149.

264 EBRAHIM RASOOL

caste. They sought refuge in a common Indian identity, which found expression in a variety of languages, music, and culture.

Conditions were hard for the early Muslims in South Africa, and these difficulties persisted in various forms for about three hundred years. The political exiles were serving out banishment orders or jail sentences; in fact, one of the first prisoners on Robben Island was Shaykh Madura, a Muslim leader who was exiled and in whose footsteps Nelson Mandela followed.[14] In a speech to Muslims later, it was clear that, from his grave, Mandela sought inspiration and solace when he spent his many years as a prisoner on Robben Island.

The slaves were the property of the Dutch masters and subjected to the usual conditions of abuse. The indentured labor system was the British compensation for labor after they had formally outlawed slavery but remained in need of labor.[15] The conditions were brutal; the laborers toiled unceasingly and enjoyed no rights, and the chances of ever returning to their countries of origin were remote.

Anti-Muslim Practices

Particularly in the Cape, the Dutch banned and outlawed the practice of Islam. Disobedience carried one of three consequences: confiscation of property, imprisonment, or execution. This law remained in force for about one century and resulted in the absence of any visible Islam in the form of mosques and other institutions.[16] Furthermore, the apartheid system introduced by the National Party in the 20th century deemed both the ethnic and religious identities of Muslims to be inferior, with no recognition for the practices of Islam, which was considered a "false faith" by the apartheid state and its theological bedrock, the Dutch Reformed Church.[17] Apartheid was the ultimate expression of Christian nationalism and was infused into every aspect of life alongside the racial separation and the systematic dispossession of Black South Africans.

The last two apartheid projects—discrimination and dispossession—were rooted in a Christianizing and civilizing mission. Additionally, whites conceived of themselves during the Cold War as a bulwark against an anti-Christian, Communist tide engulfing the African continent. As with all non-apartheid ideologies and philosophies, Islam, too, was seen as subversive to the apartheid

[14] Mountain, *Unsung Heritage*, p. 107.

[15] Giliomee and Mbenga, *New History frica*, p. 149.

[16] R. E. van der Ross, *Up from Slavery—Slaves at the Cape* (Cape Town: Ampersand Press, 2005), pp. 71–72.

[17] Muhammad Haron, "Three Centuries of NGK Mission amongst Cape Muslims," *Journal of Muslim Minority Affairs* 19, no. 1 (1999): p. 115.

CONFRONTING ISLAMOPHOBIA   265

ideology because although apartheid deemed mixed marriages illegal, imams were solemnizing marriages across color lines, mosques were welcoming of all races, and Muslims were also showing leadership in the struggle against apartheid as they had in the struggles against slavery and colonialism. Muslims may well have been Prospero's and Miranda's "abhorred slave, which any print of goodness will not take" and whose "vile race had that in't which good natures could not abide."[18]

Standing for Justice

Alongside enslaved Muslims were also exiled religious leaders who led the anti-colonial struggles in Indonesia, and once exiled to the Cape in South Africa, they continued their opposition, and therefore, from the early years of slavery, one such banished spiritual leader, Shaykh Yusuf of Makassar, made his place of banishment a refuge for escaped slaves, a place of spiritual healing for the broken-hearted, a site of restoration of identity for those removed from their homelands, and a place of dignity for the dehumanized. Islam was the integrator. Muslims were respected for their dignity in the face of oppression, Muslim leadership was welcomed in the struggle against colonialism and apartheid, and Islam was seen as a source of inspiration for justice, peace, and equality. This contention was evidenced from the dubious campaign by Muslims not to obey the colonial burial rules in a smallpox epidemic[19] as well as the inspiration that Muslims drew from campaigns led by Mahatma Gandhi, the prominence of Muslim names like that of Yusuf Dadoo, Moulvi Cachalia, Ahmed Kathrada, and Abdullah Abdurahman, together with his daughter, Cissie Gool. The leadership of the broad liberation movement and sacrifices made by prominent Muslims like Imam Abdullah Haroon and Ahmed Timol, who were tortured to death by the Security Police, gave rise to Muslim organizations like the Call of Islam, which fought apartheid alongside other South Africans. Throughout the 350 years of Islam in South Africa, even at the bitterest moments of suffering and at the height of slavery, to be a Muslim was to belong, in a context of marginalization.

Emerging from a Long, Dark Night

It would be wrong to exaggerate the extent of Muslim involvement in the anti-colonial and anti-apartheid struggles because Muslims, too, vacillated

[18] Shakespeare, *Tempest*, Act I: Scene ii.
[19] Achmat Davids, *The History of the Tana Baru* (Cape Town: 1985), pp. 85–87.

between the impulses of co-option to apartheid and liberation from it and between preserving ritual Islam and advancing liberating Islam. But at the time of Nelson Mandela's release from prison and the preparation for democracy at the hand of a negotiated settlement, enough Muslims had made their mark in the struggle against apartheid to identify the Muslim community as a force for good and a community of virtue, and to identify Islam as a religion that had an inclusive and confident impulse for fairness and humaneness. These were the Muslims who took active roles in the broad liberation and interfaith movements or who aligned their Islamic vehicles to the immediate objectives of the liberation movement for a humane, equal, nonracial, free, and democratic society.

Muslims' experiences in South Africa have evolved from severe suffering; deprivation of rights (including the right to worship as Muslims); discrimination and prejudice; institutionalized racism and religious intolerance; the demonization of non-apartheid ideologies like Islam, African nationalism, and communism; and the humiliation visited upon the Other through systematized and institutionalized discrimination.

For Muslims today, looking back and utilizing a contemporary lexicon that includes a word like *Islamophobia*, this humiliation may be seen as a manifestation of Islamophobia. An analysis of a state not recognizing Islamic beliefs and Muslim people may strengthen that conclusion. The application of such discrimination—delegitimizing the Muslim identity, not registering Muslim marriages, forcing parents to register Muslim children as "illegitimate"—would stand out today as the nadir of the practice of Islamophobia. Yet South African Muslims progressed to being equal and free contributors to their society. What are the insights we can gain out of the long history of the evolution of the Muslims of South Africa that can be useful to other contexts?

Battening the Hatches: Resisting the Hurricane

Mindful of this condensed history of Islam in South Africa and using the power of hindsight, it would be useful to interrogate the concept of Islamophobia and the notion of hostility toward Muslims as it may have manifested in South Africa. The apartheid tragedy, the United States' rage after 9/11, Israeli occupation in Palestine, the Bharatiya Janata Party's excesses in India, the assault on the Uyghurs in China, the plight of the Rohingya in Myanmar, genocide in Bosnia, forced assimilation in France, and the many instances in which Muslims have suffered at the hands of others cannot simply be put under the label of *Islamophobia* or *hostility toward Muslims*. Shakespeare's *The Tempest* shows us a broader template of bigotry.

There remains a need to both analyze the causal factors and to determine calculated, strategy-driven processes and actions for lasting solutions. Shortcuts exacerbate our victimhood and allow us not to take responsibility for solutions, thus incapacitating us for agency. In interrogating the slavery, colonialism, and apartheid visited upon Muslims in South Africa, we can begin to make some tentative observations.

Locating the Anti-Muslim in the Anti-Human

Isolated from a broader context, the suffering of Muslims over three centuries would appear as an affirmation of Islamophobia and hostility to Muslims. Indeed, the Dutch and British colonialists may have had a combination of fear and hatred of Muslims, but this motivation was not the only one for what they did. They needed labor to maintain a supply line from their colonies to the colonial center. The colonialists also needed systems to maintain law and order in the colonies. They would not allow interruptions to the process of plunder and accumulation from anti-colonial forces, so they dealt with them.

The South African experience shows how the Dutch were also systematically dispossessing and exterminating the Khoisan in the Cape as well as fighting frontier wars against the Xhosa and the Zulu in the East.[20] Farther north in Africa, Europeans had unfolded the most reprehensible transatlantic slave trade of Africans who were either displaced or killed.

Apartheid institutionally discriminated against Muslims but not simply as Muslims. They were discriminated against also as nonwhites: as Malays, Indians, Africans; as merchants who should not be allowed into certain markets; and as adherents to a "false faith."[21] Christian liberation theologians, too, were made to suffer. The same Afrikaners were followers of Hitler and subscribed to anti-Semitism. Communists also bore their share of repression.

A denigration of the Other as subhuman justifies such inhumane and heinous crimes. Shakespeare's *The Tempest* is an illustration of exactly what this project entails. Colonialism, apartheid, and other systems that systematically discriminate, humiliate, and eliminate the Other must be based on an idea of superiority and inferiority, the indispensable and the dispensable, human and less than human. In South Africa, this idea centered on whiteness, Christian-ness, and the civilized-ness of the oppressor. These were the core constructs of superiority that allowed for callous and inhuman behavior by fairly educated people. Conversely,

---

[20] Giliomee and Mbenga, *New History*, pp. 73–75.
[21] Haron, "Three Centuries," p. 115.

268 EBRAHIM RASOOL

constructs of inferiority were constructs around the non- or subhuman-ness of the colonials.

Avoiding Muslim Exceptionalism

We must always be cautious of elevating one form of hatred or bigotry as the defining feature of what is being done to people, at the expense of other forms that also cause suffering. Islamophobia, racism, sexism, anti-Semitism, xenophobia, homophobia, and all related intolerances are manifestations of prejudice and discrimination that, in turn, are the offspring of ignorance and fear of the Other. It reflects an inability to manage difference, always coveting another's power, freedom, or land and resources. It, therefore, becomes important to look beyond the given—the form in which the prejudice, discrimination, or intolerance presents itself—to determine or analyze what in essence and at the core is being coveted or appropriated and to devise the appropriate responses to it.

Colonialism banned and criminalized the practice of Islam. Apartheid was the political expression of Christian nationalism, and Islam was regarded as a "false faith," and its adherents were humiliated.[22] But Muslims were also removed from the areas where they grew up and were dispossessed of their property, and certain professions were proscribed for them.[23] These changes occurred in a context of general dispossession and subjugation of the colonized and oppressed and the even more severe brutalization and dehumanization of other Indigenous peoples. The Khoi and the San, as first peoples, were subjected to genocide, while the Xhosa and the Zulu were forced violently off the land. The South African experience should also be viewed in the context of an intolerance of all ideas and ideologies different from the ruling ones, including communism, African nationalism, militant liberalism, liberation Christianity, and others, in addition to Islam.

Was this Islamophobia and hostility to Islam, or was it a variant on the theme of a general intolerance of and attack on the Other? Were Muslims the ultimate source and target of this brutality and others the collateral damage? Or was Islamophobia the specialized weapon of choice against Muslims within a general war on Blacks and other ideologies? The evidence suggests that Muslims did suffer but not exclusively. They suffered under a general yoke of intolerance and oppression that we today call Islamophobia, which was a tailor-made weapon for one component of the many who opposed colonialism and apartheid.

---

[22] Haron, "Three Centuries," p. 115.
[23] Giliomee and Mbenga, *New History*, p. 264.

South African Muslims, from the earliest arrival to the moment of freedom, did not believe that their suffering was only because they were Muslims. Had they subscribed to the uniqueness of their situation of oppression, and had they monopolized victimhood for themselves and elevated their pain, they would have been unable to recognize the suffering in others, to make common cause with them, to enter with them into life-and-death struggles for survival, and to adopt a set of common objectives that would realize freedom from oppression and a state of equality.

The post-apartheid challenge that faced the Muslim community was what they were going to do when the common enemy of colonialism and apartheid was defeated. Would Muslims retain the impulse to goodness and virtue? Would we still be able to maintain the balance of being both distinct from, and connected to, the broader society? How would we want the wrongs of the past to be righted in the new South Africa that was at hand, for society as well as for Muslims? As it turned out, Muslims contributed to a nationally transformed society with benefits for all and a better dispensation for Muslims as Muslims.

From Exclusivity to Solidarity

Through long periods in the history of South Africa, Muslims were the victims of Islamophobia but always as fellow sufferers, not exclusive victims. This realization was the point of empathy and common cause that offered a path to solidarity and joint struggle. On one hand, failing to recognize Islamophobia as part of the broader struggle for survival and human dignity in current conditions, we make it impossible to reach out and build partnerships, coalitions, and alliances. On the other hand, by elevating Islamophobia and conferring a status of uniqueness on Muslim suffering, we lessen the possibility of collaboration with millions of other victims. We also run the risk, through extreme rhetoric and violent methods, of adding Islam and Muslims to such victims' list of things to fear and combat.

The opportunities that emerge from a nonexclusive perspective to Islamophobia and an ability to locate Islamophobia alongside its other siblings like racism, xenophobia, homophobia, anti-Semitism, sexism, and others are that many Muslims in India can make common cause for greater dignity and inclusiveness with the Dalits, who also face severe exclusion and indignity. Muslims in the United States can make common cause with other immigrants like Latinos who experience xenophobia and daily face deportations and the separation of families, as well as African Americans through the Black Lives Matter campaigns who bear the brunt of racism. Muslims in the United Kingdom can make common cause with other minorities—both ethnic and religious—who

270   EBRAHIM RASOOL

have a daily battle with a dominant Anglo-Saxon, Protestant culture. Muslims in France can make common cause with African immigrants who, too, face discrimination regularly. And Muslims have natural allies with women in society, who carry the daily burden of sexism.

What Muslims globally can learn from South African Muslims is the art of politics and, specifically, *how* to engage in the politics of cooperation. South African Muslims learned that where we share common values with other communities, we have the prospect of principled alliances through interfaith and Abrahamic movements. Where Muslims share the strategic objectives of a free society, they enter into strategic coalitions like liberation movements with nationalists, communists, and liberals. And where we need immediate short-term cooperation, we enter into the politics of the popular front. Although Muslims in South Africa have actively engaged in the anti-apartheid struggle, Muslim minorities elsewhere, in contexts of Islamophobia against them and other forms of discrimination against fellow citizens, have been loath to enter into alliances, coalitions, and popular fronts. They often stand on misguided theological reasoning that their religion prohibits such, or they fear exacerbating their suffering through such visibility.

"Even against Yourselves . . . "

In post-apartheid South Africa, one moment had the greatest potential for Islamophobia and hostility against Muslims. A group of Muslims were inspired in 1979 by the revolution in Iran and posited the idea that the "only solution [was] Islamic revolution," which they used to try to influence the anti-apartheid struggle for their narrow and exclusivist pursuit of an Islamic State. This group became the most active component of People against Gangsterism and Drugs, an organization that evolved into an urban terror group. Under the guise of fighting drugs and crime, they targeted drug merchants and politicians whom they disliked, bombed the homes of criminals and rival Ulema (the body of Mullahs (Muslim scholars trained in Islam and Islamic law) who are the interpreters of Islam's sciences and doctrines and laws and the chief guarantors of continuity in the spiritual and intellectual history of the Islamic community), and terrorized the tourist infrastructure of Cape Town. They began to undo three hundred years of trust and coexistence between Muslims and their compatriots. At this moment, acceptance of Muslims could have become fear of Muslims, and fear could have turned into hatred of Muslims and Islam in a country where we had all fought injustice side by side over three centuries. It was the courage of the Muslim leadership to stand up to this group and to refuse to be cowed by fear or silenced by false solidarity that dissipated the terror group and rallied the broader community.

So often, Muslims find themselves understanding the ultimate causes of the anger that burns within them, but at the same time they recoil from that which is said and done in the name of Islam and Muslims, as a response to those causes. When those Muslims, ostensibly responding to real conditions of provocation, appropriate the symbols and language of Islam for an agenda of terror and mayhem, then there can be no solidarity in the name of Islam, despite our recognition of the causal factors. We become complicit in that which creates a genuine fear of Islam and Muslims when we do not contest unequivocally the Islamicness of violence against civilians and divisive rhetoric.

All of these feed into a vicious cycle. Like the proverbial chicken-and-egg debate, does Islamophobia breed extremism, or is extremism the cause of Islamophobia? Frankly, it does not matter any longer—the one feeds the other, and both must be collapsed and their high priests disarmed. Our voice must be the first and the loudest in condemning the hijacking of our religion, lest we cede the ground to the Islamophobes. Unless we do this, every side will find a historical antecedent to justify itself and its actions, scrambling to occupy the moral high ground in an endless contest for victimhood. The process to undo this vicious cycle, to collapse extremism, and to ensure that we systematically tackle Islamophobia—in word, deed, and attitude—is one that relies on the other not to make the first move but to work simultaneously, in good faith, and one that relies on our removing each other from being the other's hostage.

Being in, and of, the Land

The South Africa of Nelson Mandela opened conditions of democracy, human rights, and freedom within which Muslims could emerge from the margins, find a home, and regain their voice. But our voice cannot be one that remains implacably faithful to the heartlands from which our forebears were either forcibly removed or from which they departed to seek a better life, free from either stultifying poverty or authoritarian oppression. We are not in a new land to recreate the old heartland with our inherited prejudices, to indulge our misconceptions about democracy or rights, to heighten our expectations of exclusivity and exceptionalism, and to deepen our sense of identity as exclusively or primarily religious (Muslim), ethnic (Arab), or national (Somali). We need to insert the reality of where we *are*, not only where we are *from*. We need to recalibrate our identity to include being South African, American, or European and to adopt positive norms that come from that, while infusing some of our culture, values, and practices into that society, thus enriching it.

In South Africa, we did not understand democracy as compromising the sovereignty of God but as the platform from which to create space for the better

272 EBRAHIM RASOOL

worship of God. The condition for the effective use of that space is participation in individual and organized capacities, and not simply Muslim-only organized formations. Muslims are also civic, professional, sporting, economic, and political beings. Being part of the fabric of society is the immunization against Islamophobia and anti-Islam hatred. We learned this lesson on the eve of democracy when I convened the National Muslim Conference and we gathered our thoughts to insert our aspirations as South Africans, as well as South African Muslims, into the new Bill of Rights and the Constitution of our free, nondiscriminatory, and democratic society.

This becomes possible when we weld together the ability to be focused on the ultimate objectives of Islam and the higher intents of being Muslim and the ability to integrate into our new societies. We can be both *in* (inhabitants) and *of* (citizens) the land when we carefully discern among isolation, assimilation, and integration. They are not synonyms but words with nuanced, significantly different paths to coexistence.

Isolation denotes coexisting in the same space; it signifies a form of separateness whereby, for example, a Muslim community can live without learning the language of the country, knowing fellow citizens, and participating in the national and community life because the Muslim community members have their own schools and their own mosque with an imported imam, and they believe that while they earn a better living there, they are uncontaminated by the West. *Assimilation* means to become the same. This demand is often made of Muslims and other immigrants upon entering a country such as France. You are required to leave your religion, language, culture, dress code, and identity at the border and to adopt everything from the new country completely. This isolation is unacceptable.

The South Africa of Nelson Mandela chose the mode of coexistence to be one of *integration* but in the sense that fundamentally carries the root word *integrity*. Muslims entered into a compact whereby we would respect the integrity of the whole society, which includes being free of prejudice against all. In turn, we would have our integrity as Muslims respected to be free to worship, to carry our markers of identity, and to enjoy the equality we share with others. This made us *in*, and *of*, the land.

Secular or Secularist?

Given South Africa's complex relationship with religion under apartheid, we needed as an important first step in rebuilding the fabric of our post-apartheid society in order to redefine the relationship between the state and religion. How would we move from the Christian-national ideology, adopted as the clarion call by the architects of apartheid, that justified apartheid ideology as divinely inspired and the quest of a nation for Lebensraum? Would we ever again want religion manipulated by a ruling party, or would we want to insulate society from such religious influence? Could we ignore the fact that while there was a state Christianity, there also emerged a liberation theology to challenge that from among Christians?[24] Despite its repressed status, there were Muslims who saw Islam as fundamentally oriented toward justice and, therefore, joined in struggle against apartheid. How would we simultaneously insulate society from the misuse of religion and recognize the liberating ethic of a diversity of religions?

In resolving this conundrum, we learned further lessons in nuance. We could forge a relationship between the state and religion whereby the state is neither *theocratic*, in the sense of adopting an official religion or making such a state religion's prescripts those of society, nor *secularist*, in the sense of the state opposing any religion by banning the practice of religion or their visible symbols. Rather, South Africa was described as *secular*.[25] The state was above and equidistant from all religions; it provided for freedom of worship of all religions and for freedom of belief or nonbelief. It would foster cooperative relations with religious communities.[26] The state would make provisions for such communities, such as sites for worship and burial as well as the observance of the most important rites and holy days of the diversity of faiths.

Furthermore, the regulation of religious communities would be through trust in each community, as individual citizens and collective congregants, to abide by the Bill of Rights and Constitution, which would balance freedom of speech with the prohibition of hate speech—equality for a community with equality for all communities.[27] Rights and freedoms claimed for yourself translate into the responsibility to ensure that even those with whom you are uncomfortable would enjoy those same rights.

Conclusion: *Was na i'l fulk* ("But Construct an Ark!")

The instruction to Noah to construct an ark[28] in anticipation of an inspired storm sheds light on these lessons from South Africa. There may be elements that would be useful against the tempest, the storm, or the hurricane of Islamophobia

[24] *The Kairos Document* (Institute for Contextual Theology, 1985), http://wp.production.patheos.com/blogs/markbraverman/files/2011/06/The-Kairos-Document-1985.html.

[25] Albie Sachs, *Interfaith Solidarity—a Guide for Religious Communities* (Cape Town: Institute for Justice and Reconciliation, 2004).

[26] Constitution of the Republic of South Africa, ch. 2: Bill of Rights (1996), https://www.gov.za/documents/constitution/chapter-2-bill-rights.

[27] Constitution of the Republic of South Africa, ch. 2: Bill of Rights.

[28] Quran ch. 23, Mu'minun, v. 27.

274   EBRAHIM RASOOL

that, for the foreseeable future, would be a reality for Muslims. Right-wing populism remains a political constant, and Muslims continue to face discrimination
and deprivations as part of an immigrant underclass, which they are bound to
resist.

But the challenge lies in the metaphorical ark—the mode of resistance. How
do you resist the scourge of Islamophobia without entrenching its core narrative
that you are the danger you are purported to be? The South African experience
provides a few guidelines, and the relatively constructive and warm relationship between Muslims and their fellow South Africans show the success thereof.
Muslims cannot conduct their resistance in the unsuccessful way that Caliban
and his cohorts had done in Shakespeare's *The Tempest.* A bumbling alliance led
to an equally bumbling putsch because they ignored the central advice Caliban
provided: they failed to counter the cunning, to match the knowledge of, and
to apply better intelligence than the colonial master. Rather, they preferred an
overwhelming belief in the righteousness of their cause and the inevitability of
victory. Thus they played into his hand and failed:

> '[T]is but a custom with him [Prospero] in the afternoon to sleep: then thou
> mayst brain him, having first seized his books; or with a log batter his skull. . . .
> [R]emember, first to possess his books; for without them, he's but a sot. . . . [B]urn
> but his books. He has brave utensils,—for so he calls them.[29]

In a globalized world, harnessing the power of communication technology,
coupled with the demands of global security, the world is saturated with
stereotypes of Muslims, equivalent to Shakespeare's image of the wild, savage,
and masterless man,[30] that characterize Muslims as undeserving of empathy,
justifying the departure from purportedly civilized values in dealing with the
civilizational, if not existential, threat posed by Islam and Muslims. The ark will
have to confront this battle for characterization, this battle for ideas, this battle
for the mobilization of the middle ground, by resisting the easy caricaturing of
Muslims and by locating values like justice, human rights, and coexistence as
equals at the center of the battle for ideas. The solution lies in making common
cause with other victims of discrimination, dispossession, and marginalization,
not from the edges of society but from the mainstream.

---

[29] Shakespeare, *Tempest,* Act III: Scene ii (emphasis added).
[30] Nichols, *Progress,* p. 436.

Index

For the benefit of digital users, indexed terms that span two pages (e.g., 52–53) may, on occasion, appear on only one of those pages.

Tables and figures are indicated by *t* and *f* following the page number

Abbott, David, 109
Adityanath, Yogi, 194–95
Advani, L. K., 186–87
AfD (Alternative for Germany), 76–77, 81–83, 88–90, 92–93
Alekseyeva, Anna, 154n.19
Al Hussein, Zeid Ra'ad, 233–35
Alliance against Islamo-Phobia and Anti-Muslim Hate (CLAIM), 91–92
Allport, Gordon A., 142n.50
al-Qaeda, 176–77, 223
Alternative for Germany (AfD), 76–77, 81–83, 88–90, 92–93
Ambedkar, Bhimrao, 194, 213
American Center for Law and Justice (ACLJ), 52–53
American Conservative Union (ACU), 54, 63–64
American Freedom Law Center, 66
Amrani, Saad, 169
Annan, Kofi, 252
Asad, Talal, 27–28
Association for the Protection of Race and Religion (Ma Ba Tha), 246–47, 251
Aung San Suu Kyi, 236–37, 243–44, 249–52
Auroux, Jean, 126–27
Aziz, Sahar, viii

Babri Masjid Mosque destruction, 16–17, 186–87, 201–2, 204, 205, 210–11
Bachman, Michele, 68
Bailey, Shaun, 96
Banks, Aaron, 101–2
Bannon, Steve, 54, 71
Bastrykin, Alexander, 151–52
Bayraklı, Enes, 90
Beinart, Peter, 53–54
Belgium
    affecting and alienating Muslims in, 178–80
    current attitudes toward immigrants and Muslims in, 176–77

far-right political parties in, 14–15
government structure of, 15, 173–74
GWOT in, 14
Muslim migration to, 171–73
overview of, 14, 169–71, 180
police abuse in, 14, 169, 172–73, 174–75
rise of anti-immigrant and anti-Muslim sentiment in, 174–76
terror attacks in, 176–77
toward a *vivre ensemble* in, 180
Benslama, Fethi, 34
Beydoun, Khaled, viii, 17–18
Bhagwat, Mohan, 192
Bharatiya Janata Party (BJP), 16–17, 183, 186–89, 190–97, 201–2, 204–6, 207, 208–9, 215–16
Binder, Leonard, 27
Blanquer, Jean-Michel, 115
Bobako, Monika, 143–44
Bonikowski, Bart, 58
Bonnefoy, Laurent, 123
Bouvet, Laurent, 113–15, 116–17
Breivik, Anders Behring, 86–87
Briant, Emma, 101–2
Britain
    Brexit in, 12–13, 97–106, 108, 111
    components of populism in, 103–4
    Conservative Party of, widespread Islamophobia in, 106–10
    from the fringe to ruling-party policy in, 106–10
    great replacement theory and, 105, 108
    GWOT and, 94–95
    hate crimes in, 12–13
    international stage and, 101–5
    overview of, 12, 94–96, 110–11
    populist campaign for Brexit in, 97–106
    Prevent program in, 95
    refugee crisis in, 98–101, 100*f*
    September 11th attacks and, 94–95

276 INDEX

Britain (cont.)
  Tory Party, widespread Islamophobia in, 106–10
  white genocide and, 105
Broder, Henryk, 86–87
Browne, Andrew, 108
Buchanan, Pat, 161
Bush, George W., 7, 18, 19, 60–62, 79–80, 223

CAA (Citizenship Amendment Act), 16, 183–84, 191–96, 203–4
Calderone, Sarah, viii
Cambridge Analytica (CA), 102–3
Camus, Renaud, 47, 118–20
Čaputová, Zuzana, 136–37, 141
Carlson, Tucker, 161
Castaner, Christophe, 122
Center for Security Policy (CSP), 51, 66
Chaturvedi, Vinayak, 185
Chen Quanguo, 226–27, 229–30
China, Islamophobia in. See Uyghur Muslims
Christian nationalism, 3, 7–8, 38–40, 264, 268
Ciotti, Éric, 116
Citizenship Amendment Act (CAA), 16, 183–84, 191–96, 203–4
clash of civilizations, 3–4, 32–33, 59–60, 62
Clinton, Hillary, 54–55, 56–57
contesting spatialization of Islamophobia in urban India
  beef ban and, 205–6
  BJP and, 201–2, 204–6, 207, 208–9, 215–16
  CAA and, 203–4, 208–9, 212–13
  exclusionary citizenship, 208–9
  ghettoization and, 210–12
  Hindutva and, 201–3, 204–8
  illegal occupations and, 208
  new spatial orders and, 204–8
  overview of, 201–3
  reparative citizenship and, 212–14
  Shaheen Bagh case and, 209–17
  urban citizenship and, 203–4
  urban segregation and, 207
  urbicide and, 214–17
COVID-19 pandemic, 16, 158–59, 164, 187, 194–95, 210, 225–26

Darmanin, Gérald, 124
Darusman, Marzuki, 246
Dean, Howard, 42
Defferre, Gaston, 126–27
Derrida, Jacques, 28–30
Deutsche Islamkonferenz (DIK), 83–84
displacing and disciplining Muslims in India
  accelerating settler-colonial agenda, 188–91

BJP and, 183, 186–89, 190–97
CAA-NRC in, 191–96
communications blackout during, 189–90
endangering citizenship and, 191–96
February 2020 pogrom in Delhi and, 196–99
Hindutva and, 4, 16, 183–87
Kashmir and, 188–91
overlapping frameworks and, 184–87
overview of, 15–17, 183–84, 199–200
Saffron nation and, 199–200

Eastern Europe
  class dimensions of, 143–47
  geographic dimensions of, 143–47
  Islamophobia without Muslims in, 134–37, 136t
  not the contact hypothesis and, 141–42
  overview of, 132–35, 148–50
  peripherality and, 143–47
  population of Muslims in, 137–39
  quantitative studies of Islamophobia in, 139–41
  racial dimensions of, 143–47
  regional variation in, 136–37
  spatialization effects in, 138
  "without Muslims" in East and West and, 137–39
Eatwell, Roger, 45–46
Ellison, Keith, 9, 63–64
Ellmers, Renee, 64–65
El-Tayeb, Fatima, 77–78
Ethridge, Bob, 64–65
Europe. See also Belgium; Britain; Eastern Europe; France; Germany
  anti-Judaism and, 14
  economic problems in, 10–11
  immigration to, 9–10
  national variation in, 11–14
  overview of, 6–9
  right-wing populist parties in, 4
  scapegoating in, 10–11
  white Christian identity in, 9–11
European Islamophobia Report, 90–91

Farage, Nigel, 12, 97–98, 99–102, 103, 105
Farmer, John, viii, 14–15
Federation of Student Parents' Councils (FCPE), 113–15
Fico, Robert, 136–37
Fidesz party, 141
Five Star Movement (Italy), 45
Flemish Interest Party (formerly Vlaams Blok), 14, 174–76

Foucault, Michael, 119
France
  colonialism of, 13
  contemporary emergence of the "Muslim Problem" in, 124–28
  from "Great" to "Small" replacement in, 118–21, 128
  Islamization in, 123–24, 128
  mainstreamization in, 112, 119
  opportunistic repositioning of the far right in, 128–30
  overview of, 13, 112–13, 131
  radicalization in, 122, 124–25
  rhetorical cohesion of the Islamophobic bloc in, 121–24
  secularism in, 116–17
  September 11th attacks and, 124–25
  series of anti-Muslim events in, 113–18, 114f
  strikes in, 125–28
  veiling in, 113–15, 116, 121–22, 124–25, 130
Freedom of Conscience Defense Fund (FCDF), 52
Freedom Party (Austria), 10, 89, 128–29
Freedom Party (Netherlands), 128–29

Gaddie, Ronald Keith, 39
Gaffney, Frank, 53–55, 71
Galzi, Olivier, 116
Gandhi, Indira, 210–11
Gandhi, Mahatma, 16, 185–87, 213, 265
Gay, Vincent, 125–26
genocide. See Rohingya genocide
Germany
  AfD in, 76–77, 81–83, 88–90, 92–93
  belated right-wing populism in, 80–83
  Berlin Wall in, 79
  colonial amnesia in, 77–78
  connecting to the Islamophobic international and, 88–90
  GWOT and, 79–80
  hate crimes in, 90–91
  history of racism in, 77–79
  Kaiserreich in, 75, 76, 77, 83
  legal Islamism and, 84
  media coverage in, 86
  overview of, 11–12, 75–76, 92–93
  polling in, 11–12
  postcolonialism and, 77–80
  post-Nazism and, 77–80
  refugee crisis in, 81–82
  remembrance culture in, 78–79
  response to Islamophobia in, 90–92
  reunification of, 77–80

roots of Islamophobia in, 77–80
September 11th attacks and, 79–80, 83–84
state praxis, hegemonic idea, and violence in, 83–88
USSR's fall and, 79–80
volkisch antisemitism in, 78–79
Ghertner, Asher, viii, 16–17
global Islamophobia overview
  Asia, 15–19
  definition of Islamophobia, 3–4
  demographics and migration, 2–3
  Europe, 6–9
  general tenets, 3–4
  GWOT, 1–2
  Hindu, Han, and Burmese supremacy, 15–19
  human rights violations, 2
  increased interest in topic, 1
  Islam as inherently violent, 9
  Muslim identity, 2
  right-wing populism, 3–6
  scapegoating of Muslims, 6
  September 11th attacks, 2
  spread of Islamophobia, 1–3
  United States, 6–9
  white Christian nationalism, 6–9
Global War on Terror (GWOT)
  Belgium and, 14
  Britain and, 94–95
  civilization as under attack in, 61–62
  framing of Islam in, 61
  Germany and, 79–80
  overview of, 1–2
  Russia and, 157, 166–68
  United States and, 58, 60–62
  Uyghur Muslims and, 18, 222–26
Godse, Nathuram, 185–86
Goldsmith, Zac, 96
Golwalkar, M. S., 185
Goodwin, Matthew, 45–46
Gorka, Sebastian, 54
Govil, Stuti, viii, 16–17
great replacement theory, 47, 105, 108, 118–19, 124, 128
Greven, Thomas, 97
Gross, Jan, 133–34
Grover, Varun, 194
Gujarat Pogrom, 186–87, 197–99, 204–5
Guterres, António, 236–37
GWOT. See Global War on Terror

Hafez, Farid, viii, 10–11
Haider, Jörg, 10
Hajjat, Abdellali, 119

278 INDEX

Hamid, Shadi, 47
Hansen, Thomas Blom, 205
Hassan II, 127
hate crimes, 12–13, 90–91, 94, 104, 168
Hetherington, Marc, 50
Hewstone, Miles, 43
Hickman, Mary, 146–47
Hindutva, 4, 16, 183–87, 201–3, 204–8
Hindutva (Savarkar), 184
Hochschild, Arlie, 56–57
Holmes, Stephen, 147
Hope Not Hate, 12–13, 96, 98, 107
Hopkins, Katie, 106
Hopkins, Najib, 138
Hopkins, Teeple, 138
Huntington, Samuel, 8–9, 32–33, 59, 60, 62

immigration, 2–3, 6–7, 9–10, 30–32, 164–
68, 171–73
Independent Group of Experts on Hostility to
Muslims, 91
India. See contesting spatialization of
Islamophobia in urban India; displacing
and disciplining Muslims in India
intergroup bias, 40–43
Islamism, 11, 13, 28, 34, 84, 88, 92–93, 116–18,
120, 121–22, 123, 124, 270–71
Islamization, 11–12, 64–65, 81–83, 88–89, 123–
24, 128–29
Islamophobia. See global Islamophobia
overview

Jaffrelot, Christophe, 187, 194n.62
Jiang Zemin, 18, 223–24
Johnson, Boris, 99–101, 106–7, 108, 109–10
Jones, Robert, 44–45

Kaczyński, Jarosław, 133
Kalmar, Ivan, viii, 10–11, 13–14
Kaya, Ayhan, 145–46, 240–41
Kayaoglu, Ayşegül, 145–46
Kepel, Gilles, 123
Keskinkilic, Ozan, 83
Kessel, Patrick, 116–17
Khalid, Umar, 199
Khan, Imran, 59
Khan, Sadiq, 96, 106–7
King, Desmond, 48
King, Peter, 70
Kjaersgaard, Pia, 128–29
Krastev, Ivan, 147

Laliwala, Sharik, 213

Laruelle, Marlene, 162–63
Leave.EU campaign (UK), 12, 97–98, 101–
5, 111
Lee, Ronan, viii, 18
legal Islamism, 84
Le Pen, Jean-Marie, 130
Le Pen, Marine, 10, 45, 105, 112–13,
124, 128–30
Lewis, Andrew, 50
Lewis, Bernard, 8–9, 59–60
Lübcke, Walter, 91
Lyon, David, 222–23

Ma Ba Tha, 246–47, 251
Macron, Emmanuel, 117–18, 122, 130
Mahmood, Saba, 34
Mair, Thomas, 104
Majlesi, Ava, viii, 14–15
Mandela, Nelson, 271
Marcos, Subcommandante, 143–44
Markell, Patchen, 26–27
Mason, Lilliana, 41–42, 43
Massad, Joseph, vii–viii, 7
Mauroy, Pierre, 126–27
McCain, John, 68–69
Merkel, Angela, 24, 108–9
Messerschmidt, Astrid, 78–79
migration, 2–3, 6–7, 9–10, 30–32, 164–
68, 171–73
Milli Goruş movement, 84–85
Minkenberg, Michael, 80
Mishra, Kapil, 196–97, 199, 214–16
Mitterrand, François, 125
Modi, Narendra, 4, 16, 186–87, 188, 197–99,
204–5, 227
Mohammed, Marwan, viii, 10–11, 13
Mondon, Aurelien, 145
multiculturalism, 23–24, 25–27, 28, 30, 34–35,
81, 88, 157, 162, 173–74
Muslim Youth in Germany, 84–85
Mutz, Diana C., 48–49, 51
Myanmar, Islamophobia in. See Rohingya
genocide

Nationalist Front (France), 10, 45
National League for Democracy (NLD), 243–
44, 249–52
National Register of Citizens (NRC), 191–
96, 208–9
National Socialist Underground (NSU), 87–88
Nemtsov, Boris, 156
New York Police Department (NYPD), 70–71
9/11 attacks. See September 11th attacks

969 Movement (Myanmar), 246–47
Norquist, Grover, 54
NRC (National Register of Citizens), 191–96, 208–9
Nu, U, 240–41

Oakes, Nigel, 102–3
Obama, Barack, 7, 9, 58, 62–63, 64–66, 67–70
Odoul, Julien, 115–16
Omar, Ilhan, 71–72
Orbán, Viktor, 45, 105, 132, 136–37, 141, 145, 149
orientalism, 8–9, 59–60, 101, 134, 148–49, 224
Orientalism (Said), 59, 259

Palin, Sarah, 64–65
Park51, 64–65
Patel, Eboo, 42
Patriotische Europaer gegen die Islamisierung des Abendlandes (Pegida), 81–82
Pegida, 81–82, 88
Perry, Samuel, 38–39
Pettigrew, Thomas, 142n.50
Phillips, Judson, 63–64
politics of vulnerability
  authoritarianism and, 49–51
  Christian nationalism and, 38–40
  demography and, 43–47
  discounting of anti-Muslim discrimination and, 48–51
  end of white Christian America and, 43–47
  group identity and, 40–41
  intergroup bias and, 40–43
  mega-identities and, 41–43
  Muslim ban and, 36–37
  opposition to Muslims' rights and, 51–55
  overview of, 36–38, 55
  perceptions of threat and, 43–47
  social dominance orientation and, 48–49
  social identity theory and, 48
  state responses to, 53–55
  threat in Europe and its impact on American dynamics and, 45–47
  US partisanship and, 41–43
Pompeo, Mike, 54, 228
populism, definition of, 4–5, 58, 97
Povinelli, Elizabeth, 26
price of recognition
  assimilation and, 24–25, 30–31
  costs of recognition concepts and, 26–28
  democracy and, 28–30
  demography and, 30–32
  difference concepts and, 24–26

Europeanness and, 30–32
immigration and, 30–32
multiculturalism and, 23–24, 25–27, 28, 30, 34–35
one Islam and the many and, 28–30
overview of, 23, 35
September 11th attacks and, 33
social inclusion and, 25
sovereignty and, 26–28
US pluralization of Islam and, 30–35
who has to pay, 26–28
Primakov, Yevgeniy, 156–57
Putin, Vladimir, 154n.19, 156–57, 161, 164–65, 166–67, 168

Rai, Mridu, 190–91
Ram Janmabhoomi movement, 205–6
Rashtriya Swayamsevak Sangh (RSS), 184–86
Rassemblement National, 115, 117, 128–29, 137
recognition, price of. *See* price of recognition
Redman, Eric, 66–67
Reed, Adolph, Jr., 24
Reich, Wilhelm, 144–45
Robinson, Tommy, 106
Rohingya genocide
  attitudes toward religion, ethnicity, and race and, 237–41
  Buddhist nationalism and, 244–52
  democracy and, 244–52
  hate speech and, 245–52
  historical context for, 237–41
  from indigenous to foreigners and, 241–43
  international law and, 235–36
  map of Myanmar and, 234f
  national demographics and, 237–41
  overview of, 233–37, 252–53
  rights restrictions from 1962 and, 241–43
  Tatmadaw and, 233–35, 236–37, 239–40, 242–44, 251–52
Rougier, Bernard, 123
Rubin, Mark, 43
Rushdie, Salman, 124–25
Russia
  Chechen wars and, 157, 167
  complex history of Muslims in, 153–62
  COVID-19 pandemic and, 158–59, 164
  "good" and "bad" Muslims in, 154–57, 160
  GWOT and, 157, 166–68
  migrants from former Soviet States in, 158–60
  national security law politics in, 166–68
  native Muslim populations in, 154–57
  overview of, 151–53, 168

280 INDEX

Russia (*cont.*)
  politics of migration in, 164–68
  public opinion and relations with Muslims
    in, 162–64
  rise of ethnonationalist populism in, 160–62
  September 11th attacks and, 166–67
  Ukraine and, 165–66
Ryan, Louise, 146–47

Said, Edward, 59, 259
Salvini, Matteo, 45, 137
Sarrazin, Thilo, 86–87
Saudi Arabia, 29, 149
Savarkar, V. D., 89–90, 184–86, 187
Schäuble, Wolfgang, 88
Schneiders, Gerald, 87
Scott, Rick, 64–65
Selod, Saher, vii–viii, 7, 8–9
September 11th attacks
  Britain and, 94–95
  France and, 124–25
  Germany and, 79–80, 83–84
  overview of, 2
  price of recognition and, 33
  Russia and, 166–67
  United States and, 7, 58
  Uyghur Muslims and, 222–25
Shah, Amit, 192
Shaheen Bagh (neighborhood), 193–94, 196–
  97, 209–17
Shortle, Allyson F., 39
Simpson, Jim, 51
Smith, Rogers M., 48
Social Democratic Party of Germany (SPD),
  80–81, 86–87
South Africa
  anti-Muslim practices in, 264–65
  avoiding Muslim exceptionalism in, 268–69
  being in, and of, the land in, 271–72
  cape of storms in, 261–66
  emerging from a long, dark night in, 265–66
  from exclusivity to solidarity in, 269–70
  Islamism in, 270–71
  locating the anti-Muslim in the anti-human
    in, 267–68
  Muslims as slaves and outlaws in, 261–66
  overview of, 257–58, 273–74
  resisting the hurricane in, 266–73
  roots in slavery and exile in, 263–64
  secular or secularist in, 272–73
  standing for justice in, 265
  Tempest and, 258–62, 266, 267–68, 274
  template of colonialism in, 258–61

  today's post-apartheid Muslims in, 262–63
spatialization of Islamophobia. *See* contesting
  spatialization of Islamophobia in
  urban India
Spivak, Gayatri Chakravorty, 26
State of Hate report, 96
Storch, Beatrix von, 82–83
Strike Hard against Violent Terrorism campaign
  (2014), 18, 225, 226, 227, 228–31
Suhay, Elizabeth, 50
Suu Kyi, Aung San, 236–37, 243–44, 249–52
Swiss People's Party, 128–29

Tajfel, Henri, 40–41, 48
Tatmadaw, 233–35, 236–37, 239–40, 242–
  44, 251–52
Tazamal, Mobashra, viii, 12
Tea Party, 56–57, 60, 62–63, 64–65, 70
Tell Mama (organization), 106–7
Tempest, The (Shakespeare), 258–62, 266, 274
Thein Sein, 244–45, 248, 249–51
Trilling, Daniel, 99
Tropp, Linda, 142n.50
Trump, Donald
  ascendancy of, 70–72
  birther movement and, 68
  Brexit and, 102–3, 104–5
  class dimensions of supporters of, 144–45
  India visit of, 198–99
  influence of, 36
  Islamophobia of, 7, 36–37, 54–55, 56–57
  price of recognition and, 24
Truschke, Audrey, viii, 16

Uddin, Asma, vii–viii, 7–8
UKIP (United Kingdom Independence Party),
  12, 97–98, 100f, 103–4, 106, 140
Union Solidarity and Development Party
  (USDP), 244, 249, 250–51
United States
  anti-Sharia bills in, 9, 66–67
  ascendancy of Trump and, 70–72
  birther movement and, 67–70
  clash of civilizations and, 59–62
  demographic changes in, 8
  founding of, 6–7
  future of, 70–72
  ground zero mosque controversy and, 64–66
  GWOT and, 58, 60–62
  immigration to, 6–7
  "Obama is a Muslim" claim and, 67–70
  overview of, 6–9, 56–57, 70–72
  partisanship in, 41–43

pluralization of Islam in, 30–35
populism and ethnonationalism in, 58
racism in, 9
September 11th attacks and, 7, 58
Tea Party's rise in, 62–64
white Christian nationalism in, 6–9
xenophobia in, 6–7, 9
Uyghur Muslims
distinctness of, 17–18, 222
GWOT and, 18, 222–26
Han supremacy and, 4, 17–18, 221–22
identity and society of, 219–21
mistreatment of, 4, 18
overview of, 17–18, 218–19, 231–32
September 11th attacks and, 222–25
terror of Chinese counterterrorism
against, 226–31

Vadum, Matthew, 51–52
Valeurs actuelles (magazine), 117, 119
Valls, Manuel, 112–13, 121–22
vulnerability, politics of. *See* politics of
vulnerability

Walker, Scott, 69–70
Wallerstein, Immanuel, 143

war on terror. *See* Global War on
Terror (GWOT)
Warsi, Sayeeda, 94, 106
Western civilization, 7, 8–10
white genocide, 105, 108–9
Whitehead, Andrew, 38–39
Wigmore, Andy, 101–2
Wilders, Geert, 128–29
Williams, Mark, 64–66
Willis, Hazel, 43
Winter, Aaron, 145
Wirathu, 246–49, 251

Xi Jinping, 59, 221–22, 226
Xinjiang. *See* Uyghur
Muslims

Yerushalmi, David, 66–67
Yudina, Natalia, 162–63

Zelensky, Volodymyr, 156
Zeman, Miloš, 136–37, 140–41
Zemmour, Éric, 118–19
Zimmerer, Jürgen, 77–78
Zobel, Malisa, 80
Zuckerberg, Mark, 246